# HOMEPORT

## Campobello - Saint John - St. Martins

### 1780-2000

IMAGES *of our Past*

# HOMEPORT

## Campobello - Saint John - St. Martins

### 1780-2000

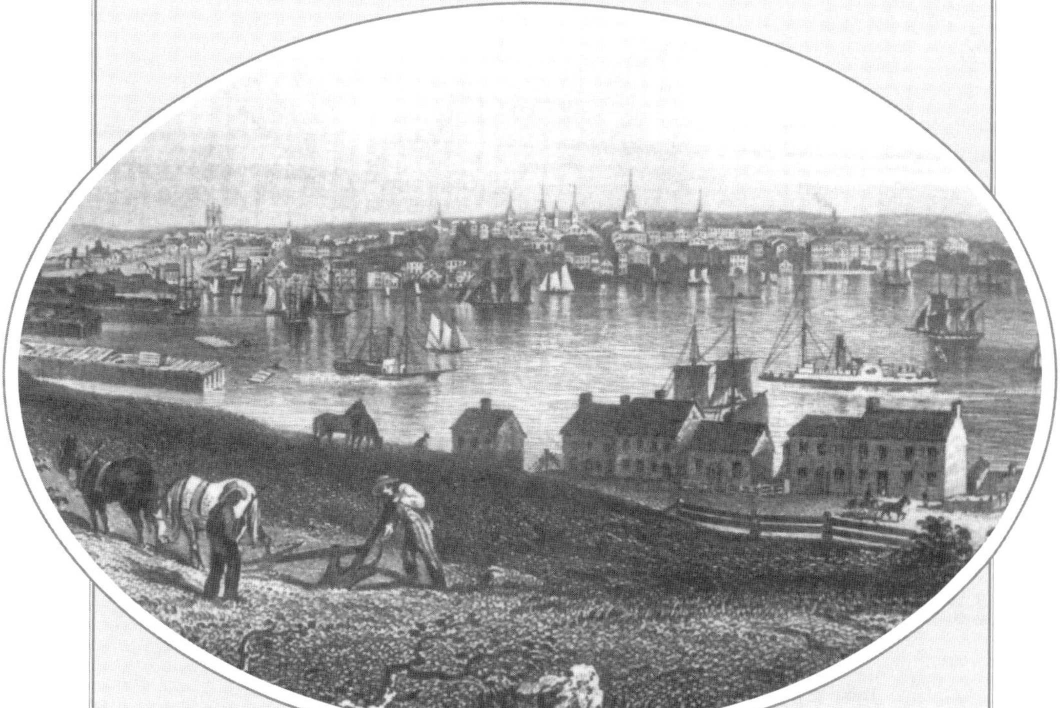

HAROLD E. WRIGHT
DEBORAH STILWELL

NIMBUS PUBLISHING LTD

Nimbus Publishing Limited
PO Box 9166
Halifax, NS B3K 5M8
(902) 455-4286

Design: Joan Sinclair

Printed and bound in Canada

Cover photo: South Market Wharf, c.1925. See page 48

Title Page: View of Saint John from Portland, c. 1845. Chesley Drive is in the foreground with Long Wharf at the left. Navy Island is at the right. This illustration is by John W. Hill, a prominent nineteenth-century American artist.

**National Library of Canada Cataloguing in Publication**

Wright, Harold E
Homeport : Campobello - Saint John - St. Martins, 1780-2000 /
Harold E. Wright, Deborah Stilwell.

(Images of our past)
ISBN 1-55109-387-1

1. Saint John (N.B.)--History--Pictorial works. 2. Campobello (N.B.)--History--Pictorial works. 3. St. Martins (N.B.)--History--Pictorial works. I. Stilwell, Deborah, 1966- II. Title. III. Series.

FC2497.37.W748 2002 971.5'32 C2002-901696-7
F1044.5.S14W748 2002

Canada

The Canada Council for the Arts | Le Conseil des Arts du Canada

We acknowledge the financial support of the Government of Canada through the Book Publishing Industry Development Program (BPIDP) and the Canada Council for our publishing activities.

# *Dedication*

*We wish to dedicate this work, first, to those who assisted us by providing information and photographs for this book, and second, to all those over the past two hundred years whose lives were impacted by the rising tides of the Bay of Fundy.*

# Acknowledgements

We wish to thank those individuals and organizations who helped us put this book together. Those who provided photographs are recognized on the photo credits page. Those who gave information or other forms of assistance are: Stu Trentkowsky, Bob Elliott, Kari Watson of Print Digital, Bill McKnight, Melissa Woodcock, Horace Meating, Rick Smith, and Norton Wyse, all of Saint John; the Saint John Port Authority; Maureen Venzi of Calgary; Betty Mabey of Campobello; Barbara McIntyre and Faye Marks of St. Martins; and Lieutenant Commander Ray Stacey of British Columbia.

We are grateful to Dan Soucoup and Nimbus Publishing for bringing this book to market. We trust our effort will be both informative and entertaining. While we have made every effort to ensure the accuracy of the information and its presentation, we invite any reader with additional information to contact us.

Our final words of thanks go to our spouses, Owen and Cheryl, and our children: Nicholas, Cassandra, and Jeremy; and Jessalyn and Jason. While we were tucked away with our photographs, research notes, and computer, they didn't forget about us, nor did we forget them.

*Deborah L. Stilwell*
*Harold E. Wright*
June 24, 2001
St. Jean de Baptiste Day,
Saint John

# *Contents*

*Introduction*

# The Bay, Saint John and Its Outports

## THE BAY OF FUNDY

For millennia, indigenous people used the Bay of Fundy and the inland waterways of New Brunswick for travel, fishing, and trade. In Mi'kmaq lore, a giant whale angered the god Glooscap and created such a splash with his mighty tail that to this day the water sloshes back and forth, producing the enormous tides of the Bay of Fundy. Geologically, this awe-inspiring natural phenomenon was created 350 million years ago, some 100 million years before the first dinosaurs roamed the earth.

The tides of the Bay of Fundy are truly one of the world's great natural wonders. Twice daily on an average tide, one hundred billion tonnes of water flow into and out of the bay, creating rip-currents, swirling whirlpools, and a tidal amplitude reaching 16 metres at the bay's head. This volume of water ebbing and flowing is estimated to be two thousand times greater than the daily discharge of the Gulf of St. Lawrence. The immense energy of the Fundy tides powers a highly productive, rich, and diverse natural ecosystem, by turns shaping the environment, the economy, and the culture of the Saint John region.

The rich aquatic feeding grounds around Campobello, Deer, and Grand Manan islands make the Bay of Fundy one of the world's most accessible sites for viewing marine mammals. Every summer up to fifteen species of whales come to the bay to mate, play, and feast. The stirring of deep, nutrient-rich water into shallow surface water causes immense blooms of plankton—passively floating food that nourishes all marine life. Some of the whales feeding here are the finback, humpback, minki, North Atlantic right, sei, orca (killer), and blue whale. As well, the bay contains a number of shark species: basking, porbeagle, white, and, the fastest of all, the mako.

Along the Fundy Coast the tides have left ample evidence of their power and might. At Hopewell Rocks the tide has carved and sculpted towering forms of red sandstone. Topped by evergreens, these irregular stacks resemble huge flowerpots and stand as one of many Fundy marvels. At St. Martins, the constant tidal action has carved out enormous sea caves, and with each receding tide, vast, nutrient-rich mudflats are exposed in the Minas Basin.

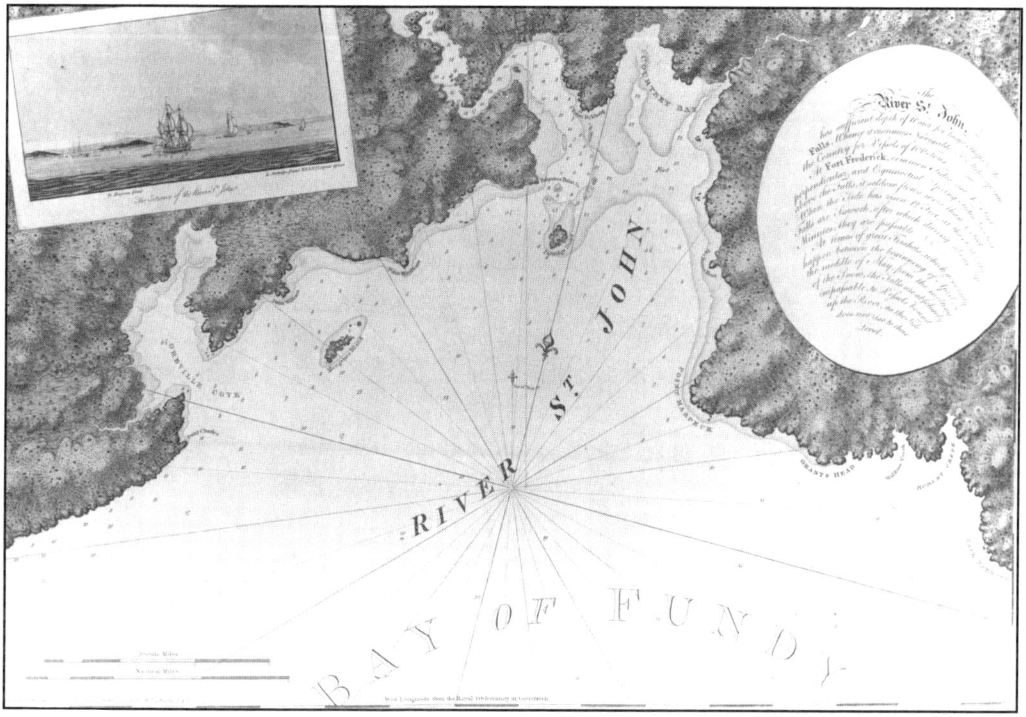


**ENTRANCE TO THE RIVER ST. JOHN, 1780, BY JOSEPH F.W. DESBARRES**

*This chart shows many features still recognizable in today's harbour, but with some unfamiliar names: Lorneville Cove was Grenville Cove; Point Wilham was on Taylor's Penninsula; Manawagonish Island was Meogenes Mand; Sheldon Point was Point Windham; Negro Town Point was Bruyeres Point, Lower Cove was Point Debbeig; Red Head was Des Barres Head; and Mispec was Point Maspeck. DesBarres was a military officer, engineer, administrator and surveyor. This chart was one of several depicting the coast of North America that he published in the* Atlantic Neptune. *He was appointed lieutenant governor of Cape Breton and, later, of Prince Edward Island DesBarres died in Halifax in 1824.*

## Early Settlements

These great tides provided hardships, opportunities, and adventures for aboriginals and European explorers. The Mi'kmaq and Passamaquoddy fished and hunted near the Bay of Fundy, building temporary villages wherever game was plentiful. The Spaniard Estao Gomes (Estavan Gomez) is believed to have been our first European visitor. In 1535 he identified a river on the east coast of North America as the "Rio de la Buelta" ("river of the return"), a reference to the Reversing Falls. On June 24, 1604 (St. Jean de Baptiste Day), Mi'kmaqs gathered on *Ouigoudi* (Navy Island) to watch a strange ship enter the harbour. Aboard were Pierre Dugua, Sieur de Mons, and Samuel de Champlain. After charting the harbour and making note of the reversible falls, they sailed down the bay and wintered that year on Dochets Island in the St. Croix River. This was one of the first European settlements in North America. Champlain described the challenge of sowing grain and nurturing gardens over a dry summer and of their voyages and meetings along the way with many of the Algonquin peoples. The island's isolation and unusually harsh winter severely tested the colonists; more than half the population succumbed to scurvy before the mild weather brought friendly Wabenaki Indians with fresh game.

This meeting between Europeans and aboriginals led to a trading system that operated well into the nineteenth century. In 1632, Charles la Tour established a small fur-trading post at Portland Point, setting the stage for early French rivalry and conflict in the area. In 1645, La Tour's rival, the Sieur d'Aulnay, forcibly took over the post.

Rivalries between France and England in the seventeenth and eighteenth centuries affected the colonies in North America as the balance of power swung from one nation to the other. The struggle was settled in 1758 when Colonel Robert Monckton defeated the French at Fort Martignon. In 1762, James and Richard Simonds arrived at Portland Point where they established a trading post; with their partner, William Hazen, they built and operated a successful trading business until the American Revolution seriously curtailed their operations. Also in the mid-eighteenth century, the English established Conway, a small settlement on the west side of the Reversing Falls.

## The City of Saint John

Attacks by American privateers and the threat of native unrest spurred the British Army to build Fort Howe in 1788. Five years later, fourteen thousand American Loyalists arrived at the mouth of the river, having been promised land, food, and supplies. They founded the towns of Carleton and Parrtown, which amalgamated in 1785 to form the city of Saint John. The city of Portland was amalgamated in 1889.

The inhabitants of this settlement endured many hardships during its early years. Lands were granted, property cleared, rock blasted away for roads, and simple frame dwellings were built. Commerce started between Saint John and other settlements in New Brunswick, Nova Scotia, and the West Indies. A political system similar to the British model was adopted. Saint John's first Common Council met in a tavern.

By the mid-nineteenth century, the community had changed dramatically from a small town to a bustling urban centre with maritime commerce quickly becoming the mainstay of the local economy. Fish, furs, masts for the Royal Navy, livestock, grains, and other foodstuffs were traded, and shipbuilding began. The Loyalists soon recognized the value of New Brunswick's forests, and they developed a shipbuilding and lumber trade based at the port of Saint John. Through the early and middle 1800s, New Brunswick lumber was highly prized throughout Britain, and the shipbuilding, shipping, and timber trades flourished at the port.

The geographic location of the city, with the St. John River providing a highway from the New Brunswick hinterland, placed Saint John in a good position to profit from the timber trade. The development of New Brunswick timber resources during the Napoleonic Wars contributed to Saint John's growth into a major port with important shipping interests. Prosperity brought many changes to the city: houses, wharves, and stores were built in great quantities; rents increased; and wages were high due to a shortage of labour. This prosperity did two things for the city: it supported the timber trade as a mainstay of the economy, and it attracted immigrants from Great Britain.

Napoleon's military successes in the 1790s and the first decade of the nineteenth century convinced the British government that a secure timber supply was vital to its national interests. Thus, the English government looked to its North American colonies. The necessary development of new sources for lumber demanded changes in both the timber trade and the merchant marine, and this required the cooperation of businessmen. Shipowners and merchants lobbied for, and secured in 1809, tariff protection for the more costly British North American timber. With the market protected, colonial wood enjoyed preferential treatment for the next three decades. In New Brunswick, this arrangement allowed the number of timber transports built annually and their annual cumulative tonnage to grow substantially. After 1815 Saint John's economy began to diversify into business concerns other than those directly connected to the timber trade, and these began to emerge as important employers and commodity producers. "The timber trade remained important, but it was increasingly challenged by shipbuilding, construction, saw milling, and a variety of small crafts and trades."

During the next four and a half decades, shipping, shipbuilding, and the timber trade created a thriving economy in New Brunswick. New outports of registry opened in St. Andrews in 1823 and Miramichi in 1826. Great Britain's expanding industries—with ever-increasing appetites for timber—forced further expansion of the merchant marine; and New Brunswick builders and owners reaped the benefits of this continued economic expansion. Despite fluctuations during this 45-year period, there was an enormous net increase in the number of vessels constructed for immediate sale on the British market.

Saint John experienced many changes during the 1840s and 1850s. In 1839 the harbour ferry *Victoria* began providing service between the west and east sides of the harbour. There was also the incorporation of gas lighting, the installation of a public water supply from Lily Lake (the first in North America), the building of the lunatic asylum in 1848 (the first in Canada), and the construction of a bridge at the Reversing Falls rapids. International events stimulated shipping and shipbuilding. The opening of the China Sea trade and the Crimean and American Civil wars were positive influences on the growth of Saint John industries. The discovery of gold in California in 1849 and in Australia in 1851, along with increased emigration from Great Britain, created an unprecedented demand for vessels to transport people as well as goods between Europe and new settlements worldwide. In the 1850s, a wharf was built at Reeds Point to service passenger steamships.

Saint John became a major immigrant port-of-entry, with an estimated three million immigrants and seamen passing through the Partridge Island quarantine station during the nineteenth and twentieth centuries. These immigrants brought new talents and trades, ideas, capital, and what all local residents feared—disease. Epidemics during the nineteenth and twentieth centuries killed thousands of new immigrants and residents.

The shipyards of Saint John and the outports of St. Martins, Deer Island, Campobello, St. Andrews, Miramichi, Sackville, and many smaller communities along the Bay of Fundy thrived throughout the mid-nineteenth century. As the fourth largest shipbuilding centre in the world, the shipyards around the Saint John harbour launched an average of two ships every week during this "golden age" of shipbuilding, and the port was extremely active.

The end of our golden age started in the late 1860s, due in part to the greater use of steel-hulled steam vessels throughout the world and also to lower labour and material costs and more efficient economic operations in Ontario and Quebec, where the railways made it cheaper to ship goods by land. Coupled with these conditions was the economic impact on Saint John of Confederation in 1867. This union, based to a large degree on population and political influence, caused a shift in the economy from the Maritime provinces into the central part of the country. The building of ships in New Brunswick began to decline about 1865, although local ownership continued to expand until 1879.

On June 20, 1877, Saint John was hit by the "Great Fire," which erupted at York Point and burned out of control for nine hours, destroying the business and residential heart of the city. More than thirteen thousand people were left homeless, eighteen were killed, and $28 million was lost in property damage (with less than 25 per cent of this amount covered by insurance). This fire could well have meant the downfall of Saint John had it not been for the determination and spirit of the citizens, and the generosity of communities from all over North America and Great Britain, which sent relief in the form of cash, food, clothing, and building materials. Architects, engineers, masons, carpenters, and labourers came from all over the continent to aid in the rebuilding of Saint John. The prophecy that "From these very ashes and ruins a brighter, a more glorious and more prosperous city will arise" came true, for within five years Saint John's fire-damaged district was rebuilt.

The 1877 fire gave many businesses the opportunity to shift their capital from the shipping business to banking, land transportation, merchandising, and other land-based service industries. Saint John shipowners continued to invest $8 million in wooden ships because they "blindly believed that never will come the day when...sailing ships shall be forced from the great carrying traffic of the world."

The effect of the 1877 fire and its aftermath on local tradesmen was devastating. Hundreds lost their jobs, and many were forced to adapt their trades to furniture, statuary, architectural ornamentation, and building construction. A few New Brunswick shipping firms modernized their fleets and remained active in the international scene, but most marine entrepreneurs, reacting to a decrease in freight rates that began in the mid-1870s and to Canadian government policies promoting landward development, redirected their capital from the sea to enterprises they expected would be more lucrative. By the turn of the century, New Brunswick's role in international shipping and shipbuilding existed only in memory.

In the 1880s and 1890s, Saint John's industrial capital, employment, and output increased, but the population decreased. In 1882, Mr. P. R. Edictor, in an address to the Ladies' Society of the Congregational Church, speculated that in fifty years' time Saint John would have a population of 468,000 people. An elevated, rapid-transit, double-tracked railway would skirt the South End, and the one harbour ferry would be increased to three. On the social side, Edictor predicted that "rum and intemperance have now for many years been unknown evils, and the jail is the most rickety, unused building in the city, while the police are getting rich in peaceful avocations."

Saint John rested its hopes for continuing prosperity on the port.

The Canadian government at this point was using Portland, Maine as the Canadian winter port. In 1889 the Canadian Pacific Railway completed the "Short Line" from Montreal through Maine. In 1894, the threat of resignation of two Saint John members of parliament provided incentive to the federal government to grant a $25,000 subsidy to the Beaver Line to use Saint John during the winter. This experiment proved successful, and in 1896 Ottawa stopped using Portland and directed traffic to Saint John.

By the end of the nineteenth century, steel-hulled ships had almost replaced wooden vessels and the wooden ship building boom had ended. Norton Wyse, a research volunteer at the New Brunswick Museum, has been using port registries to identify ships, shipyards, and shipbuilders. Although still incomplete, his research indicates some five thousand vessels were built in the province. For example, in Saint John alone he has identified 72 yard owners, of which the Olive Family of Carleton built 87 vessels between 1812 and 1867.

By the late nineteenth century, population expansion had also begun west of New Brunswick as Canada became home to European immigrants seeking new lives. Railways were becoming an important transportation mode and local businesses realized a rail link with the rest of Canada was essential to the survival of Saint John. Each winter, the St. Lawrence River froze and ice prevented the port of Montreal from handling goods. As rail links developed in the late nineteenth century, Saint John became Canada's winter port.

Over the next twenty-plus years, harbour facilities were improved and expanded. The increase in grain shipments due to the development of rail links with Western Canada created the need for a grain elevator. The first grain elevator was built on the west side in 1893; the building of a second elevator on the east side followed. The port was described as "not a pretty place, but it was busy, where ships from all over the world came to load and unload in the winter port … [and the] Saint John longshoremen were more honest than those anywhere else, and more efficient."

Peacetime port activity was supplemented during World War One when the port assumed a major military role. Through the major ice-free industrial centre in the Maritimes, ships carried munitions, food stuffs, horses, machinery, and troops overseas. More than twenty thousand New Brunswickers flocked to the recruiting stations to "Fight for the Empire." At home, fuelled by the spark of patriotism, women replaced men in the factories. At this time, the port was changing from a regional port handling local goods to an international port shipping products from across Canada to the world. Construction of the Saint John drydock, which had been halted during the war, resumed and the drydock was open for business in 1923.

The end of World War One brought economic hardship coupled with the disastrous effects of the worldwide Depression of the 1930s to Saint John. The city was again on the brink of economic disaster. In 1927, Saint John sold its harbour facilities to the federal government. And not a moment too soon; in June 1931 a major portion of the west side dock facility burned. Quick federal aid saved the city's economy as the federal government rebuilt the wharves in concrete and steel. In 1934 Navy Island Terminal was created and a new channel to replace the Z-shaped channel was completed. Another federal relief project was the construction of the municipal airport in Millidgeville. A new Boston ferry, the SS *Saint John*, as well as a new harbour ferry, the *Loyalist*, began operating. Now Saint John could service national and international customers by land, sea, and air.

The outbreak of World War Two again brought both economic prosperity and the threat of attack from Germany. Fear of submarine and air attack was so great that several forts were established around the harbour. This fear proved reasonable, as two U-boats did penetrate the Bay of Fundy to Saint John and St. Martins; however, the financial benefits generated by the war eclipsed the fear of attack. Longshoremen played a vital role in keeping the port running smoothly: "In wartime their work is an absolute necessity. They are the front line along with everybody else but in that front line they are prominent, taking an important part in making it possible for supplies of all kinds to be conveyed. So when you hear the unloading of a ship, in the night or day, pay a tribute to the men who are doing this job and doing it well, knowing its importance, and proud of doing their best for the general welfare. It is a good thing there are longshoremen and while they are on duty, and 'getting on with the job' all should be well in the harbour."

At the Saint John drydock, hundreds of warships and merchant vessels were built and repaired. The story of AMC *Jervis Bay's* heroic defence of its convoy is still commemorated in Saint John today. The corvettes HMCS *Saint John, St. Croix, St. Stephen, Moncton*, and the frigate HMCS *Fredericton* proudly carried these New Brunswick community names into battle against the German navy. Then, as in previous periods, the end of the war brought a temporary slowdown in economic activity for Saint John.

In 1948 a new customs and immigration building opened in Saint John, renewing the transportation link with the CPR that had stopped at the time of the 1931 port fire. In 1951, the following ship and rail lines called in Saint John: Cunard, Manchester, Cairn Thomson, Newcastle and Leith, Furness, Swedish American, Capo, French Lines, Canadian Pacific, Canadian National. The shipping lines provided service to ports in Canada, the United States, Central and South America, the Caribbean, Europe, the British West Indies, South and East Africa, Australia, and the Far East.

The 1950s, 60s, and 70s saw many changes in the physical appearance of Saint John. Wartime housing was built in the Rifle Range and Portland Place areas of the North End, and suburbs emerged in Forest Hills, Champlain Heights, and Millidgeville. A massive urban renewal program replaced slum housing and workers' tenements in the Main Street area and in the East End, where wooden buildings were replaced by concrete office buildings, highways, landscaped areas, and shopping malls. Port activity reached new heights and the prosperity promised a bright future. Pugsley Terminal berths were constructed between 1948 and 1952. Ten years later Long Wharf Terminal was extensively renovated. In 1968 the look of the harbour changed when the Saint John Harbour Bridge was completed, almost a hundred years after it was first proposed.

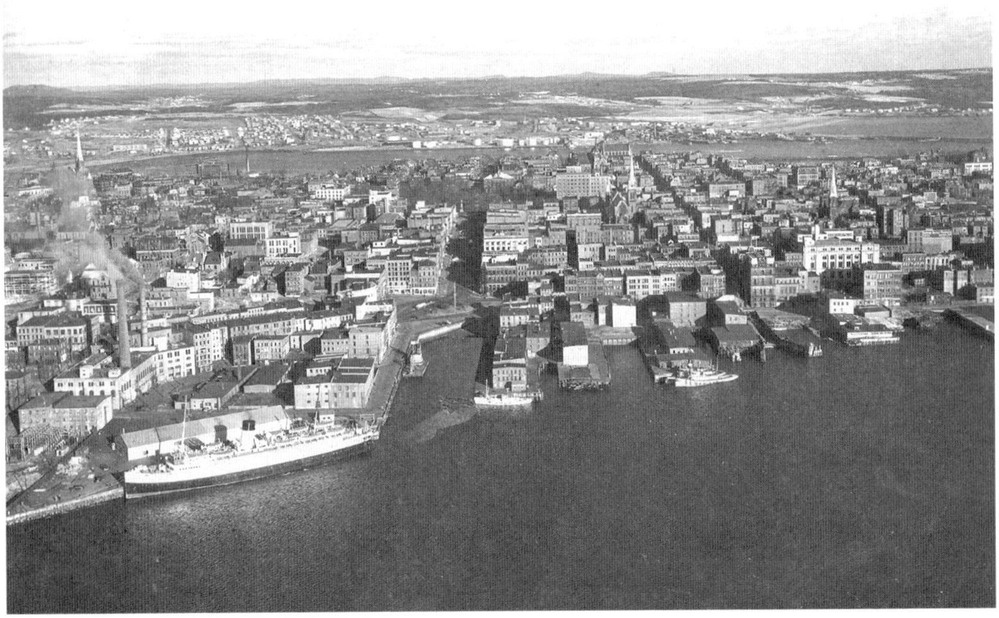

**MARKET SLIP, 1950** *Much has changed since this photo was taken, both along the waterfront and in the areas of the city visible here. The Dominion Coal Company is gone, replaced by the terminal for the* Princess Helene. *Freedman & Sons and the pilot station at South Market Wharf, as well as the slips down to the ferry landing at Princes Street, became coast guard property. McAvity's is gone, and the area at the right is now Pugsley Park. Starting at the left is the steel frame of the YMCA, under construction in 1950, and the Dock Street power plant. Dock Street, renamed St. Patricks Street, is the location of the Canada Games Aquatic Centre. In the background is Courtenay Bay before the causeway was constructed, Simonds Regional High School on Bayside Drive, and the hills and forests, which became Forest Hills and Champlain Heights and the Irving Oil refinery.*

Port business continued to develop in response to changes in the marine industry, and in 1972 Saint John entered the containerized shipping business at the Rodney Container Terminal. By the middle of the 1970s the port of Saint John was serviced by thirteen container lines. In 1975, a forest products shed was designed specially for handling palletized material using forklifts. With increasing mechanization of port industry, fewer workers were needed. Trucking companies gained popularity over rail with shippers because of lower transport costs and increased efficiency.

In the 1980s and 1990s, Saint John continued to prosper. In 1985 the Barrack Point Potash Terminal opened, handling potash mined in the Sussex area. Potash remains a significant commodity for the port and is sold to Mexico, South America, and other global markets. Half of the world's known potash is found in New Brunswick. Throughout the 1980s and '90s, the Saint John Shipyard constructed naval frigates, the McAllister Place shopping area grew, the oil refinery expanded, the natural gas pipeline from Sable Island was constructed through southern New Brunswick to the United States, and the cruise ship business grew in St. Andrews and Saint John. In 2000 the Lantic Sugar Refinery closed, ending an association with the port that was more than 85 years old.

Shipping lines operating from Saint John in 2000 included: Kent, Spliethoff, Wallenius Wilhelmsen, Tramarco, Gearbulk, NSCSA, Oldendorff, Star Shipping, Christensen Canadian African, Ecuadorian Line, Egyptian National Lines, Pakistan National Shipping Corporation, Spliethoff's Bevrachting-Skantoor B.V., and Turkish Cargo Lines. Cargo was shipped to or from ports worldwide. As it had for almost two hundred years, Saint John maintained the outport's international connections.

## The Outports

For many years the Passamaquoddy hunted, fished, and harvested clams and sea urchins at what they called "A bah quiet," which was later named "Port aux Coquilles" by the French. In 1767 Captain William Owen received a grant of "the Outer Island, then called Passamaquoddy." Three years later, Owen and 38 settlers went to the island and named it Campobello.

The new settlers planted oats, peas, barley, wheat rye, clover, hemp, flax, potatoes, turnips, apple, and plum trees, and cleared and fenced land for hay. They traded cured fish, lumber, potash, shingles, cordwood, and salted pollock with the West Indies. By mid-century, cod, haddock, hake, herring, pollock, and mackerel fishing was the primary island industry.

Summer visitors have been going to Campobello since 1855. Boston and New York businessmen bought the Owen property in 1881, building luxurious hotels that they leased to private management and selling land to both wealthy visitors and island residents.

James and Sara Roosevelt and their one-year-old son Franklin D. visited Campobello Island in 1883. James purchased several acres of land upon which he constructed a summer home. At that site, the Roosevelt Campobello International Park was established in 1964 following a gift of the cottage and its grounds to the Canadian and United States governments. Now more than 100,000 people visit the cottage each year. Although seafood harvesting and other occupations related to the fishing industry remain the mainstays of Campobello's economy, tourism is rapidly increasing its economic impact on the island.

Deer Island is home to many species of mammals (including whales, seals, and dolphins), birds (including eagles, osprey, and blue heron), and fish. A tour of the island reveals numerous rocky beaches, fishing harbours where fishing boats lie at the wharves, and a variety of architectural styles with many large, old homes once owned by navigators. The island is accessible by car ferries. At one end of the island are two government ferries, and on the southern tip is Eastcoast Ferries, a private service that operates two ferries. One ferry runs from Eastport, Maine and the other from Campobello Island.

Adventure Tourism took off with whale watching tours becoming increasingly popular with tourists. Along with this new industry came a heightened awareness of the need to protect these beautiful giants of the sea. Cline Marine is Quoddy's original whale-watching company. In business since 1986, the eco-tourism company offers each visitor an opportunity to see whales in their natural environment—and on their own terms. Although the company cannot guarantee that visitors will see a whale on every outing, their policy is: "If a whale you don't see, your second trip is FREE." During 2000 they had a 99 per cent success rate in whale sighting.

St. Martins was established by a detachment of the King's Orange Rangers after the American Revolution. The settlement was originally called Quaco, a derivative of the Mi'kmaq word *Goolwagagek*, meaning "Land of the hooded seals." The name was changed to St. Martins by Matthias Moran after his parish name in France, but Quaco is still found in the place names of Quaco Head and West Quaco.

Shipbuilding became the principal industry of St. Martins, where the first vessel, the schooner *Rachel*, was built in 1805 by David Vaughan. The last square-rigged ship built at St. Martins was the barque *Kismet*, in 1882. In the intervening years, 238 square-rigged vessels had been built. As well, 149 schooners were built between 1805 and the launch of the *Quaco Queen* in 1917. These ships were built in St. Martins as well as in other nearby communities such as Tynemouth Creek, Salmon River, Gardners Creek, Melvins Beach, McCumber Beach, Vaughans Beach, West Quaco Creek, Browns Beach, and Black River. Many of these vessels were then outfitted and registered in Saint John.

Intimately tied to the area's shipbuilding industry was the lumber business. During the winter months, trees were felled for later use in the construction of ships. Sawmills refined the lumber for overseas shipment, while pulp was taken by barge to Saint John and to mills in Maine. Lobster fishing was another prominent industry. Today few fishermen live in the village of St. Martins, but men like Bill Holland, Andy Gallant, Kent Belding, Jim and Troy Mannette, and Matthew Mawhinney continue the proud fishing traditions of their forefathers.

In 1874 the steamer *Earl Dufferin* carried freight and passengers on a regular schedule to Saint John. This service continued until the opening of the St. Martins to Upham Railway in 1878, which operated at a cheaper rate. The railway also opened St. Martins to tourism. By 1908 W.E. Skillen was advertising St. Martins as "The Favorite Route for Tourists and Sportsmen. St. Martins is famed for its trout fishing and is rapidly gaining notoriety as a moose hunting ground."

St. Martins remains a quaint little seaside village. Its charm is its future as tourists continue to visit the village, where the homes of shipbuilders and captains are now bed & breakfasts or heritage inns. Huttges's canteen at the Caves continues to provide good food at reasonable prices. The crown jewel of St. Martins, however, is the Fundy Trail.

The Fundy Trail Parkway is a two-kilometre corridor along the northeastern coast of the Bay of Fundy between Fownes Beach in St. Martins and the western boundary of Fundy National Park. Examples of most of the ecosystem dynamics of the bay—including the nutrient-rich saltmarshes, tidal flats, and the dramatic tides—may be seen within this area. The Fundy Trail Parkway is a seasonal, multi-use coastal access network that includes a reduced-speed roadway with scenic lookouts, a pedestrian and bicycle trail, and footpaths to the beaches and river estuaries, as well as an interpretive centre at Big Salmon River.

## Chapter 1

# Our Shipbuilding Tradition

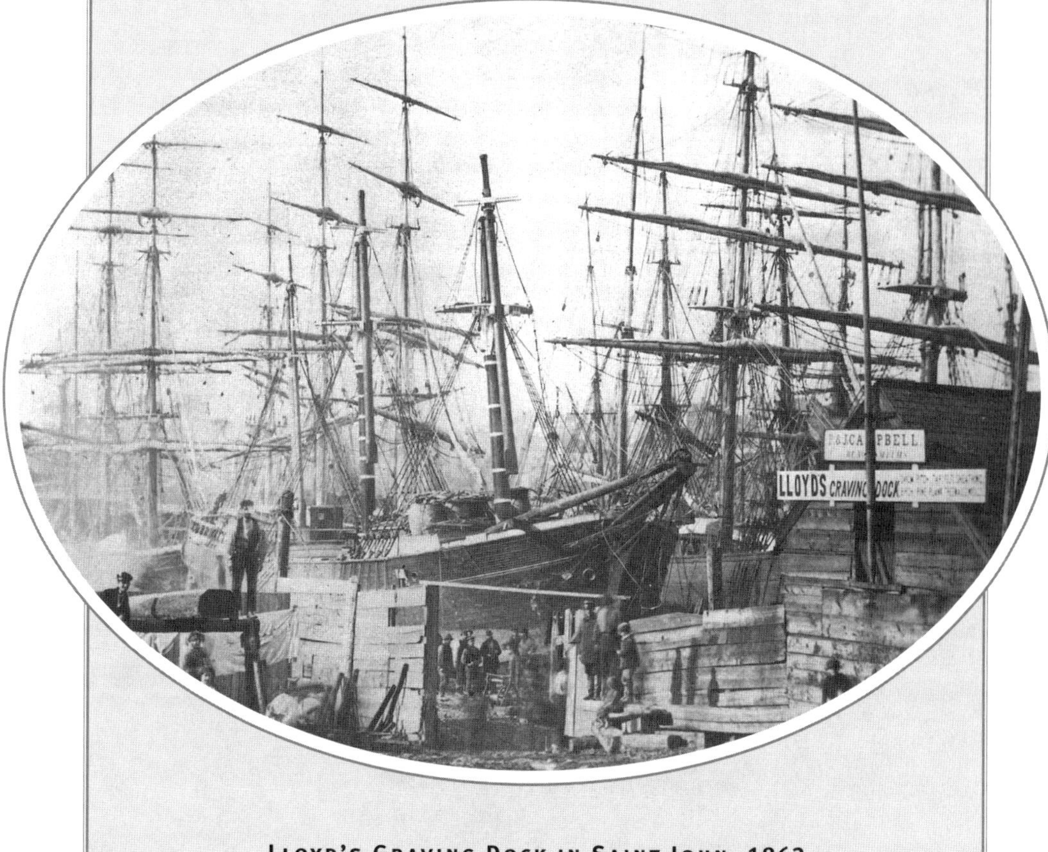


**LLOYD'S GRAVING DOCK IN SAINT JOHN, 1863**

John F. Lloyd's graving dock and P. & J. Campbell's blacksmith shop at York Point provided immediate repairs to damaged vessels. This sea of masts shows just how busy York Point was in the 1860s. Members of the Lloyd family were involved in related industries: one was a surveyor at the Customs House, Edward was an engineer, and John ran a grocery at 32 Mill Street. By 1869, John F. was a ship's carpenter living on Mill Street next to his graving dock, and his brother James was a clerk living on Brussells Street.

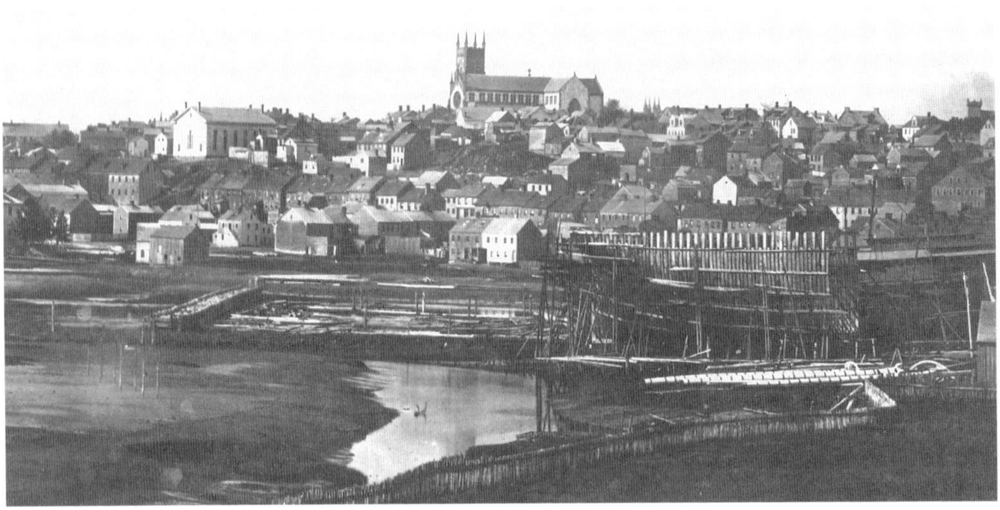

**COURTENAY BAY, 1863** Several of the buildings shown here still exist. Left to right, the three churches are the Brussels Street Baptist Church, Exmouth Street Church, and the Cathedral of the Immaculate Conception. In the right foreground is a ship under construction.

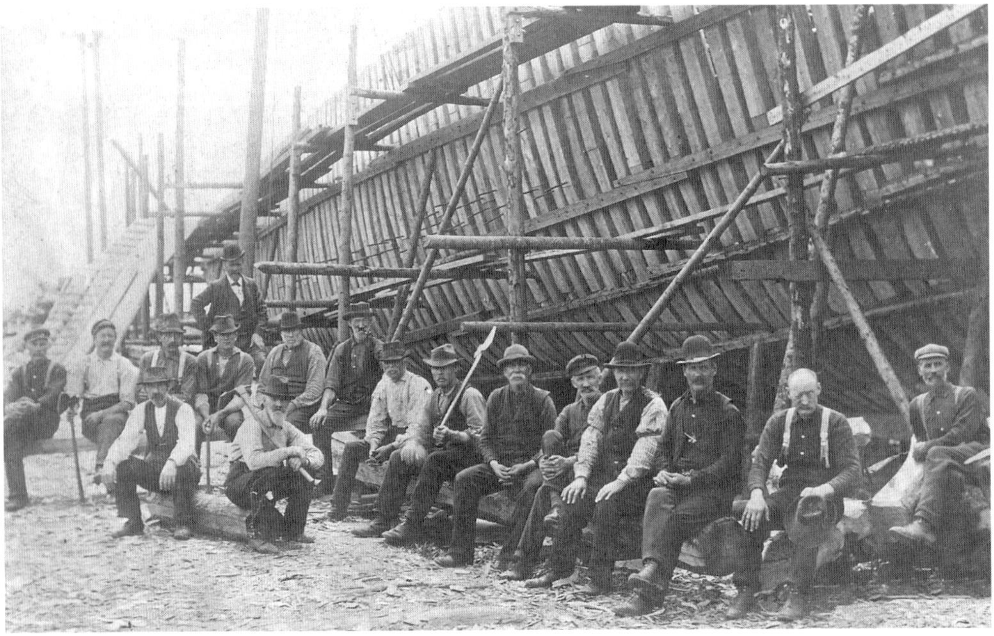

**A LYNCH SHIP, C.1870** This could be the *Rock Terrace*, one of more than twenty-four ships built by David Lynch. Launched from Lynch's Mill Pond yard in June 1875, the *Rock Terrace* was the first vessel owned by Troop & Sons, one of the largest shipping fleets in Saint John history. In January 1888, the *Rock Terrace* hit a coral reef outside Guam. Unable to reach harbour, the crew abandoned ship and the vessel drifted for another five months before driving aground off Tarawa. Note the tools used by the shipbuilders, that all the men are wearing hats, and that only one man is clean-shaven.

**DAVID LYNCH, c.1880**

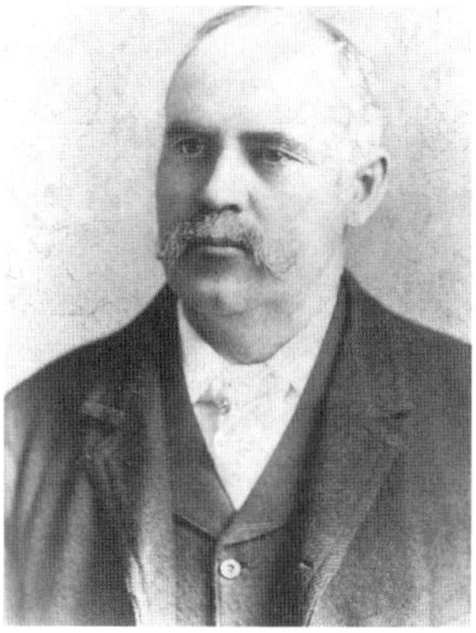

David Lynch, from Londonderry, was probably the most prominent New Brunswick shipbuilder. From his shipyard at Mill Pond (at the foot of Main Street where Tim Horton's now stands) he launched some of the largest and best of the New Brunswick wooden sailing ships. Ship-building and its related industries provided the economic lifeblood of Saint John; and the Irish, like Lynch, played roles as shipowner, builder, labourer, and crew. "The integration of this large immigrant population was further complicated by a virtual Irish monopoly of the unskilled labour of the port and the concentration of a large part of the Roman Catholic population in the low-cost housing of York Point." Lynch was born in 1836 and died in 1904.

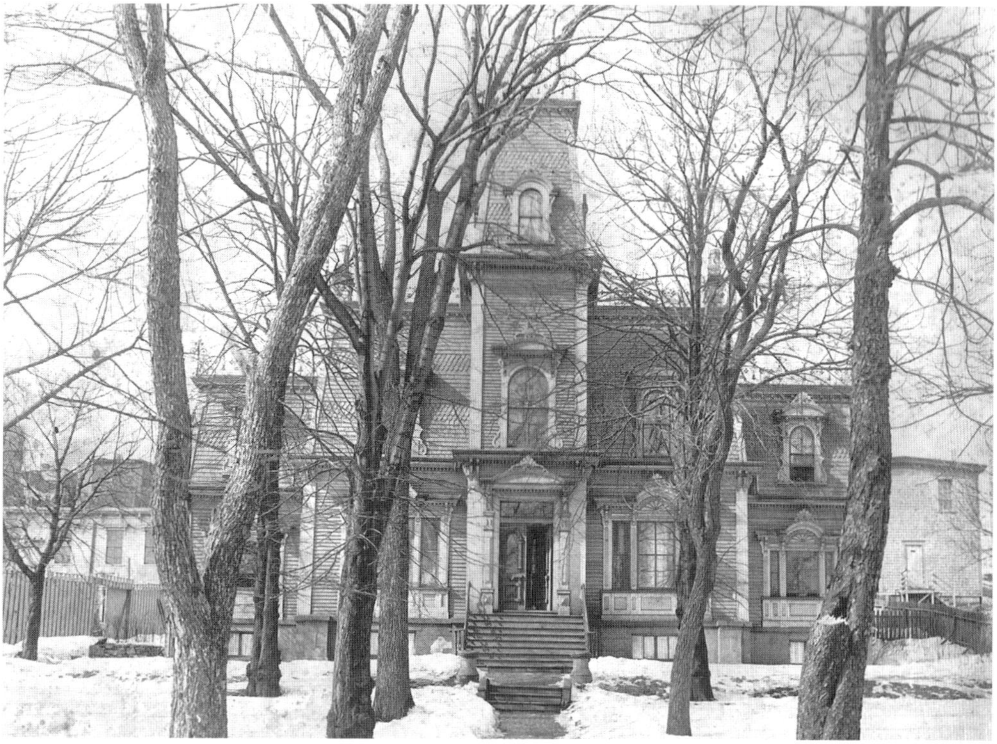

**142 PARADISE ROW, c.1900**

Prominent shipbuilders lived in houses that were testaments to their successes. Originally built for shipbuilder John Owen, the house pictured here was bought by David Lynch in 1881. Lynch had the house "thoroughly remodelled, the ceilings made higher, rooms enlarged, staircases improved ... another story, or Mansard roof ... added, with projecting tower and lookout." Lynch's grandson, Charles, the well-known Southam News columnist and war correspondent, was born here. The building was demolished in the 1970s for the Garden Street overpass expansion.

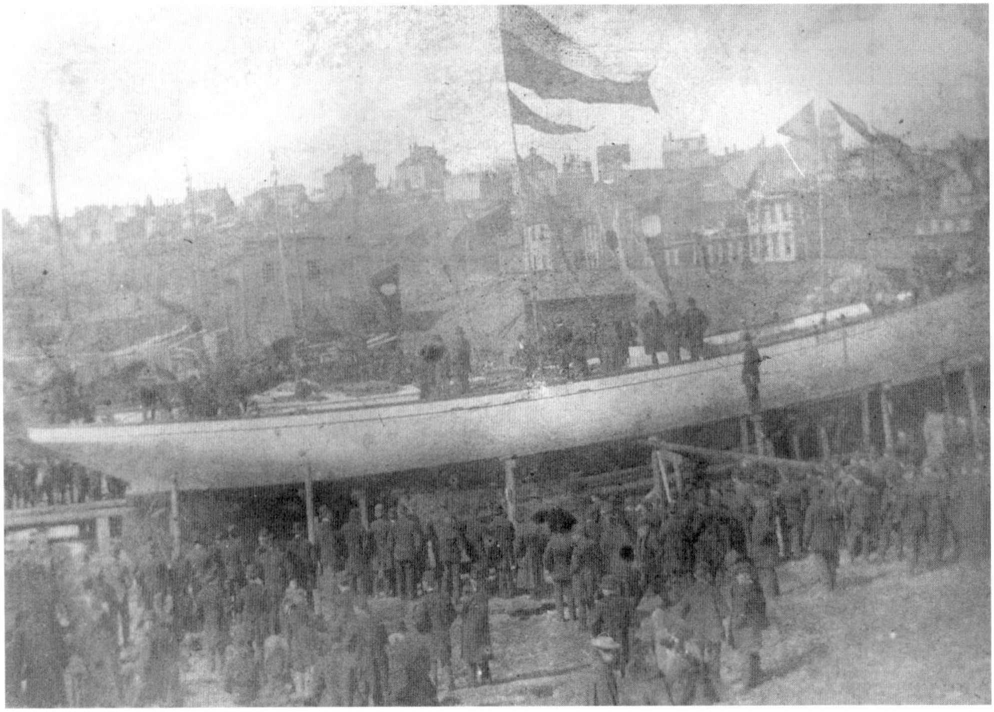

**SCHOONER LAUNCH, 1894** Built by David Lynch, the pilot schooner *David Lynch* was launched from the Hilyard shipyard at the foot of Harrison Street (where the HMCS Brunswicker building now stands). In the background is Douglas Avenue.

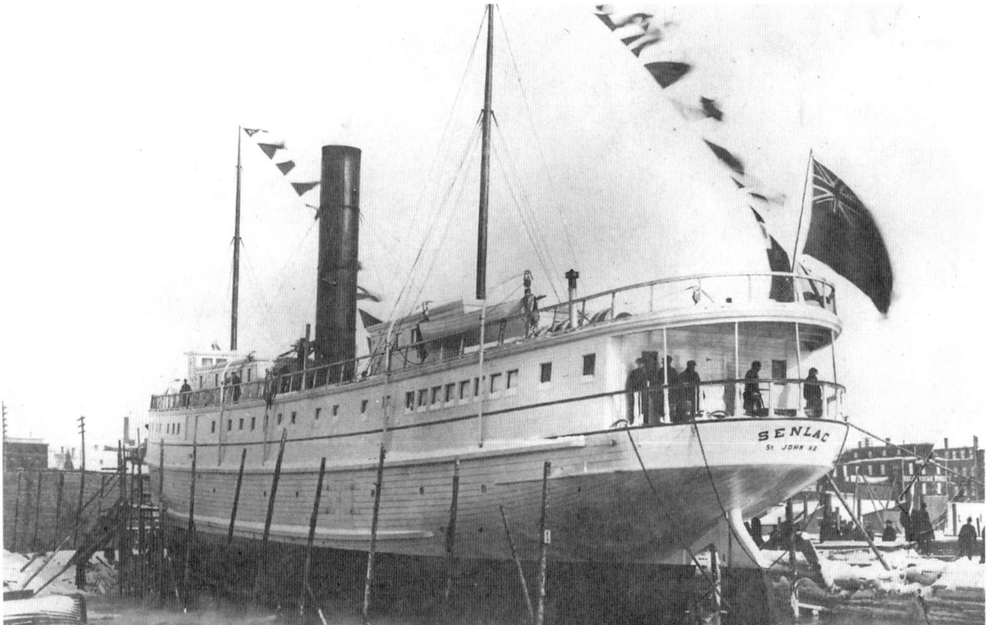

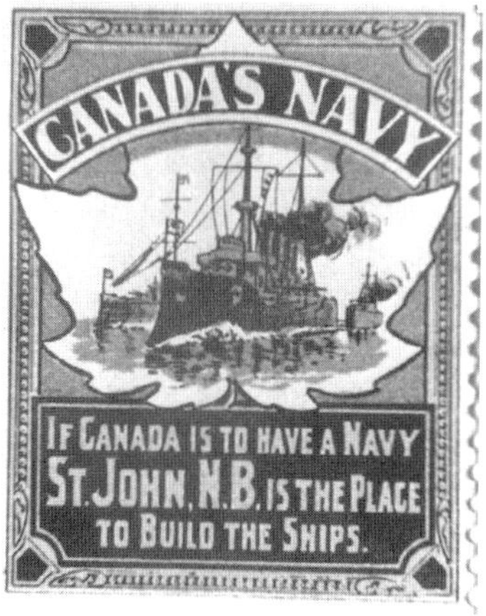


### Promotional Stamp

By 1909 the Canadian government was evaluating proposals to build a Canadian navy, with ships to be either purchased from England or built in Canada. In the same year the Saint John Board of Trade produced this promotional stamp to sway the decision toward building the ships in Saint John. In 1910 the Canadian government purchased two British ships, HMCS *Niobe* and *Rainbow*, and thus was created the new Royal Canadian Navy. Two of the gun barrels from HMCS *Niobe*, formerly used on coast defence mountings on Partridge Island during World War Two, are now on exhibit in Saint John.

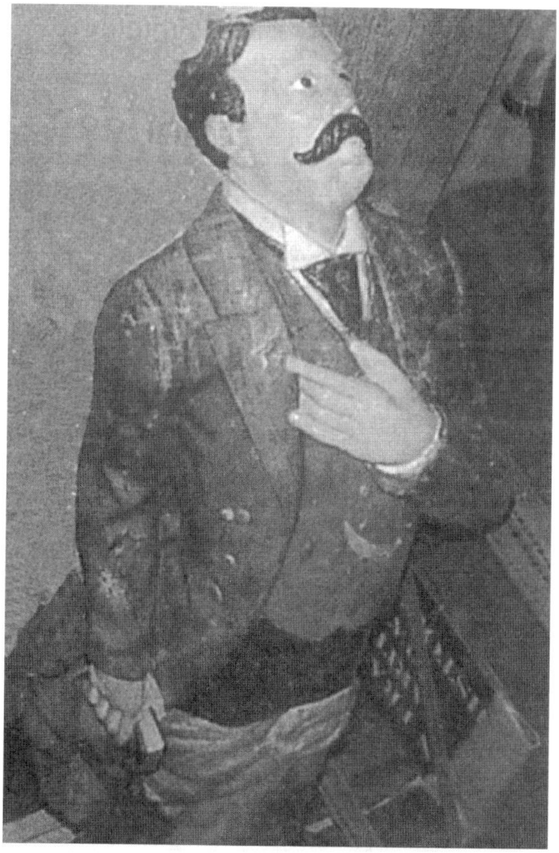

### Howard D. Troop Figurehead, 1998

The four-masted steel barque *Howard D. Troop* was built by Robert Duncan in Glasgow in 1892. After the death of Troop in 1912, the ship was sold to James Rolph Jr. of San Francisco. She was renamed the *Annie M. Reid* and broke up in 1934. In 1980 Harold E. Wright visited the San Francisco Maritime Museum and noted the figurehead of Howard D. Troop aboard the square-rigged ship *Balclutha*. Upon return to Saint John, he informed the New Brunswick Museum, which attempted to repatriate this significant figurehead to Saint John through purchase, replication, or exchange. That effort was not successful.

### Hilyard Shipyard, 1904

AT LEFT

The steamer *Senlac* was built for William Thomson & Co. by David Lynch. The carpenters were supplied by George V. Beatteay. The *Senlac*, launched in January 1904, served the coastal route along Nova Scotia's South Shore, PEI, and Newfoundland. She was destroyed by fire in 1915. Shown to the right of the yard is McCready's Vinegar Pickle Works.

**WAR MONCTON, 1917 AND 1919**

The Grant & Horne Shipyard built the sister ships *War Moncton* and *War Fundy* (launched August 1918), and the *Cutty Sark* (launched December 1919). "All the hustle and bustle in and around the yard. Butts piled up here, piles lying everywhere, lumber stacked sky-high, the buzz of the saw as it plies its way through the heavy timbers, the noise of the axe, all combine to make the scene one of real activity. Fully one hundred men are employed in preparing the blocks and erecting the derricks at present, and this number will be increased next week to five hundred." Native yellow birch and spruce were used for framing and planking the vessels. The 2,300-tonne wooden steamer *War Moncton* was launched from the Grant & Horne Shipyard at Courtenay Bay on May 29. At launch, her anchors were to check the ship as she left the ways, but her stern stuck fast in the mud. It took ten minutes for the tugs *Neptune*, *Alice R.*, and *G.D. Hunter* to move her. The *War Moncton* was then towed to Pier 6 where she received her engines. The *War Moncton* and her sister ship, the *War Fundy*, were built for the Imperial Munitions Board; but since the war had already ended, the *War Moncton* never saw active service and was scrapped not long after completion.

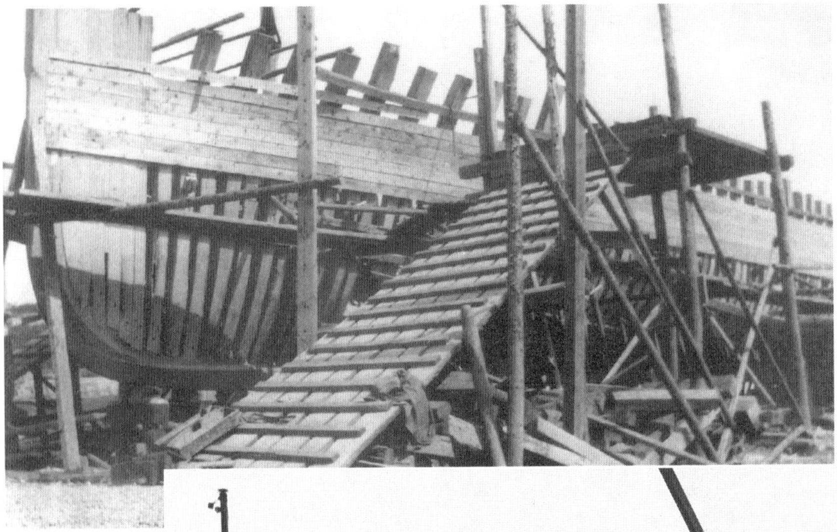

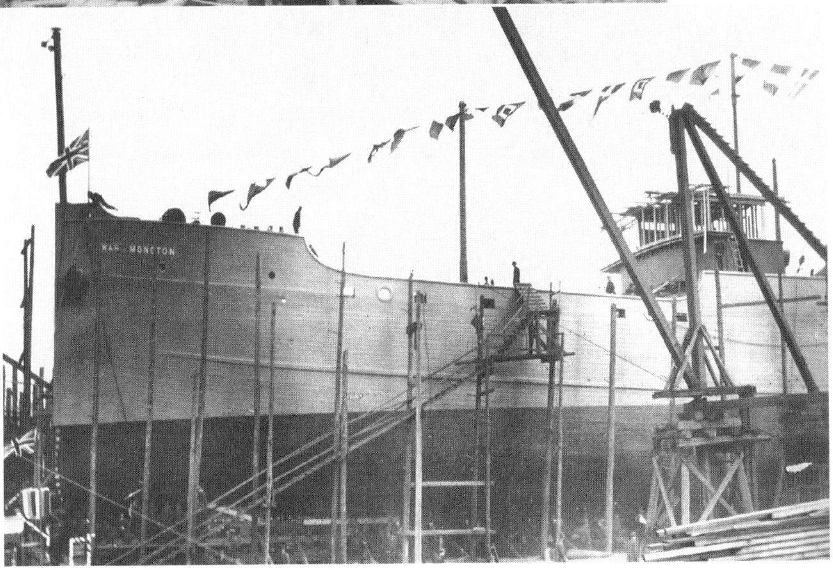

**Straight Shore Shipyard, 1918**

This image shows construction of the four-masted schooner *Randfontein*, which was laid down immediately following the launch in June 1918 of her sister ship, the *Dornfonteino*. The *Randfontein* was launched on February 4, 1919. Fraser Dunlop, who worked on the *Dornfontein,* remembered: "Well, then, from there they put him at what they called doing the work of a beatler. Now the work of the beatler was this, he had a wedged tool, a wedge-shaped tool on a long handle. Oh, a handle I suppose about three feet long, maybe four feet long, and there were two of them that worked together on this proposition and they were putting oakum into the cracks of this ship. They would put this strip of oakum at the

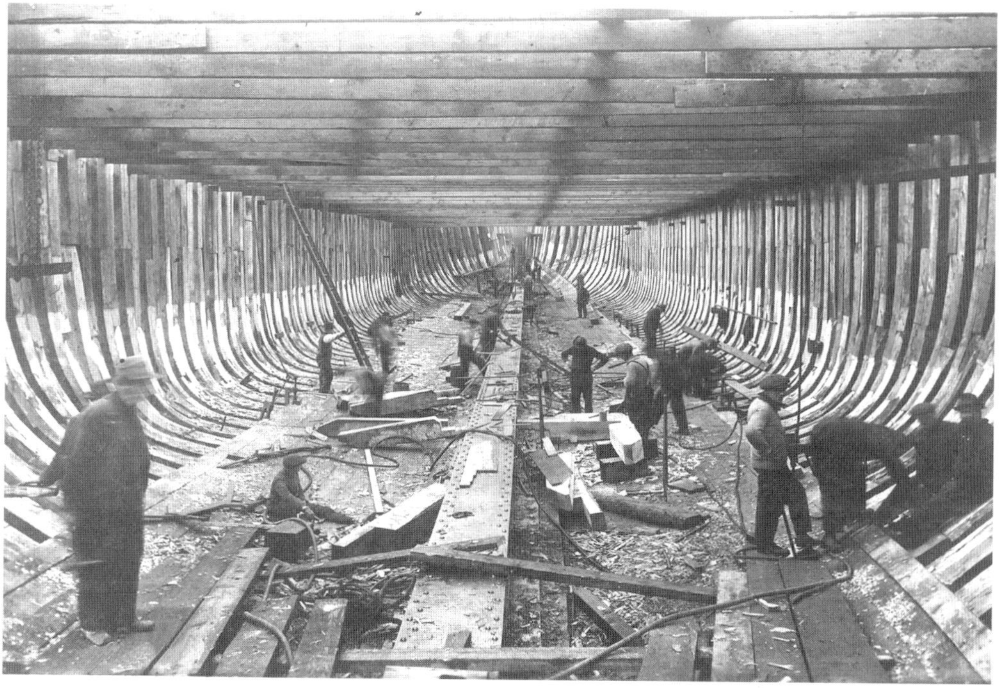

crack and then take this wedge-shaped tool and put it against the oakum and then the second fellow with the mall would hit this tool and drive this oakum into the crack until they couldn't get any more pounded in there. And Roy went to work at that. He worked at that for a couple of hours, and he was the fellow that was using the maul. There were, I suppose, two dozen of these fellows working on the side of this ship, and after a little while he noticed that the other crews, two men in a crew, were changing off every so often. One fellow held the wedge and the other fellow did the pounding, but this fellow that had been working with Roy, he was just holding the wedge and Roy was doing the pounding, hour after hour. So Roy said, "Look fellow, I think I could hold that little thing and I'd let you do the pounding for a while." Well, that was it. The fellow had to acknowledge that he was putting it over on Roy so they settled that. But that was Roy's work there for I don't know how many days, but at least while we were there he was a beatler, and he didn't seem to enjoy the name. It struck him rather funny, for he could laugh about it as well as anyone, and inform us every once in a while that was his office at the ship. He was a beatler."

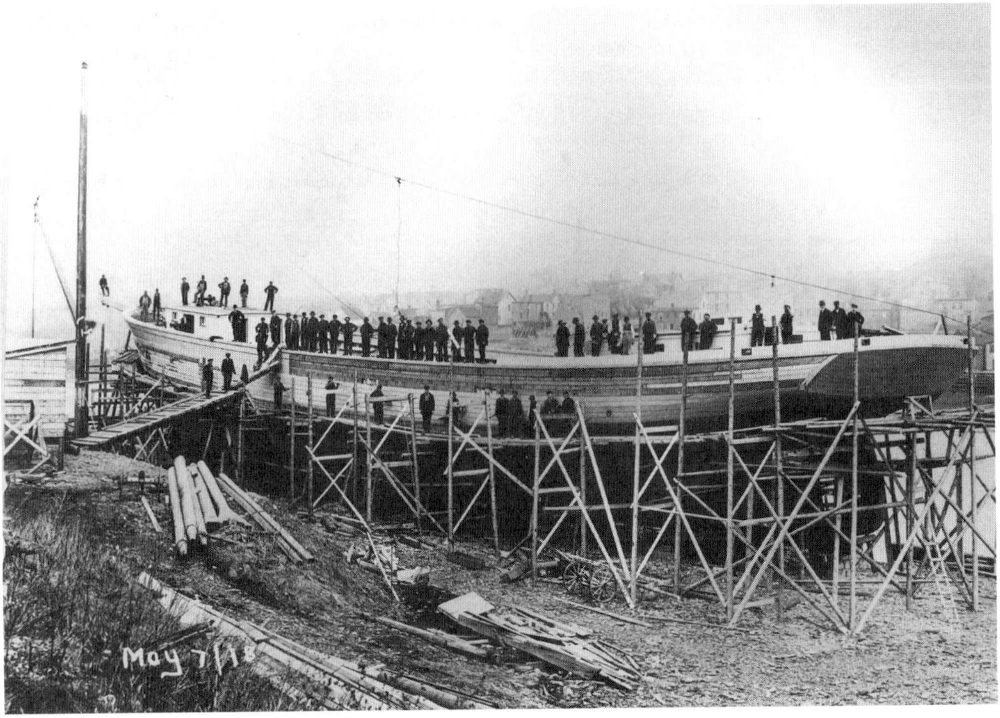


LAUNCH OF THE *DORNFONTEIN* (ABOVE) AND ITS MAIDEN VOYAGE (BELOW)

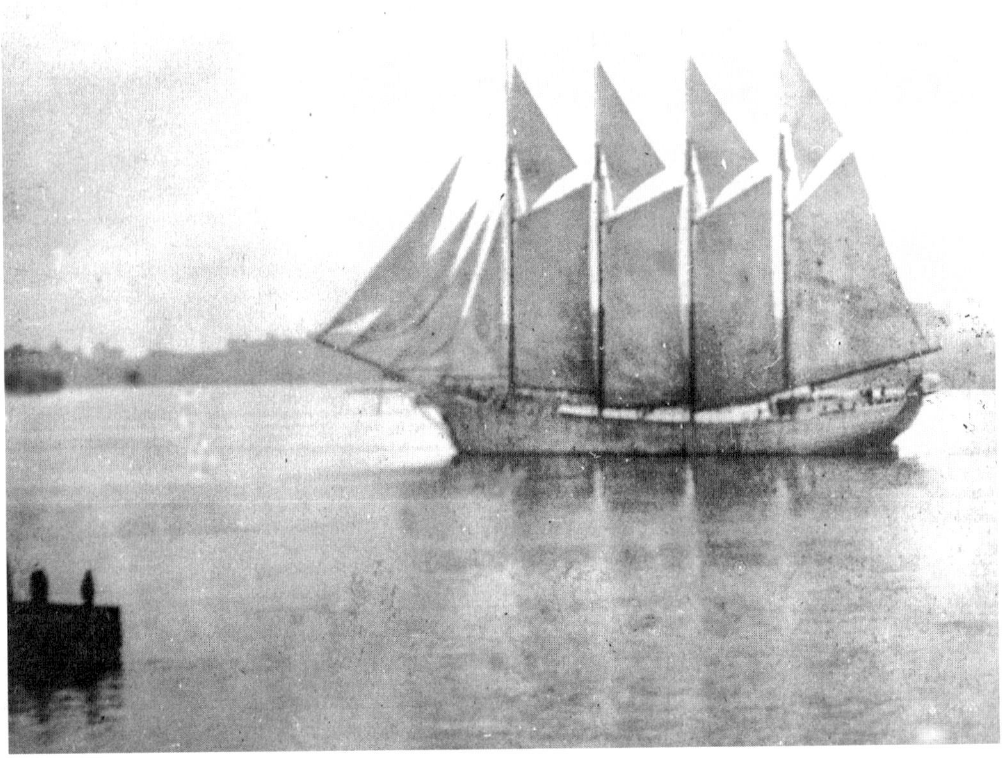

TOP LEFT

## *Dornfontein*, May 7, 1918

On June 11, 1918, at two o'clock in the afternoon, thousands crowded the shores near the Reversing Falls to witness the launch of the four-masted schooner *Dornfontein*. Built by D.A. Saker of the Marine Construction Company, *Dornfontein* was laid down in October 1917. She was 172 feet in length, had a beam of 40 feet, and registered at 695 tonnes. The keel was made of Douglas fir. Birch, Bayshore spruce, and Virginia oak were also used in the construction. Standing in the centre holding the small plank is Albert Patterson of West Quaco with his sons. To his right is son Gordon. The fourth man to the right of Gordon, standing under the wire, is son Charlie. A third son, Isaac, is also on the deck.

**Maiden Voyage,**

BOTTOM LEFT

The *Dornfontein* left Saint John fully loaded and carrying a large deckload of lumber. Twenty-five miles off Brier Island, Nova Scotia, the German submarine U-156 surfaced and fired two shots across her bow. "After taking from the ship all her valuables and foodstuffs, as well as a large quantity of gasoline, the Germans started a fire in her forecastle and another in her after cabin, and the ship burned to the water's edge." Some research suggests that this vessel was rebuilt and renamed the *Netherton*, which was destroyed by fire in August 1920.

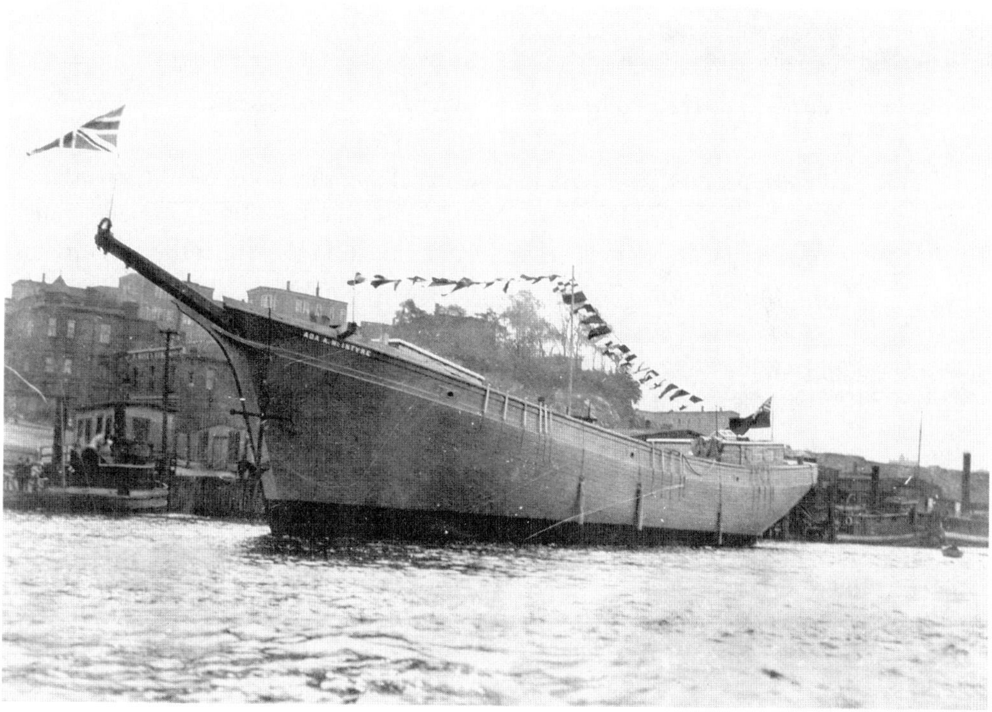


**Outfitting, 1918** The *Ada A. McIntyre* was launched at Moss Glen on the Kingston Peninsula on September 25, 1918. She was brought to Indiantown for outfitting. In 1923 she was lost off the coast of Maine.

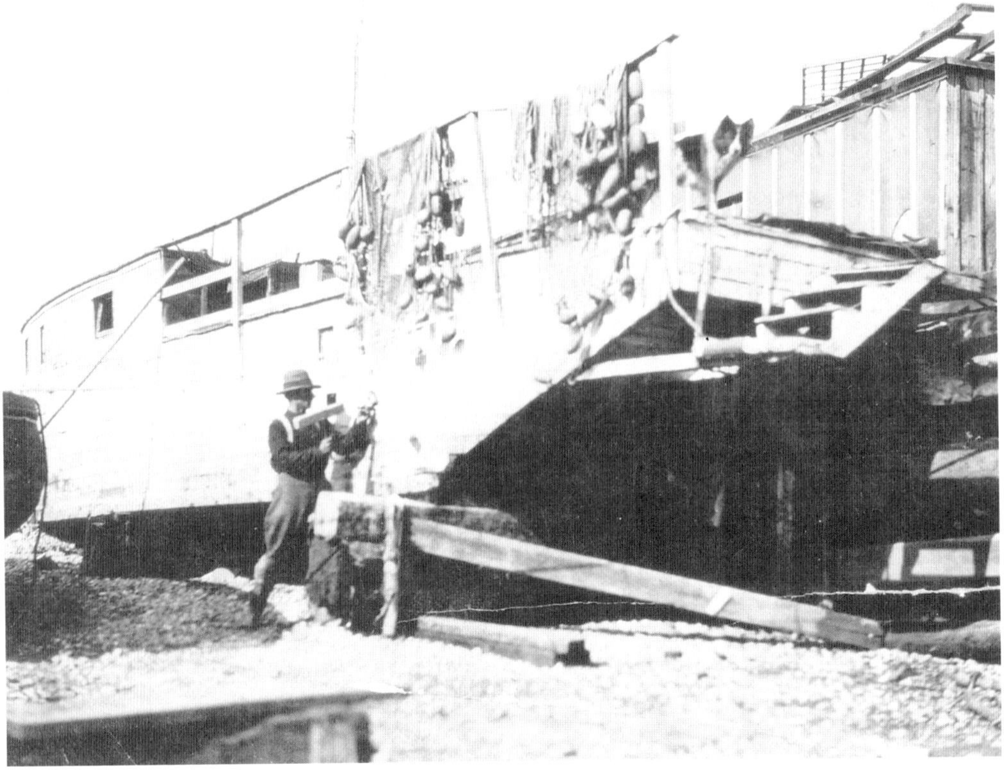

**Eel Boat, May 1930**

Fred Lord of Navy Island is shown caulking the motor boat *Milwaukee,* which was owned by his brother Charles. The Lord brothers made annual trips up the St. John River to Grand Lake for eels, which they exported to the United States. Fred and his family lived on Navy Island for over two generations. Navy Island had originally been reserved for the British Royal Navy, but the city of Saint John leased the land to fishermen. In 1927 the city sold Navy Island to the federal government. Fred Lord was killed in an industrial accident at the port in November 1930.

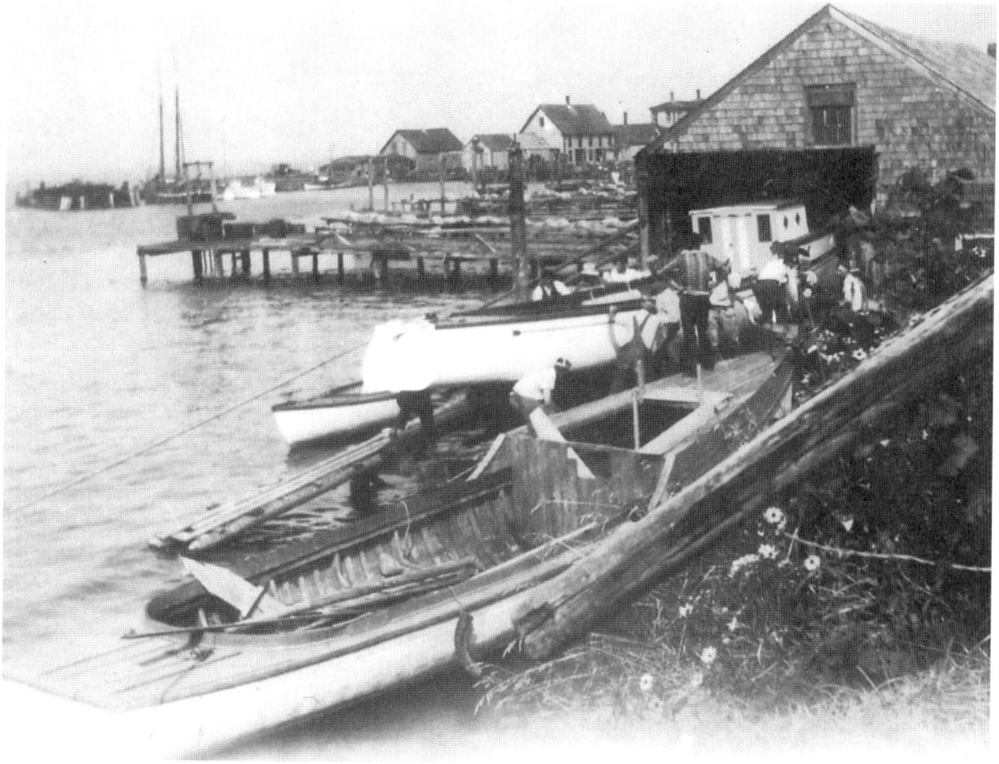

**Campobello Boatyard, c 1940**

Morris and Varne Fletcher and their father, Blan, operated a boatyard from the early years of the twentieth century until 1982. The brothers built various crafts: Varne fashioned models of tall-masted ships that once plied the Bay of Fundy, and Morris, who also worked at Jackson Brothers' fish-processing plant, built lobster boats made of oak and cedar. A finished boat cost about $10,000 plus the Morrises' labour. Varne died in 1983 and Morris died in 1987.

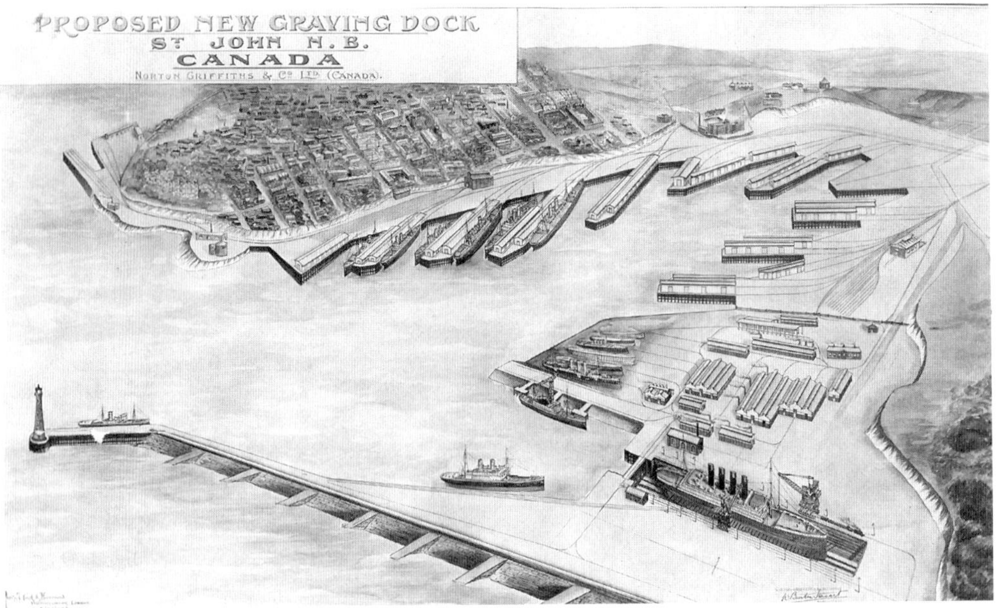


**Proposed Graving Dock, August 9, 1911**

Saint John's member of parliament, William Pugsley, pushed for the construction of a drydock for years. This was not a new dream—efforts to secure a modern drydock went back well into the third-quarter of the nineteenth century. Pugsley was successful in having the Norton Griffiths Company of London put forth this scheme in 1911. Construction of the drydock and the Courtenay Bay breakwater began in 1912, but the outbreak of war in 1914 slowed construction until 1916 when the Norton Griffiths Company went into receivership.

## Construction of Graving Dock, 1922

TOP RIGHT

In 1918 the Saint John Drydock and Shipbuilding Company Limited restarted the project to build a drydock. Excavation started in Courtenay Bay on October 15, 1918, and was finished on July 21, 1921. Concrete was started in July 1921 and finished on September 22, 1923. On October 29, 1923, Governor General Baron Byng of Vimy, opened the 1,500-foot drydock, then the largest in the world. The drydock was separated by a central caisson, which could provide two working docks. The office building shown at the left still stands.

**The first ship, 1923**

BOTTOM RIGHT

The Norwegian steamer *M.H. Kongshaven* was badly damaged when she ran aground on the southwest ledge of Brier Island in October 1923. Captain John Palander took his vessel into the drydock in time for the official opening by His Excellency, Baron Bing of Vimy, Governor General. The steamer *Kongshaven* was on a voyage from Philadelphia to Saint John to load potatoes for Havana, Cuba, when she grounded. The ship's stern post had been broken off near the deck and carried away with the stern's shoe. Several plates were badly bent and punctured and she had taken on several feet of water. She had made her first trip to Saint John in March 1922.

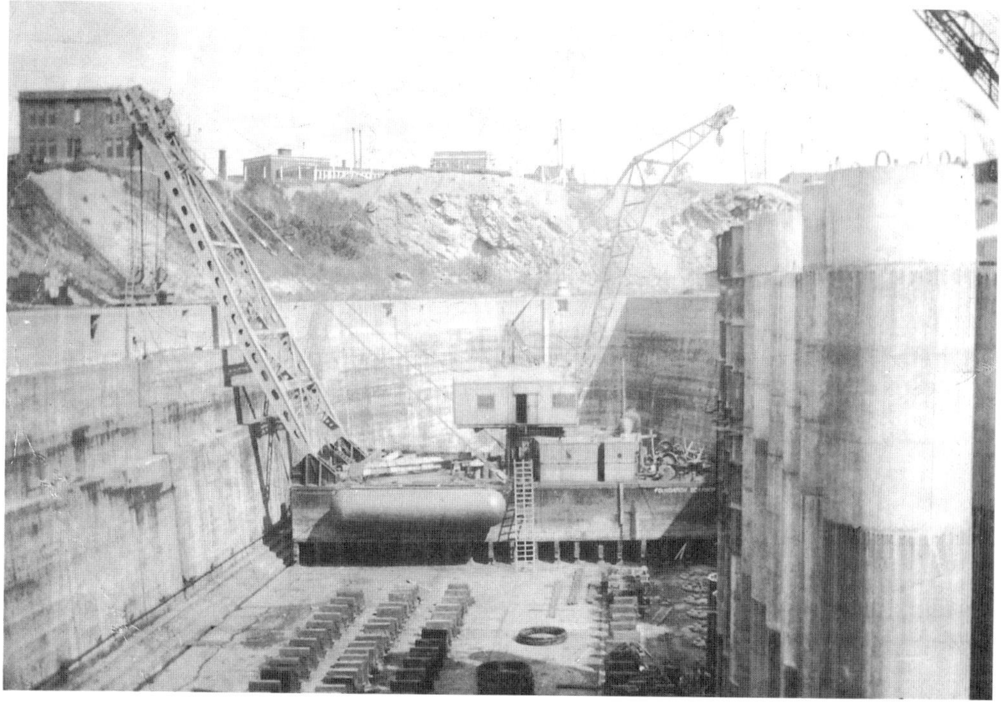

CONSTRUCTION OF GRAVING DOCK (ABOVE) AND THE FIRST SHIP (BELOW)

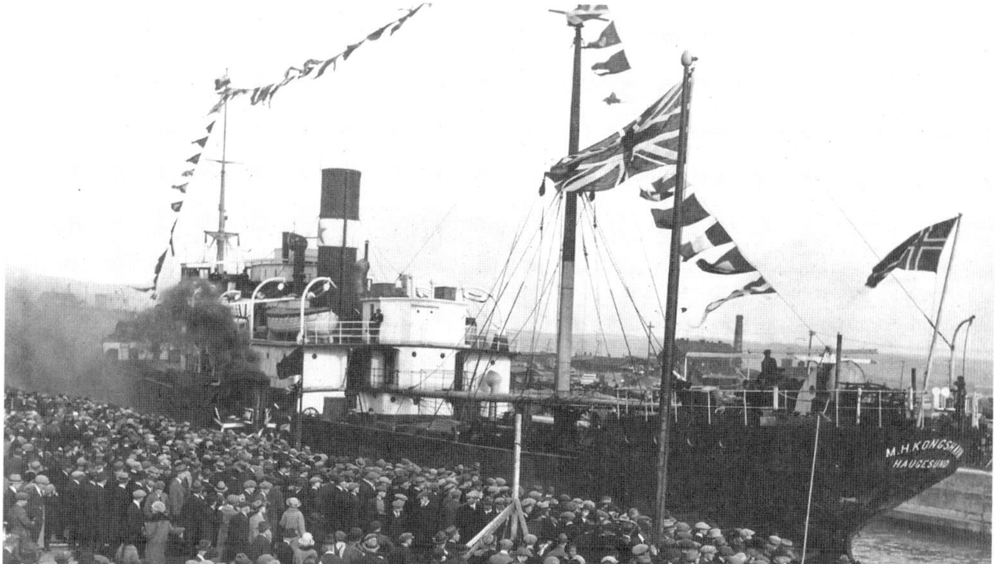

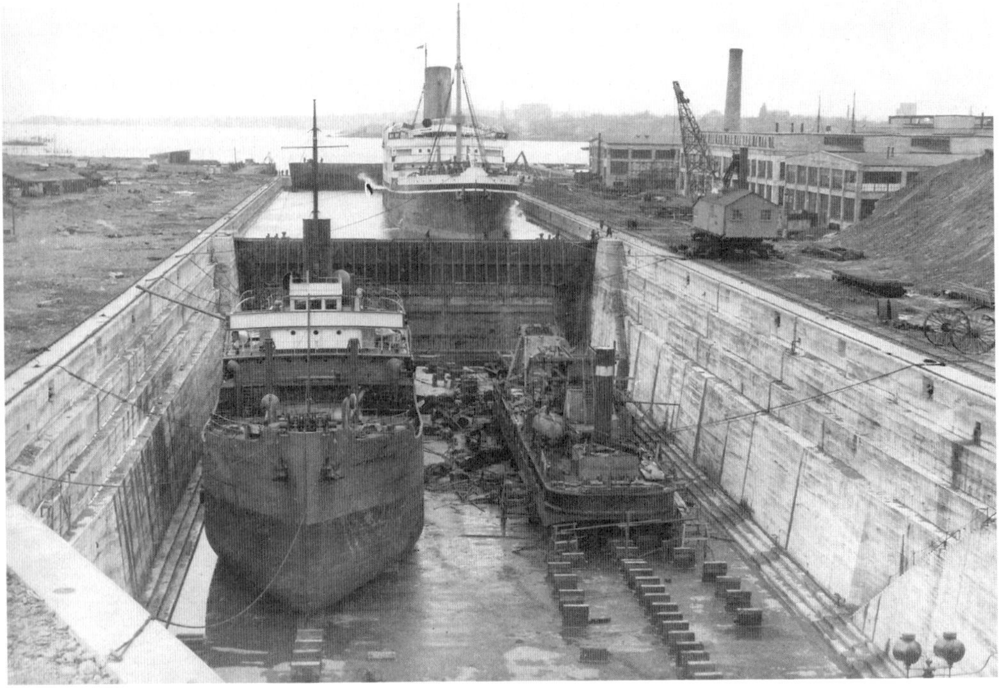

**GRAVING DOCK, 1930**

The Saint John Drydock and Shipbuilding Company Limited billed itself as one of the largest in the world. While the head office was in Saint John, the executive office was in Montreal. The outer dock, shown with the CPS *Marloch*, was 650 feet long and 125 feet wide, with 42 feet on the sill. The inner dock, shown with the SS *Emperor of Montreal* and the dredge *Leconfield*, was 500 feet long. When this photo was taken, the yard had a marine railway dock system with a 2000-tonne deadweight capacity, electric dewatering pumps, ten 15-tonne electric capstans, one 15-tonne travelling crane, and one 60-tonne fixed derrick on the fitting-out wharf. The yard also had floating and locomotive high-capacity cranes, as well as dredges and tugboats. The yard also did structural steelwork, providing the steel for the New Brunswick Museum and the Saint John General Hospital.

**RAIL FERRY, 1926**

TOP RIGHT

The Saint John Shipyard built this rail ferry for the PEI service. Named the *Scotia II*, it replaced the original *Scotia,* which had been built in 1915. By 1921 islanders were agitating for a new ferry service across the Strait of Canso. A Royal Commission on Maritime Claims agreed: "*Scotia I* was unsuitable for the Island service, and Prince Edward Island was inappropriate for automobile traffic. Passengers travelling by automobile had to load their cars on railway flatcars for the trip—a pleasant novelty in 1920, but an unacceptable nuisance ten years later." *Scotia II* was still being used in the mid-1960s to handle peak traffic.

RAIL FERRY, 1926

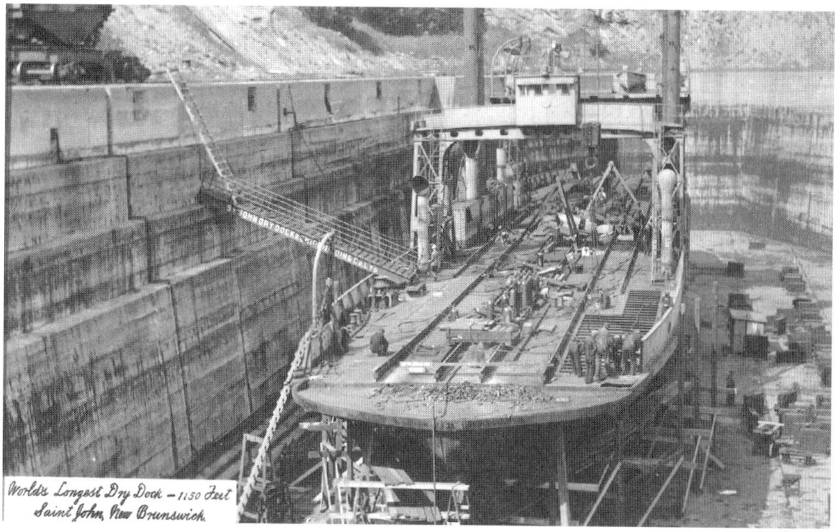


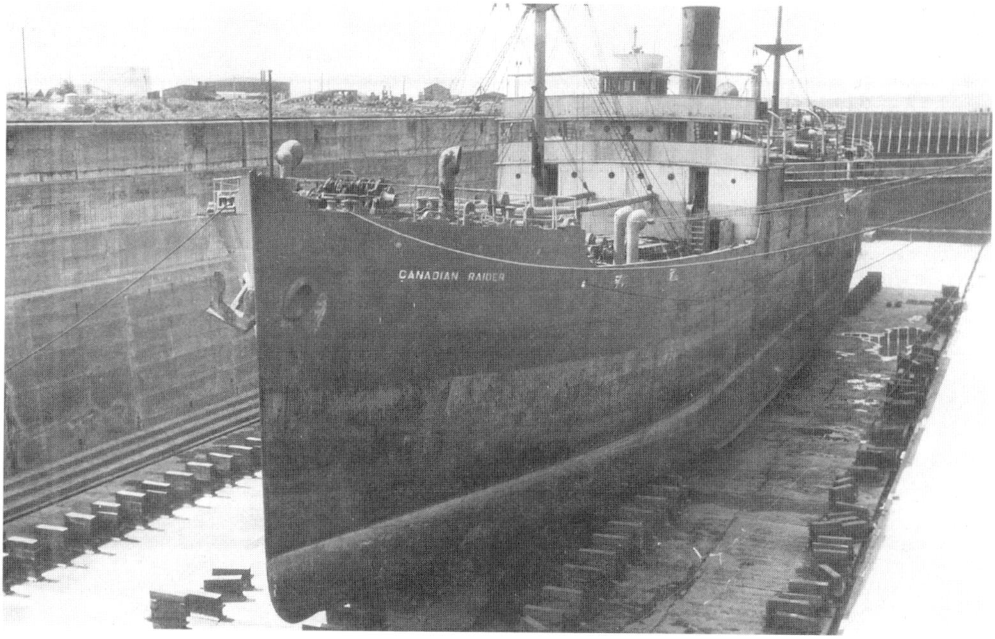


***CANADIAN RAIDER*, AUGUST 1929**

The presidents of the Saint John Drydock and Shipbuilding Company were James Playfair (1918-1934), Frank M. Ross (1934-1945), and Charles N. Wilson (1945-1959). In 1959 Wilson sold the company to K.C. Irving. From then until the 1990s, Saint John Shipbuilding constructed and repaired numerous vessels, including the oil rig *Bow Drill III, Abegweit II,* the tanker *Kurdistan*, the Arctic icebreaker *Canmar Kigoriak*, the *Grand Manan IV*, *Aime Gaudreau*, MV *Hudson*, the coast guard ships *Robert Foulis* and *Thomas Carleton*, the *Princess of Acadia II*, the MV *Esso*, and the current Kent Line fleet: *Irving Arctic, Canada*, *Eskimo*, *Wellington Kent* (former *Irving Nordic*), *Kent Express*, and *Kent Sprint.*

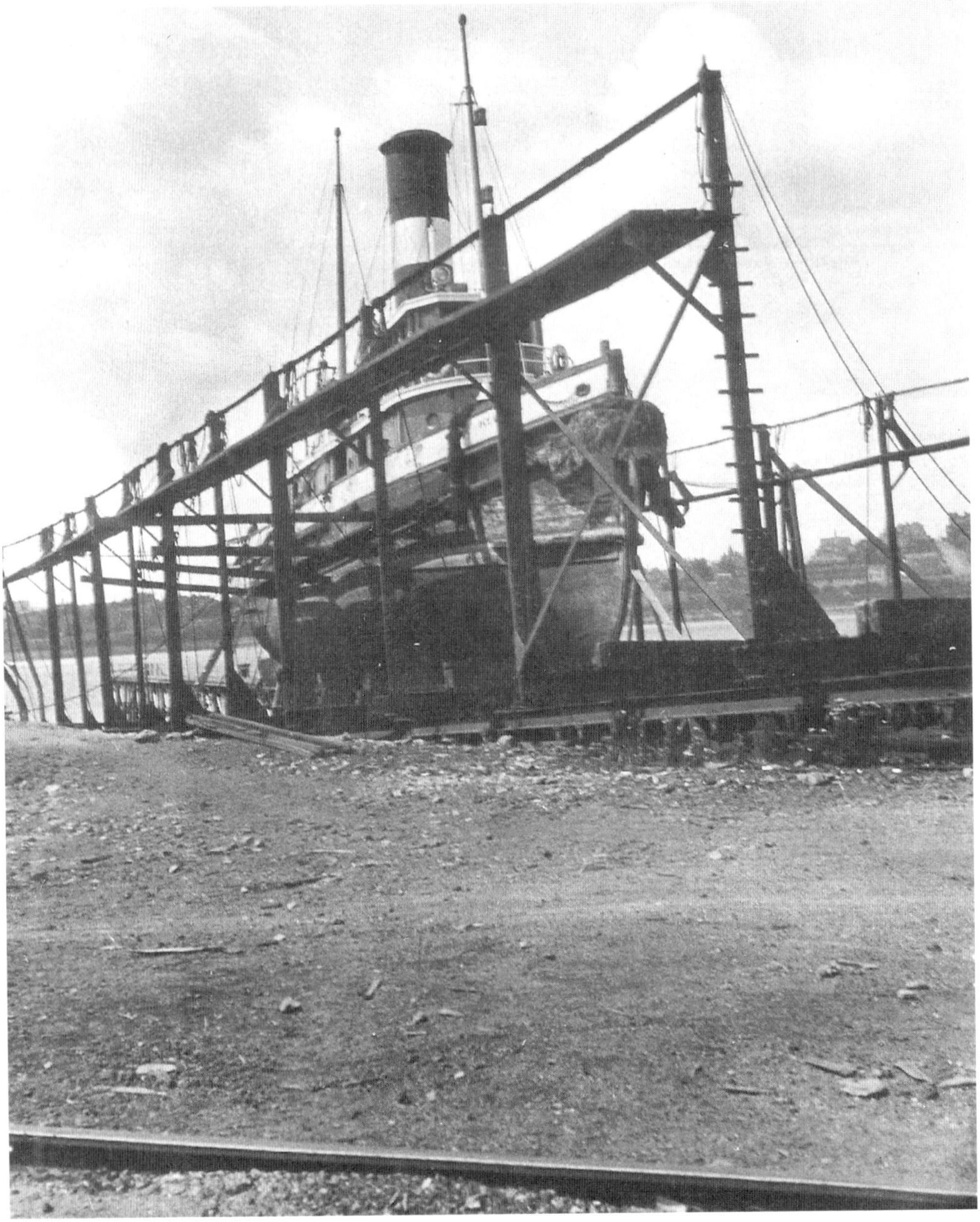

**Ocean Hawk, August 1929**

The tugboat *Ocean Hawk*, owned by Saint John Drydock and Shipbuilding Company, is shown in the slipway at the drydock. Tugboats are the workhorse of a harbour, and there are several well-known tugs throughout our history, including the *Lord Kitchener, Foremost #43, Ocean Osprey, Rockswift, Ocean Kiwi, Ocean Snipe, Neptune, Franklin, Irving Birch, Gregory, Irving Teak*, and *Ocean Hawk II.*

**CORVETTE K-148, DECEMBER 1940**

This is the stern of HMCS *Amherst*, the first of three Flower-class 1939-1940 corvettes built at Saint John Drydock. She was laid down on May 23, 1940, launched on December 4, 1940, and commissioned on August 5, 1941. She arrived at Halifax on August 22, and after workup joined Newfoundland Command in October. She had one 4-inch gun, one two-pound gun and two 20-mm Hedgehog depth charges. She was steadily employed as an ocean escort for the succeeding three years, during which time she was involved in two particularly hard-fought convoy battles: ON.127 (August 1942) and SC.107 (October 1942). Her only real respite was between May and November 1943, when she underwent a major refit at Charlottetown, including the extension of her fore-

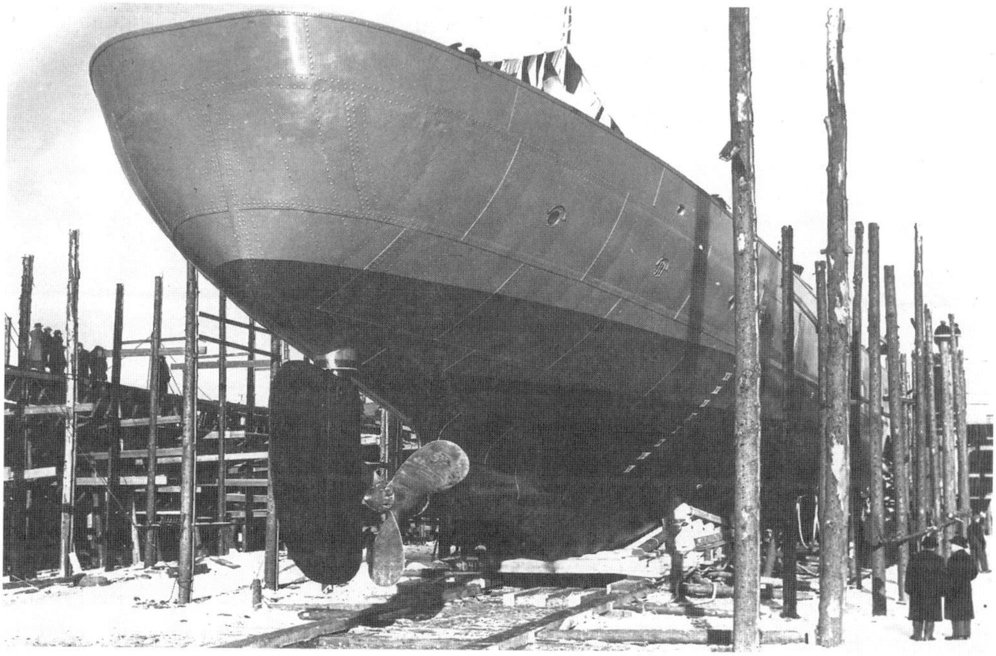

castle. After workups at Pictou she returned to the North Atlantic grind until September 1944, when she began another long refit, this time at Liverpool, Nova Scotia. Following workups in Bermuda in January 1945, she joined Halifax Force, but in March was lent to EG.C-7 for one round-trip to the UK. HMCS *Amherst* was paid off on July 16, 1945, at Sydney, and placed in reserve at Sorel. Sold in 1946, she served in the Venezuelan Navy as *Federacion* until broken up in 1956. In addition to the three corvettes, Saint John Drydock built eight 4700-tonne cargo ships and three 700-tonne coastal vessels, and outfitted or repaired a few hundred merchant vessels and warships (such as AMC *Jervis Bay*, SS *Taronga Park* for Australia, HMCS *St. Croix* and *St. Stephen*, and the battleship HMS *Ramielles)*. After the war, the drydock built several other ships for the Canadian Navy, including HMCS *Miramichi II*, HMCS *Protecteur*, HMCS *Preserver*, and HMCS *Fundy II*. HMCS *Miramichi II* was commissioned on July 30, 1954, and paid off on October 1. On October 9, 1954, she was transferred to the French Navy and renamed *La Lorientaise*. HMCS *Fundy II* was commissioned on March 19, 1954, and paid off on March 31 when she was transferred to the French Navy and renamed *La Dunkerquoise*.

**THREE CORVETTES, 1941**

All three Flower-class corvettes are shown here. HMCS *Amherst*, launched on December 4, 1940, is at the right. To her stern is HMCS *Sackville*, launched on May 15, 1941. (HMCS *Sackville* is now preserved as a memorial in Halifax.) In the background is HMCS *Moncton*, laid down on December 17, 1940, and launched on August 11, 1941. Commissioned at Saint John on April 24, 1942, *Moncton* arrived at Halifax on May 12. She was the last of the RCN's initial Flower-class programme to be completed, owing to heavy demands on her builder for repair work to war-damaged ships. After workup she joined WLEF, Halifax; and when the force was divided into escort groups in June 1943, she became a member of EG. W-5. HMCS *Moncton* remained in this service until transferred in January 1944 to the West Coast where she was assigned to Esquimalt Force, of which she remained a member until VJ-Day. In the course of

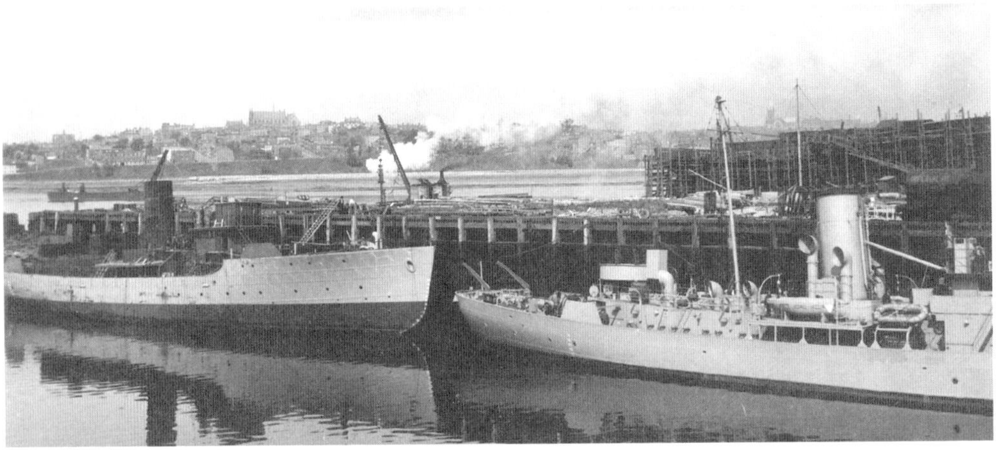

an extensive refit at Vancouver from May 5 to July 7, 1944, *Moncton's* forecastle was extended. She was paid off at Esquimalt on December 12, 1945, and sold for conversion to a whale-catcher at Kiel. She entered service in 1955 as the Dutch-flagship *Willem Vinke* and was broken up at Santander, Spain, in 1966. Another warship repaired at Saint John Drydock was HMCS *Fredericton*. Launched in 1941, she was assigned to WLEF until July 1942, when she joined Halifax Force (Aruba Tanker Convoys). In September, after one round trip to Aruba, she was placed under U.S. operational control to escort New York-Guantanamo convoys. She arrived in New York for the last time on February 21, 1943. After a major refit at Liverpool from June 9 to October 10, 1943, and workups at Pictou, she joined EG. C-1 and for the next ten months was employed as an ocean escort. She left Londonderry on September 30, 1944, for convoy ON.256 and, upon arriving in Canada, went to Saint John for a two-month refit. This was completed in mid-December, and in January 1945 the ship proceeded to Bermuda for a three-week workup. In February she joined EG. C-9, with which she was to spend the balance of the war as ocean escort. *Fredericton* was paid off on July 14, 1945, at Sorel and broken up in 1946. In 1987 Saint John Shipbuilding laid down the first of nine (contract total twelve) frigates for the Canadian Navy. Included was HMCS *Fredericton*, the only New Brunswick-named vessel, and she perpetuates the proud service of the first HMCS *Fredericton*. When this contract finished, Saint John Shipbuilding built two vessels for Kent Lines Ltd., the *Kent Express* and *Kent Sprint*.

**HMCS *SAINT JOHN*, MARCH 26, 1944**

The River-class frigate HMCS *Saint John*, K456, was built by Canadian Vickers Ltd. in Montreal. She was laid down on May 28, 1943, and launched on August 25, 1943. Lieutenant Commander W.R. Stacey, RCNVR, brought his ship to Saint John on a courtesy call. After a parade, Mayor Wasson (shown here standing to Stacey's right) presented the ship with a piano, a washing machine, a gramophone, records, books for a library, a serving tray, water jug, cigarette box, and ash trays. The officer at the left is Brigadier Gerry Anglin, Commander of District #7. The three men at the right are — Skaling, Gerry Terry, and Paul Barry. Stacey commanded HMCS *Saint John* during her attack on U-247. Under command of Oblt. Gerhard Matschulat, U-247 had one sunk ship to her credit, the British fish trawler *Noreen Mary* on July 5, 1944. The *Saint John* used depth charges to sink U-247, with the loss of all fifty-two hands, on September 1, 1944, in the English Channel near Lands End. HMCS *Swansea* was given shared credit for the sinking. In December 1944, the *Saint John* escorted convoys JW.62 and RA.62 on the north Russia run to and from Kola Inlet. Lt.Cmdr. Stacey was on leave when she sank her second U-boat. U-309, under command of Oblt. Herbert Loeder, was depth-charged by *Saint John* on February 16, 1945, in the North Sea. All forty-seven hands were lost. *Saint John* arrived at Cardiff for repairs on February 27, 1945, and, when these were completed in April, proceeded home for tropicalization refit at Saint John from May to October 1945. HMCS *Saint John* was paid off November 27, 1945, at Halifax where she was placed in reserve in Bedford Basin until sold in 1947 for scrap at Sydney. Stacey was mentioned-in-despatches on June 8, 1944, for service in the Atlantic, and awarded the Distinguished Service Cross on March 21, 1945, for "services in destroying an enemy submarine." Her ship's bell and other memorabilia are on exhibit at the Trade and Convention Centre in Market Square (Saint John). Farley Mowat, in his book *Grey Seas Under*, misidentified the *Saint John* as a British trawler. In November 1956 the Saint-class tug *St. John* was commissioned, named in honour of Father Jean De Brebeuf, a Jesuit missionary. She was paid off in 1972.

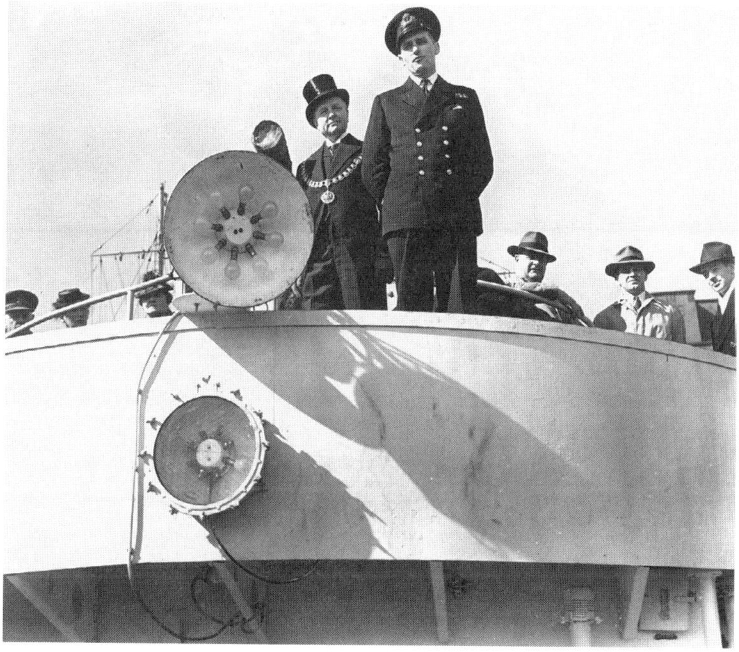


Our Shipbuilding Tradition 19

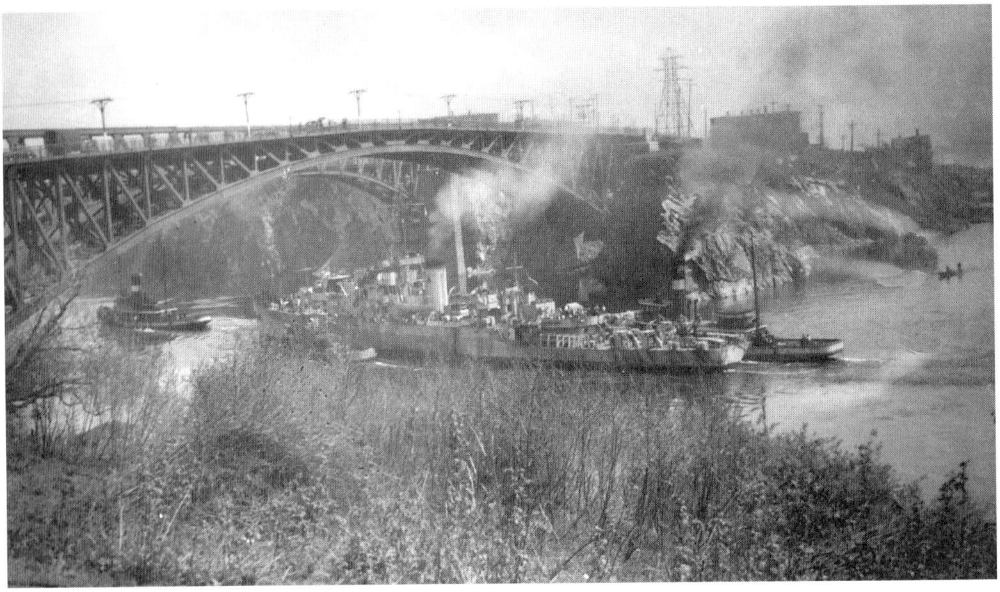

**HMCS *LA HULLOISE*, 1945**

This ship, pendant K-668, was built by Canadian Vickers of Montreal. She was laid down October 8, 1943, launched on October 29, 1943, and commissioned at Montreal on May 20, 1944. *La Hulloise* arrived at Halifax in June 1944. She had a crew of eight officers and 133 other ranks. She proceeded to Bermuda in July for workup, and on returning was assigned to EG.16 at Halifax. In October she was reassigned to EG.25, and transferred with it to Londonderry in November 1944. She spent the remainder of the war in UK waters, based variously at Derry and Rosyth. On March 7, 1945, with HMCS *Strathadam* and HMCS *Thetford Mines*, she took part in sinking U-302 in St. Georges Channel, with the loss of all forty-eight hands aboard the U-boat. Late in May she sailed for Canada to undergo tropicalization refit at Saint John. She is seen here proceeding under the Reversing Falls Bridge to the Long Reach for sea trials. Work was completed October 19, but the Pacific war had ended by then, so she was paid off at Halifax on December 6, 1945. Recommissioned for cadet and new entry training in 1949, *La Hulloise* was largely operational until November 23, 1953, when she was paid off for conversion to a Prestonian-class ocean escort. She was commissioned as such on October 9, 1957, pendant 305, and remained in service until paid off on July 16, 1965. She was broken up at La Spezia, Italy, in 1966.

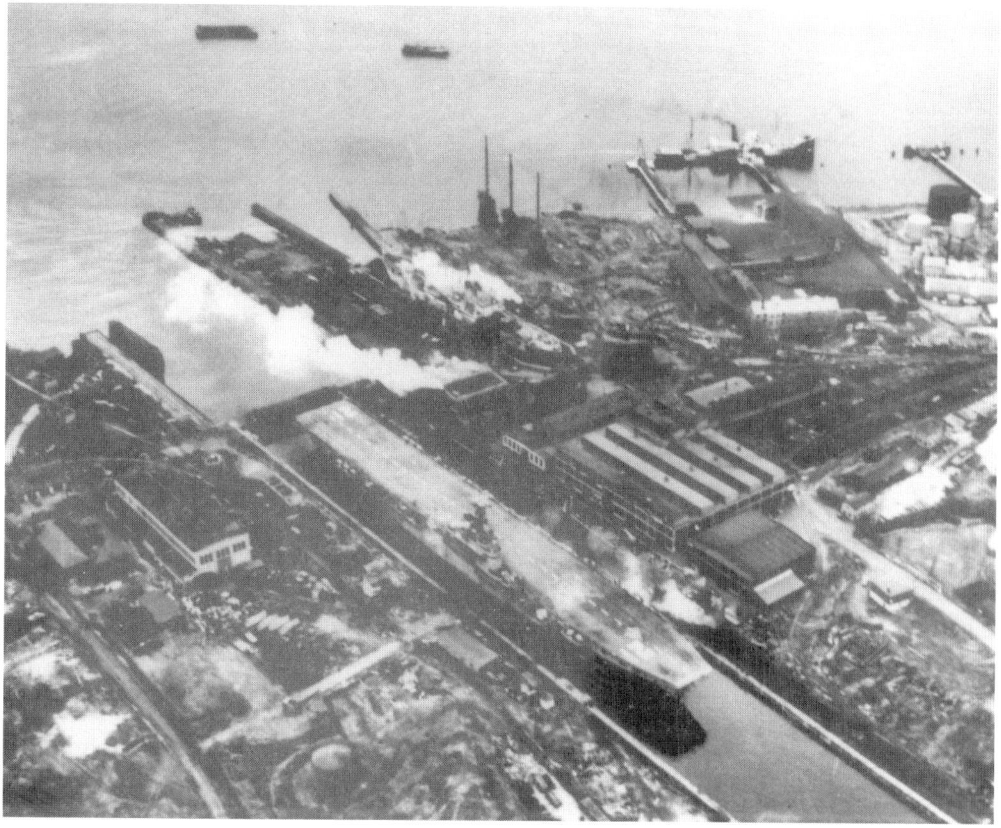

**HMCS *MAGNIFICENT*, 1948**

The *Maggie* was borrowed from Britain's Royal Navy as a replacement for HMCS *Warrior* (which was too small for the Canadian Navy's requirements). The larger Majestic-class *Magnificent* was built by Harland and Wolff, and was laid down on December 12, 1942. She was launched on May 20, 1944, commissioned on March 14, 1946, and handed over to the RCN in Halifax on April 7, 1948. Her first call to Saint John was in September 1948 when she underwent a nine-day, below-waterline examination and routine maintenance. There were nine New Brunswickers amongst her crew, including Harold Hinch and Dell Lynch of Glen Falls, Neil Flicknell, Robert McCann, and Robert Horncastle of Saint John, and Carl Robertson of Hampton. *Maggie* participated in numerous training exercises, travelling the world and showing the Canadian flag in such places as Oslo, Havana, Lisbon, and San Francisco. During the 1956 Suez Crisis she arrived in Port Said, Egypt, with a deckload of 233 vehicles and 406 army personnel as Canada's contribution to the UN Emergency Force in the Middle East. On June 14, 1957, *Magnificent* was paid off at Plymouth and given back to the Royal Navy in exchange for the first, and only, carrier ever to be bought by the RCN, HMCS *Bonaventure*. *Magnificent* was recommissioned as HMS *Magnificent*, placed in reserve, and later sold for scrap in Faslane, Scotland, in July 1965.

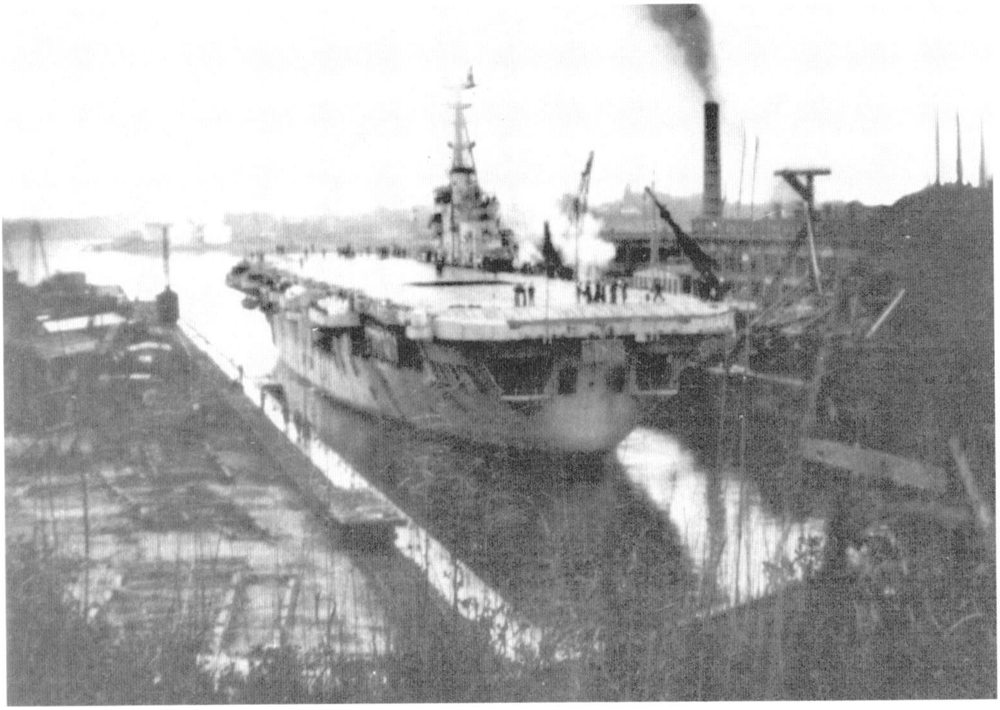

**_Maggie_, 1949**

The *Maggie* had a crew of twelve hundred and defensive armament of thirty 40-mm Bofors Anti-Aircraft guns. Her aircraft numbered between thirty-four and thirty-seven, and included Hawker Sea Furys, Grumman Avengers, and Fireflys, and Sikorsky HO4S helicopters. Her second commanding officer was Commodore Gus R. Miles, OBE, of Rothesay, who commanded from August 1948 to August 17, 1949. He lost command of his ship when the vessel went aground off Yarmouth. She was brought into the drydock for repairs which took several months. The *Maggie*'s third trip to the drydock was in December 1950 when she underwent painting, inspection, and a general overhaul.

**Bow reconstruction, 1951**

TOP RIGHT

On her final trip to the drydock, the *Maggie* had her buckled bow-plates, damaged on a rough crossing from Scotland, replaced. The carrier which replaced the *Maggie* was HMCS *Bonaventure*. The *Bonnie* served with the RCN from 1957 until 1970 and was in the Saint John Drydock a few times for refit.

**Ring's Boat Repair, c.1953**

BOTTOM RIGHT

Grenville Ring followed his father Wellington in operating his own boat repair yard. Born on Portland Street, Grenville specialized in the repair and restoration of wooden boats. He died in 1978, but his shipbuilding tools are in the New Brunswick Museum. His son Bob, grandson Geodie, and granddaughter Lisa followed in his footsteps. All three now carry their captains certification. Lisa is one of seven female captains in Canada.

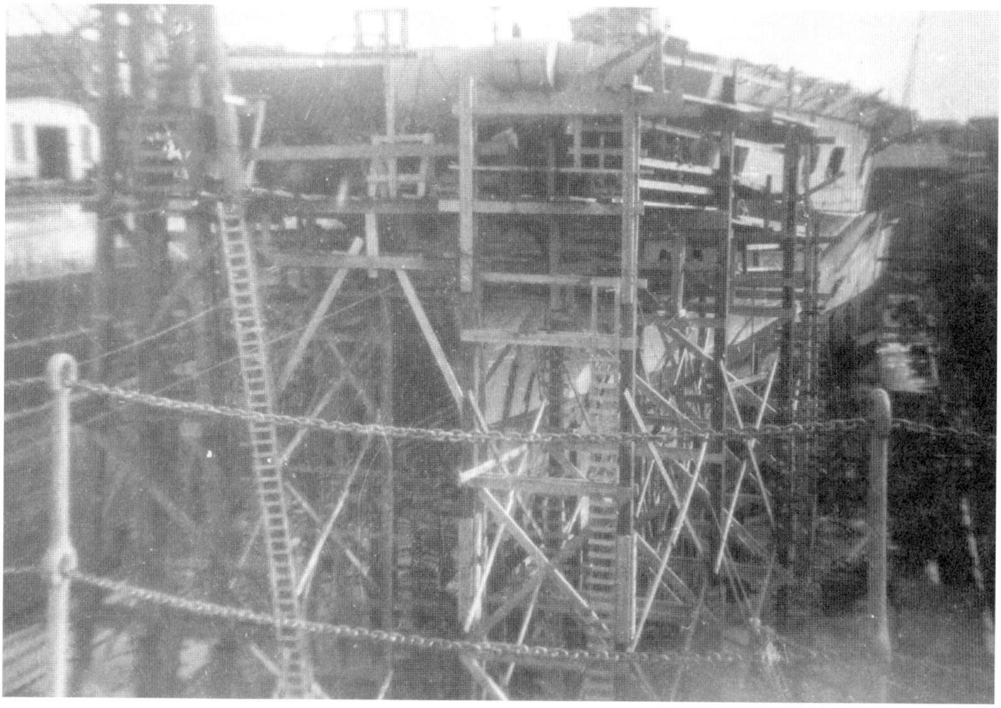

BOW RECONSTRUCTION ON THE *MAGGIE* (ABOVE) AND RING'S BOAT REPAIR (BELOW).

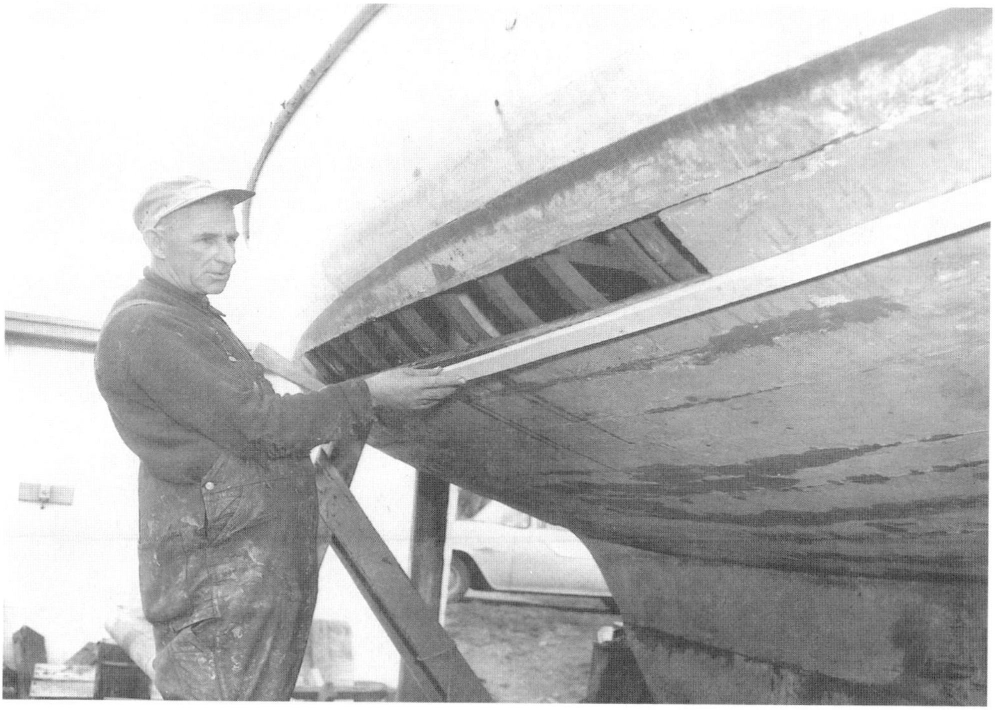

**EGERIA, 1994**

In January 1994, the New Brunswick Museum, in partnership with Parks Canada, launched a marine research expedition to the Falkland Islands. The objective was to document the ship *Egeria*. Resting in Stanley Harbour since 1872, the hulk of the *Egeria* is the most complete remnant of a mid-nineteenth century New Brunswick-built merchant vessel located to date. This chance survival preserves valuable information concerning shipbuilding techniques once employed in New Brunswick. The expedition used state-of-the-art photogrammetry survey

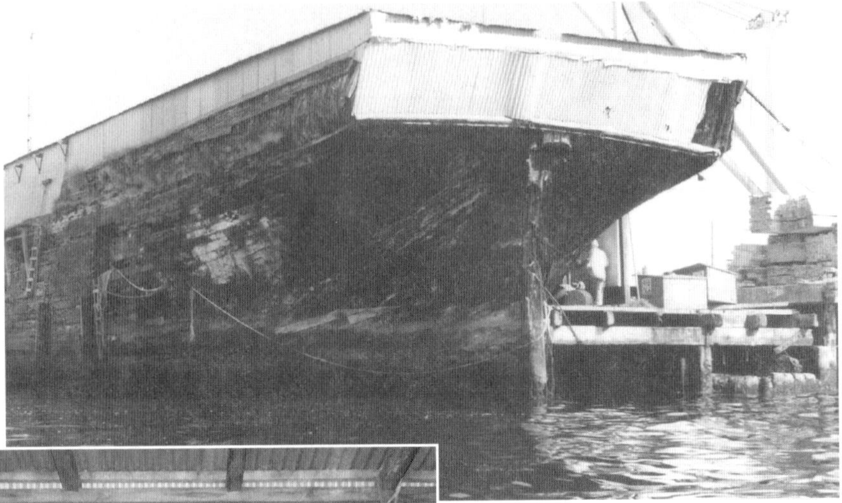

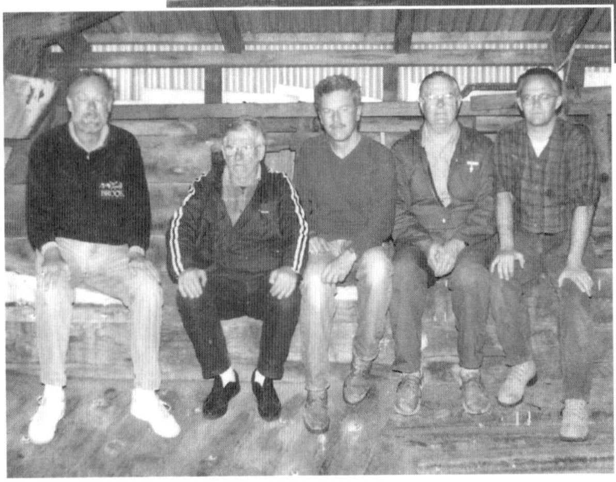

techniques, photography, and video to record information on the ship's construction. Shown on the wharf at the right is lumber for new home construction in the Falklands. The name stamped on the lumber was "Irving," the only evidence of home the survey team had for the three weeks it was in the Falklands. The team examined the remains of another New Brunswick-built sailing vessel, the Miramichi-built barque *Actaeon*, launched in 1838, as well as the Nova Scotia-built World War Two minesweeper *Protector III*. The expedition was in the Falkland Islands from January 13 to February 2, 1994, and the team members were, left to right: John Bell and Alec Barbour from Parks Canada; Robert S. Elliott, New Brunswick Museum; Eric Lawson, Marine Research Associate; and Harold E. Wright, Saint John historian.

Chapter 2

# Navigational Aids, Shipwrecks, and Salvage

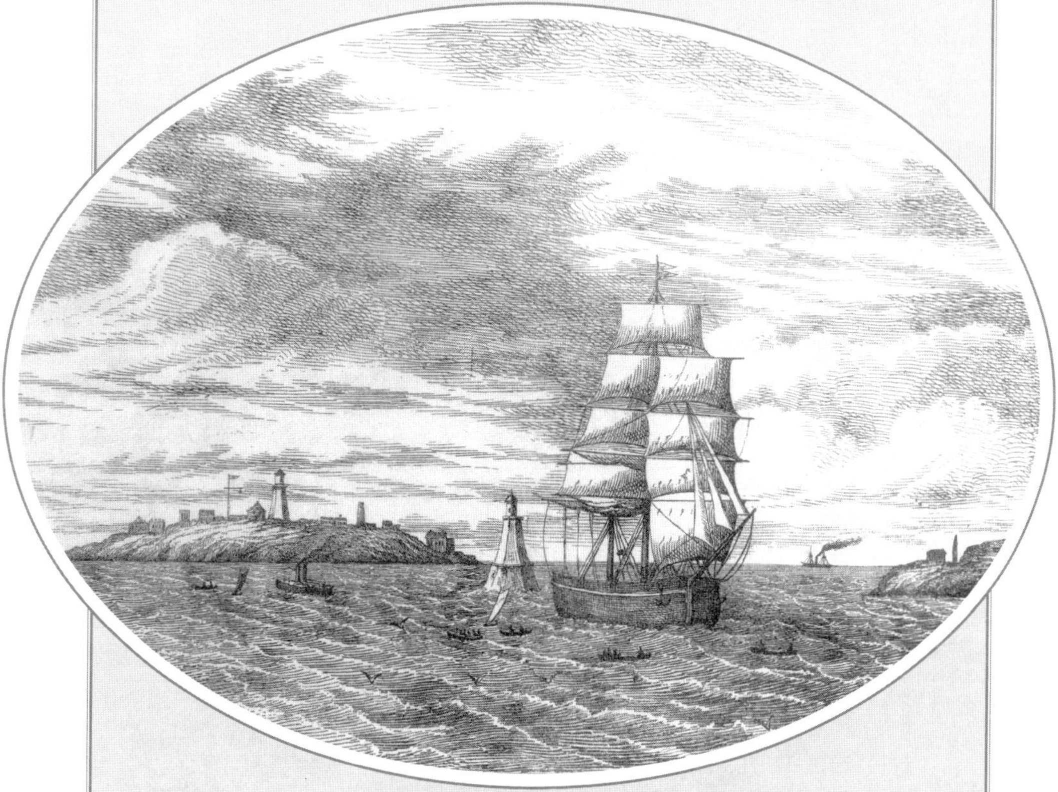

**SAINT JOHN HARBOUR, 1871**

This view shows the location of the Sand Point Beacon Light, Negrotown Point, where the breakwater was built a few years later, and Partridge Island, with its lighthouse, signal station, and fog alarm. The main harbour channel was between the island and Negrotown Point. It was not until the twentieth century that the main channel was relocated to the east of Partridge Island.

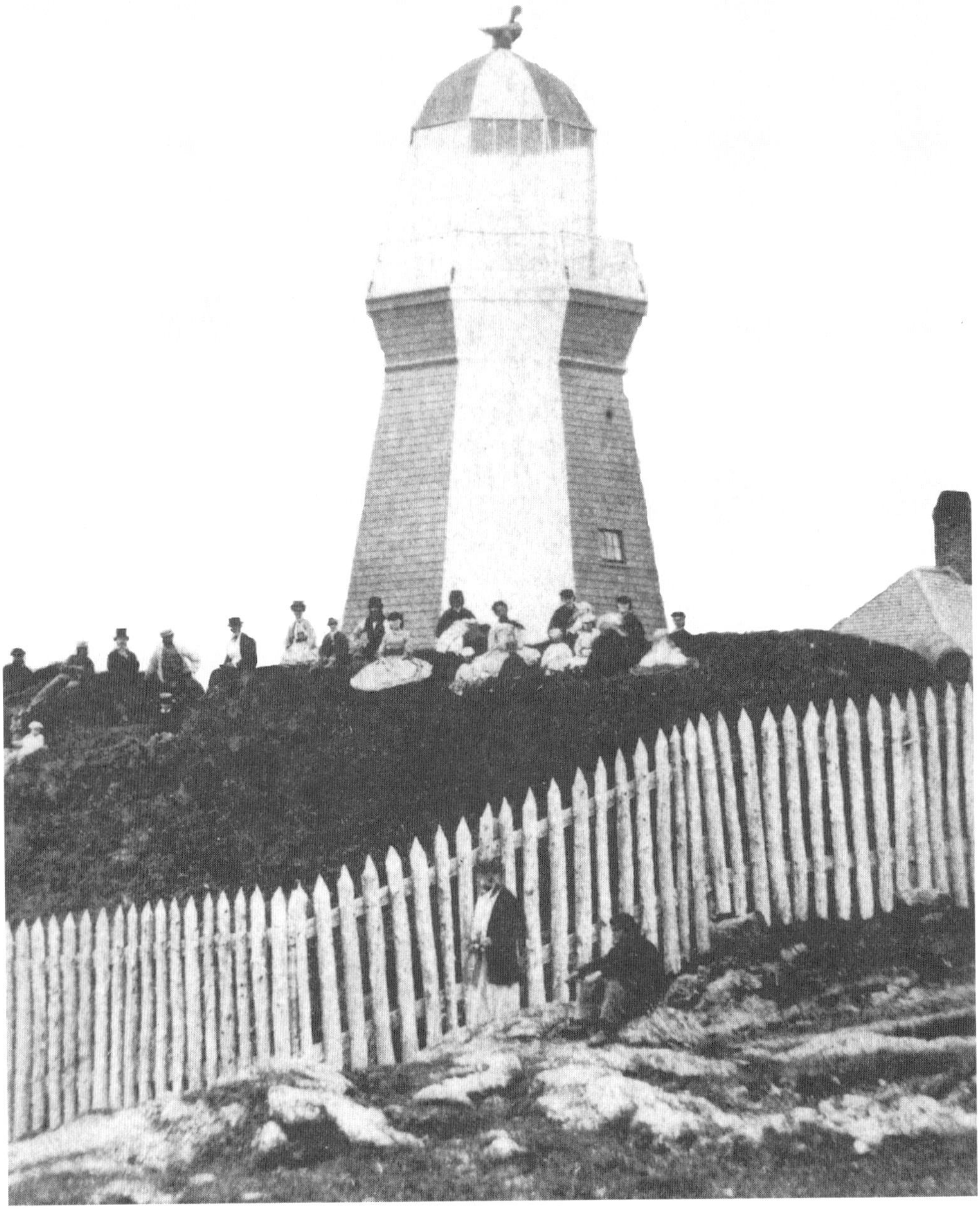

**PARTRIDGE ISLAND, C.1866** New Brunswick's first lighthouse was built here in 1791, and a light was maintained at this site for almost two hundred years, with the last keeper serving into 1989. The original lighthouse burned in a midwinter fire in 1832 and was replaced by the lighthouse shown here. This light was modified in 1880 but replaced in 1910; the current tower was built in 1959. The people seated around the light are from Saint John, visiting the island for a picnic. The man in the foreground is Dr. George J. Harding; standing is his boatman Paddy Flynn. Partridge Island was also the site of a quarantine station and Saint John's principal fortification.

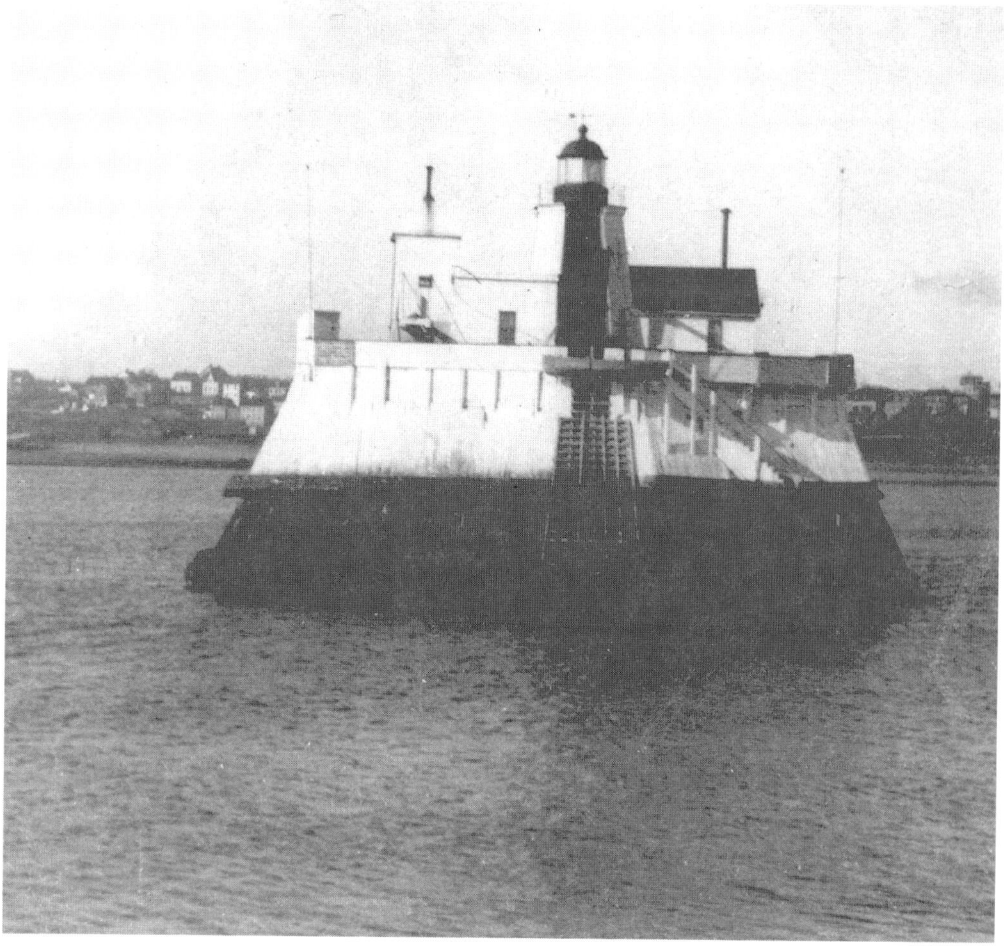

**Sand Point Beacon Light, c.1910**

The first lighthouse on the end of the harbour bar was erected in 1827 with living quarters for the lightkeeper. "In fog or storm the alarm of the Beacon Light was sounded and for many years there was no mechanical contrivance to perform this service. Fastened to the iron tongue of the bell was a strong cord which passed through a small hole in the door into the bedroom occupied by the keeper of the light, and while seated reading he would have the cord in one hand and would pull it about every five minutes, causing the clapper to send forth its sharp note of warning to the seamen. Sometimes the keeper of the light would have to keep the bell clanging for long hours at a time, and would continue his regular tugging on the rope even while lying on his bed to rest his weary body, though not to sleep. Later the bell was worked by mechanical device." The first beacon light was destroyed by fire in 1866. Later, harbour developments made this lighthouse redundant, so on August 20, 1913, it was soaked with oil and set afire, burning to the water's edge. The *Princess of Acadia* ferry terminal is now in the approximate location of the sand bar.

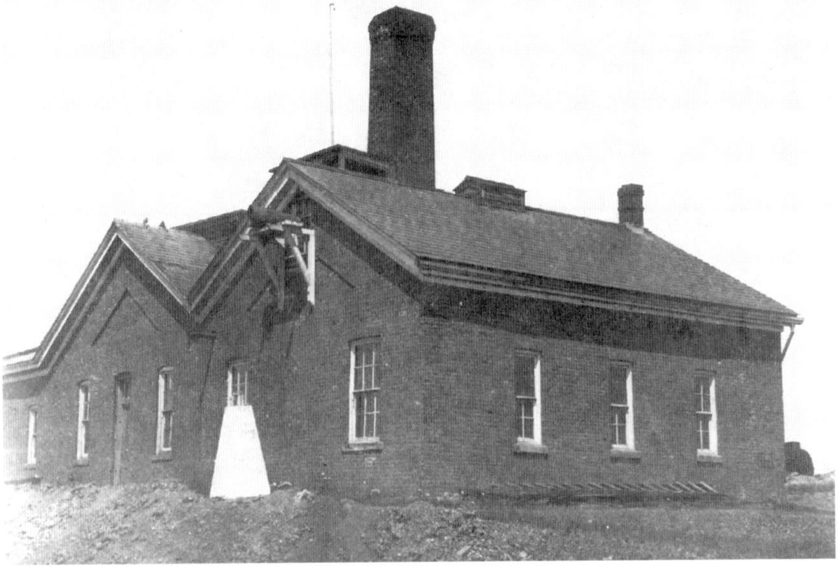

**PARTRIDGE ISLAND FOGHORN, JULY 1922** The world's first steam fog alarm, built on Partridge Island in 1859, was replaced in the 1880s by the building shown here. In 1930, diesel engines replaced the steam plant, making this the first station in Canada to function under air pressure produced from semi-diesels. In 1998 the Canadian Coast Guard shut down the Partridge Island alarm.

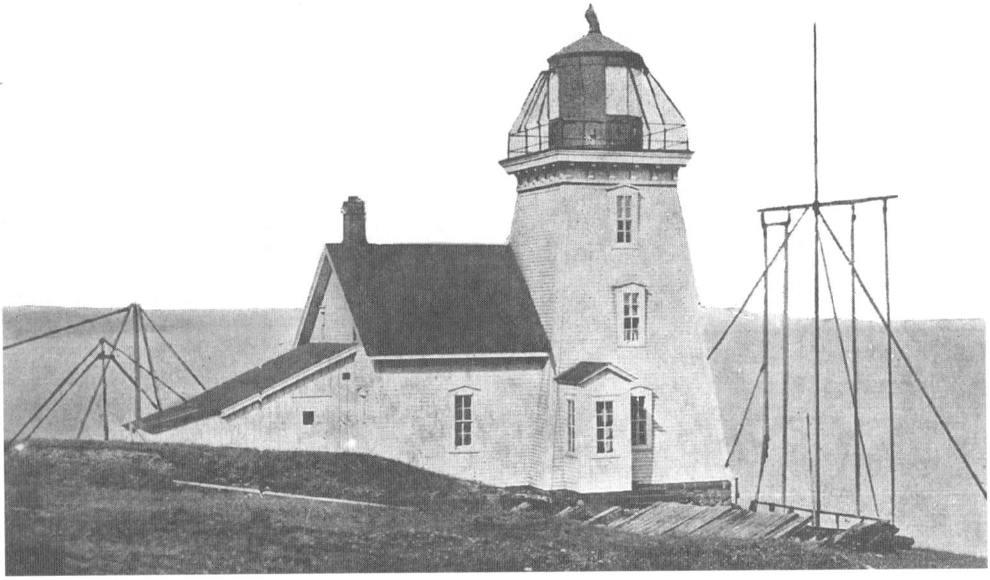

**ST. MARTINS LIGHT, 1911** The original light at Quaco Head was built in 1835 on the rocks just beyond the headland. The light shown here was destroyed by fire and a second light was built on the headland. In 1968 the present tower replaced the second light, whose lantern house is now part of the St. Martins Visitor Information Centre. Today's foghorn was built at the same time as the present light.

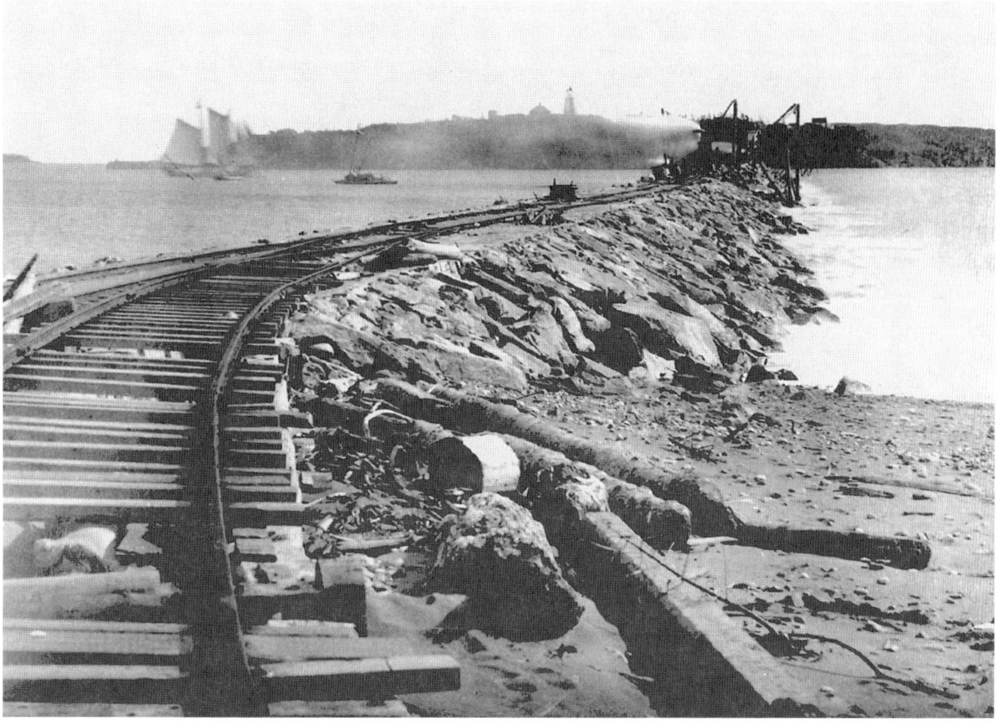

**NEGROTOWN POINT BREAKWATER, OCTOBER 1886**

In December 1872, the city of Saint John recognized that a "breakwater should be run out … at Negro Point." In January 1873 the Chamber of Commerce petitioned the minister of public works to build a breakwater or seawall "being such that a structure connecting or partly connecting it with the mainland would … render the Harbour practically a means of safety." In August 1874, tenders were received for construction of the breakwater, with J. Duffy and Company the successful contractor. In the fall of 1875, notice was given to shipping that construction was well underway and "will prove dangerous to vessels and craft passing through the Channel." Stone for the breakwater was quarried at the Carleton beaches, Pokiak, Clifton, Musquash, and St. George. Work was completed in 1877. The breakwater initially ran two-thirds the distance from Negrotown Point to Partridge Island. A small lighthouse was established at the end of the breakwater to mark the north channel between the island. This light was dismantled in 1927. As early as 1902 there were calls for the extension of the breakwater to the island. One of these calls, in 1909, made the suggestion that the island "may be made an amusement resort, to be in fact 'Coney Island' of Saint John." In 1914 funds were allocated to complete the breakwater but construction was delayed until a contract was awarded in 1958 to Foundation Maritime Ltd. of Halifax. Work on the breakwater extension was completed in 1962.

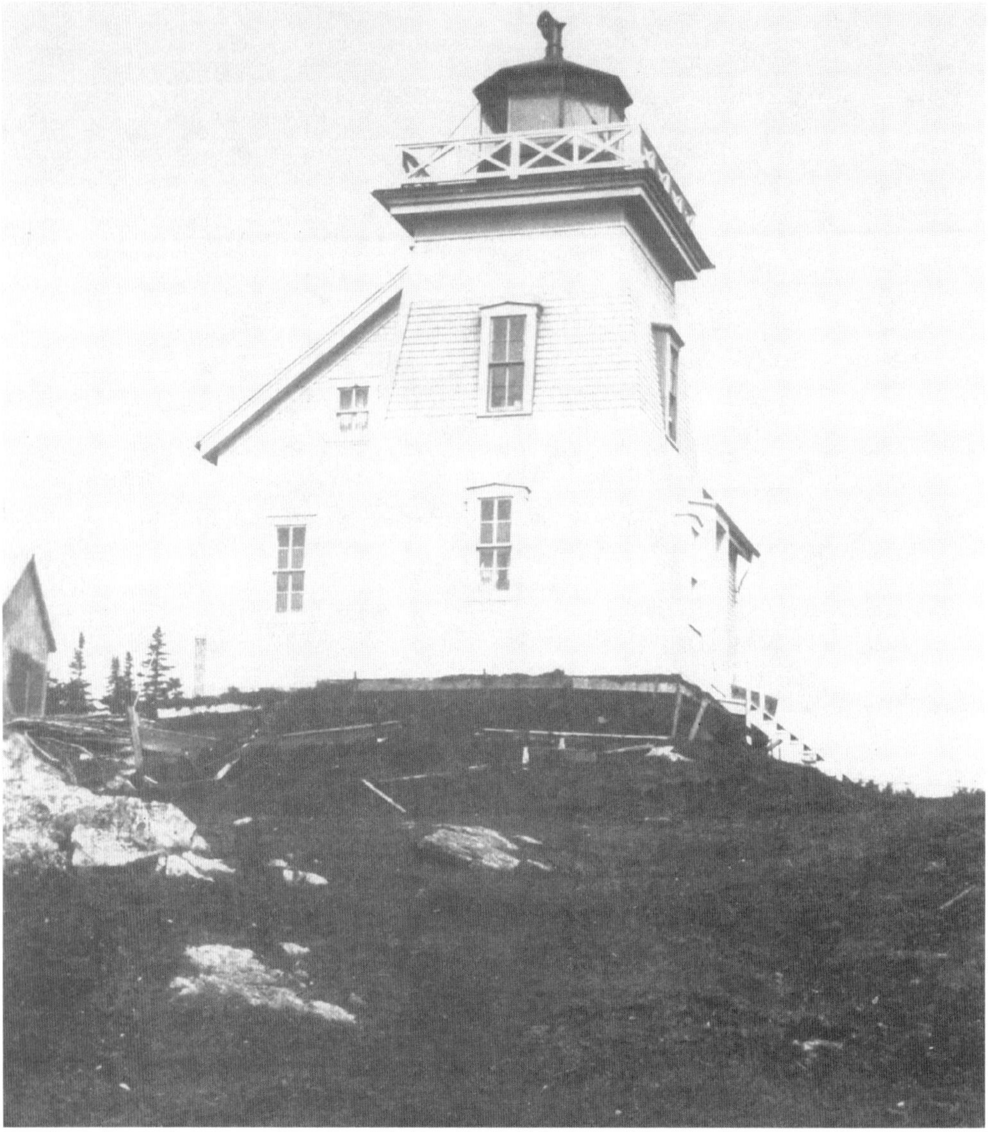

**MUSQUASH HEAD, 1920**

The Musquash Head light, also known as the Western Head light, was built in 1879 atop a two-hundred-foot cliff overlooking the entrance to the Musquash River estuary. The light shown here was replaced by a steel-reinforced tower in 1959. A foghorn was added in 1967. This light is located near Black Beach in Lorneville, apparently the only graphite/shale beach in North America. The light was automated in 1987, with the keeper's dwelling being moved off the property and sold. The Lorneville Community and Recreation Association is trying to acquire the Musquash Head lighthouse. The group wants the 108 acres of nearby land for a hiking trail it is building down to Black Beach.

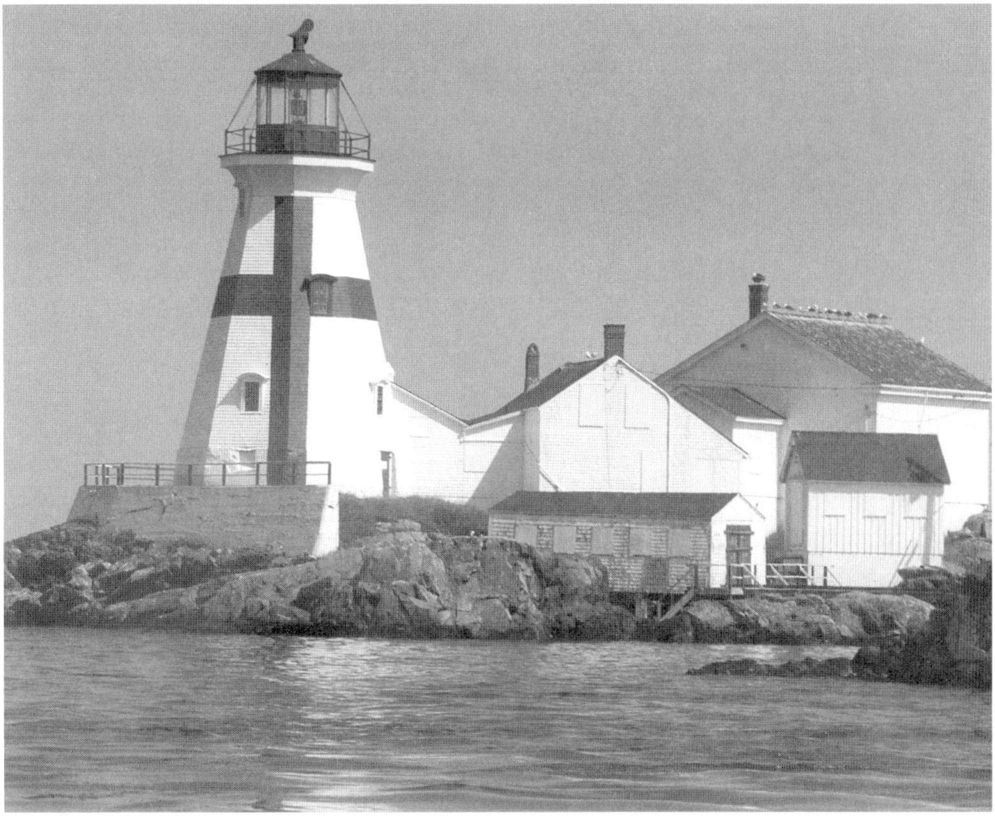

**HEAD HARBOUR, 1999**

The Head Harbour, also known as the East Quoddy light, was built in 1829, which makes it the oldest light tower in New Brunswick. The white octagonal wooden tower is 15.1 metres tall, and has a red St. George Cross daymark on one side. This distinctive pattern has been on the tower since about 1867. The light station was de-staffed and automated in 1986. There are plans for the restoration of this historic building, now one of the most photographed lighthouses in the province. There are also plans to establish a whale rescue centre at Head Harbour. This gives it the potential of becoming a world-class tourism site combining eco-tourism, lighthouse preservation, and the saving of marine mammals.

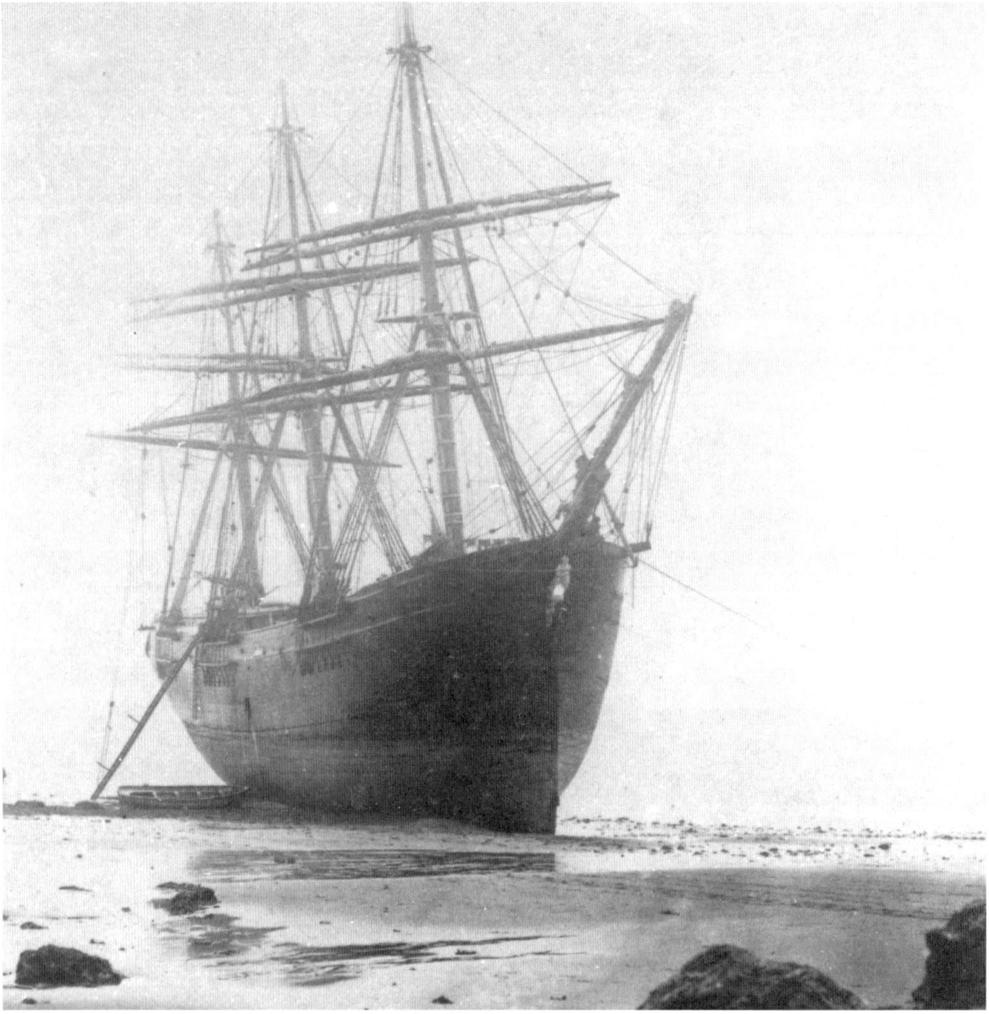

**A St. Martins Vessel in France, 1890**

New Brunswick vessels sailed the seven seas. Inherent dangers posed by storms, reefs, shoals, and other forces of nature caused many ships to be lost or, like this unidentified St. Martins vessel in France, to be driven ashore. In 1999 the Quaco Historical and Library Society published a small book titled *Shipbuilding in St. Martins*, in which was recounted the story of what happened to one St. Martins vessel: "The *Sarah Sloan* was built at St. Martins by Hugh McQuiston and launched in 1864. Hugh McQuiston sailed with his ship as he hoped to sell her in Matanza. She set sail from Saint John for Cuba at the height of a heavy gale; shortly after passing Partridge Island it began to snow; madly she raced on in the darkness ad struck about nine o'clock. All was mad confusion, nothing could be saved; the masts snapped like pipe stems; the crew and captain were swept overboard and all drowned with the exception of one crewmember, Charles Turner, who clung to some drifting cargo and was carried to the shore and dashed upon the rocks… The place where the *Sarah Sloan* struck is what is now known as Long's Eddy, about a mile from Bishop's Head, Grand Manan."

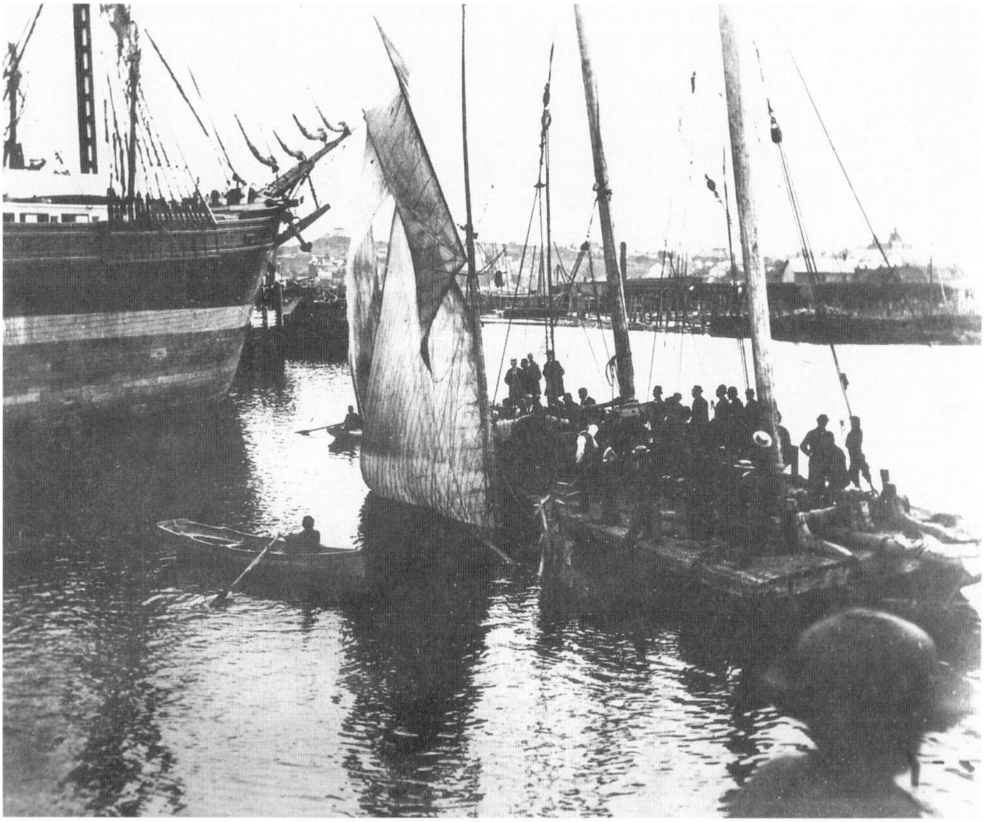

**YACHT RECOVERY, 1894**

In the Corporation Cup Race on August 21, 1894, the yacht *Primrose* was struck by a squall off Mahogany Island and sank. Eight men drowned: Samuel Hutton (a member of the Paris Crew), Fred Priest, George Heathfield, Albert Akerly, Henry Bartlett, James Hurley, William Russell, and Harry Hoyt. The four survivors were Howard Holder, Thomas H. Miles, Fred S. Heans, and James McKeever. On August 28, with just mast and sails visible, the *Primrose* was raised and towed to Sand Point. Harry Hoyt's was the only body recovered.

The *Primrose* disaster was immortalized in a poem by Peter J. Hanlon. Part of that poem reads:

> The *Maple Leaf*, Ross's boat, was seen with flag flying at half-mast;
> The people quickly gathered, while the news spread round the town,
> That Hutton and seven of his crew in the Primrose had gone down
> Dismay was seen on every hand and sorrow in each face.
> The people could not realize that death had won the race.

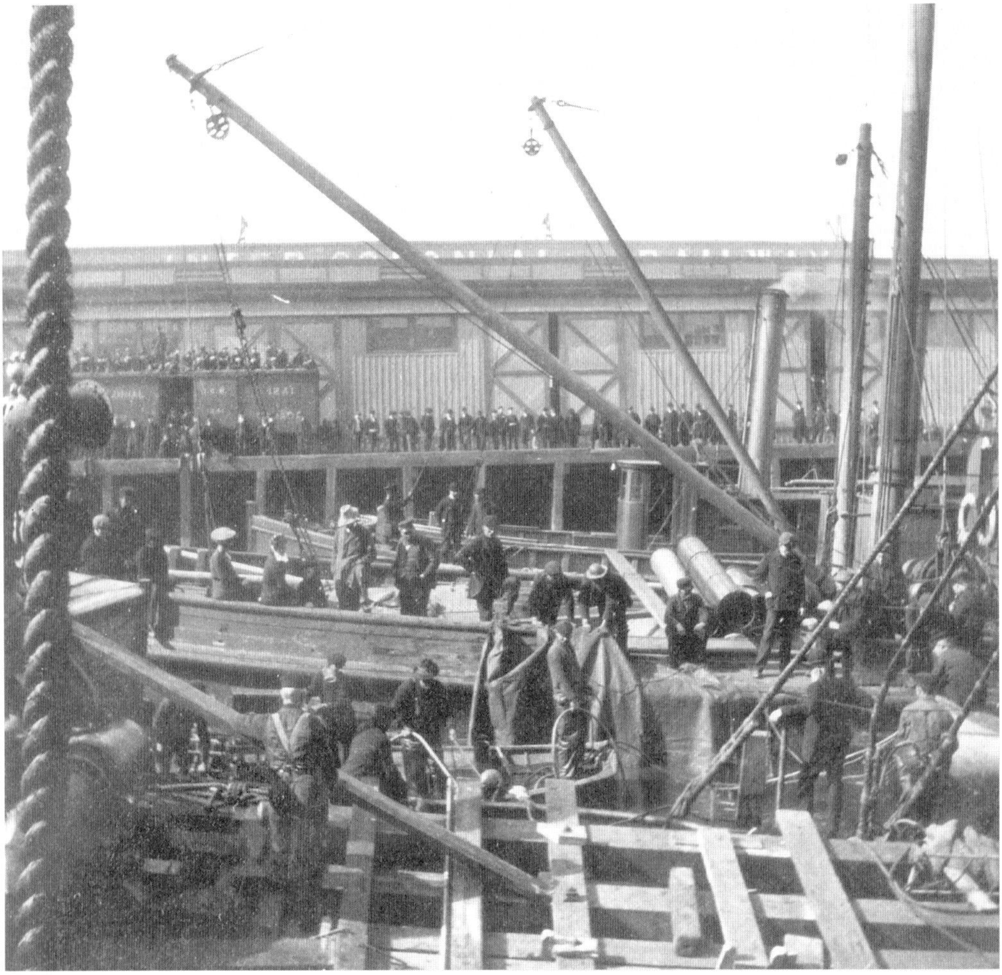

**DIVER, c.1900**

This unidentified diver is going down on the SS *Parision*. Perhaps it is Diver Lahey, who was working in the port at the time. One 1905 newspaper account stated:

> "Diver Lahey is at work in front of the Sand Point wharves looking for any articles that have been lost there. He is carrying on operations on his own account, and on Wednesday succeeded in raising a two-wheeled truck belonging to the CPR and a large bar of railroad iron. Diver Lahey has also been carrying on some prospecting work near the reef off PARTRIDGE ISLAND, and has located the bell buoy sunk there a few years ago, also an old bell lost about thirty years ago. To raise the bell buoy is a bigger task than he cares to undertake with the machinery at his disposal, but the find is too valuable a one to lose, so he will blow it to pieces with dynamite and then bring up the parts. There is in the bell buoy a large quantity of pig iron and considerable brass, probably 6 or 7 hundred dollars worth all told, so the diver will be repaid for his efforts."

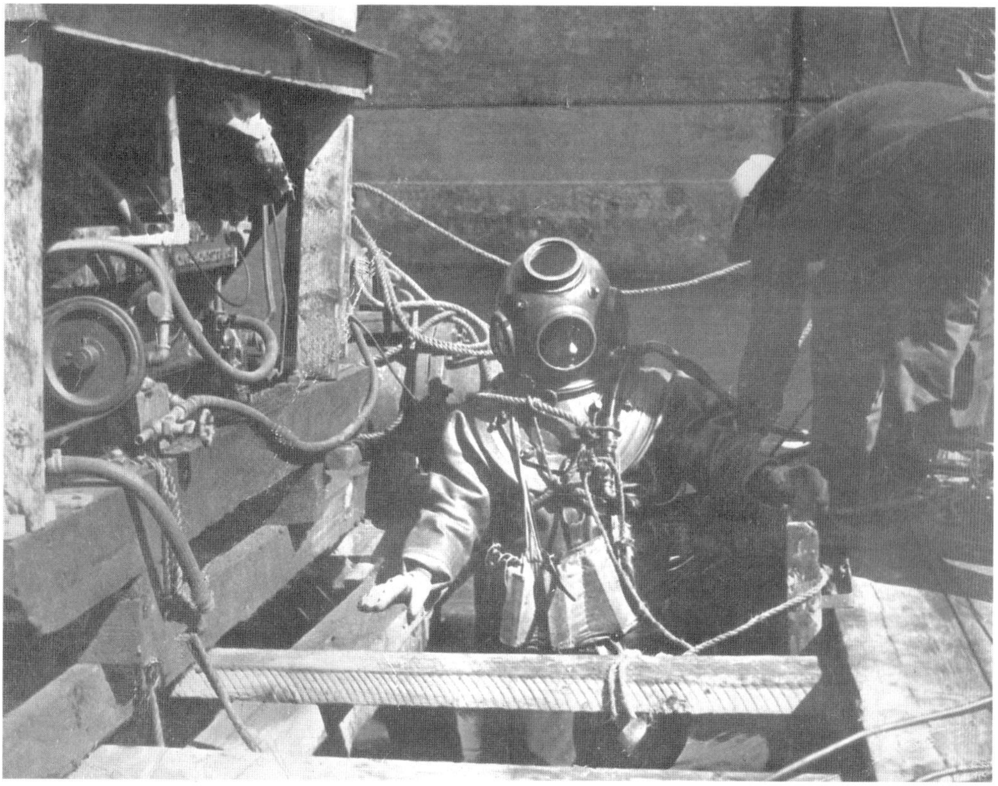

**DIVER PRICE THEODORE 'SPIKE' PALMER, C.1950**

Price Palmer was born in Parrsboro, Nova Scotia on October 22, 1906, and joined the merchant marine as a young boy. He sailed in tall ships and steamers until the outbreak of World War Two. He joined the Royal Canadian Navy on May 5, 1941, where he obtained the rank of chief petty officer and the trade of deep-sea diver. His first wife, Beatrice E. Hutchings, died while he was on service in the Atlantic. He was discharged on June 18, 1945. In 1947 he married Grace LeCain of the Annapolis Valley, then moved to Saint John where he went to work for C.N. Wilson at the drydock inspecting the hulls of vessels requiring repair. He also dove in the harbour on sunken barges and ships, and recovered the bodies of drowning accidents. Spike died on June 1, 1968.

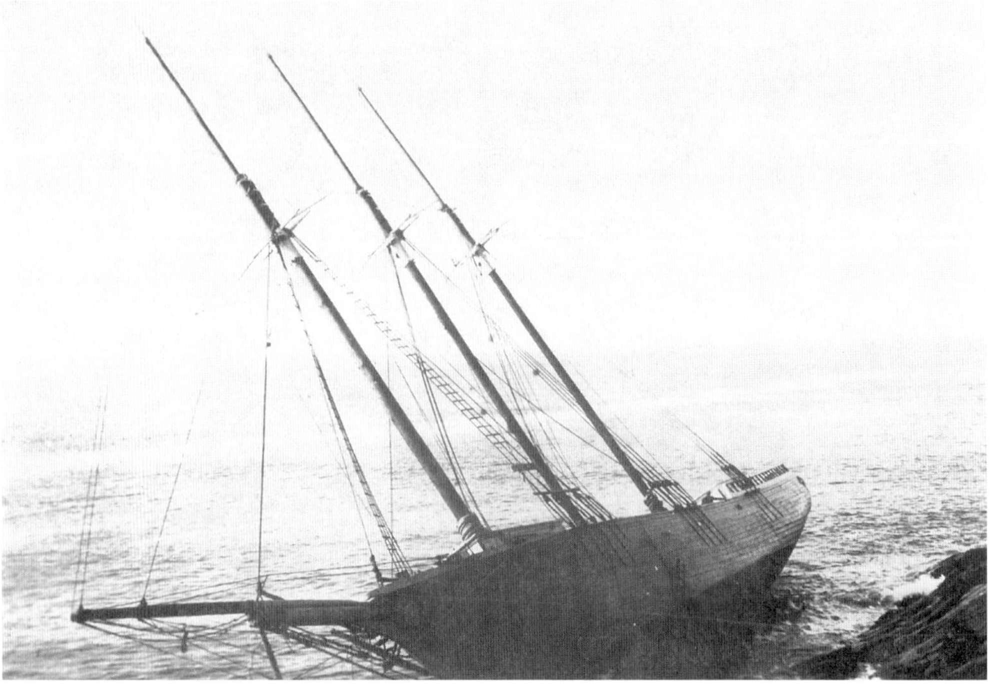

**_Edith McIntyre_, 1921, and Seaplane _Pelican_, 1920**

The 149-tonne schooner *Edith McIntyre*, built in Windsor, Nova Scotia, went down on August 2, approximately 1.5 miles west of Tiners Point. The *Pelican* (below) apparently ran into engine problems and landed on Black Beach. Over the period of a few months the parts were received and the engine repaired. One of the stories about this incident states that the American owner took the plane up for a test flight and continued on to New York, without paying his host the money owed him for a few months' stay.

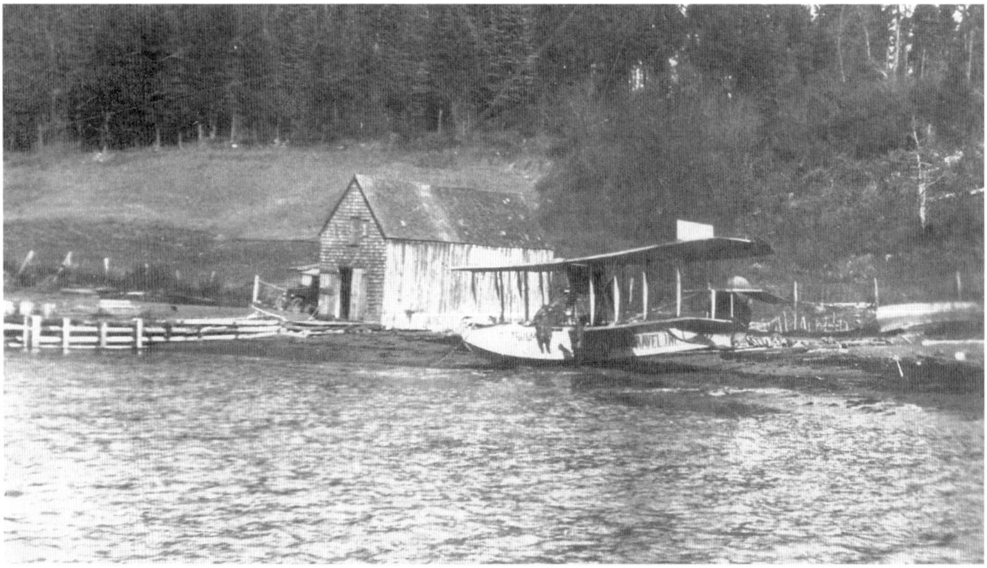

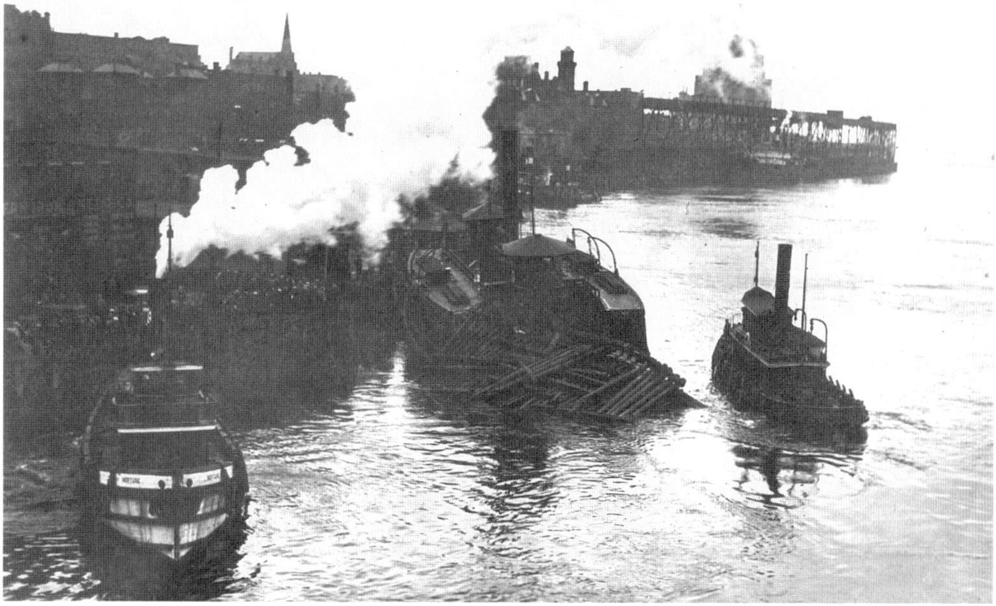

## *Ludlow* Crash, 1928

On the morning of April 23, 1928, the ferry *Ludlow* crashed into the southern wing of the east side ferry entrance at low tide. Seventy-two feet of piling and sheathing fell across the *Ludlow*, doing damage to her upper structure. The passengers were standing at the other end of the ferry preparing to disembark. Some $20,000 damage was done to the ferry, the pier, and the tug *Neptune*. The report on the accident, written by Fred S. Heans, Master Carpenter (who survived the sinking of the *Primrose* in 1894) and Captain Andrew J. Mulcahy, Port Warden, stated, "We made a thorough investigation into the cause of the accident in an effort to fix the responsibility and if possible to suggest necessary steps, which should be taken to safeguard the lives of the public who must daily use the ferry. We cannot attribute any carelessness to the Master in connection with this accident, but to the conditions existing at that time caused by the freshet in the harbour, swinging the vessel out of position. Great care is necessary in handling the ferry steamers at all times and especially during the freshet season. In our opinion the damage to the east side slip was caused by the heavy pounding of the ferry boat and the more or less wear and tear on the sheathing, piling and other parts of the structure."

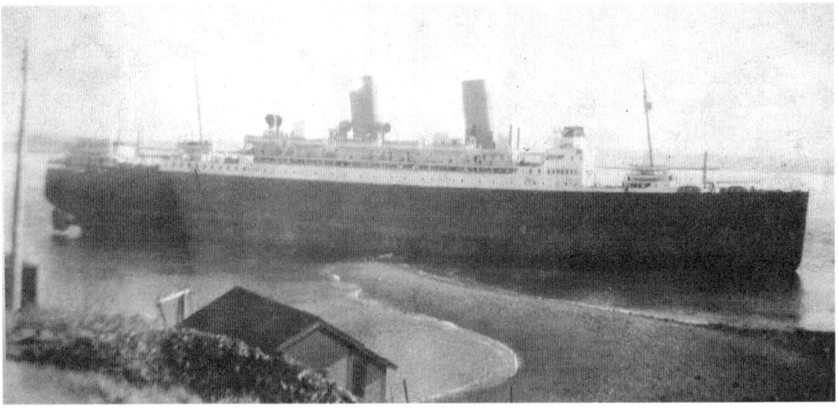

**PARTRIDGE ISLAND GROUNDING, 1929**

The *Duchess of Richmond* left Liverpool, UK, on March 8 for her first North-Atlantic crossing. On her second Atlantic voyage she stranded on the sandbar at Partridge Island where it took a few days to refloat her. She was repaired at the local drydock and set sail again for England in August. During World War Two she served as a troopship. In 1947, she was renamed the *Empress of Canada II.* On January 25, 1953, she was gutted by fire at Liverpool's Gladstone Dock.

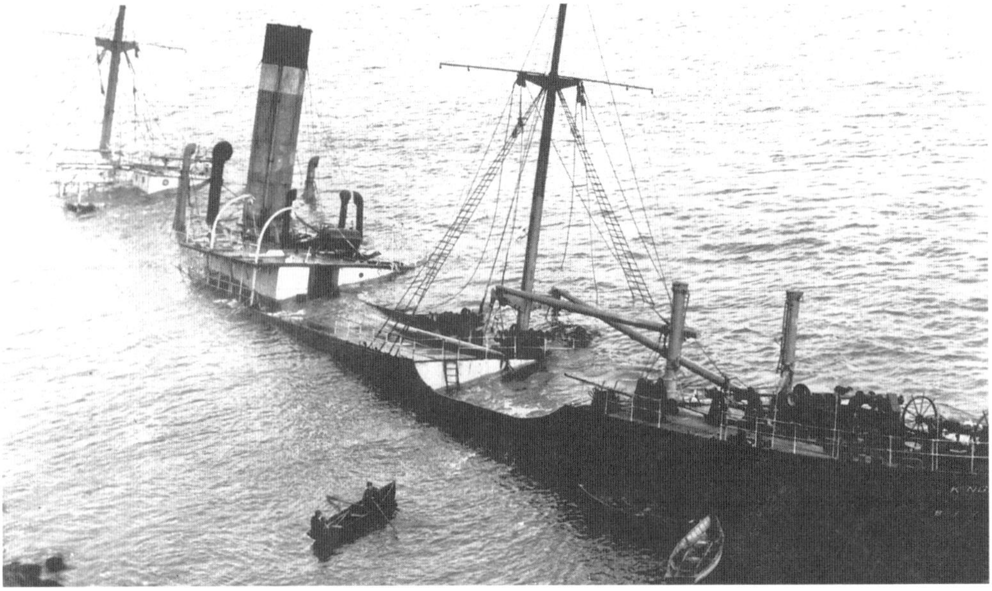

**SS *KINGS COUNTY*, 1936**

In the early hours of December 11, 1936, the captain of the Norwegian steamer *Kings County* heard the fog alarm of Tiners Point. Believing it to be the Partridge Island foghorn, he continued ahead slowly. Minutes later the ship struck the rocks during a wicked winter storm. With the ship taking on water and listing, crewman Harald Hansen, with a rope tied around his waist, jumped into the icy waters to swim the thirty metres to shore. He succeeded and all thirty-five crew-members were rescued. Hansen received bravery awards and commendations from the lieutenant governor of New Brunswick, the city of Saint John, and the king of Norway. In 1999, Harald Hansen's sons came to Lorneville to meet the people who assisted the sailors.

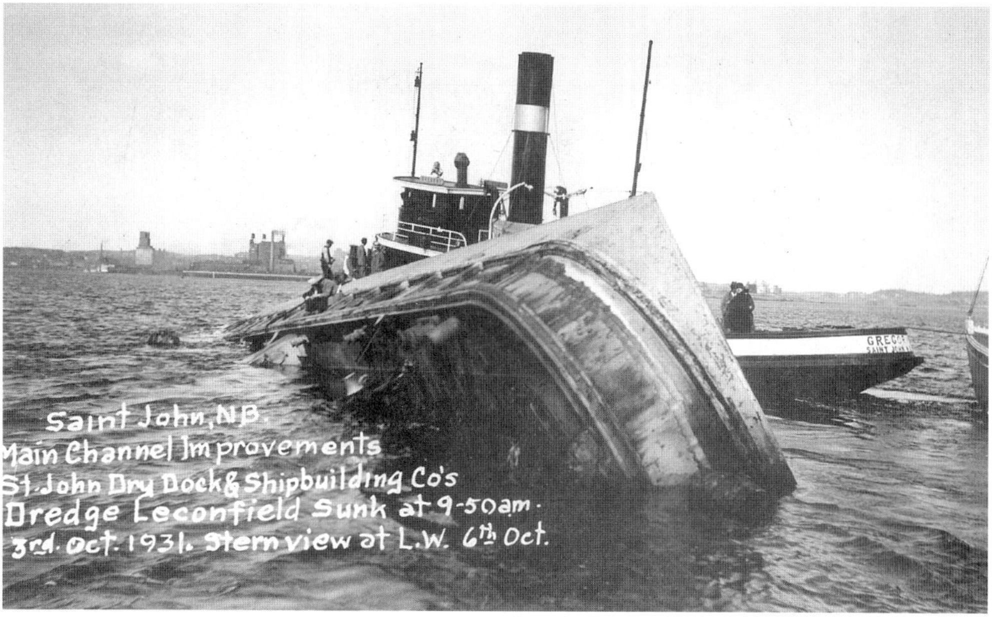


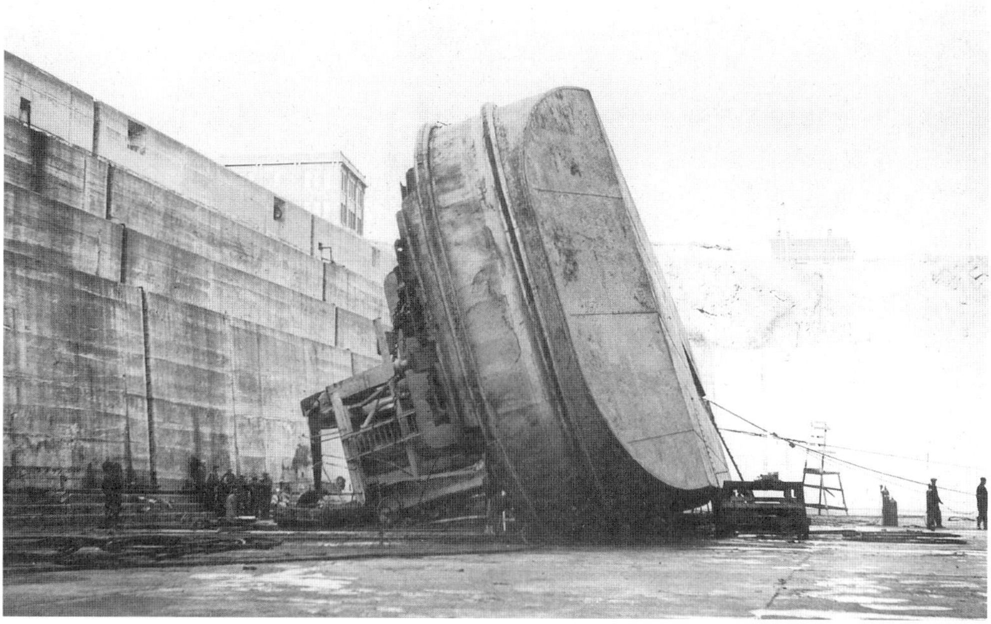

**LECONFIELD, 1931**

At 9:50 A.M. on October 13, 1931, while engaged in main channel improvements, the dredge *Leconfield* turned over and sank. At low water the stern could be seen. Buoys were set to mark her position with the tug *Gregory* standing by. On November 11, the *Leconfield* was towed into the drydock where she was inspected for damage. She was repaired and continued for many more years working in Saint John Harbour.

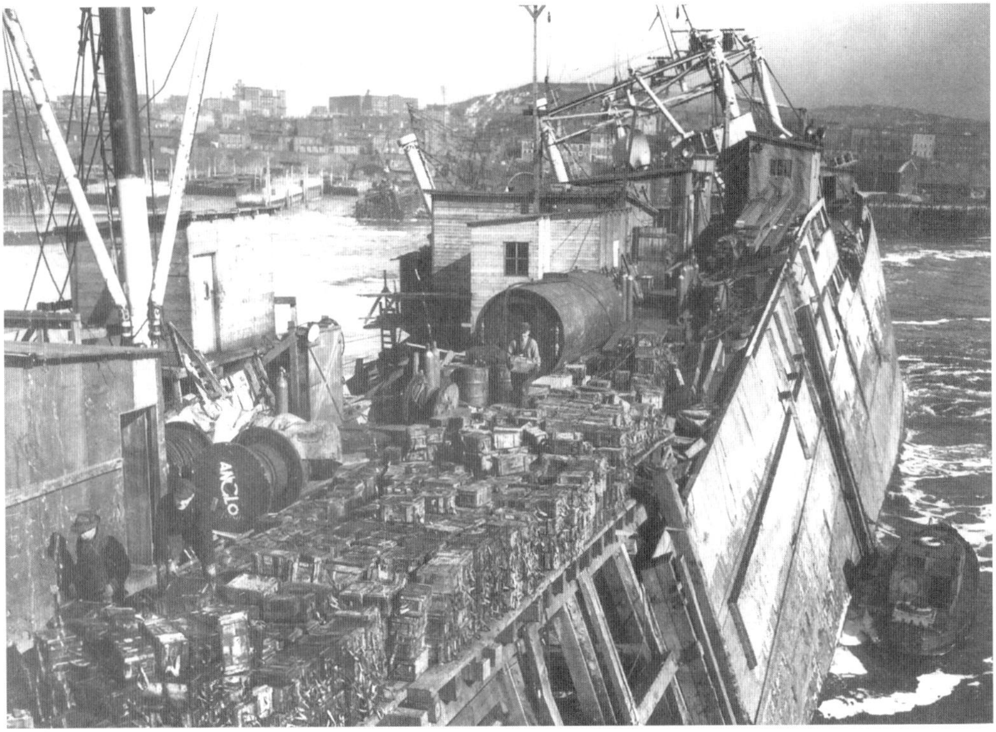

**AMMUNITION SHIP AGROUND, 1946**

On November 24, 1944, the Canadian Pacific SS *Beaverhill* went aground on Hilyards Reef while being towed by tugs from her berth. She was carrying 3,846 bags of overseas civilian mail, 1,000 tonnes of ammunition, and almost 9,000 tonnes of grain, flour, and meat. Steps were immediately taken to recover the mail and refloat the ship. When it was determined that the vessel could not be refloated, efforts were made to salvage the cargo and to remove the vessel from the shipping channel. The obstruction of the *Beaverhill* gave a peculiar twist to the harbour current, making it next to impossible to manoeuver the ferry *Loyalist* into Rodney Street slip at certain tide levels. Ferry service had to be suspended for two hours before and after low tide. In June 1945, Dean Hatfield of St. Martins received the contract to take the 2,300 cases of depth charges, 3.7-inch anti-aircraft shells, 3-inch mortar rounds, and 25 pounder shells, and dump them in one hundred fathoms of water. Instead, most of the salvaged material was taken to St. Martins, where local residents removed the brass and sold some seventeen tons of it to J.J. Freedman at South Market Slip. In all probability, the RCMP would never have found out about the operation had it not been for an explosion and fire in St. Martins. In mid-August 1945, two hundred 3.7-inch rounds and boxes of cordite, primers, and detonators exploded. On March 22, 1946, the last boxes of ammunition were taken off the Beaverhill. In December 1946 the stern of the vessel was towed thirty miles off Lepreau and sunk in three hundred feet of water. The bow was broken up and disposed of in 1947.

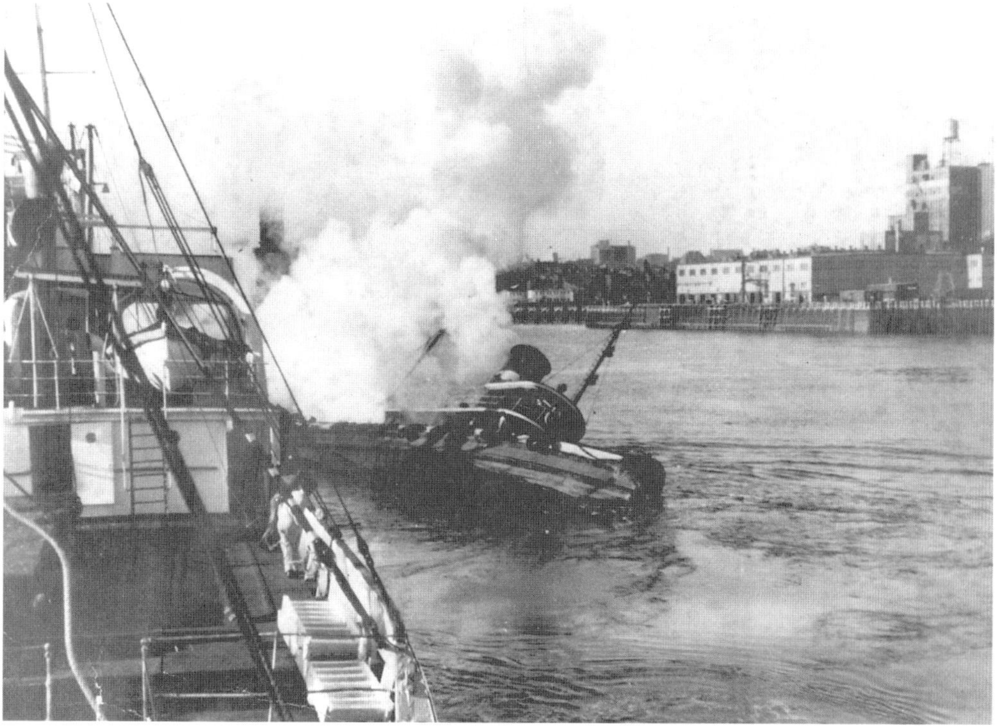

**SHIP TRAGEDY, 1953**

The *Ocean Hawk II* was built in Nova Scotia in 1940 and came to Saint John as part of C.N. Wilson's Saint John Tugboat Company. On March 19, 1953, the tugs *Ocean Hawk* and *Ocean Hawk II* were to guide the Norwegian freighter SS *Maud* with sugar for the Atlantic Sugar Refineries. Hit by the *Maud*, the *Hawk II* sank within seconds. Three members of the crew drowned: mate Thomas A. Sherrard of Fairville, deckhand Blanchard Ells of Port Greville, Nova Scotia, and cook Lloyd Lamb of Parrsboro, Nova Scotia. The survivors were William G. Hurley, captain; Herbert Carson, second engineer; William McCumber, deckhand; Judson M. Chetley, chief engineer; George Clifford, deckhand; and Robert Cole, fireman. The crew ranged in age from sixteen to more than seventy years. Clifford, Chetley, and Cole survived by hanging onto the anchor of the *Maud*. The week after the collision, when the SS *Maud* was being moved from the sugar refinery to Pier 4, the captain, Alfred Teiglande took ill at the bridge and died shortly thereafter of a heart attack. The *Ocean Hawk II* was salvaged and served until February 9, 1960, when she struck a rock at the Reversing Falls and again sank. Again refloated, the vessel carried on until being retired in 1976. The *Ocean Hawk II* ended her days as a pub and tourist bureau at Market Square before being demolished to make way for a volleyball court at Market Slip.

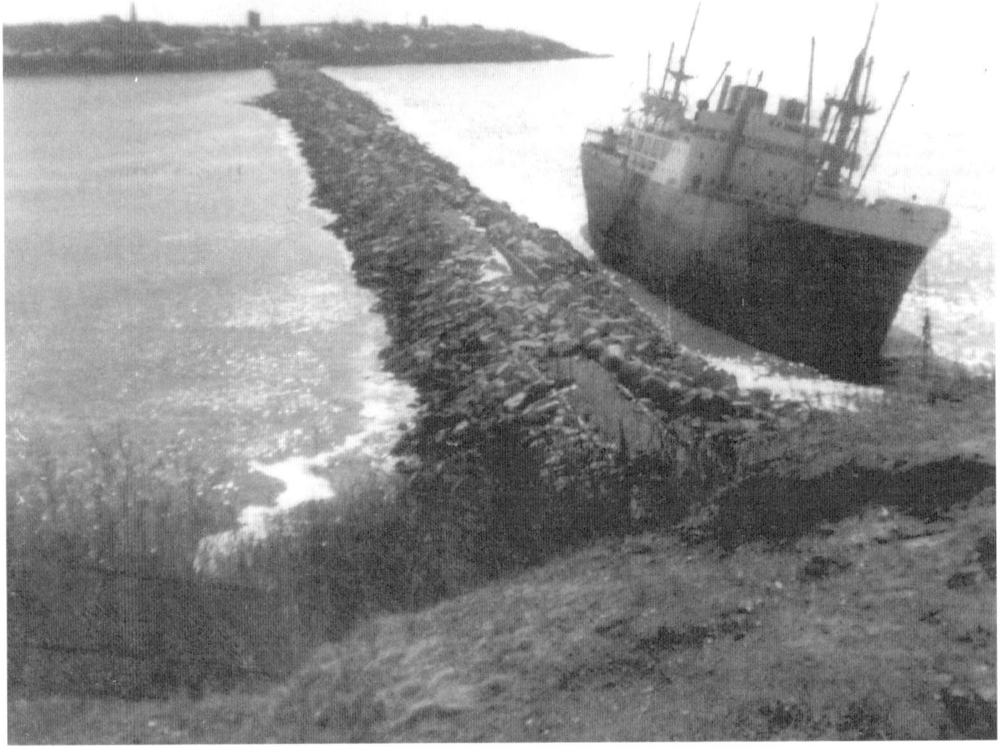

***Manes P.*, 1970**

On February 3, 1970, during a violent winter storm, the Greek freighter *Manes P.* broke loose from her anchorage and stranded on the Negrotown Point breakwater. Formerly known as the *Escalante*, the ship had been built in 1955, and had been owned by the Royal Mail Lines Limited until she was sold to Chios Navigation. With more than $1 million in damages, the owners decided to abandon attempts to salvage her, and awarded a contract to scrap the *Manes P.*

## Chapter 3

# Ship Movements

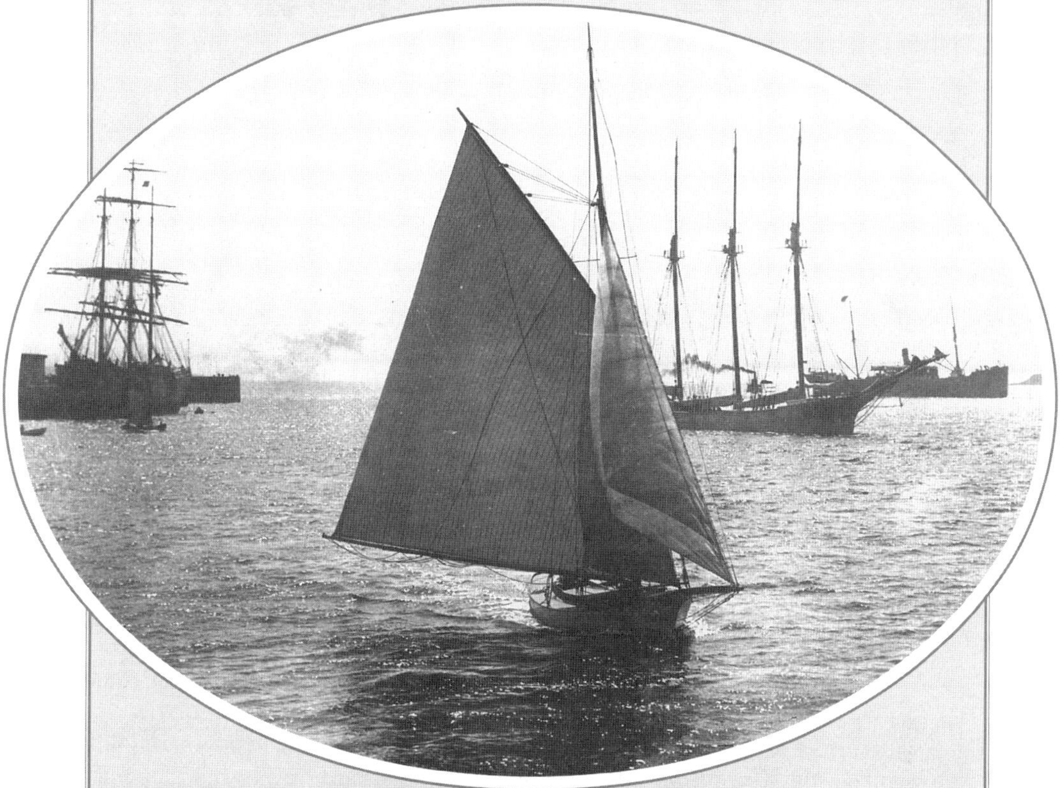

**HARBOUR BOATS, 1900**

The Saint John Harbour kept busy regardless of holidays or seasons. In December 1946, the newspaper carried this report: "The Christmas Day holiday which provided a rest period for most city workers gave port workers little relaxation as the busy rush of the last weeks went on unabated. One shipping agency noted that Christmas Day is just like any other day to us. We work right through any holiday at the peak of the season. A poll of shipping agencies on Christmas Eve showed only one of the larger companies planned to slow down operations and most of the larger shipping concerns reported last night that work continued as usual in loading and discharging operations. William A. Charlton, harbour master, stated that 'vessels that could, worked as usual, according to cargo offers.' Pre-Christmas ship movements included the sailing of the S.S. *Oakmont Park* from the Atlantic Sugar Refineries for Halifax. Her place at the refinery dock was filled immediately by the new arrival, S.S. *Hamilton Park* with a cargo of sugar from the West Indies. "

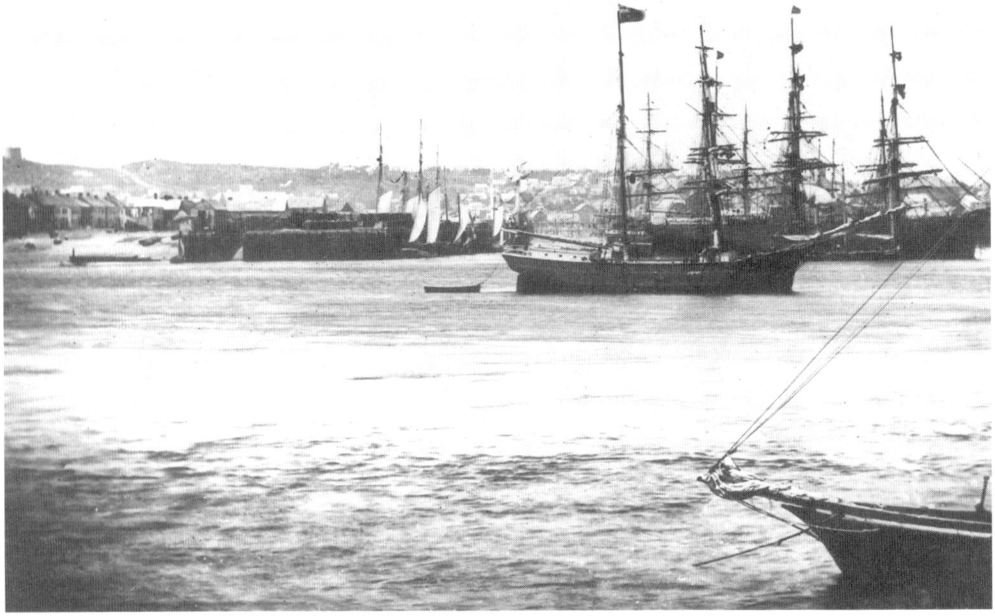

**Sand Point, c.1864**

Protection Street and the Carleton Martello Tower are shown at the left. This area was once considered as a site for construction of a drydock in 1875, when arguments for a new drydock were expressed as follows: "There is one natural feature in which St. John bears a strong resemblance to Liverpool, and that is with respect to its tides, which at both ports rise and fall about 28 feet. This circumstance, while it is a serious drawback so long as the system of loading vessels at wharves is persevered in, is an enormous advantage where docks are used. There is no doubt that, at an early day, the construction of docks will be commenced in St. John, and when this port is provided with docks its expenses to vessels will be greatly lessened and consequently its advantages for trade much increased. Indeed the use of wharves would have become an intolerable nuisance, and would have been long since abandoned in St. John, but for the fact that large vessels taking in cargoes of lumber are usually loaded from woodboats or scows, which, like the vessels themselves, rise and fall with the tide. But in unloading vessels, especially ocean steamers where haste is demanded, the greatest inconvenience and great cost are incurred, owing to the extreme rise and fall of the tide, and the people of St. John will shortly be driven to erect docks, nature thus compelling them to adopt a plan of dealing with vessels which in the end will make it impossible for any other Canadian port to compete with St. John in point of safety, cheapness and despatch. Wet docks should be built first, but dry docks should follow and when they are constructed, there will be no reason why the great bulk of the vessels which require to be overhauled, east of New York, should not come here to repair. A first-class dry dock at St. John would even bring many of Her Majesty's ships to it, instead of going to Bermuda to repair as they have to do now, for want of any dry dock at Halifax. Of course all these things would keep large numbers of men employed, would increase the population of the city and its prosperity as well."

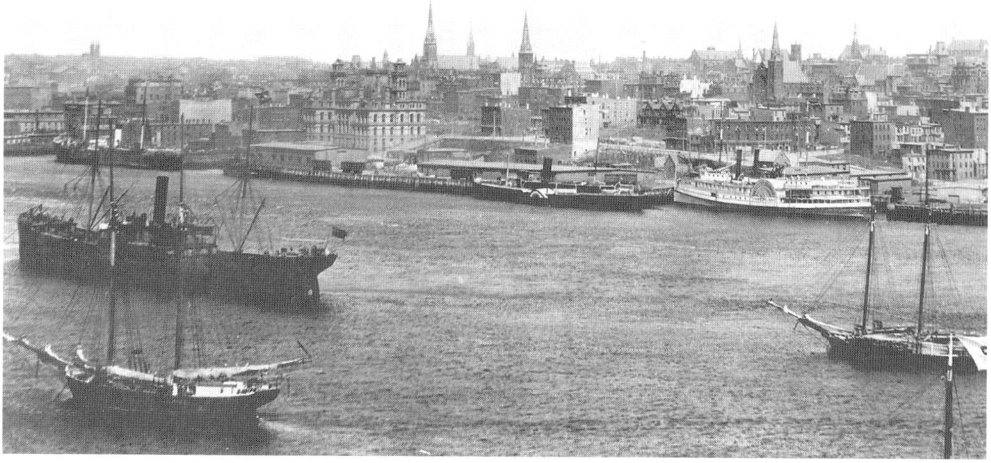

**REEDS POINT, 1890**

There are two steamboats tied up at Reeds Point, one of which is the *Cumberland.* This area is now Pugsley Terminals B and C. While these terminals are today primarily used for cruise ships, and at one time as the ferry terminal for both the Digby and Boston boats, this area was used most of the time in the past for general cargo. One of the shipping reports for 1946 stated:

> "Arousing considerable interest was the arrival of the S.S. *City of Khios*, whose last port of call was Newport News, Virginia. Registered at Liverpool, the 5,573-tonne Ellerman Line (London) vessel is carrying a cargo of 300 tons of tobacco picked up at her last port of call. The tobacco is bound for Bombay and Calcutta, India. The ship will take on general cargo here, sailing for Port Said, Bombay, Colombo, Madras and Calcutta. She left Newport News Dec. 26, arriving here at 5:30 P.M. Monday. She is tied up at Reed's Point Wharf pending the clearance of a loading pier. McLean Kennedy (Mar.) Ltd., are agents. The fairly heavy list of week-end ship movements left the port with an unofficial total of 35 vessels in port including the collier Rockwood Park, four ships at the dry dock and ships in the stream and at Partridge Island."

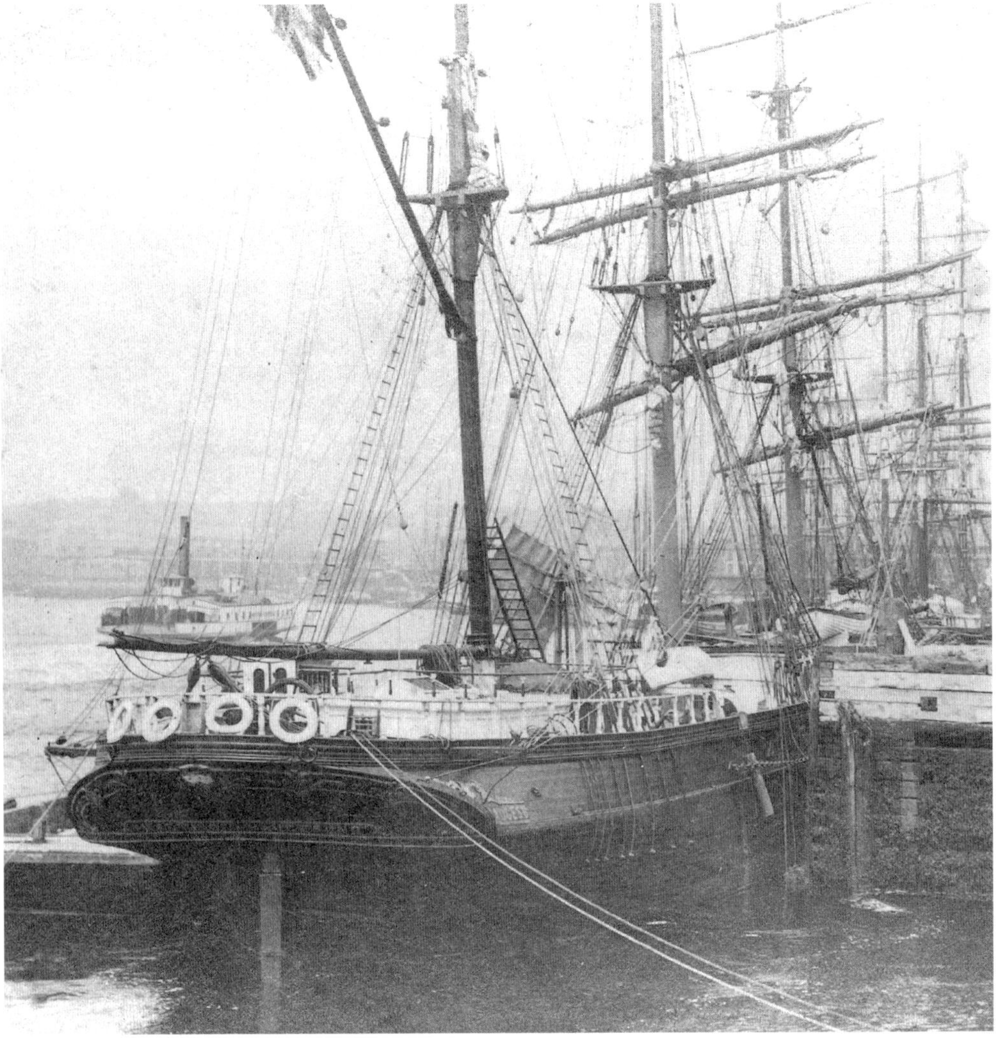

**ALONG THE DOCKS, 1902**

This stern view is probably of a foreign vessel. The nameboard on the stern is difficult to read but the second word appears to be "Hamgesund." Along the port stern are the hard-to-read letters UGESU. On the starboard side a barge is tied to the vessel, and in the background the harbour ferry, probably *Western Extension*, can be seen. The site is probably near or at Reeds Point. This image was published as a stereo view by Underwood & Underwood, Ottawa.

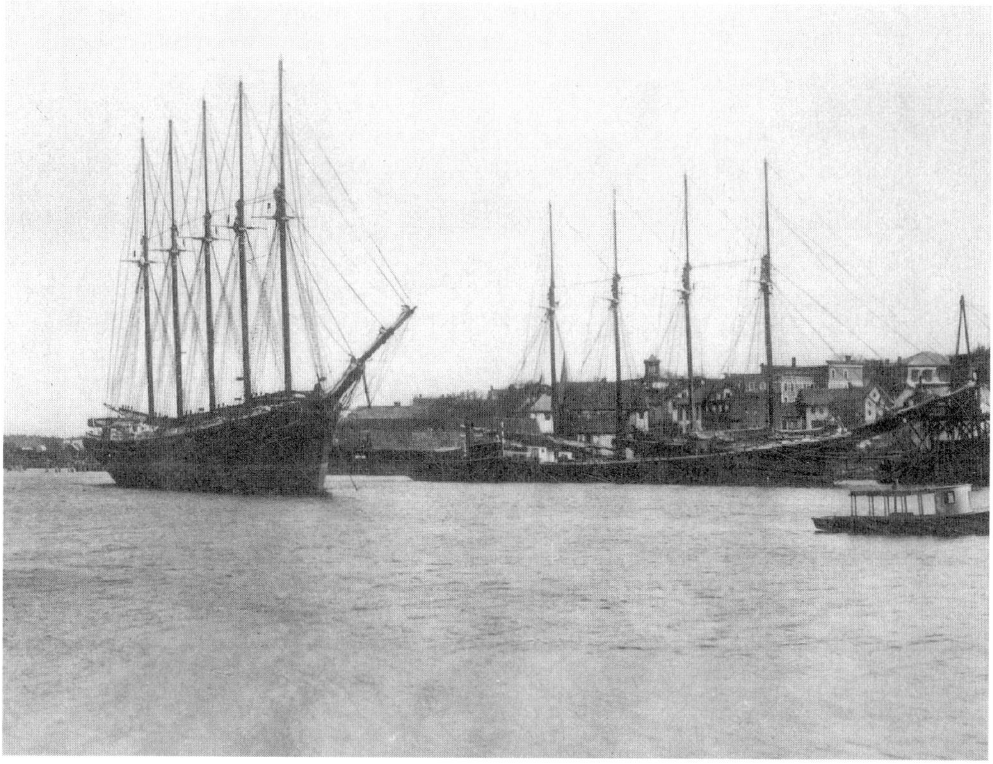

**St. Stephen and the St. Croix River, c.1900**

St. Stephen is located on the international boundary between New Brunswick and Maine. The lower part of this boundary is the St. Croix River, a Canadian Heritage River. The French explorer DeMons wintered on St. Croix Island in 1604, and in 1784 American Loyalists arrived there following the American War of Independence. By 1800 St. Stephen was an important regional port for overseas shipment of timber and lumber. Shipyards and wharves studded both sides of the St. Croix River, and the docks were crowded with tall ships loaded with lumber. St. Stephen was incorporated as a town in 1871. Then five years later, its business district was almost totally consumed by fire as eighty buildings and thirteen wharves were destroyed. By the turn of the twentieth century, lumbering and shipbuilding had all but disappeared from the area.

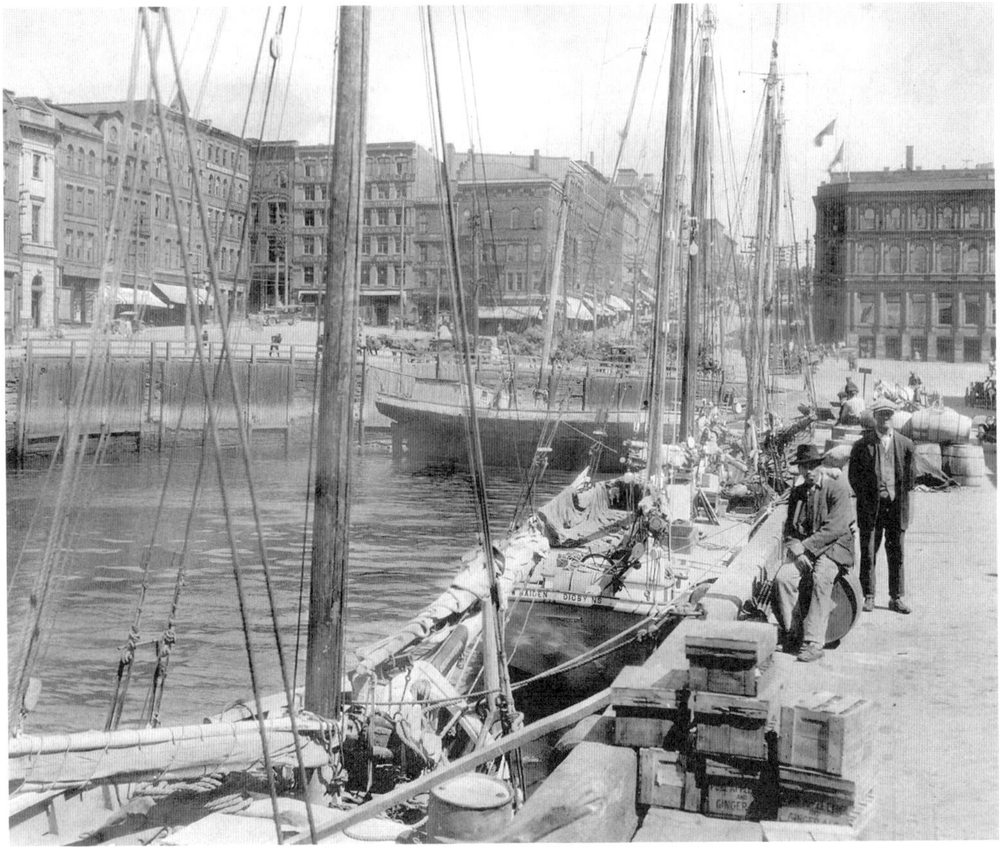

PHOTOS OF SOUTH MARKET WHARF, C.1925

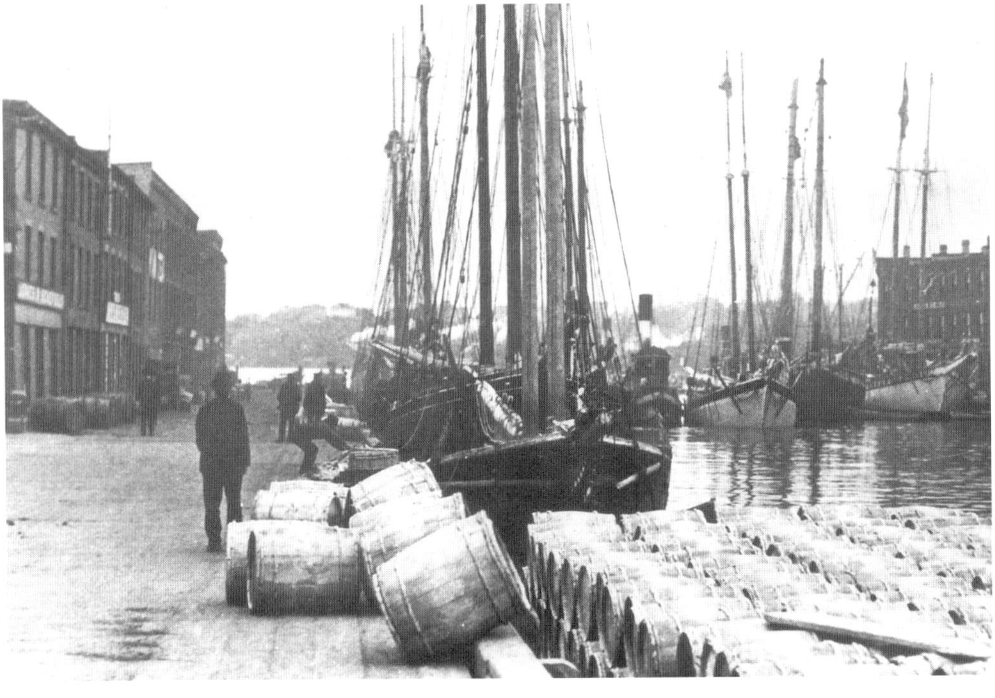

PHOTOS AT LEFT

## South Market Wharf, c.1925

The crates shown here contained pure apple cider and ginger ale, and the schooner at the left of the man on the barrel is the *Snow Maiden,* from Digby. At right a car is turning onto South Market Wharf. The view looking south of South Market Wharf shows a barge loaded with barrels which probably contain fish. In the background, Market Slip is closed in by the schooners and a tug.

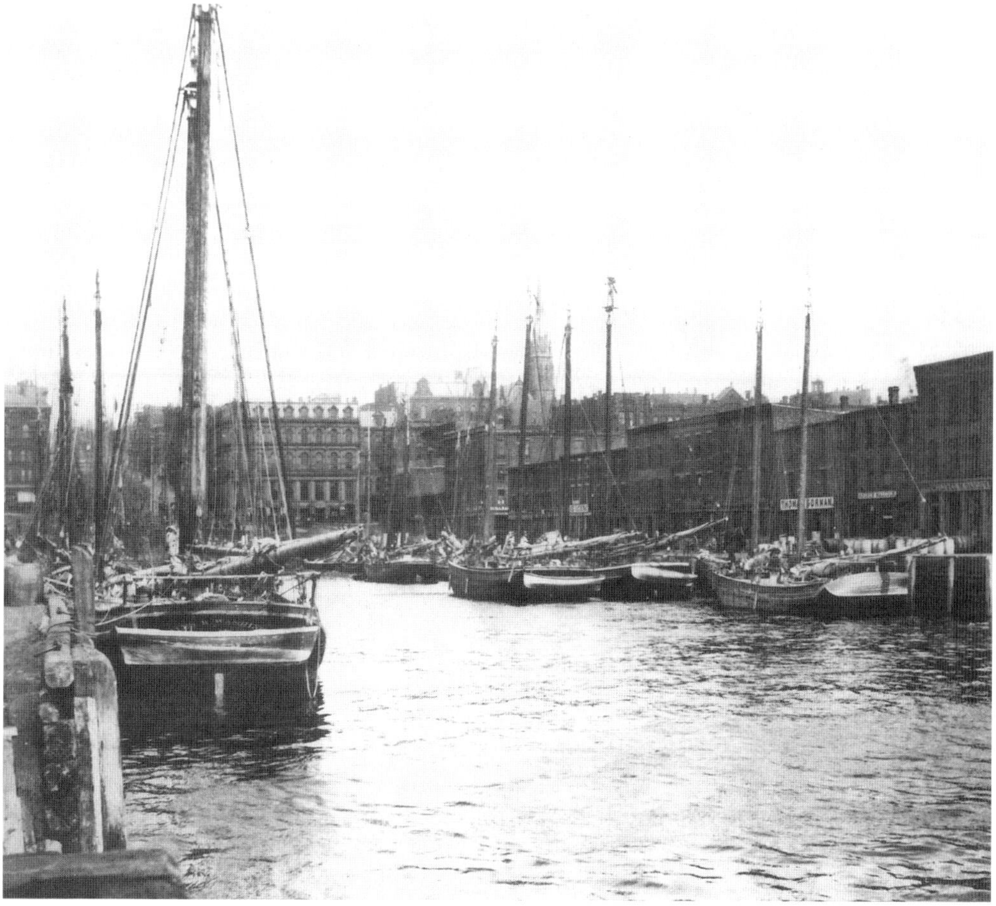

## Market Slip, 1899

On both sides of Market Slip, various cargoes are being delivered. At South Market Wharf, the last four buildings contained the businesses of Thomas Gorman, Andrew Malcolm, Wilfred M. Barlow, J. A. Galbraith, and H.W. Williams. The building at right was the West End House roominghouse for mariners. In the late 1950s, this entire area was demolished to make way for the coast guard building.

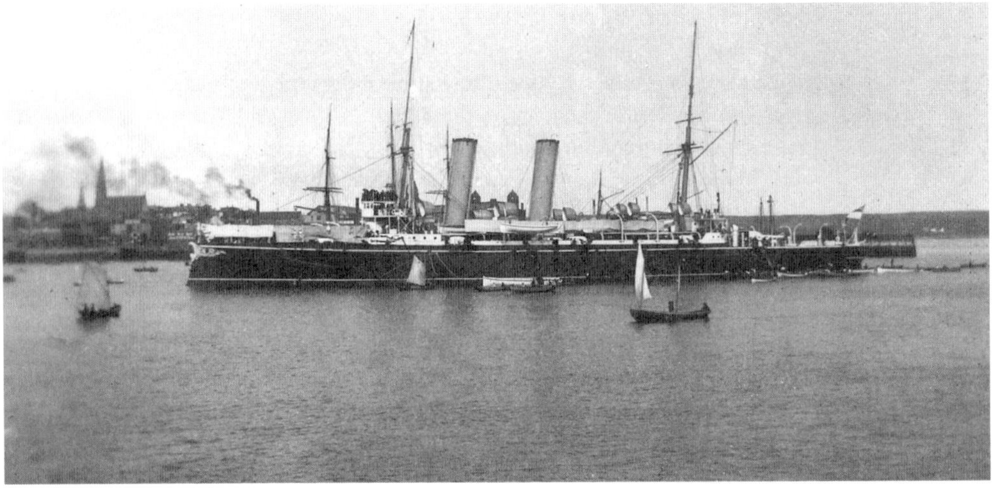

**ROYAL VISIT, 1901**

The first royal visit to New Brunswick was in 1790 when the Duke of Kent visited Saint John. In 1860, the Prince of Wales, son of Queen Victoria, came to Saint John and Fredericton. The Duke and Duchess of Cornwall and York visited Saint John in 1901, when their formal duties included presenting South Africa Medals to veterans of the Boer War. The last time a Canadian naval vessel was present for a royal visit was in 1939 when King George VI and Queen Elizabeth visited Saint John. In 1983 the Prince and Princess of Wales arrived in Saint John aboard the Royal Yacht *Britannia*.

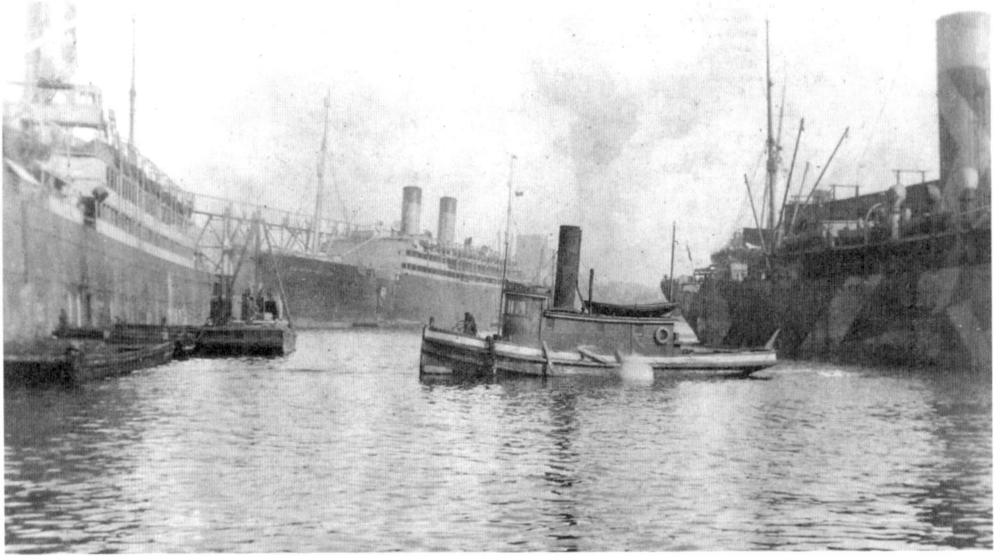

**WARTIME, 1917**

The tug *Holly* and these cargo ships are in one of the slips at the west side of Saint John Harbour. The scows at the left were used for everything from coal refuelling to cargo loading. The camouflage ship at right is a reminder that in 1917 Saint John was a major port for the shipment of war supplies overseas.

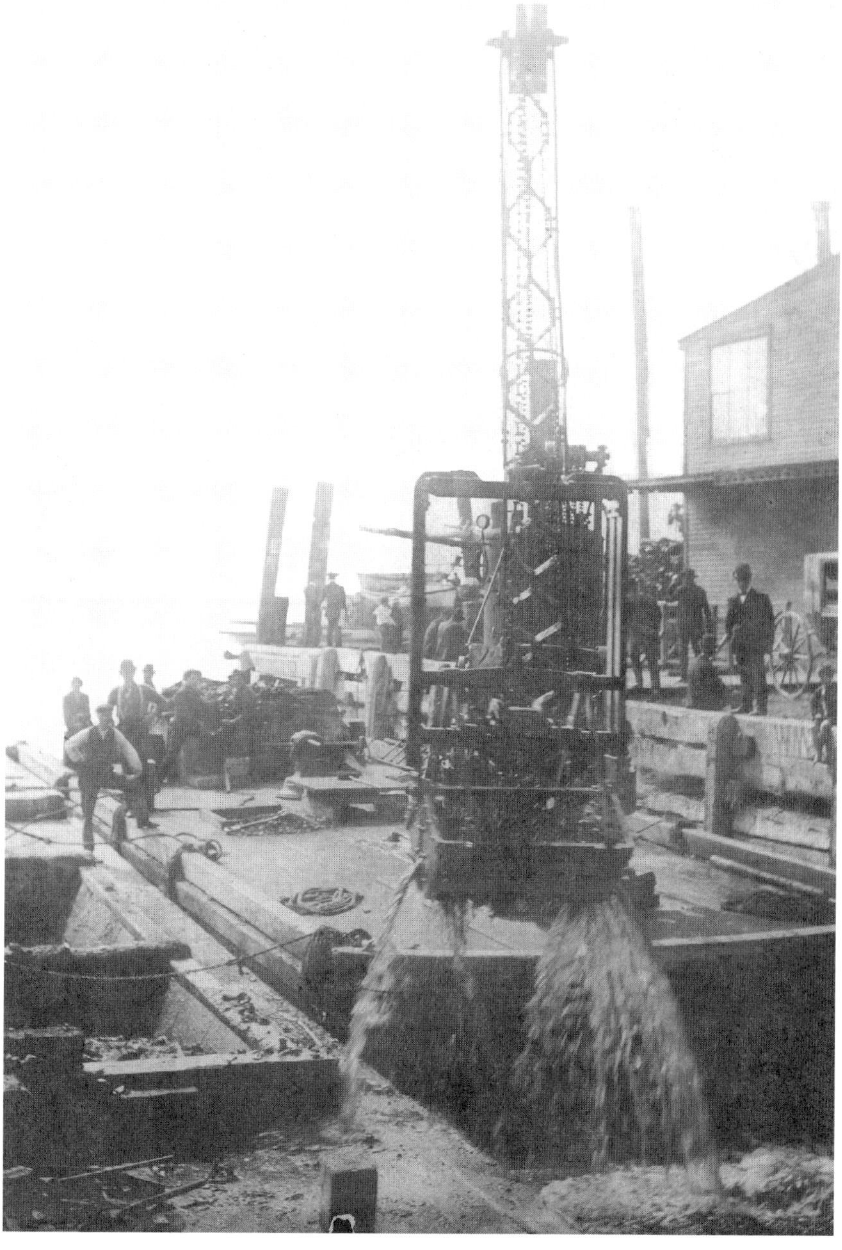

**DREDGING CREW, c.1905** George "Slim" Burley (at left with his left hand on his raised left knee) lived on Middle Street and later Water Street. His father James was a fisherman before he went to work for the Saint John Harbour ferry service. Slim worked longshore for most of his life with this dredging crew, which was supervised by Mr. Anthony, the man at the right next to the carriage. The mud from this slip was dumped onto the two barges, which were towed to the outer harbour and dumped. Slim died in 1958.

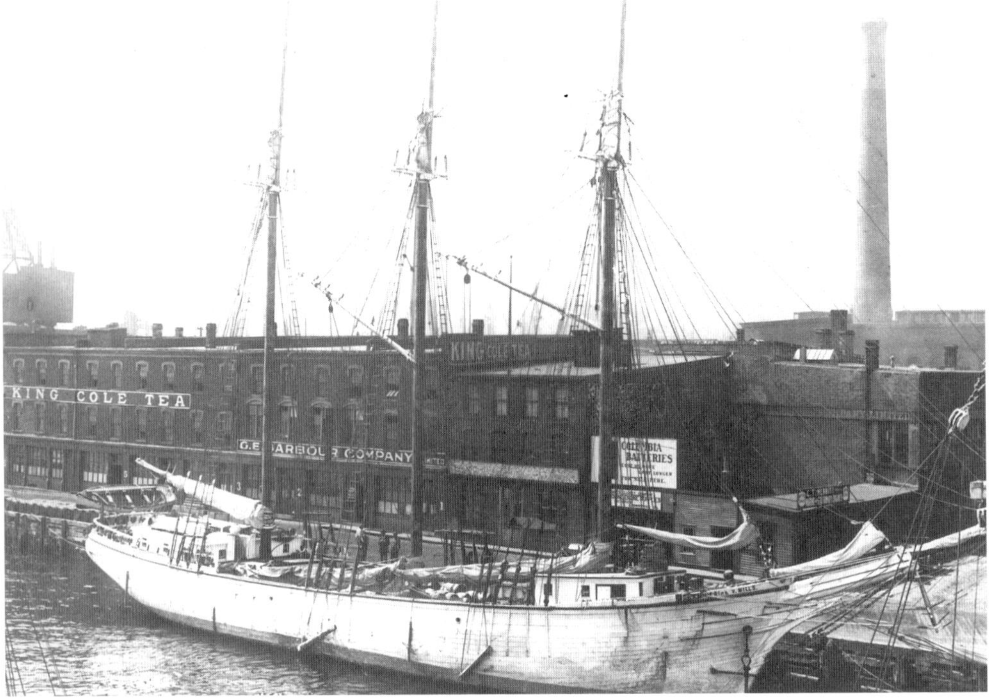


**North Market Slip, c.1920** The tern schooner *Katherine V. Mills* may have brought goods for the Barbour Company, C.T. Merritt (marine and stationary engines), or the Imperial Tobacco Company at 15 Mill Street. The chimney of the Dock Street Power Plant can be seen in the rear.

**Dredge *Fundy*, March, 1933** From March 1933 to December 1934, J.P. Porter and Sons Limited had the contract for dredging and realigning the main channel of Saint John Harbour. The seven-cubic-yard dipper dredge *Fundy* was assisted by the dredges *Leconfield*

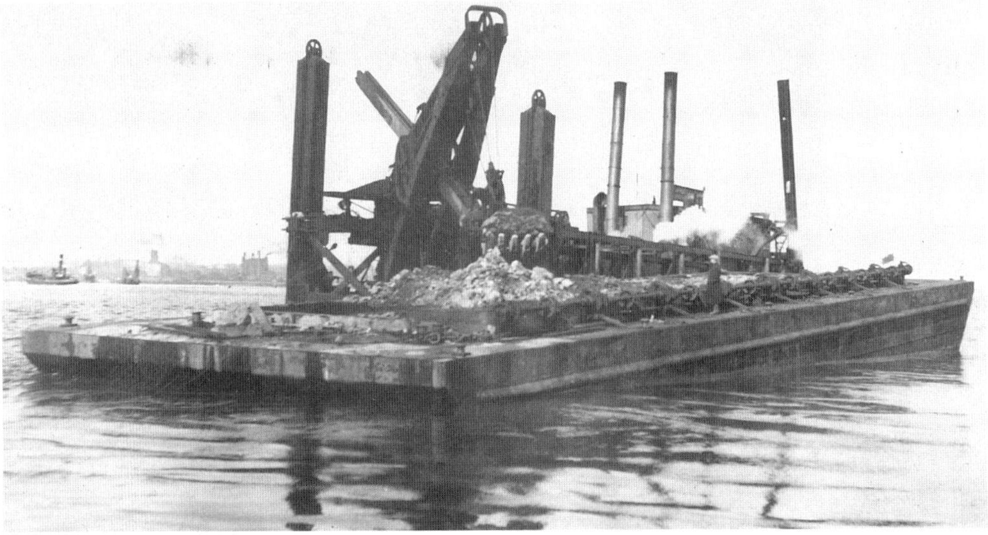

and *Orange Peel*, the steam-propelled hopper *Foremost No. 17*, and the tug *Dupre.* William Stanley of 52 Elliott Row was the dredge foreman. In his diary he made the following entry for this day:

> "Reported for duty at 9 am aboard Foremost No. 17 under Captain A.B. Small—first load—left wharf 12:45 at dredge and stopped work at 1 pm. Finish loading and lift 5:30 pm. Depart 6:10 pm South Cranberry Head, went to anchorage 6:45. Winds southwest moderate from 6:45 pm to 12 midnight, working trim and dredge at high tide."

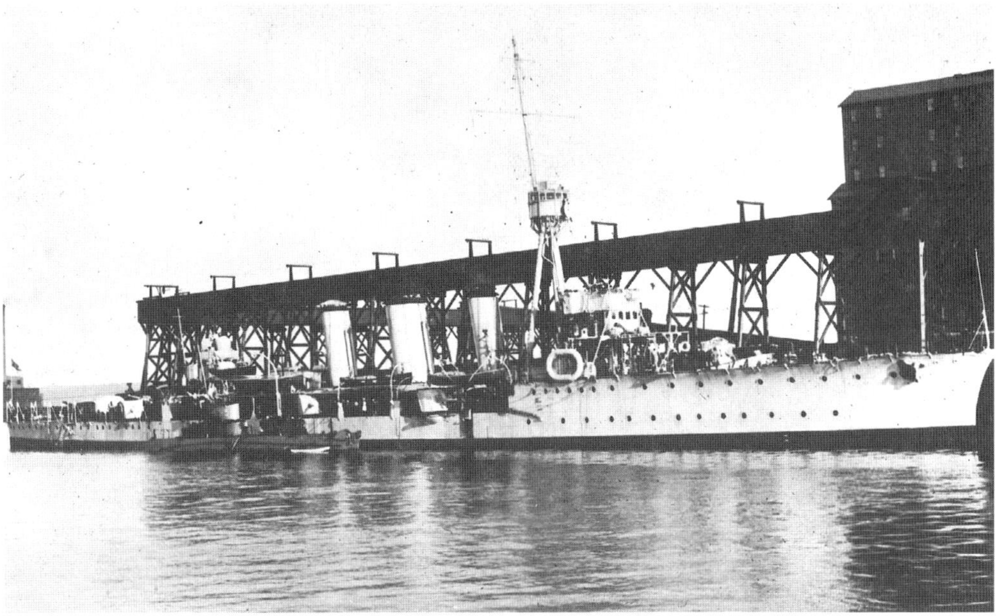

### Visiting Warships, September 24, 1921

The Arethusa-class cruiser HMS *Aurora*, and Hunt-class submarine CH-15, were just two of hundreds of Canadian, Allied, and foreign warships to call at the port of Saint John over the past two hundred years. The *Aurora* was built in His Majesty's Dockyard at Devonport and launched on September 30, 1913. She served in the Grand Fleet from 1914 to 1916, and was the first British ship in action at the Battle of the Dogger Bank in 1915. She was on hand at the surrender of the German High Seas Fleet in November 1918. *Aurora* was presented to the Royal Canadian Navy in 1920, along with two destroyers. She was commissioned into the Canadian Navy on November 1, 1920. After returning from the West Coast in 1921, she was paid off and disarmed in 1922. Submarines CH-14 and CH-15 were built by the Fore River Company at Quincy, Massachusetts, in 1917. After the war's end in 1919 Canada received the two CH-boats, which served the winter of 1921-22 at HMS *Malabar* in Bermuda where they exercised with Canadian and British ships. Upon their return to Canada, they fell victim to defence budget cuts in May 1922 and were paid off on June 30, 1922. The *Aurora* and both CH-subs were tied up at moorings in the Northwest Arm in Halifax until they were sold in 1927 to a Montreal shipbuilder for scrap.

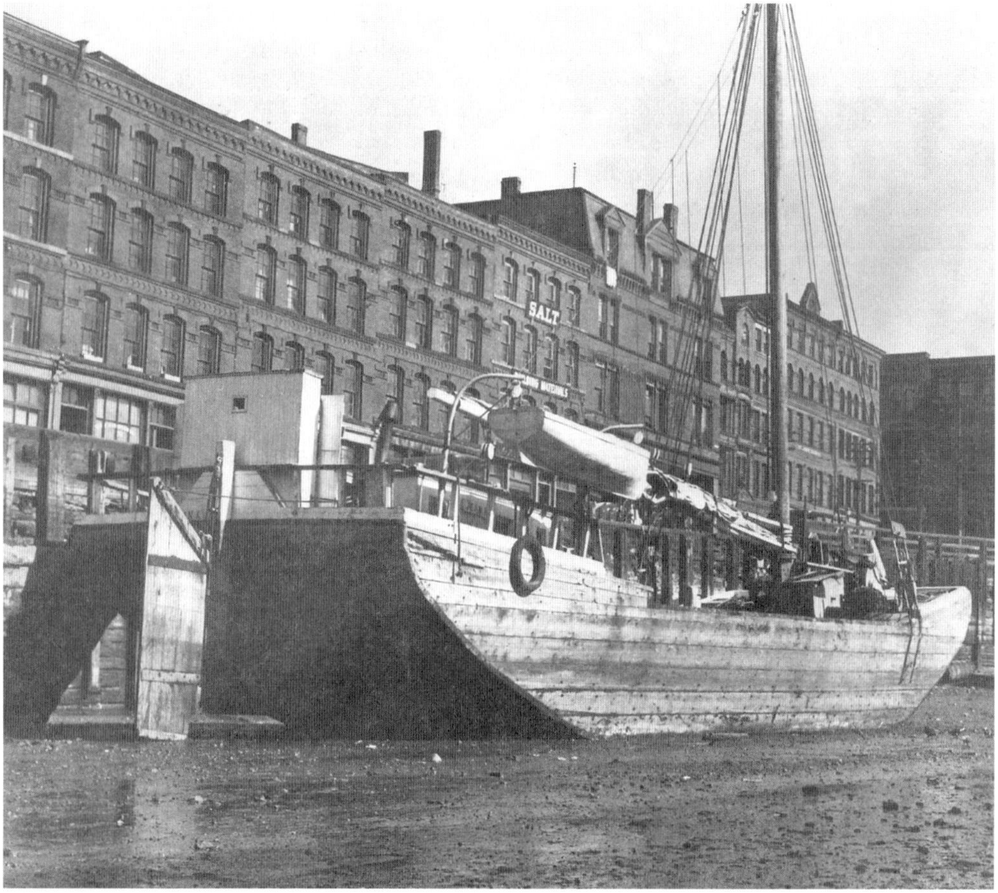


**BARGE *JEAN K.*, 1933**

The motor barge *Jean K.* was 71 feet long, built of Douglas fir, and powered by two 15-horsepower gasoline engines. Her regular runs were between Alma, Saint John, St. Stephen, Grand Manan, Parrsboro, and Yarmouth, and up the St. John and Petitcodiac rivers. Paul Kool, of Alma, had named his scow after his daughter Jean. The *Jean K.* was sunk off Saint John before Christmas in 1945.

### Stevedore Aubrey Keirstead and first mate Molly Kool, c.1938

At age twenty-three, Molly Kool of Alma became the youngest master mariner in Canada. In 1937 she wrote her mate's exam in Saint John, and in 1939 she passed her master's exam at Yarmouth and took over command of the *Jean K.* from her father. Molly was born in 1916, one of five children, and she first went to sea in 1934. She recounted her early experiences at sea, "I did the cooking. That wasn't much of a job. The old guy who was with Dad was a cook so he'd tell me how to cook. It was pretty bad, but I suppose I learned after a while. And I ran the engines, and I steered, and hoisted the sail, and did all the jobs that a sailor does. Well, an ordinary sailor doesn't do the cooking, but I was expected to do that too." When she passed her captain's exam, Kool became the second female captain in the world (the other being Russian Anna Shchetinina). Her defining moment came just at the beginning of World War Two when the Boston boat SS *Yarmouth* hit the *Jean K.* in heavy fog while leaving Saint John Harbour in the main channel. Kool was thrown overboard and came to the surface, where she held onto deals from her load of lumber. She was picked up by fisherman Cecil Akerley who took her to Partridge Island. Lightkeeper Harold Lauder called for the tug *Neptune*, which towed the *Jean K.* into Market Slip. Kool married in 1944 and soon after she left the sea. She and Cecil Akerley were reunited in 1992 at a special ceremony at the New Brunswick Museum. Today Molly Kool lives in Orrington, Maine.

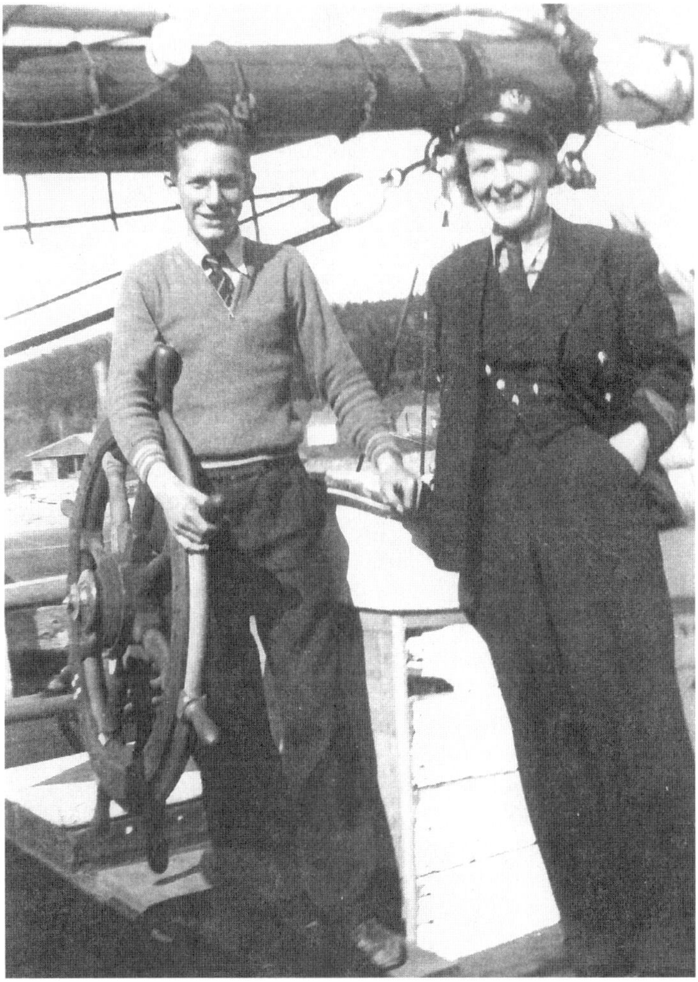

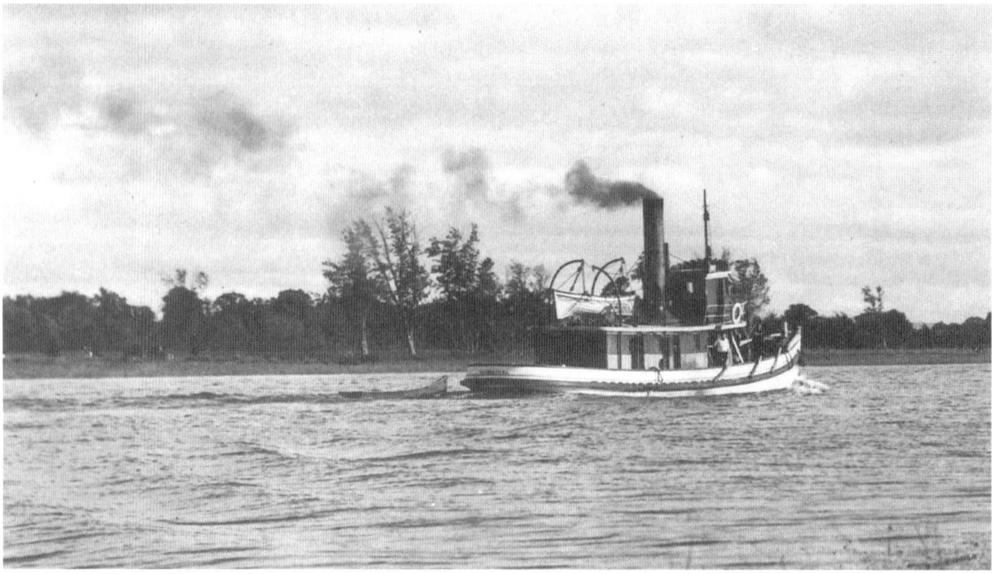

**A TUG, C.1920**

This could be the *Ocean Osprey*, which used to haul pulp down the Irish River to Saint John. She was wrecked at Canso, Nova Scotia in 1926. In 1958, the Saint John Tugboat Company bought a pre-World War Two Scottish tug, the Empire-class *Thunderer*. On April 5, 1958, she left Glasgow for the Azores en route to Saint John, arriving here on April 23. At 101 feet long, she was not an ocean-going tug so her Atlantic crossing was "quite a feat." The *Thunderer* was renamed *Ocean Osprey* II, and she was used principally to tow pulpwood along the Bay of Fundy from St. Martins to Digby and down the east coast of the United States.

**ST. MARTINS LUMBER, 1940**

TOP RIGHT

This photo at top right is probably a Pejebscot tug towing lumber from one of the portable mills in the Salmon River area into Quaco Harbour. This lumber would be unloaded and then placed onto a larger ship for transport, probably to Maine.

**SS *WEST NOSSKA*, C.1935**

BOTTOM RIGHT

This photo at bottom right shows lumber being taken from Mackay lumber scows. The loading of cargo was an activity negotiated between the longshoremen and the shipping lines. The 1920 working agreement stated: "Fifteen men, not including foreman shall constitute a gang for loading and discharging general cargo and ballast. In the case of a ship or vessel loading grain in bulk, full gangs shall be employed from the beginning of loading and men shall not lose [sic] any time when called out of hold while grain is running. In the case of deal boats, the number of men per gang shall not be less than twelve except when working two winches at a hatch, then an extra man shall be employed making thirteen in a deal gang. At no time shall there be less than six men in ship's hold when loading deals."

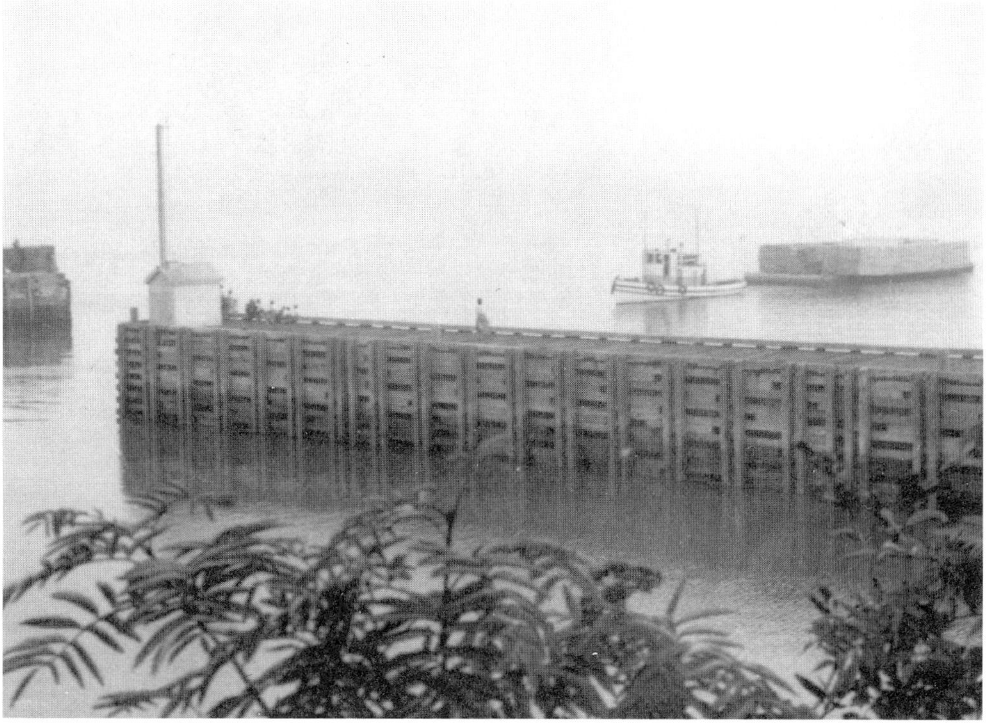

ST. MARTINS LUMBER (ABOVE) AND SS *WEST NOSSKA* (BELOW)

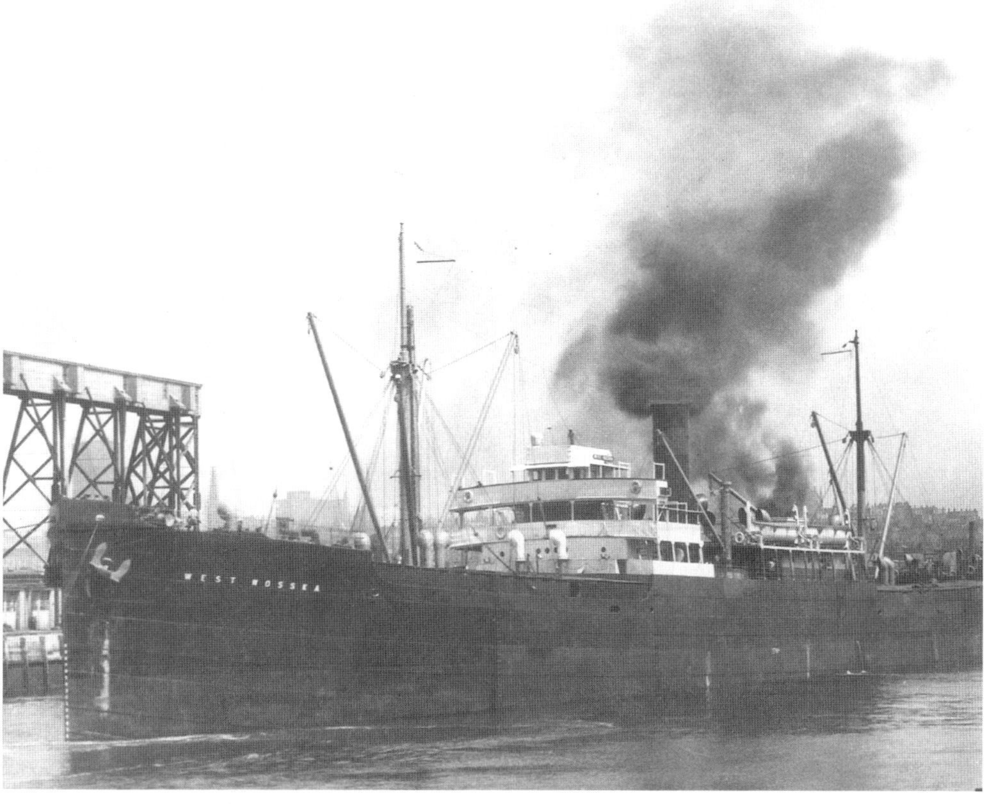

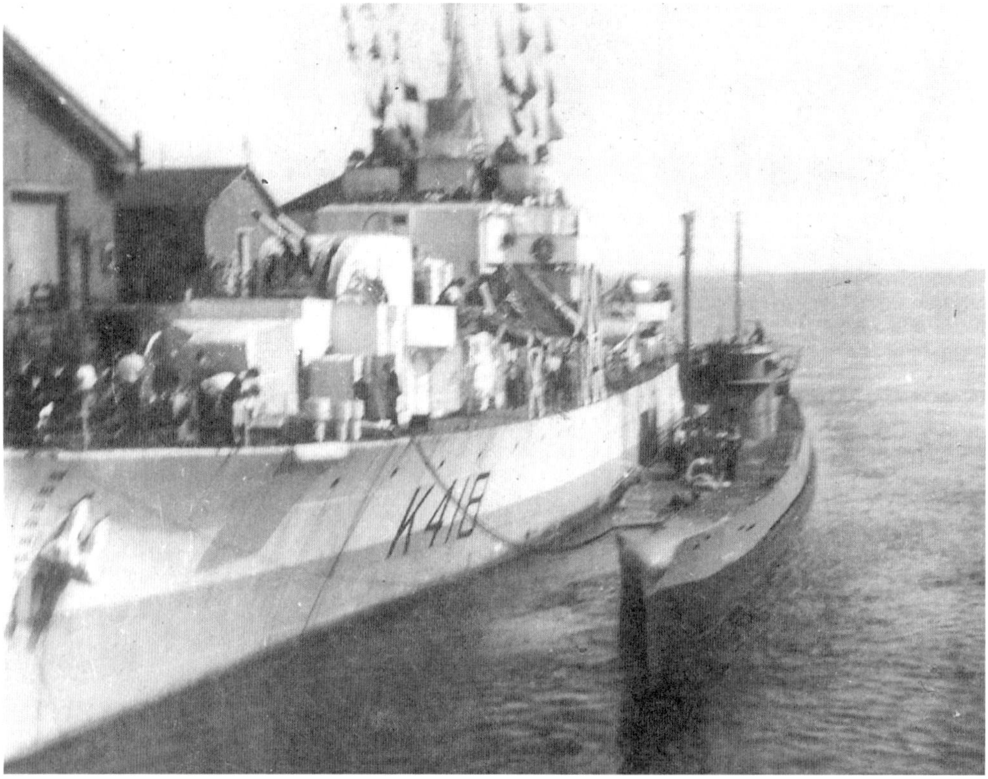

**HMCS *Joliette* and *U-889*, 1945**

HMCS *Joliette*, a sister ship of HMCS *Saint John*, was built at the Morton Engineering and Dry Dock in Quebec City. She was launched on December 11, 1943, commissioned on June 14, 1944, and paid off on November 19, 1945. *U-889* was a type IXC/40 submarine, laid down by AG Wesner in Bremen on September 13, 1943. She was commissioned on August 4, 1944 under Kptlt. Friedrich Brauecker. She had one patrol without any success in sinking Allied ships. Brauecker commanded *U-889* until May 10, 1945 when the U-boat became the first in the western Atlantic to surrender. Two days after receiving the message ceasing hostilities, *U-889* was overflown by a Liberator from the Royal Canadian Air Force. It took two low passes before a flag was seen—the Liberator had been arming the depth charges and setting the bomb sight when the submarine surrendered. The Liberator stood by until HMCS *Rockcliffe*, *Dunvegan*, *Saskatoon*, and *Oshawa* arrived on the scene. Twenty four hours after the interception, *U-889* was turned over to HMC ships *Inch Arran* and *Buckingham* and escorted to Shelburne, Nova Scotia where formal articles of surrender were signed on May 13. The following day His Majesty's Canadian Submarine *U-889* was formally commissioned in the Royal Canadian Navy. *U-889* made a courtesy call to Saint John in August 1945 under the auspices of the Navy League of Canada. While on these courtesy calls in the Maritimes, sixteen sea cadets aboard, including Bill Dalzell from No. 9 Rodney Sea Cadets in Saint John. *U-889* was transferred to the US Navy on January 10, 1946. She was scuttled at the end of 1947 after being used for torpedo trials off New England.

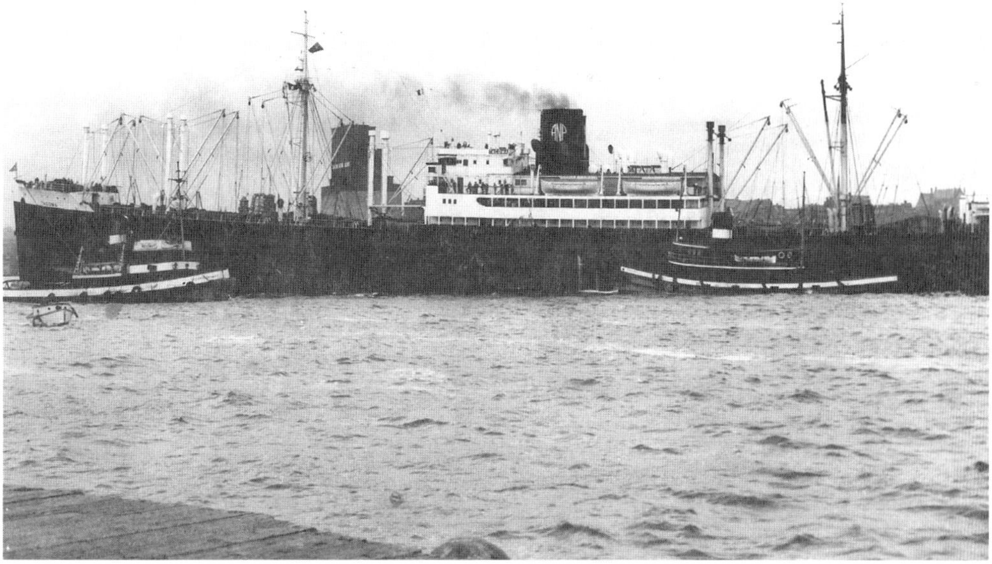

**MV *TACOMA*, NOVEMBER 1949**

When the Uruguayan ship MV *Tacoma* arrived in port, the local newspaper wrote this:

> "[she arrived] late last night and will shift to Pier 13 tomorrow to begin loading the largest single cargo of New Brunswick seed potatoes shipped through Saint John this winter. The *Tacoma* has three officers and a small group of Uruguayan cadets aboard in [the] charge of Lt. Commander Jose Nattero who made the long trip from Uruguay to Saint John on a goodwill tour and training cruise. While in port they will be guests of HMCS *Brunswicker* and will be entertained at a number of social functions and sporting activities. While in port the *Tacoma* will load some 100,000 crates and 15,000 sacks of seed potatoes for Uruguay. These tubers will be distributed among growers in the South American country. This ship also visited Saint John early in November last year carrying a group of naval cadets on a training cruise. She returned to Uruguay with a large consignment of potatoes. The *Tacoma* once served as a fuelling ship for German sea raiders and submarines and was seized in Montevideo at the time of the scuttling of the *Graf Spree*."

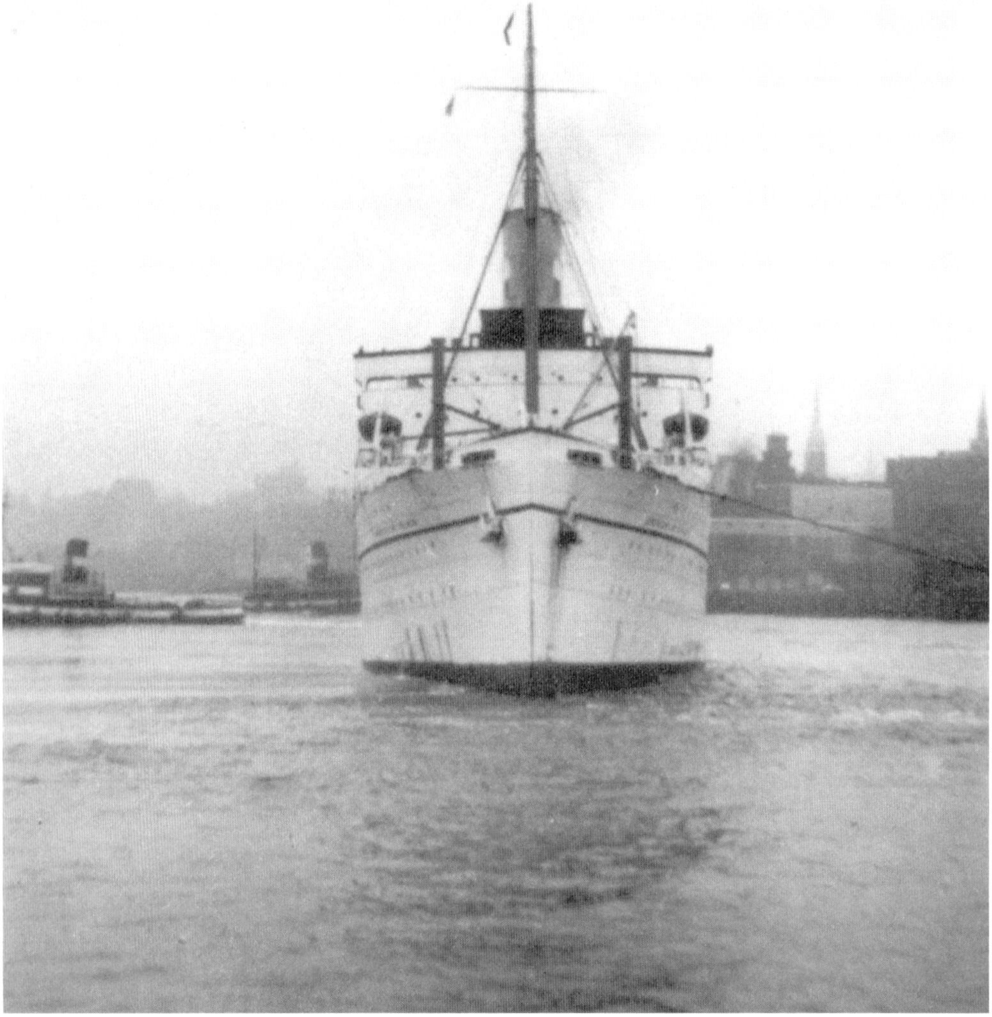

**EMPRESS OF FRANCE, 1950**

The December 1950 landing of the *Empress of France* was described in a local newspaper account:

> "Some 600 passengers, many of them making their first trip to this country, got a real taste of Canadian winter yesterday when the Canadian Pacific Steamship's *Empress of France* docked here at 3:30 P.M. in temperatures hovering around the zero mark. Commanded by Capt. S. W. Keay, the vessel carried 2,673 tonnes of general cargo to this country. She sailed from Liverpool for her first visit of the season to this port."

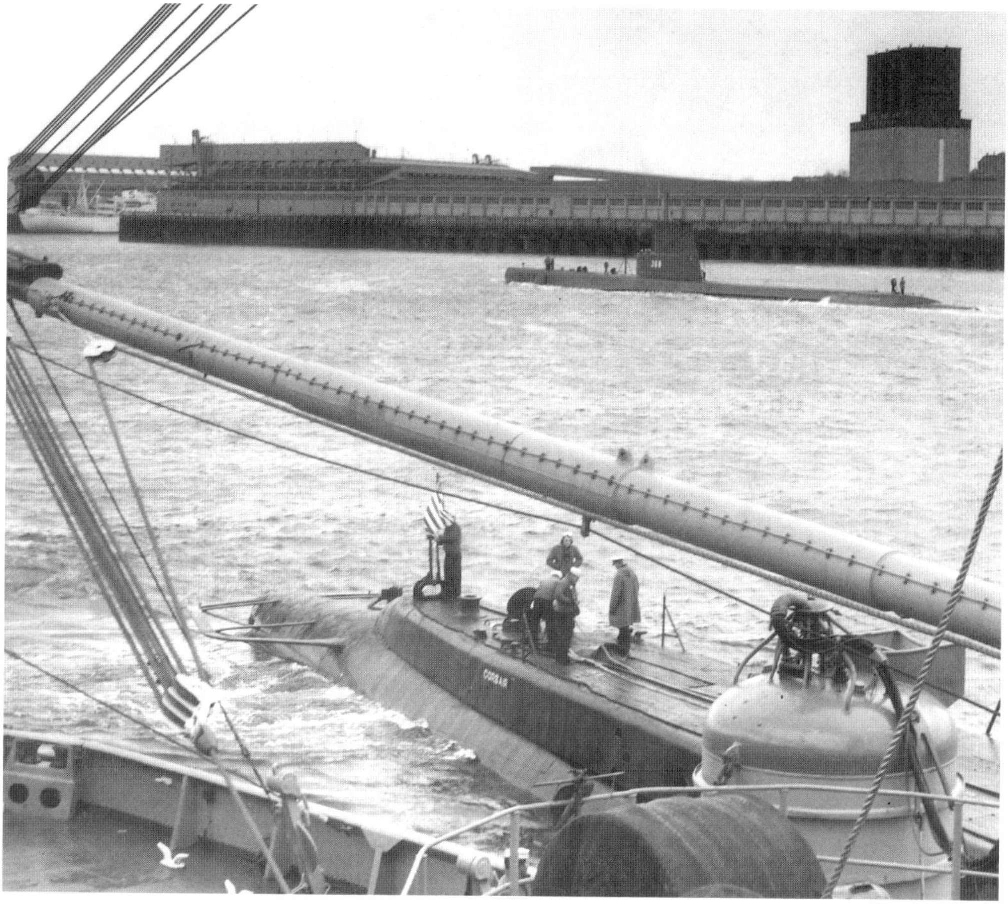

## US Submarines, November 1961

Saint John has always been visited by warships of allied countries. Some of the US warships in port have been the submarines *Dogfish*, and the USS *Corsair* and *Carp*, shown here. The Tench-class SS-435 *Corsair* was built at the Electric Boat Company, Groton, Connecticut, and commissioned in 1945. The Balao-class SS-338 *Carp* was built by the same company and also commissioned in 1945. She remained in service until 1968 when she was transferred to the naval reserve for use as a training boat before being scrapped in 1973.

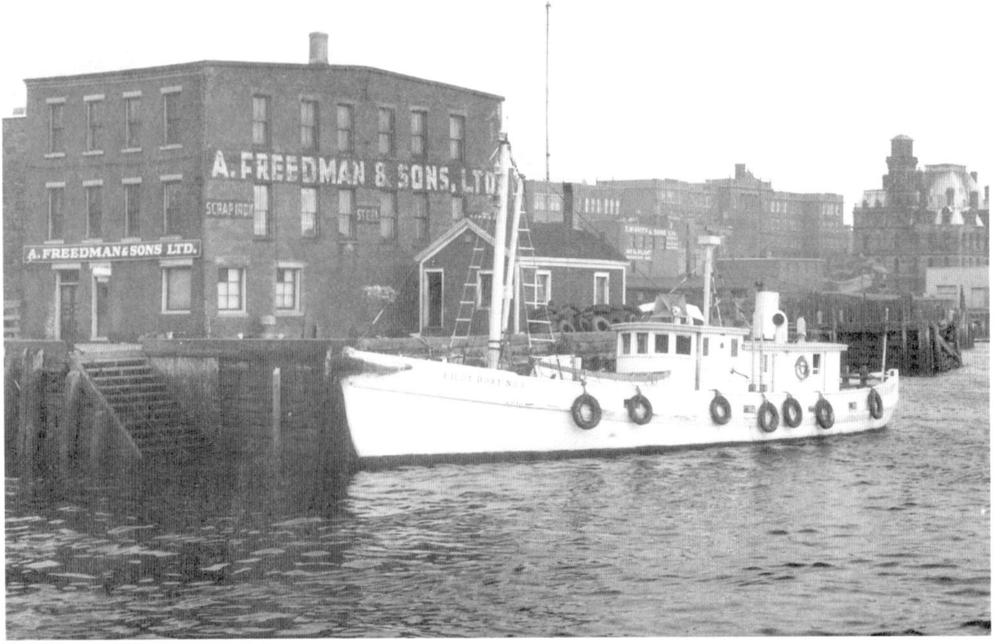


**DOOMED PILOT BOAT, 1950**

Pilot boat No. 1 is shown on the face of South Market Slip. In a dense fog and 12-below-zero weather on January 14, 1957, pilot boat No. 1 was rammed and sunk by the SS *Fort Avalon* one and a quarter miles off the Fairway buoy. Killed were pilots William J. Murray, John V. Cunningham, William P. Traynor, and Ward Poole, cook Blanchard Cosman, seaman Frank Coughlan, and engineer Donald Johnson. The decision of the enquiry by Justice W.A.I. Anglin of the Supreme Court of New Brunswick, Queen's Bench, found that the "physical cause of the sinking" was the "immoderate speed" of the freighter. In August 1958 the replacement pilot boat, No. 6, assumed duties in Saint John.

**ICE BOAT, C.1972**

TOP RIGHT

Winter navigation posed many hazards even when the ship was in port. Ice had to be removed from lines, gear, winches, and chains, both as a safety precaution and to allow longshoremen to operate the equipment for the loading and unloading of the ship.

**PIER 3, C.1970**

BOTTOM RIGHT

An unnamed Canadian Pacific boat and the MV *Jalakirti* are at Pier 2 and the MV *Jaladharna* is at Pier 3, with the tug *Rockswift* at the face of Pier 3. These vessels continued to call on the port of Saint John because of the reputation of the local longshoremen in handling cargo. A contemporary newspaper article reported:

> "During this same period the men continued to handle a great deal of bulk cargo, mail, and fruit, to name just a few. The longshoremen continued to break records in grain handling and maintain their first rate reputation … proving time and after time that no cargo is impossible to reckon with if you have the know-how … cargoes so heavy they have to be loaded aboard ship in sections … cargoes so perishable they have to be rushed into heated sheds … four diesel engines each weighing 72 tonnes … for the good name you have given this port."

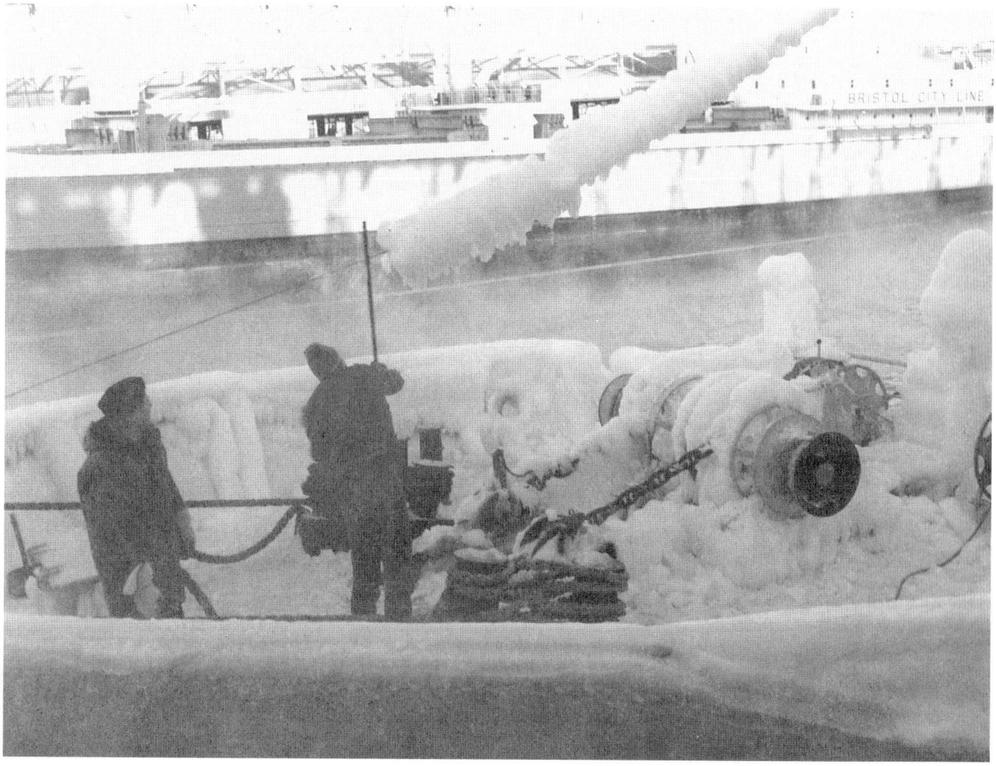


ICE BOAT C.1972 (ABOVE) AND PIER 3, C.1970 (BELOW)

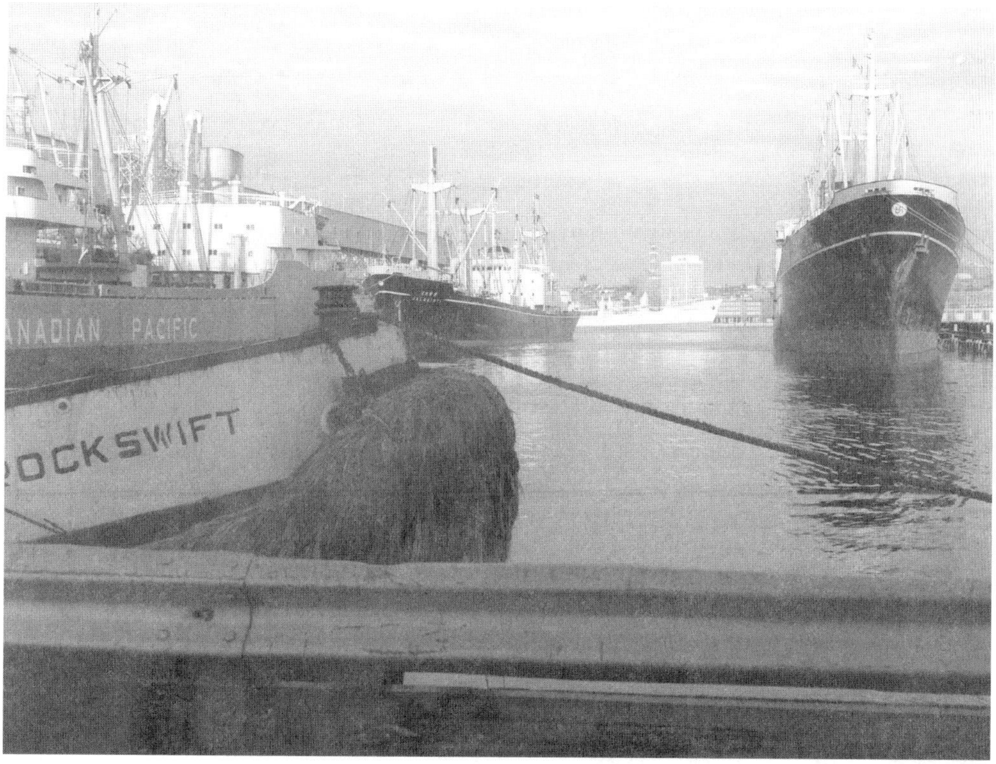

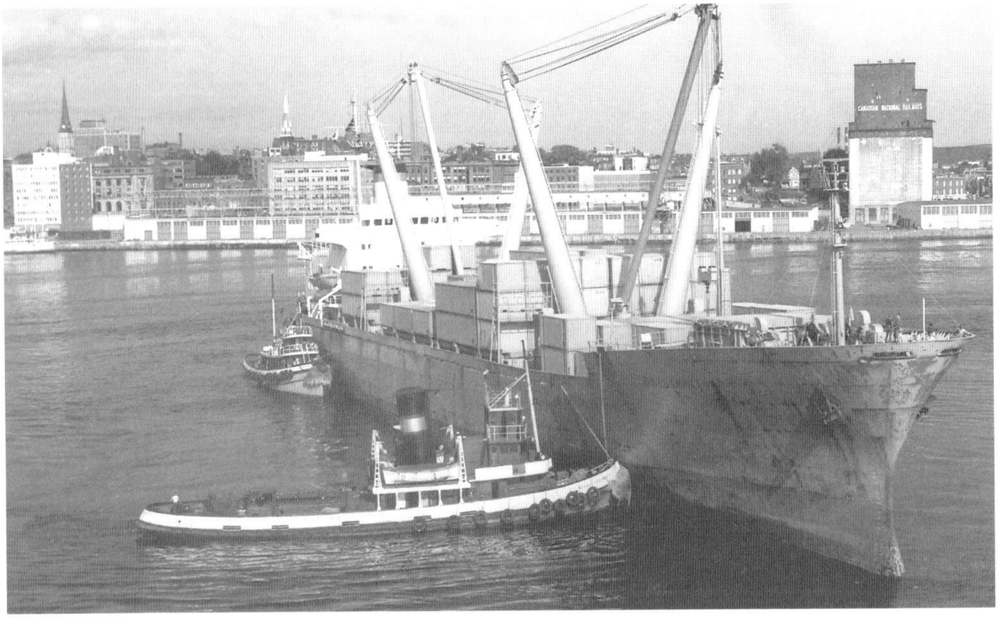

**Tug** *Assistance*, **c.1970**

The municipal government owned and leased the Saint John Harbour facilities until 1927 when the title was sold to the federal government. In 1929 the port facilities included fifteen ocean berths (ten with grain conveyors), three grain elevators, two rail lines (CN and CPR), a fertilizer storage shed, three frost-free potato warehouses, coal and oil bunkering facilities, molasses tanks, an immigration depot with hospitals at Partridge Island, a Seamen's Institute, and a good towing system. By 1947 this had changed to twenty ocean berths (eleven with grain conveyors), two frost-free potato warehouses, and the 1929 services less the hospitals, which had been closed on the island. The Saint John stevedores were described as "highly efficient, and the labour of good class and dependable."

## Gordie Halvorsen aboard MV *Irving Eskimo*, 1997

The *Irving Eskimo* was built in 1980 at the Saint John Shipyard. Saint John native Gordie Halvorsen worked as an oiler aboard the *Eskimo* for three months. During his one year with Kent Line Limited, Gordie also served on the *Wellington Kent* and the *Irving Arctic*. As an oiler, his duties included the operation and maintenance of engine-room and auxiliary machinery. Gordie had served with the Canadian Navy for three years and also for Atlantic Towing. While he was with Kent Line, he visited several ports throughout the Atlantic provinces, on the St. Lawrence, and in Maine, New Jersey, and Rhode Island, as well as in Boston and New York. In this photo Gordie is shown in the engine-room control room while the *Eskimo* was in drydock at Halifax.

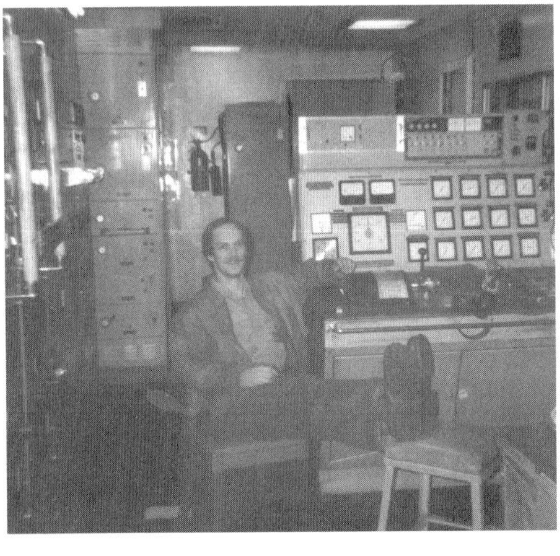

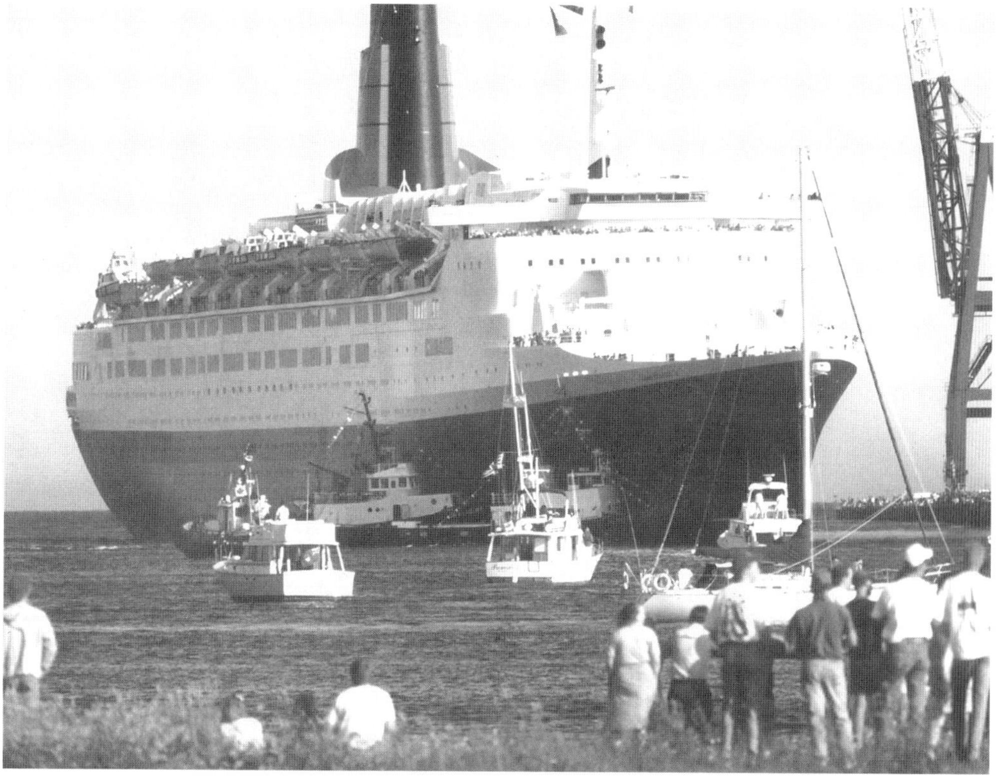

***Queen Elizabeth II*, 1995**

"Imagine a floating palace where the pleasures are unmatched." These words describe the queen of the cruise ship fleet, which made her first call to Saint John in 1995. She is seen here just as she is departing, with a glorious send-off by thousands of Saint Johners. *QE II* is the last of the great Cunard ships built for the trans-Atlantic service and is Cunard's flagship vessel, embodying the essence of British heritage and all that is Cunard. She remains the only ship offering regularly scheduled trans-Atlantic service. Discussions concerning a replacement ship for Cunard's *Queen Mary* and *Queen Elizabeth* began in 1958. On September 20, 1965, the keel was launched by *Queen Elizabeth II*, the ship was named *Queen Elizabeth II,* and the delivery date was set: May 1968. Due to continued technical problems, however, the maiden voyage of *QE II* from Southampton to New York, did not take place until May 2, 1969. Over the next few years the *QE II* reduced the number of trans-Atlantic crossings and concentrated on cruises. The outbreak of the Falklands War in April 1982 led to a change in her role as she was requisitioned for service as a troop transport. Conversion work added a helicopter flight deck and a modern communications system. The 5th Infantry Brigade boarded the ship and sailed for South Georgia on May 12, arriving on May 27. After the troops disembarked, the *QE II* returned to Southampton on June 11 where she was restored for commercial service. In 1986 she was again extensively refitted with new passenger accommodation.

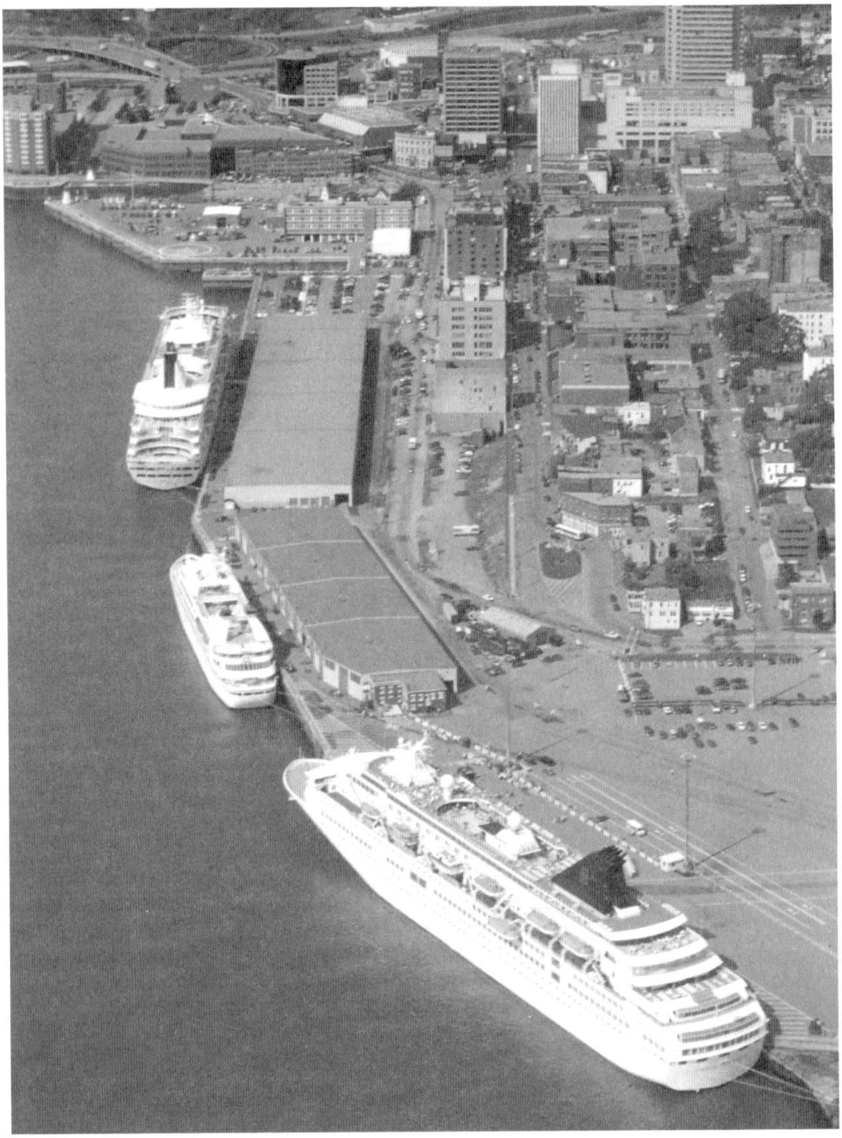

**CRUISE SHIPS, SEPTEMBER 1999**

Saint John's cruise ship industry went from zero ships in 1988 and one ship in 1989 to 67 ships in 2000. Two-hundred and thirteen vessels over that twelve-year period have brought 255,543 passengers aboard such vessels as the *Royal Princess, Seabourn Pride*, and *Norwegian Majesty*, shown here tied up from Pugsley Park down to the Lower Cove Terminal. In 1998 the cruise ship's Meet and Greet Committee was presented the President's Award at the Saint John Board of Trade's annual Outstanding Business Achievement Awards Dinner. Saint John's welcome is amazing; it creates a lasting impression for the visitor. A band plays as the passengers disembark, and a rose is given to each female passenger and a city pin to each male. Youth ambassadors in the information kiosk distribute city maps and answer questions from the passengers and crew. A town crier also welcomes the passengers. When the cruise ship departs, a lone piper pipes the ship out of the harbour.

Chapter 4

# Cargoes

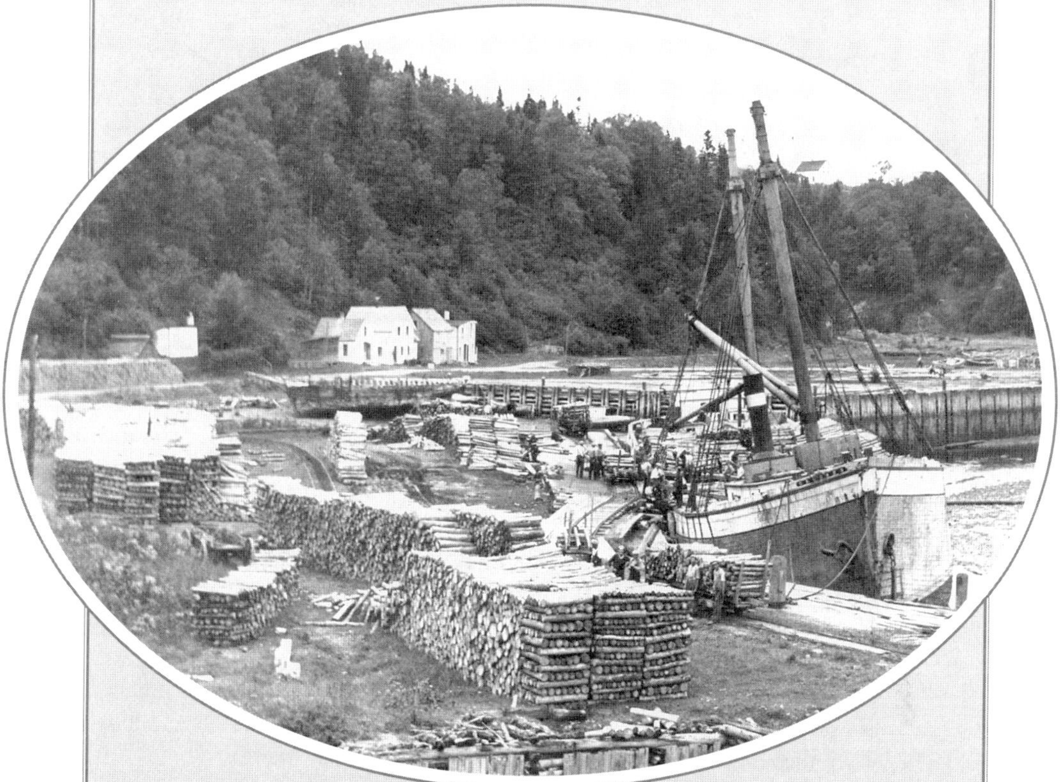

**St. Martins Wharf, c.1920**

Pulp is being loaded aboard this vessel, whose name is unclear but appears to be "*Oalgans.*" Jim Forret of Rothesay arrived in St. Martins in 1928 as a 14-year-old Scottish immigrant. He recalled the loading of pulp at the wharf: "All the wood you see came down the Irish River to the dam and was loaded onto trolleys and hauled from the dam by horses, one horse in a set of shafts hooked to the trolley on the narrow gauge railroad. The railway followed the edge of the road past the houses, then crossed the road up to the wharf. They had a switch they used to pull the empty trolley back to the dam. When the next one that was loaded came, the pulp was unloaded down a chute to the boat hold. When the hold was full they also loaded the deck. Back then the wages were $1 per day for 10 hours. I did work in the woods in 1932 for $17 per month and board."

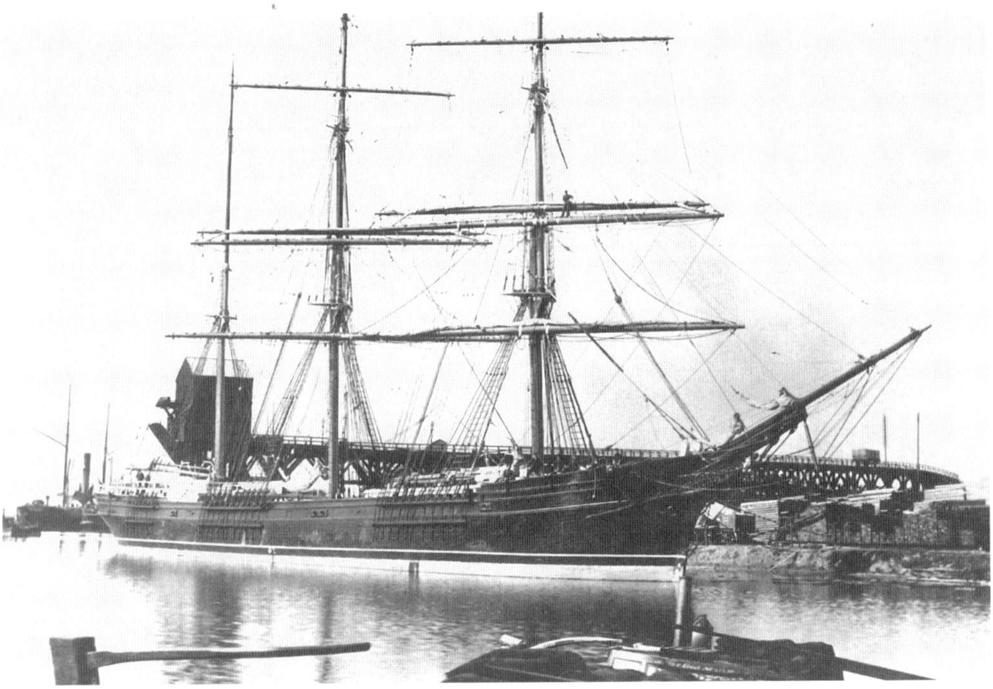

**LONG WHARF, C.1870**

Two vessels are shown here: a scow and a ship tied at the face of Long Wharf. The scow is probably loading coal from the Gibbon's Coal pocket. (Note the elevated rail trestle with the coal car.) The vessel on the inside of Long Wharf is loading lumber from the Kirk & Daniels Mill, also located here.

**FIRST SUGAR, C.1890**

TOP RIGHT

This photo by Augustus Stoerger (who owned a photo shop in Saint John between 1888 and 1892) captured the first "shipment of sugar to market from Sand Point." The cargo was handled by J. Johnston. Whether the sugar is coming or going is not apparent since at the time sugar was transported by rail to a refinery in Moncton. In 1914 Atlantic Sugar Refineries Limited built the refinery at Lower Cove, where sugar continued to be processed until the fall of 2000 when the refinery closed.

**LONG-SHOREMEN, C.1890**

BOTTOM RIGHT

Saint John longshoremen established Canada's first labour union in 1849. For the 150th anniversary of the ILA Local 273, Patti Breen published *Along the Shore, Saint John Longshoremen, 1849 to 1999*, from which this description comes:

> "Cargoes are handled amid a tangle of ropes, gears, spans, masts, derricks, and swinging booms. On deck, the whistles and calls of command, the rattle and whit of winches, the creaking of booms and drafts, the noise of chains, are confusing to ear and brain .... Huge loads of goods jerked from the hold or pier, sway and twirl as they rush through the air and swing past the heads of men. Spans of steel wire sag and sway ... longshore work is carried on in all kinds of weather. The hot glare of the summer sun, causing a blinding reflection on deck and stifling, furnace-like heat in the hold; the chill rains of autumn and early spring; and ... winter. Freezing limbs and numb fingers, and icy floors and tackle. Often economic demands result in two or three gangs working the same hatch."

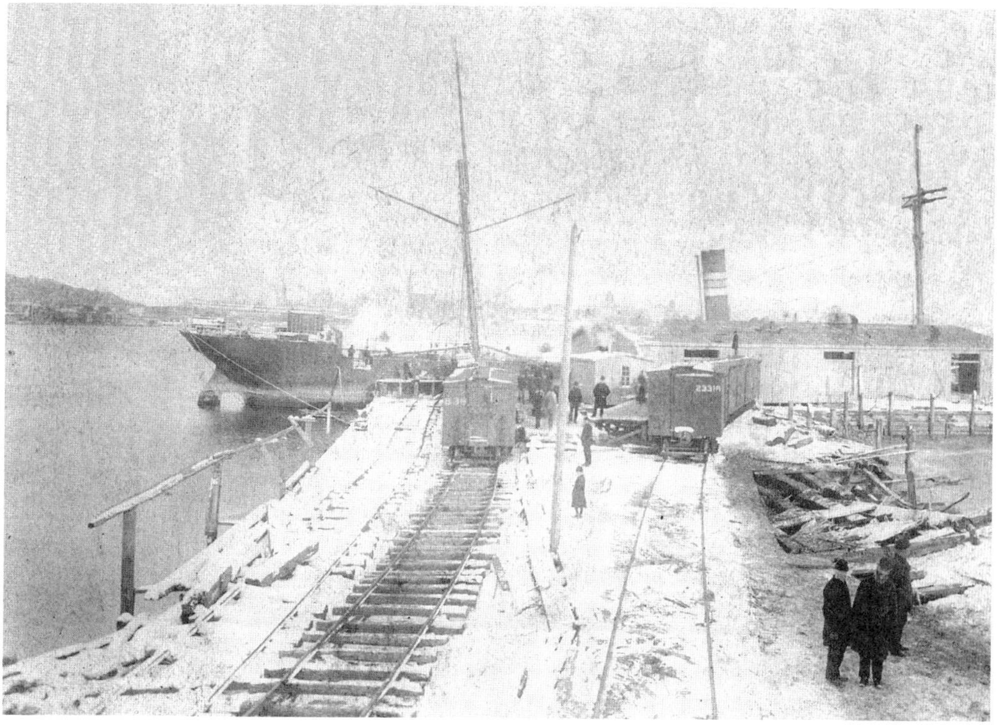

FIRST SUGAR, C.1890 (ABOVE) AND LONGSHOREMEN, C.1890 (BELOW)

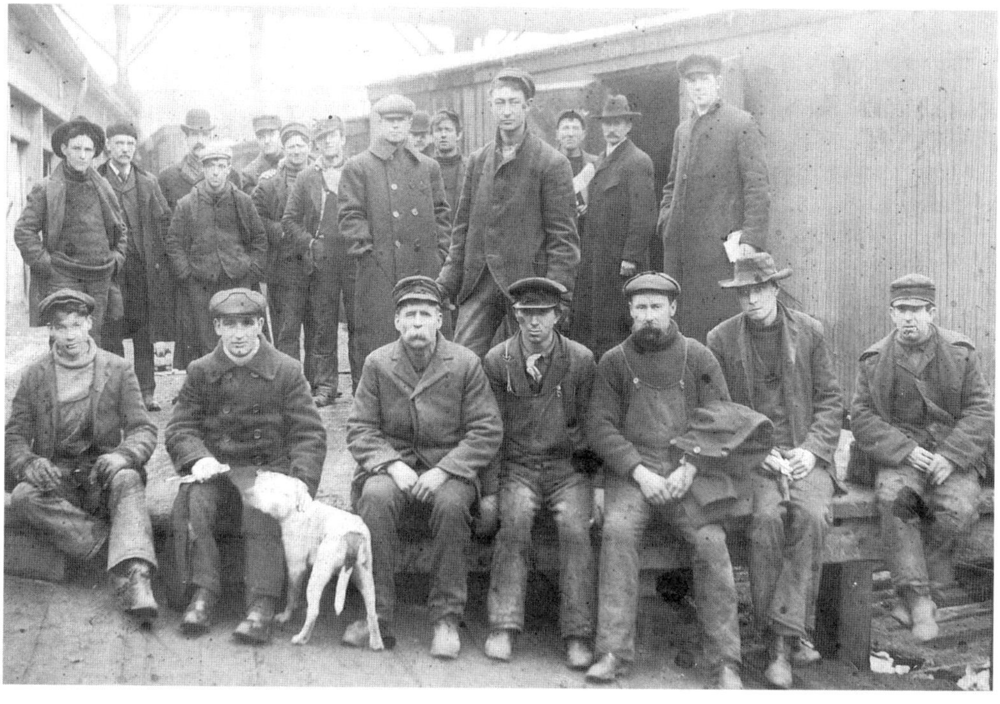

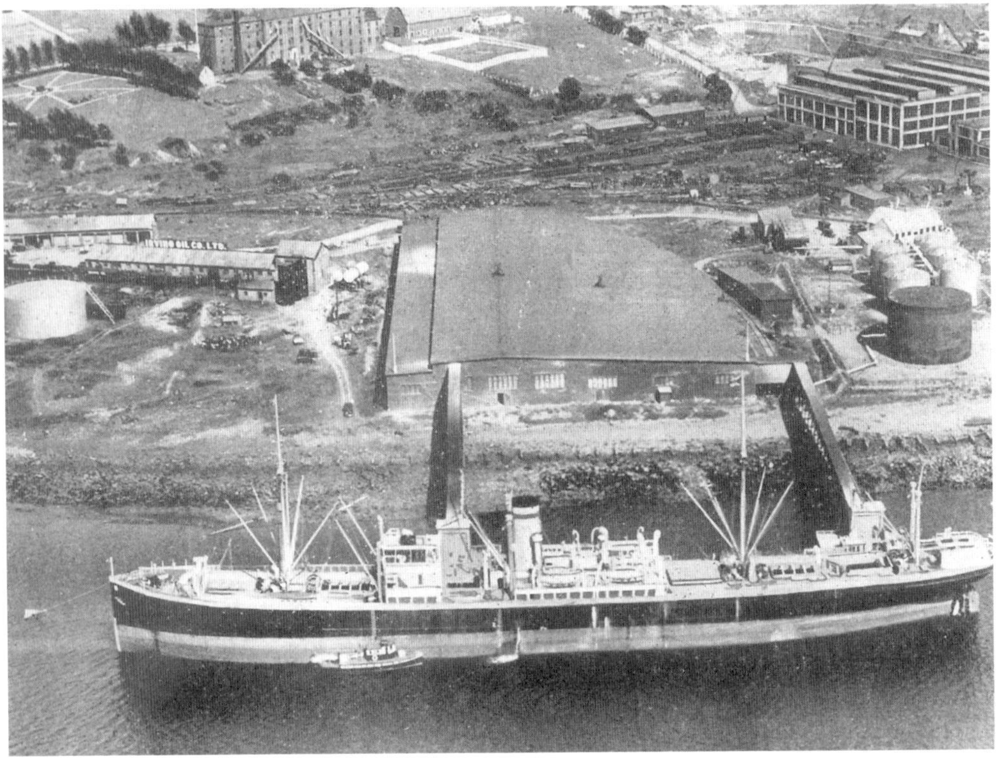

## International Fertilizer, 1937

The International Fertilizer Company opened in March 1931. At 450 feet long, 250 feet wide, and 33 feet high, it was then the largest one-storey wood building of its kind in the Maritimes. Here vessels unloaded fertilizer for distribution to other parts of Canada. The cargo was difficult to work with; because "fertilizer will compact and harden when stowed in ships, most of the work was done by pick and shovel and when the tubs were filled they were hoisted out of the hold … ships often took as long as sixteen days to unload." The company closed its Courtenay Bay plant in 1968. At the left in this photo is the Irving Oil terminal, and behind it is the poor house on Bayside Drive. At the right is Saint John Drydock. This entire area now forms part of the Saint John Shipbuilding property.

TOP RIGHT

## Pulp Shipment, August 14, 1937

The Hamburg Line *Karmoy* is shown at Pugsley wharf loading pulp for the first shipment to Germany after World War One. Note the wood stacked on top of the *Karmoy*'s deck. As is apparent from the number of men aboard the *Karmoy* and the pulp tenders, loading pulp was a labour-intensive operation. Forest products remain one of the most significant of Saint John's exports.

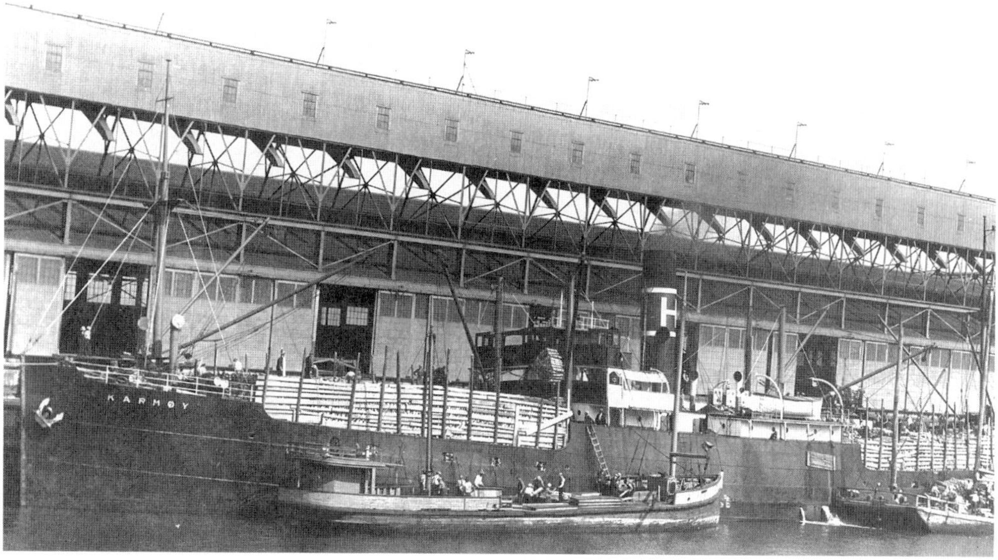

PULP SHIPMENT, AUGUST 14, 1937 (ABOVE)

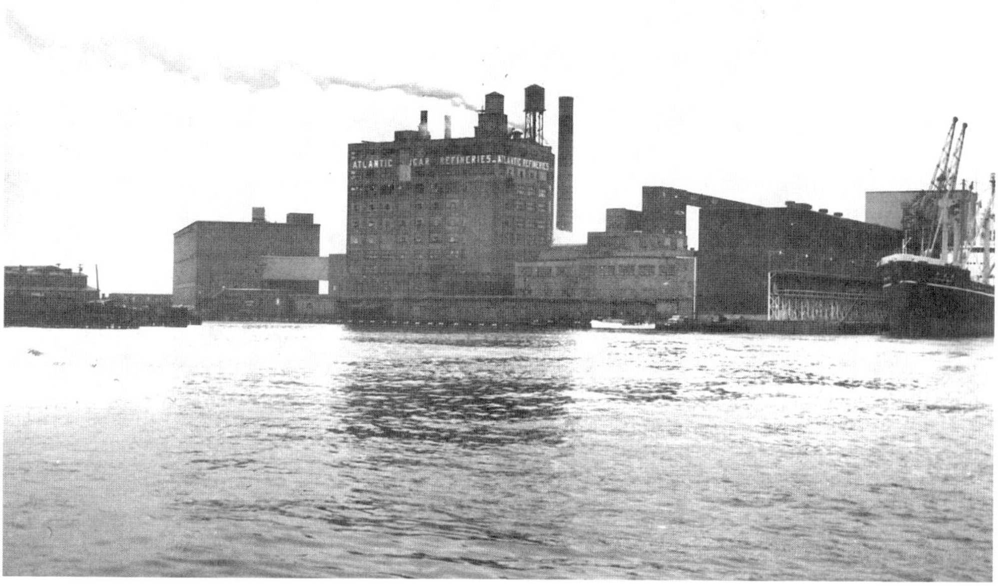

## Atlantic Sugar Refineries, c.1955

Atlantic Sugar Refineries operated at Lower Cove from 1914 to 2000. The structures shown, from left to right, are the storage and shipping warehouse, the pan and filter house with corporate offices, the melt house, and the raw sugar storage building. The long narrow building in front of the pan house is the storage warehouse. Sugar was taken off boats by crane and placed in the raw sugar shed from where it was carried by overhead conveyors to various parts of the refinery until the finished product was loaded onto rail cars.

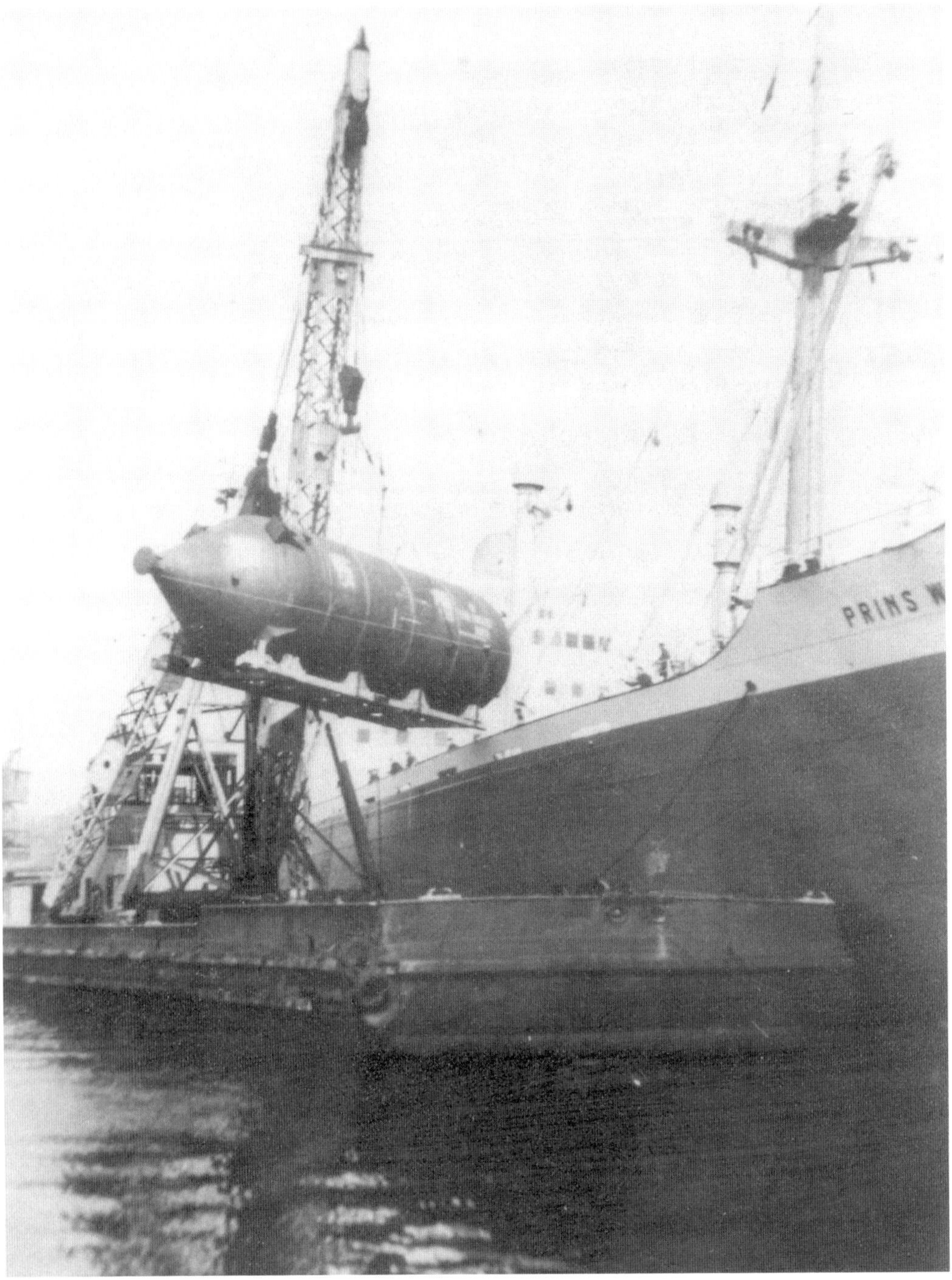


**Pulp Mill Digester, 1951**

Shortly after K.C. Irving bought the Reversing Falls Pulp Mill, the plant underwent a $20-million upgrade and expansion. This digester arrived on the *Prins Wilhelm*. After being loaded onto this barge, it was towed up-harbour through the falls to the mill.

**Flour and Apples, 1966**

The Russian freighter, SS *Neliki Luki* is shown loading flour bound for Cuba at Pier 9 while the SS *Thorstream* is shown at Pugsley A loading British Columbia apples. Cargo handling was labour-intensive until the advent of containerization in the 1970s.

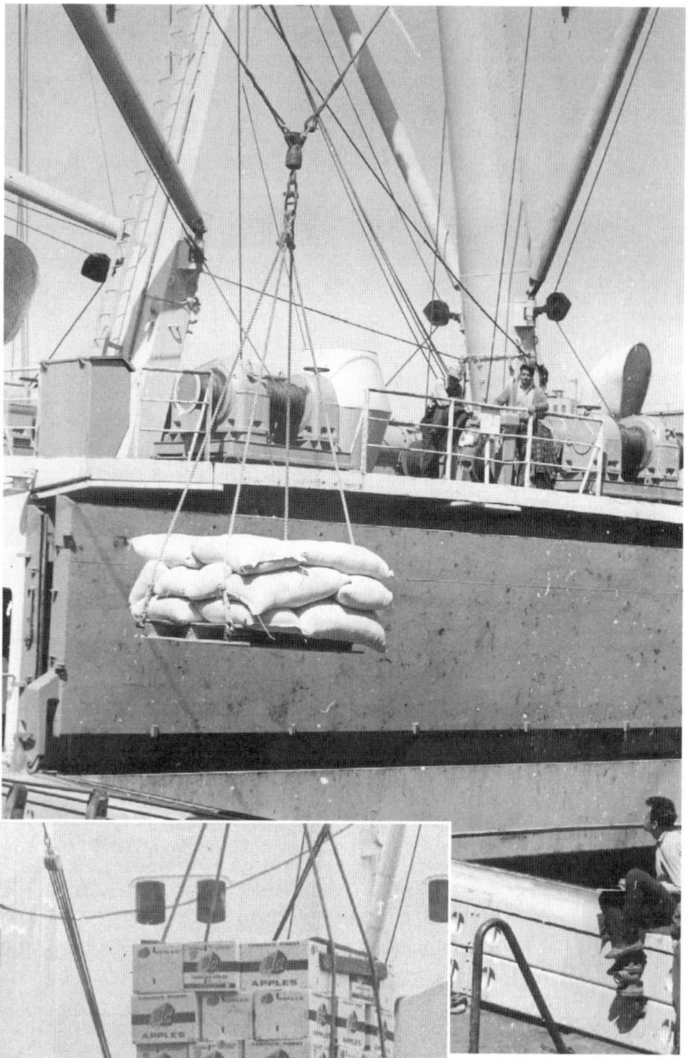

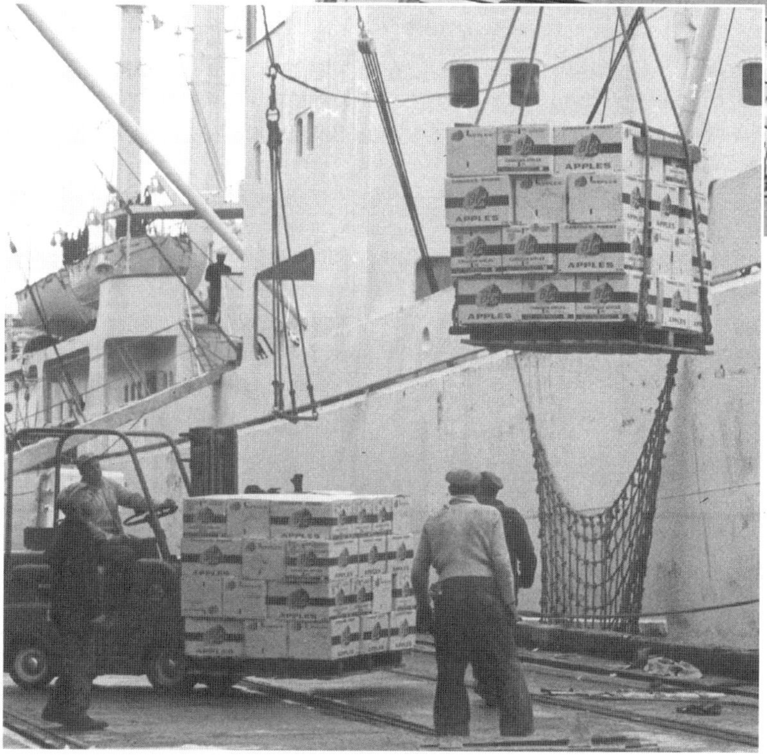

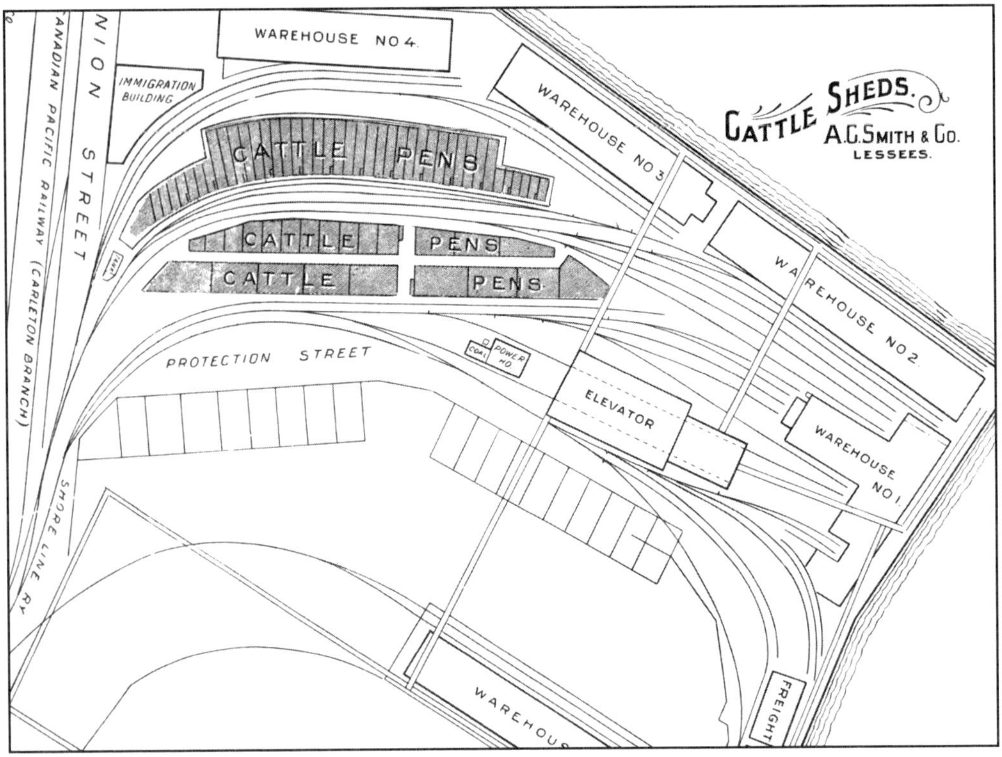


**CATTLE SHEDS, 1898, AND C.1950**

Livestock comprised an important export to the United States. A.C. Smith and Company, which leased the cattle sheds, was located at the lower west side. In 1897-98, 7,844 cattle, 4,843 sheep, and 391 horses were exported—a value of $477,415. In 1912 Commissioner Schofield presented a plan to Common Council for the removal of some of the cattle sheds near Protection Street: "… the sheds are too near the tracks used by immigrant passenger trains to be considered safe, and as they are not used at present there is no objection to their removal." In February 1933 the longshoremen went on a cattle round-up! "It was sixteen to one on Friday at McLeod's Wharf. The sixteen men … and one, small bull, only ten months old—but what a bull …. They are driven out of their stalls on the ship, a rope is put around their nose and horns and they go into a sort of cage which is hoisted to the dock. From there they pass into a runway which leads to the cars …. But when it came to the third bull—well he was temperamental and had ideas of his own. He positively refused to go where he was wanted to go and then the fun began …. With sixteen men holding onto his rope, he had a merry dance. He started on a gallop over the dock instead of into the runway and the sixteen men were sprawling all over the wharf." Another humorous animal story is told during the Second World War: "… food was rationed, [we] felt sure that just one of the many hogs being loaded that day would not be missed. After some deliberation, it was decided to dress the porker and help walk it out on its hind legs. One man placed his cap on the hog, another his scarf, another his topcoat, and finally a pair of overshoes were put on this poor animal's hind legs. Two of these gents then proceeded to stand the hog up, and each man with an arm around it, walked through the gates as if helping a somewhat intoxicated co-worker."

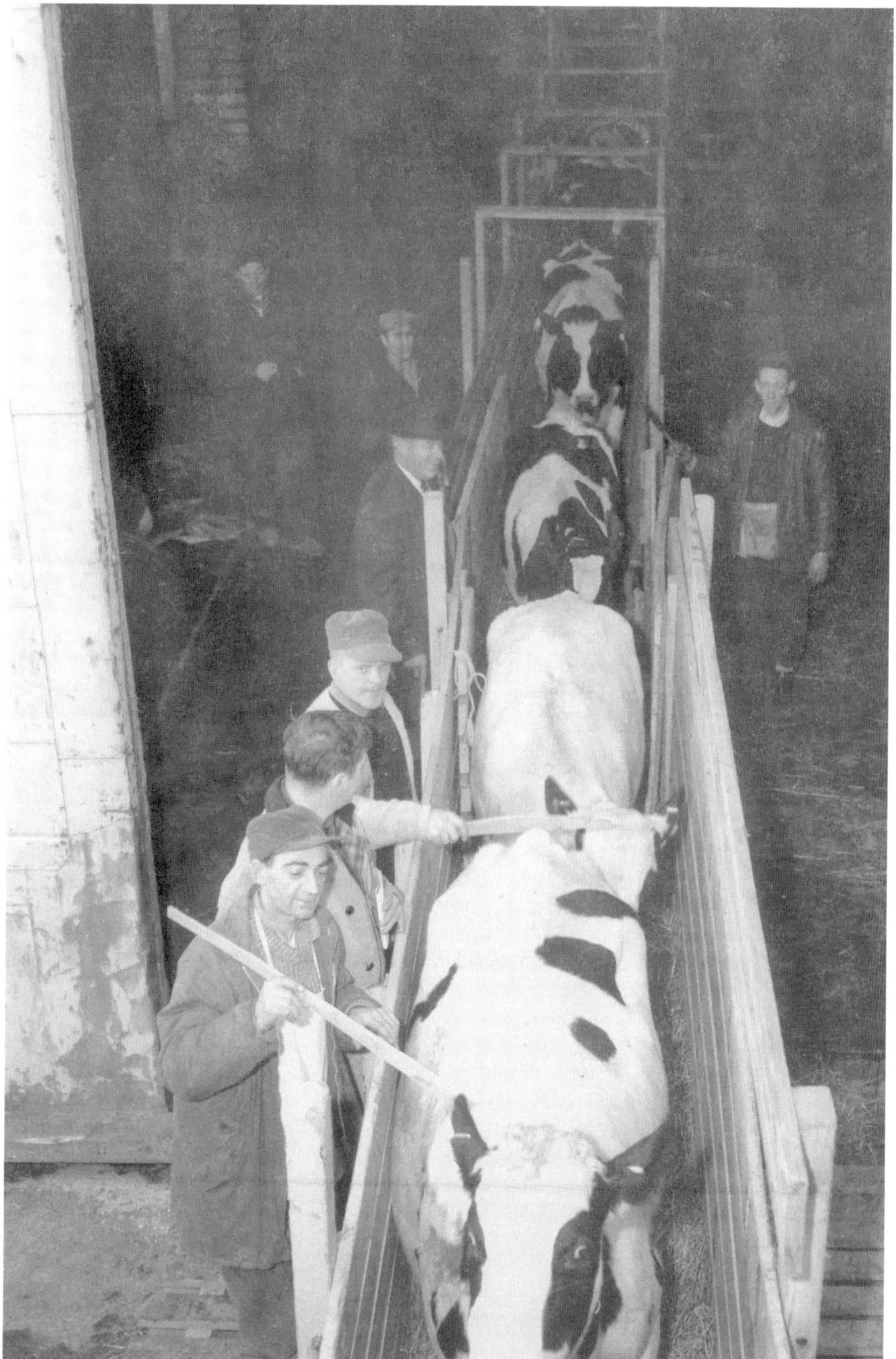

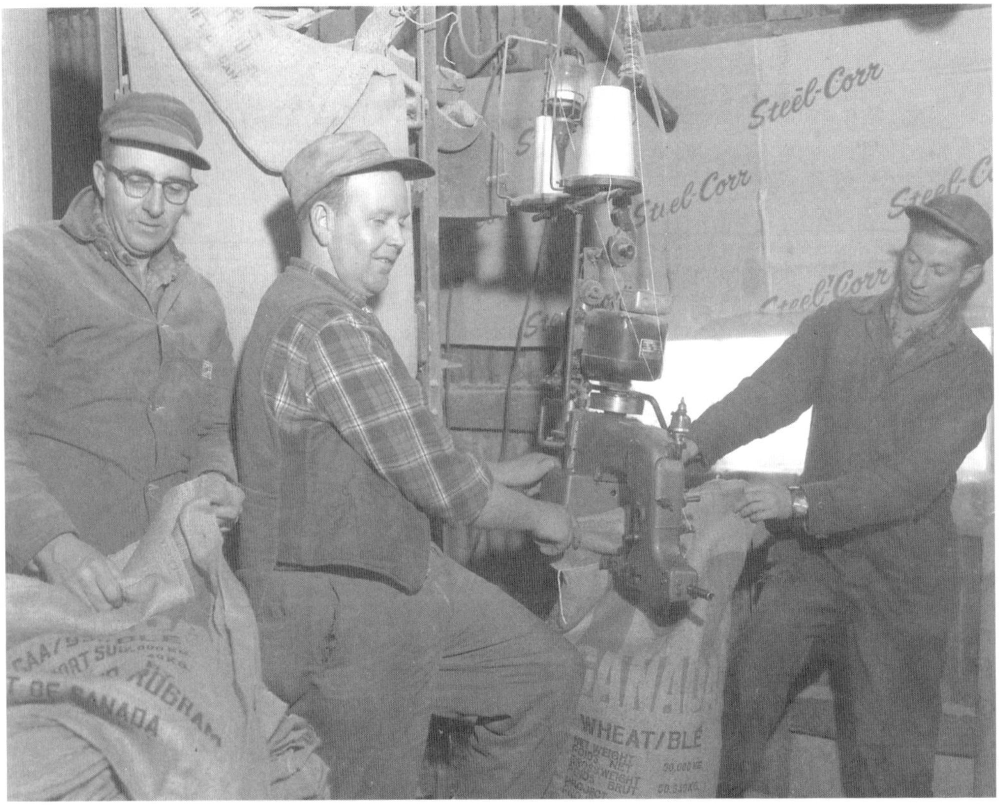


**Grain elevator, c.1972**

Grain has been a major export through the port of Saint John since the end of the nineteenth century. The CPR owned two elevators on the west side, and the CNR had one at the foot of Water Street, so total capacity in 1929 was 2,225,000 bushels. By 1947 the capacity had expanded to 3,500,000 bushels. Longshoremen (from left to right) Knobbie Walsh, Roy Gilmour, and Leo Crombie are shown filling bags bound for Port Sudan, a gift of the World Food Program. All three grain elevators have since been demolished.

PHOTOS AT RIGHT

**Loading pulp and paper, c.1970**

While pulp has been shipped from Saint John for over fifty years, paper is a more recent export. Shipped from the Forest Products Terminal on the west side of the port, paper is now a major export through Saint John. Forterm also moves containers, steel, and flour. In 1987, they moved 618,000 tonnes of cargo.

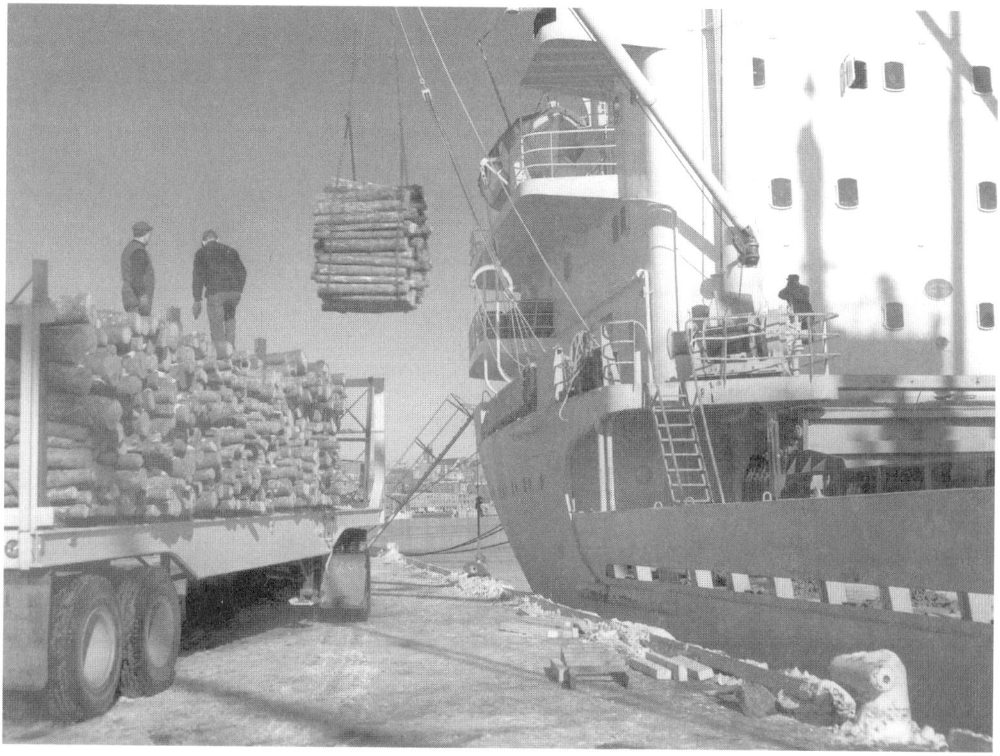

LOADING PULP AND PAPER, C.1970

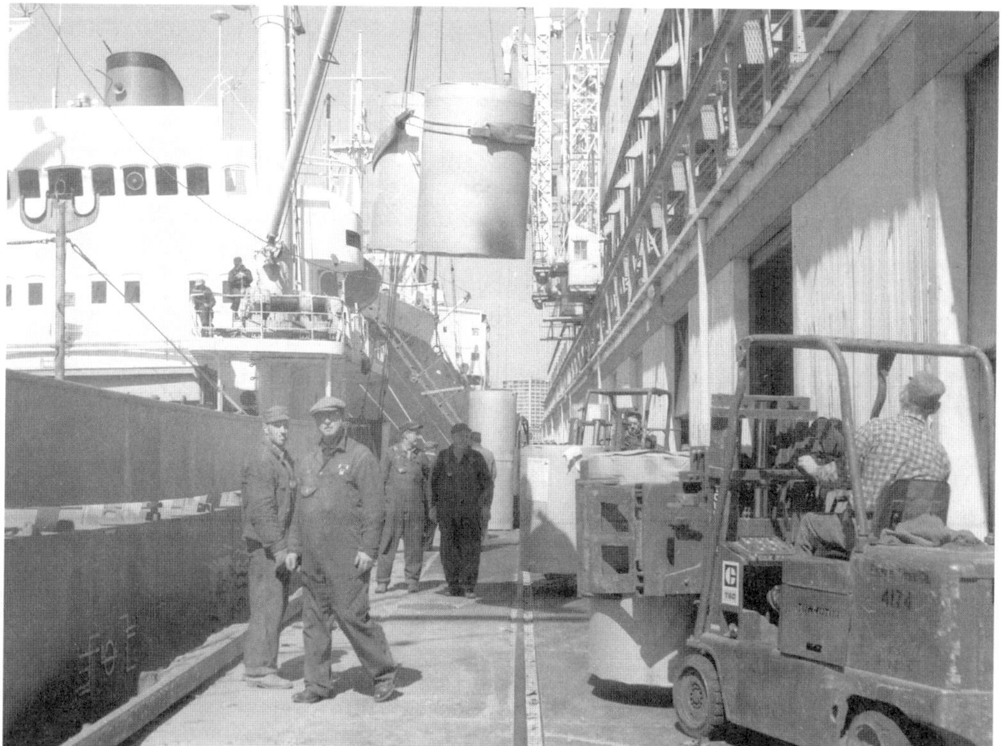

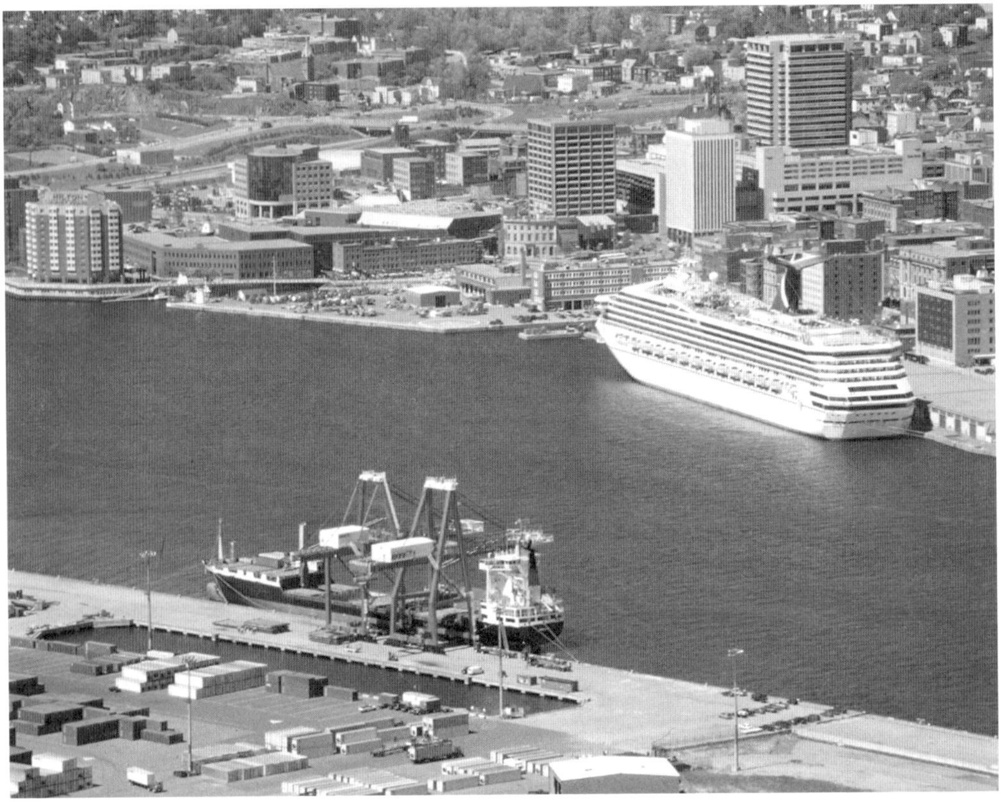

**Diverse cargoes, 1999**

The Rodney Container Terminal, opened in 1971, was originally operated by Brunterm but is now operated by BTI. The terminal's facilities include two 45-tonne container cranes, storage capacity for 20,000 containers annually, a fully computerized container and storage documentation system, and a rail vehicle ramp for rolling stock. This is the eastern terminus of the New Brunswick Southern Railroad, so containers can be assembled on-terminal or be transferred directly to/from rail. All types of bulk and containerized cargo are shipped through Saint John. At the Pugsley Terminal on the opposite side of the harbour, the cruise ship *Carnival Destiny* has brought visitors to Saint John for the day. The 2001 cruise ship schedule brought fifty-four vessels with 86,600 visitors.

*Chapter 5*

# *Saw and Pulp Mills*

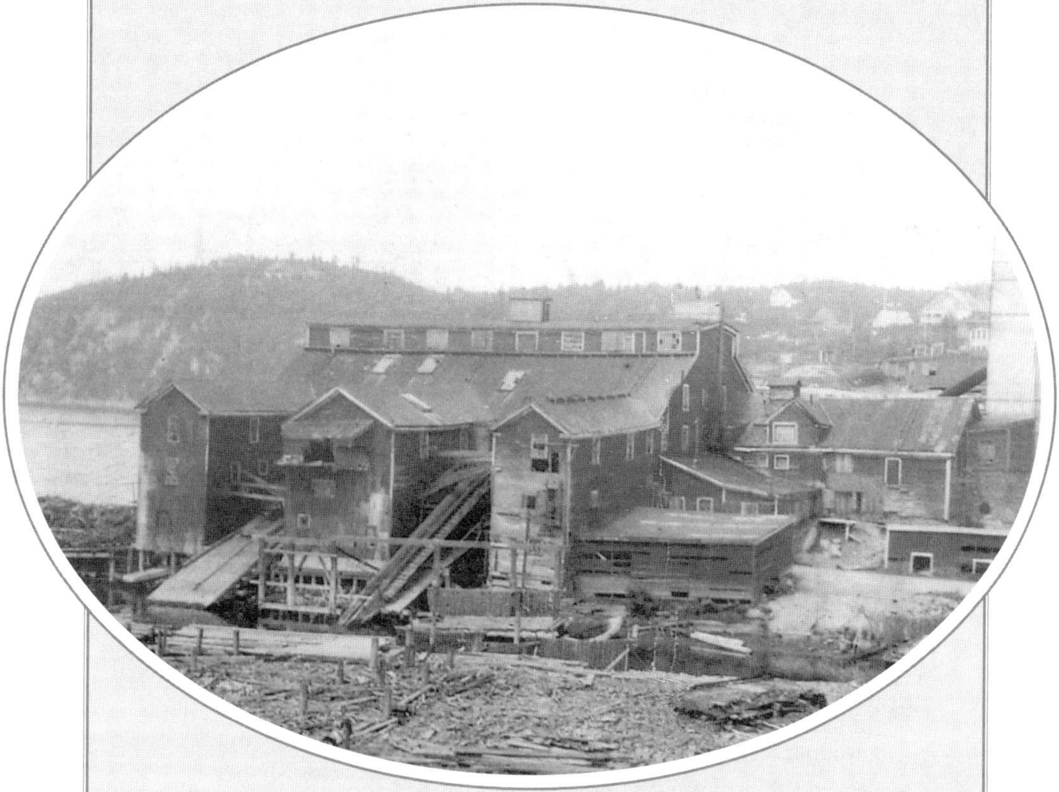

**STETSON & CUTLER MILL, SPAR COVE, C.1920**

The Stetson & Cutler Mill operated from 1867 until it closed in 1923. Water for the mill's boilers came from Newman's Brook. Frederick C. Beatteay was manager of the mill. Later his son C. Allan was also its manager. Stetson & Cutler also operated the lime kilns at Pokiok.

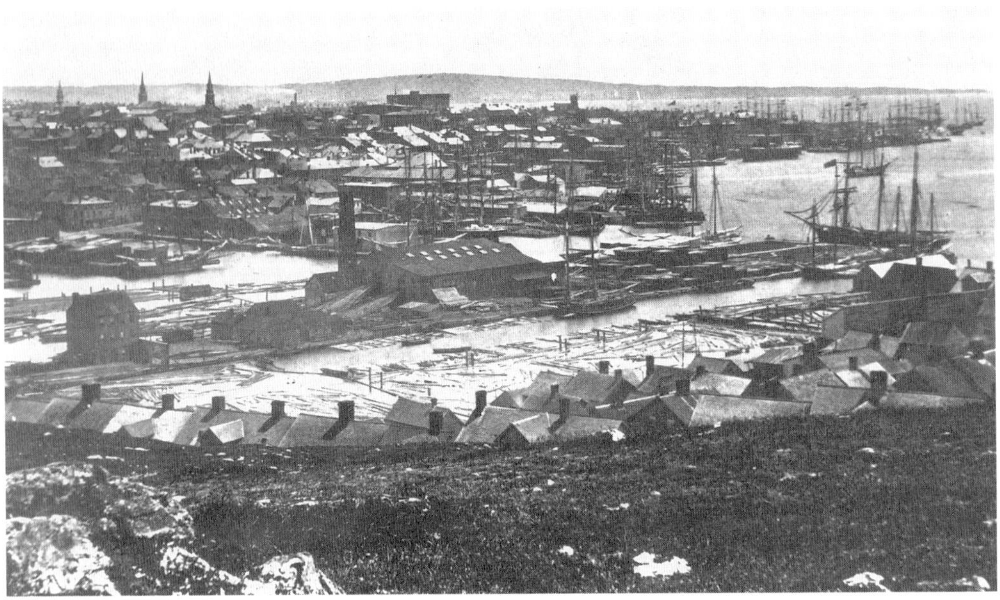

**KIRK & DANIELS MILL AND MILL POND, LONG WHARF, C.1875**

During the mid-nineteenth century, the following mills were operating in the immediate Saint John area:
Kirk & Warrels, Long Wharf (later Kirk & Daniels, as shown in this photo)
Briggs Mill, Portland Point
Anderson Mill, near the Straight Shore
Petree Mill, Straight Shore
Flewelling Mill, Straight Shore
Shives Mill, Straight Shore
Brown Mill, Marble Cove (later Murray & Gregory)
Two Mills, Indiantown (later Rankine)
Rivers Mill, Boers Head and Pleasant Point
Millidge Mill, Millidgeville
Drury Mill, Drury Cove
Jewett Mill, Millidgeville
Jewett Mill, Deadmans Cove and Reversing Falls
James Vernon Mill, South and Grand Bay
Holt Mill, Randolph
Lingley Mill, Pleasant Point
Barnhill Mill, Pleasant Point
Hunter Mill, Pleasant Point (later Miller & B Woodman)
Cushing's Mill, Cunnables Point
Goddard Mill, Union Point
Wetmore Mill, Westhead Eddy
Clark's Mill, Carleton
Calter Mill, Carleton
Adams Mill, Carleton
Robertson Mill, Carleton

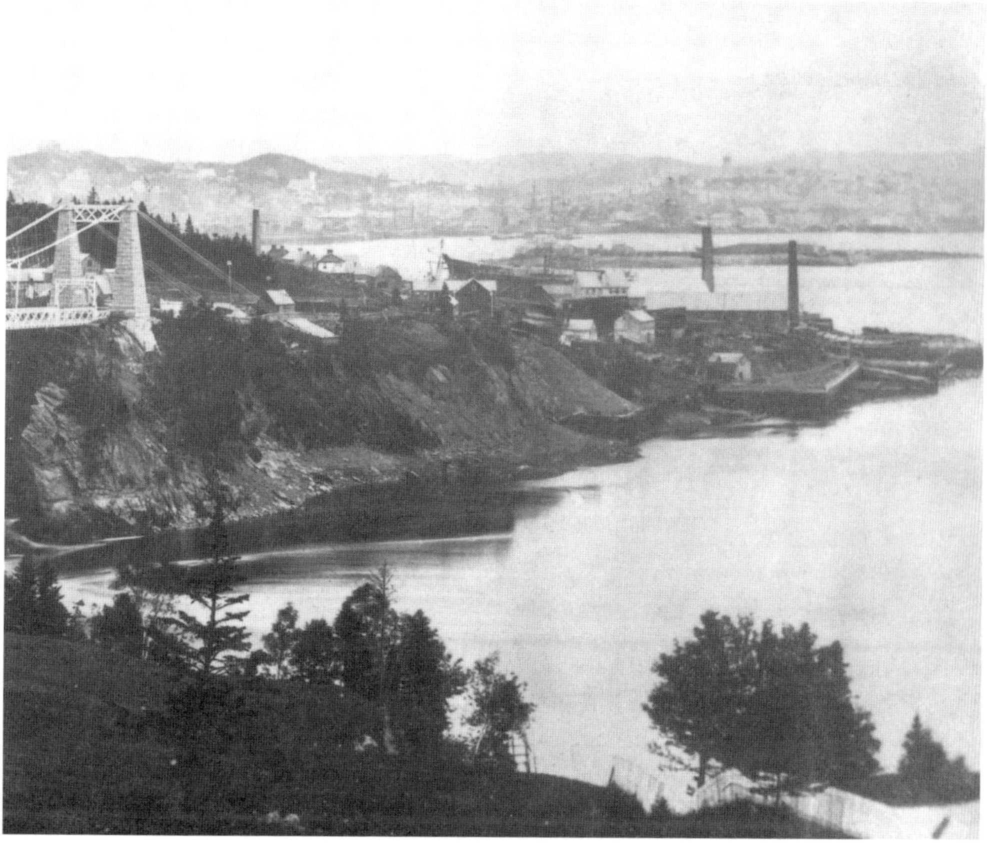

**William Shrives Sawmill, 1863**

The William Shrives Sawmill is at right, with a ship under construction behind it. This is the area of Ocean Steel on Chesley Drive. This mill produced square timber which was described as: "…not…less than ten inches square nor shorter than 16 feet (hardwood excepted, which may be twelve feet long, if not less than 12 inches square) to be square and smooth hewed, and free from knotty tops, plugs, rots, rotten or concave knots, decayed sap and worm holes, to be square butted and the taper not to exceed one inch for every 18 feet in length."

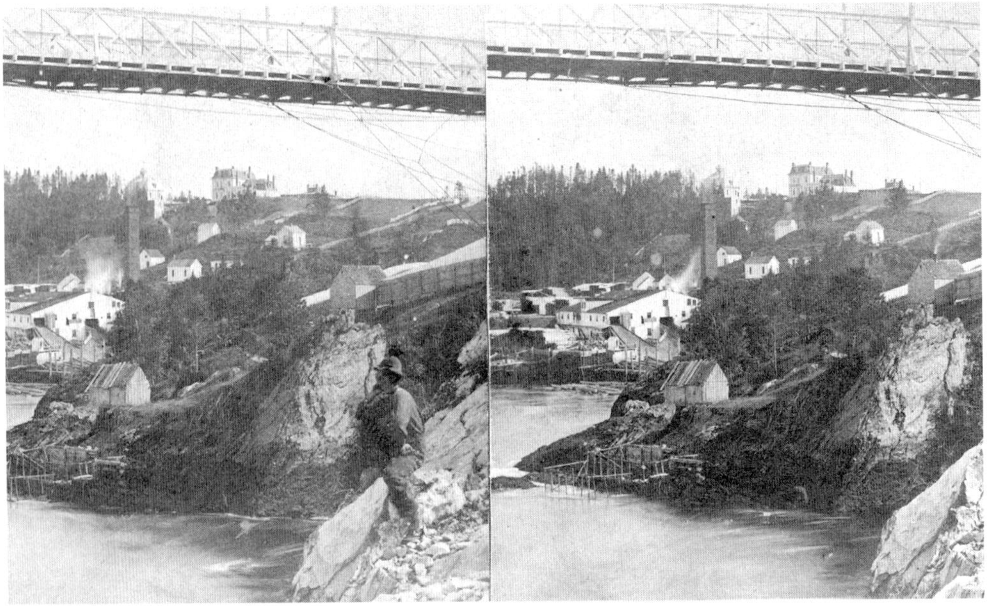

**E.D. Jewett Mill, Reversing Falls, c.1875**

Note the man sitting on the rock under the bridge in the image on the left. He is not in the image on the right. Below the E.D. Jewett Mill, a fishing weir similar to Cutch McCallum's weir from 1930 (see page 117) is visible. One of the earliest sawmills (c.1765) in New Brunswick was on the Nashwaak River. In 1770 Simonds and White built the first mill in Saint John. In 1822 Otty and Crookshank built the first steam-powered sawmill, and by 1830 there were between fifty and sixty sawmills on the St. John River and its tributaries below Woodstock. The first spruce deals were shipped in 1819 from the Miramichi and from Saint John aboard the *Amelia* to Cork, Ireland, in 1822. Spruce was considered the strong and durable lumber, while the balsam fir was considered a "weed" tree. In 1824 pine was still the primary export from Saint John.

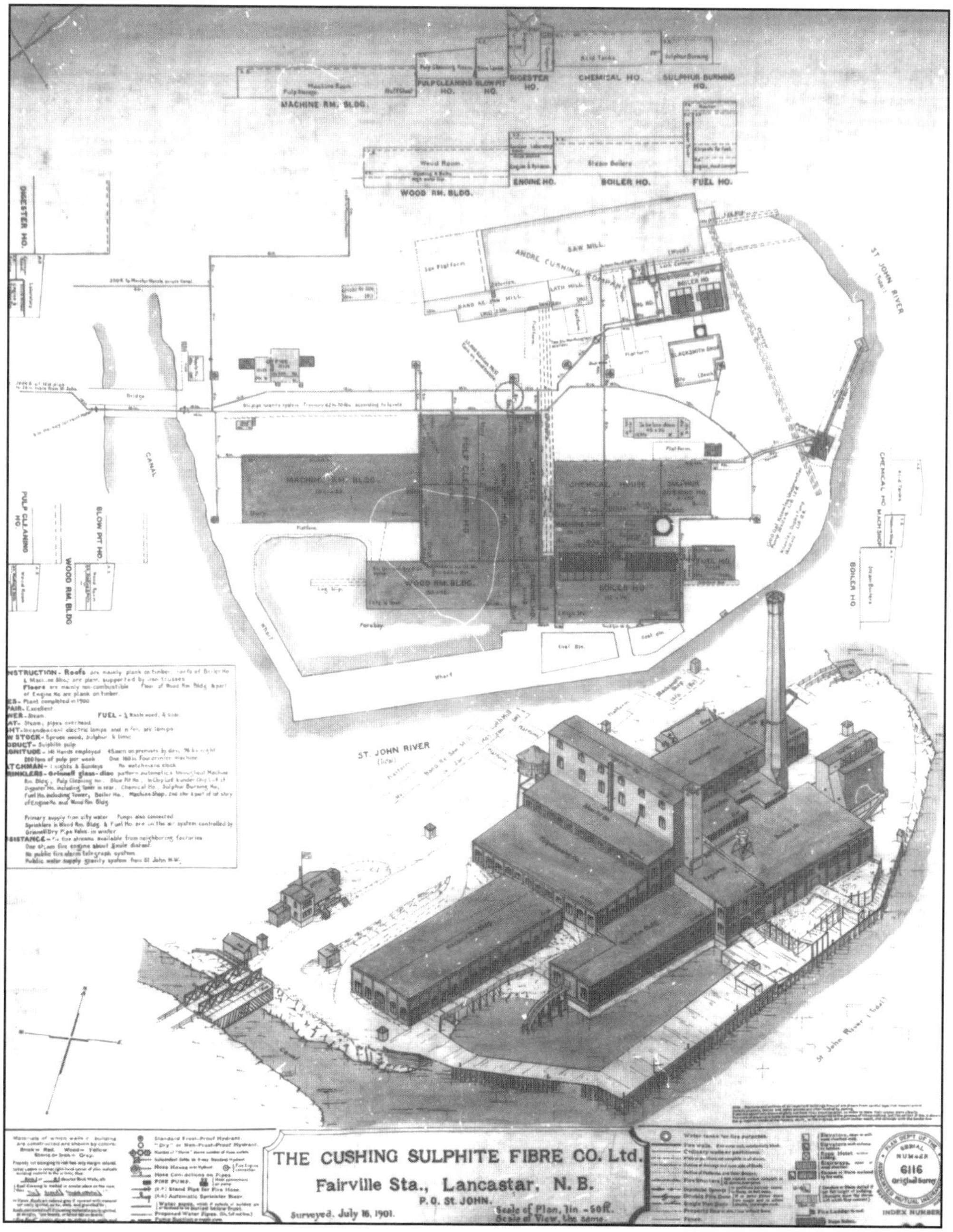


**Cushing Sulphite Mill, July 16, 1901**

This survey plan of the sulphite-fibre mill at Cunnables Point was drawn by E.H. Tenney. The mill had the following departments: machine room, wood room, pulp-cleaning house, blow-pit house, digester house, engine house, machine shop, chemical house, economizer room, boiler house, sulphur-burning house, and a fuel house. The canal was built in the 1830s by the Saint John Mill and Canal Company.

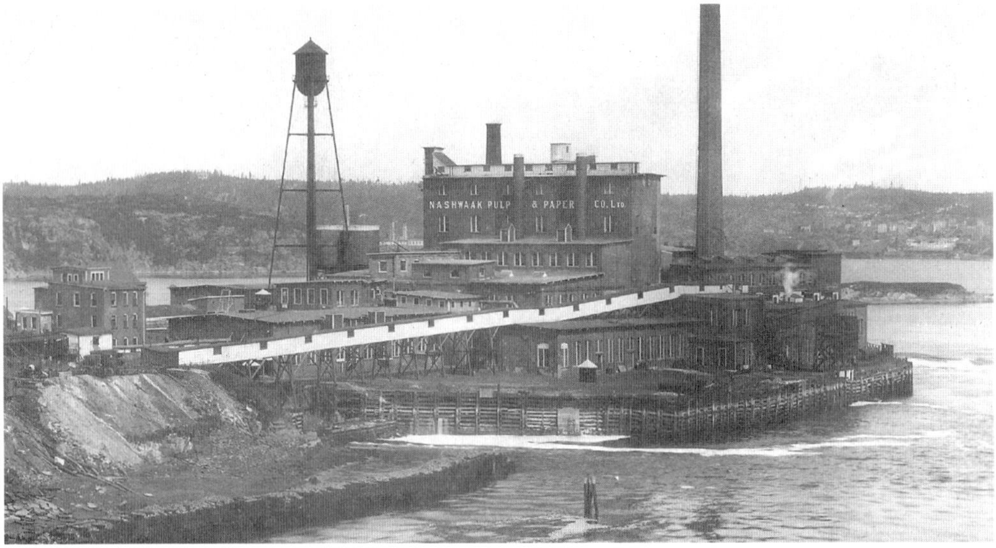


**NASHWAAK PULP MILL, C.1925**

In the 1830s, a canal had been cut across Union Point to allow navigation around the rapids, and in the 1850s Andre Cushing from Maine built the first sawmill at this site. Next to his mill was the Goddard Sawmill. In 1899 the sawmill was replaced by a sulfite mill known as the Nashwaak Pulp & Paper Company, which operated until 1932. The manager of the Woodlands Department of Nashwaak Pulp and Paper from 1923 until 1929 was Chester W. Alden of Maine. While in Saint John, Alden lived at 286 Douglas Avenue. In 1932 Nashwaak was purchased and renamed the Port Royal Pulp & Paper Company. K.C. Irving bought the mill in 1946 and renamed it Saint John Sulfite Limited. It was renamed Irving Pulp & Paper Limited in 1951 when it underwent a $20-million expansion. Since Irving took over the mill, the employees have had steady employment.

**SPAR COVE MILL, 1841**

TOP RIGHT

The Otty & Crookshank sawmill in Indiantown was purchased by Hayford & Stetson in 1881; it was later owned by Robert Rankin & Conpany. In 1824 the following quantities of wood products were shipped through the port of Saint John: 114,116 tonnes of pine and birch; 11,534,000 feet of pine boards and planks; 1,923,000 staves; 1,981 masts; 2,698 oars and oar rafts; 1,435 cords of lath wood. By 1826, wood accounted for 73.7 per cent of total exports from Saint John.

**MILLER & WOODMAN MILL, ROBERTSONS POINT, 1874**

BOTTOM RIGHT

This is Robertsons Point at the Narrows as seen from Pleasant Point in Milford. Pleasant Point was the site of the Byng Boys Club from the 1920s until the 1980s. Deals were one of the products made at this mill. A deal was "a piece of lumber between 3 and 3½ inches in thickness. The standard breadth of deals was 9 to 11 inches. Standard lengths were 10, 12, 14, 16, 18, 20, 21, 22, 23 and 24 feet. 'Merchantable deals' had to be 12 feet or more in length, trimmed square exclusive of bad knots shakes, splits, sap stain, gum seam and gum balls, plug or plugs, worm holes and auger hole or holes."

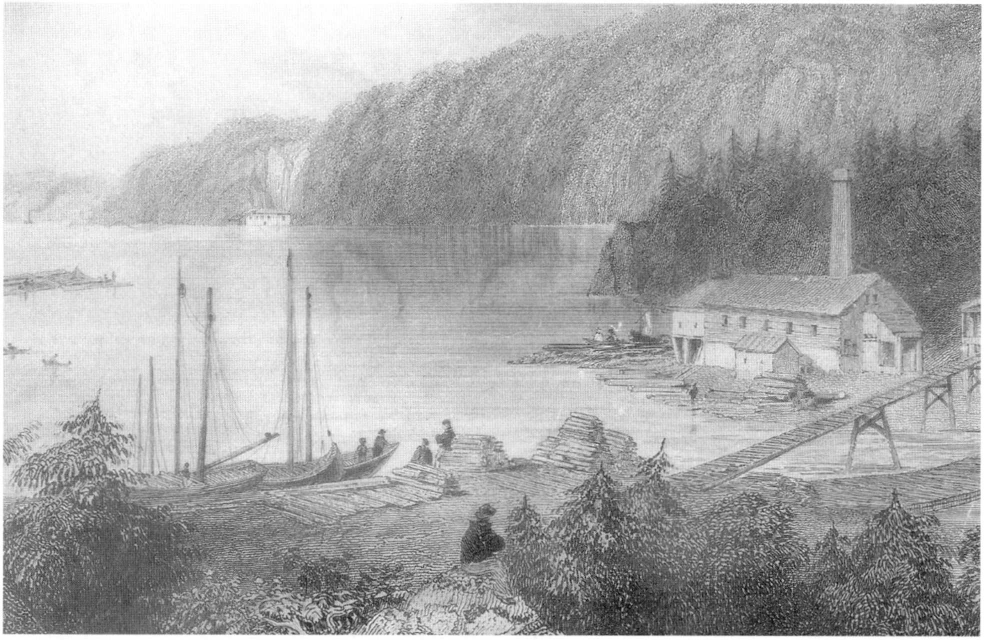

SPAR COVE MILL (ABOVE) AND MILLER & WOODMAN MILL (BELOW)

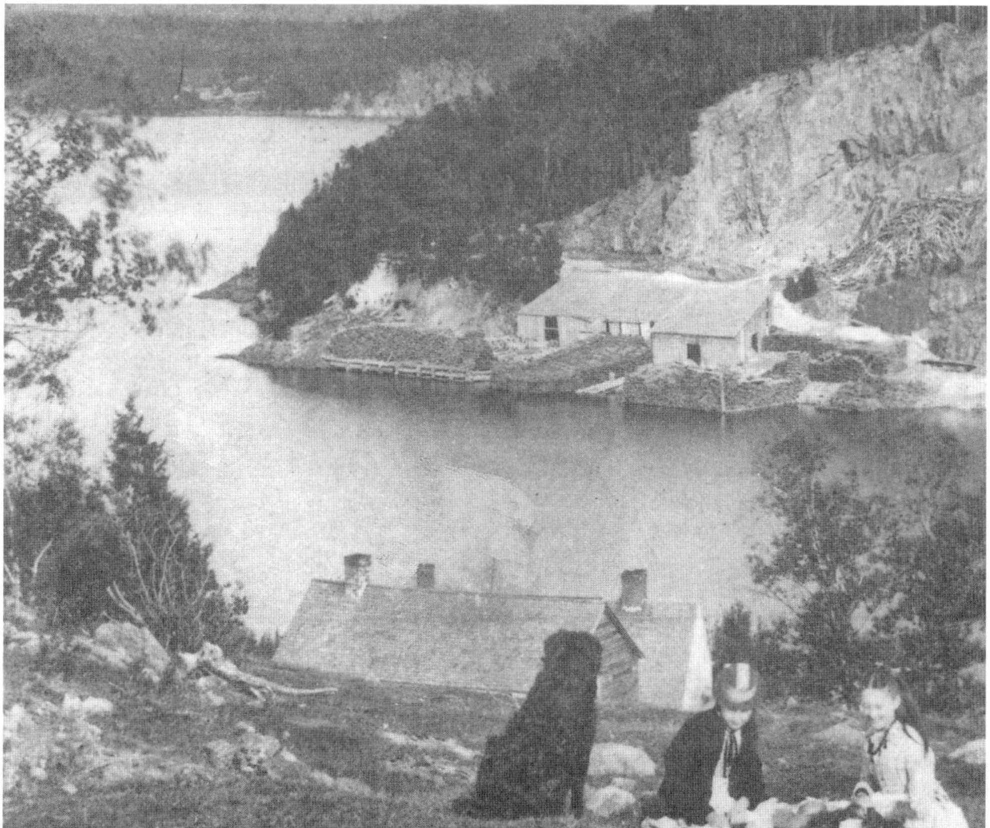

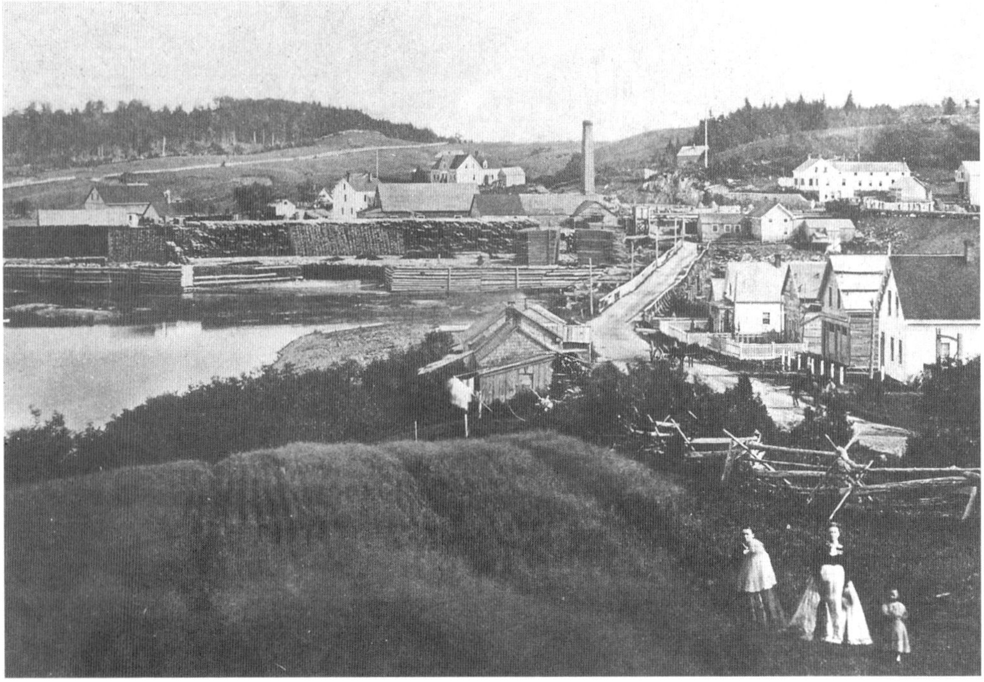

**South Bay Mill, c.1880**

The American firm of E.D. Jewett & Company was established in Saint John in 1878, contributing greatly to the industrial and commercial development of the port as extensive dealers in lumber with a large mill employing some ninety hands in Brothers Cove at Millidgeville. In 1896 their second mill, which was at Grand Bay, was for sale. This mill employed from sixty to one hundred hands. The mills produced chiefly for the United States market using Maine logs from the head waters of the St. John River. From their office on Walker's Wharf, E.D. Jewett & Company managed a number of vessels engaged in the coast trade, and owned the steam tug *Dirigo*, the most powerful tugboat in Saint John Harbour. This tug towed the famous Leary raft to Portland, Maine, and was used by the Governor General on his visit to Saint John in 1895.

**Randolph Mill, 1893**

TOP RIGHT

Archibald Randolph and Charles P. Baker's original partnership was in a lime-burning business in Randolph. By 1897, the lumbermill's output was over 21-million board feet. The mill had two gangs, three lathe machines, a stave machine, and a heading machine. The company also owned two tug boats, the *Randolph* and the *Kingsville*, which used to bring the logs downriver in booms. Behind the lumbermill was the lime quarry. In 1897, the lime kilns produced 65,000 barrels of lime.

**Mispec Pulp Mill, 1900**

BOTTOM RIGHT

Before 1870 Mispec Pulp Mill was owned by the Saint John Manufacturing Company. In 1896, it was taken over by the St. John Sulphite Pulp Company. Power for the mill was supplied by the Mispec River. Originally a woollen factory, it converted to the production of cotton yarn. In 1900 the mill manager was M.F. Mooney.

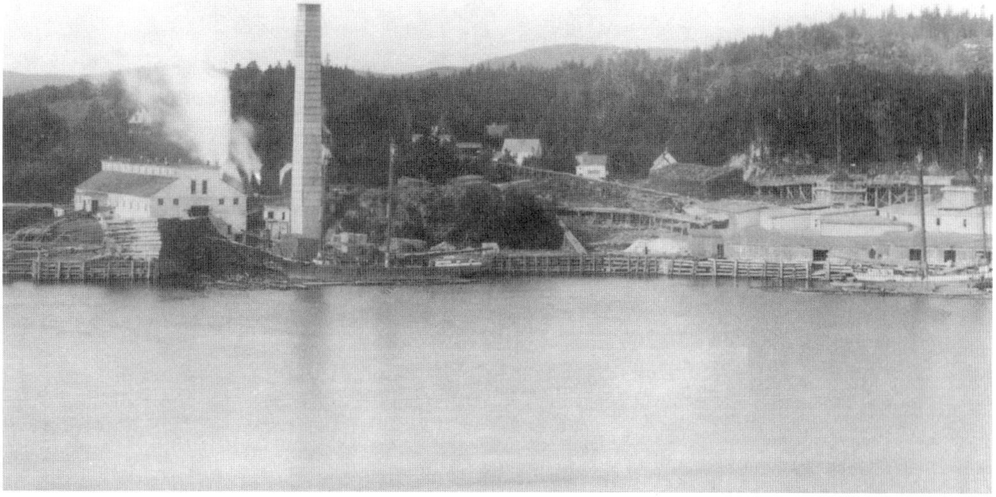

RANDOLPH MILL (ABOVE) AND THE MISPEC PULP MILL (BELOW)

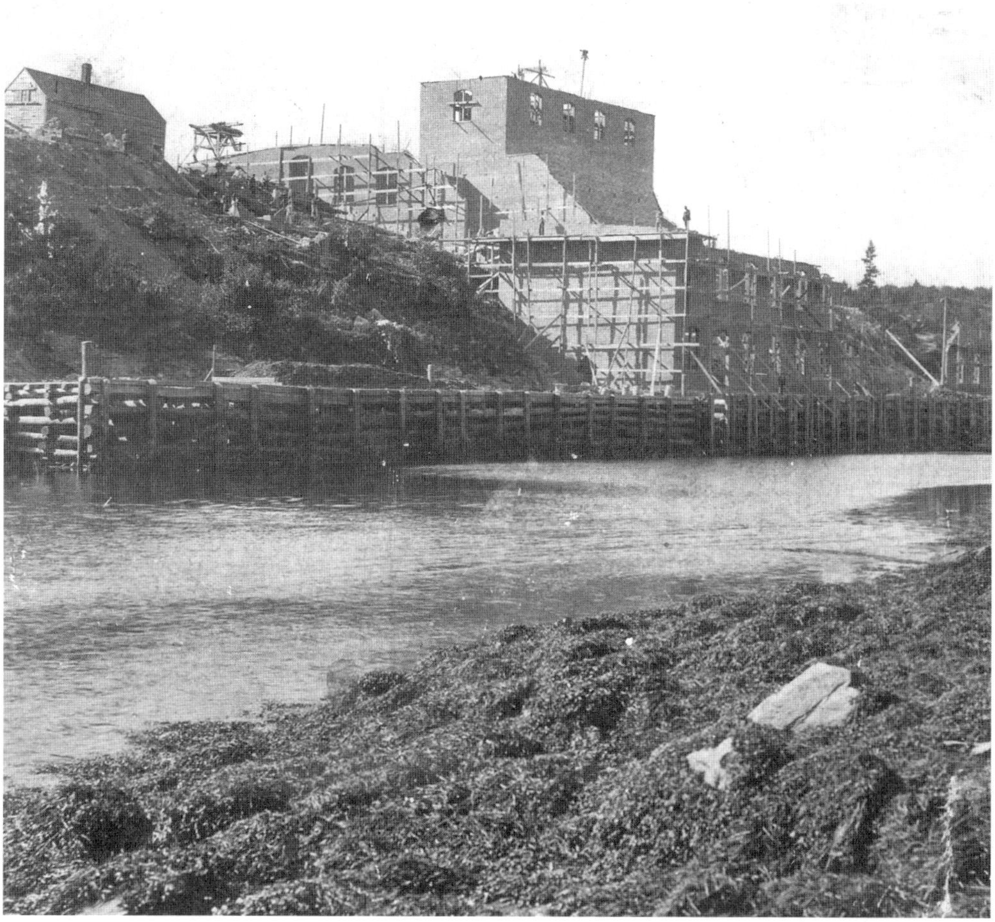

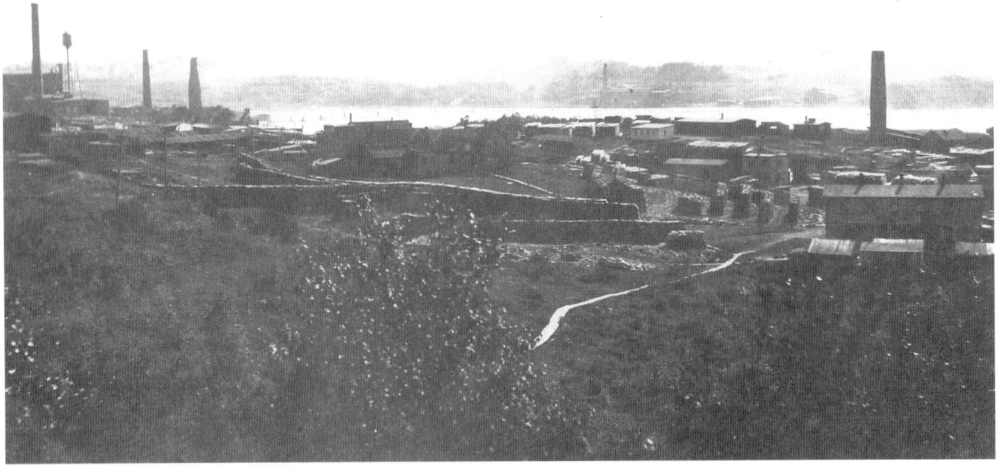

**MURRAY & GREGORY YARD, MARBLE COVE, 1921**

In 1898 there were sixteen sawmills in the Saint John area, about ten of which were owned and operated by Americans. In 1878, William H. Murray opened his mill at Marble Cove. By 1898 the mill was the largest and best-equipped in New Brunswick. It had both gang and rotary saws along with machines for making lath boxes and cooperage stock. Deals for the British market made up the mill's main product. By the turn of the century, the annual cut of spruce, pine, and cedar was about 40-million feet. J. Fraser Gregory later became a partner and the mill operated into the 1980s.

**HILYARD BROTHERS MILL, C.1910**

TOP RIGHT

In 1913 the following mills were operating in Saint John:

Randolph & Baker
Charles Miller
John E. Moore, South Bay
Stetson & Cutler, Indiantown
Murray & Gregory
Stetson & Cutler, Pleasant Point
James R. Warner
Miller Brothers
Hilyard Brothers
F.E. Sayre & Company
Edward Partington Pulp & Paper Company

**GREAT SALMON RIVER, JUNE 14, 1924**

BOTTOM RIGHT

The S.T. Company No. 1 barge, built of spruce and hardwood from the lands of the Bayshore Lumber Company, was launched at Salmon River on May 30, 1907. The masterbuilder was Albert Patterson of West Quaco, and the marine architect was W.R. Huntley of Parrsboro, Nova Scotia. The barge carried pulp and lumber from Salmon River to Bath, Maine, for the Lisbon Falls Fibre Company, Pejepscot Paper Company, and the Bowden Paper Manufacturing Company. Her registered owner was Robert Connelly, manager of the Bayshore Lumber Company. In the background of this view is the S.T. Co. No. 4 barge. Both barges were still afloat after 1932.

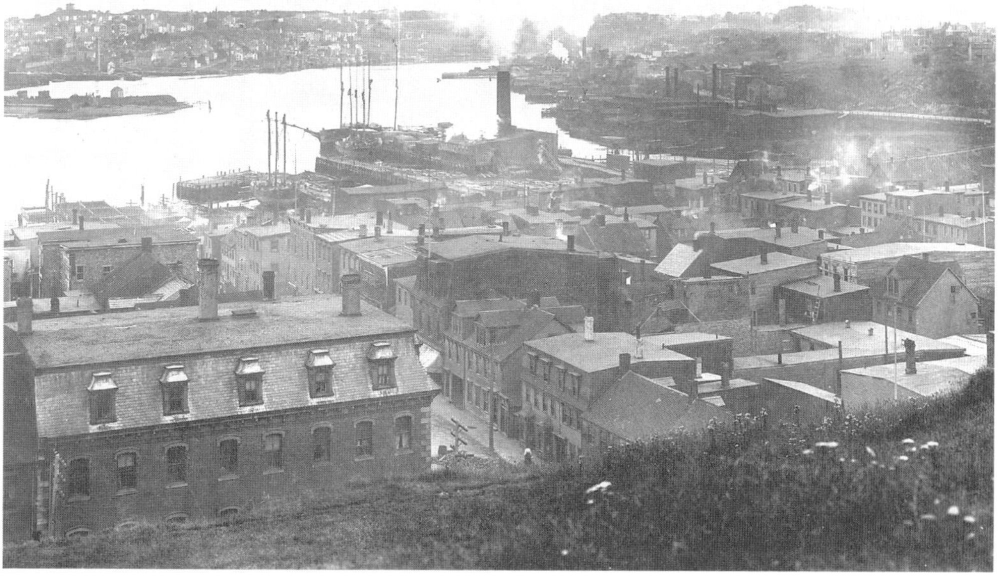

HILYARD BROTHERS MILL, HILYARD STREET (ABOVE) AND AT THE GREAT SALMON RIVER (BELOW)

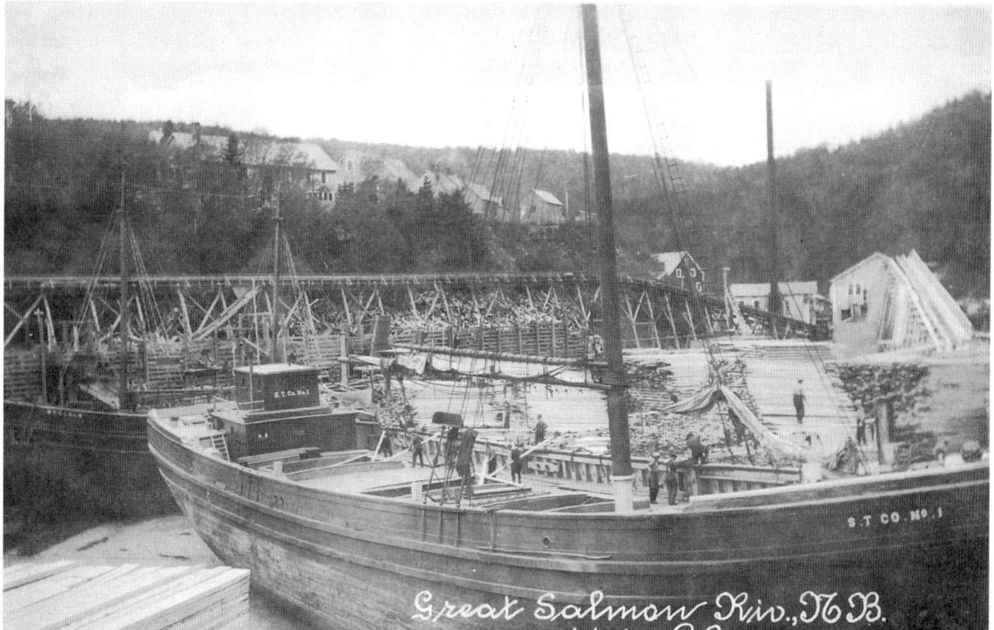

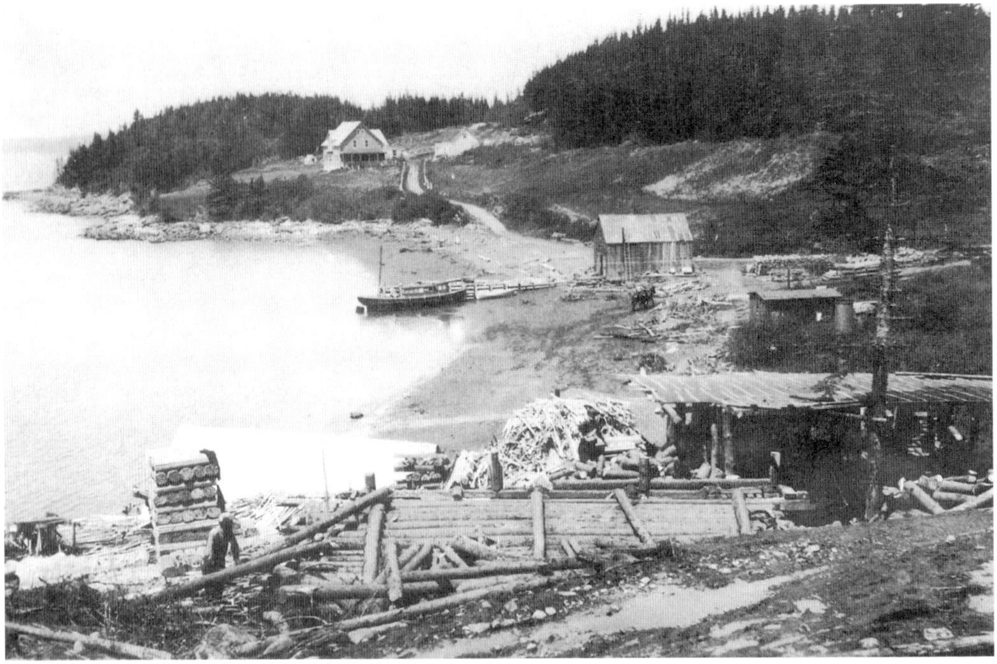

**Black Beach, c.1920**

The small mill at Black Beach was probably operated by Captain Grundmark, who lived in the house at the top of the hill. In the foreground a man is stacking logs, and on the beach another is riding a horse. During periods of bad weather the salmon fishermen pulled into Black Beach for protection. Margaret (Shannon) Splane recalls that it was either her grandfather or great-grandfather, both named John Shannon, who was given the original three-hundred-acre land grant, which included the beach. Both men were fishermen like her father, Joseph. John Shannon eventually sold the property to Captain Grundmark. The original Shannon home burned and Grundmark replaced it, but it is not known if the house shown here is the original or the replacement. Grundmark sold the property to Earl Johnson, who built several summer cottages at the beach, then sold the property to the province of New Brunswick. The beach, famous for its black sand, is now part of the Colson Cove Power Plant property. The Lorneville Community Association hopes to acquire three acres of beach property, as well as the 110-acre Musquash Light property, to develop for environmental tourism.

## Chapter 6

# *Shore Support*

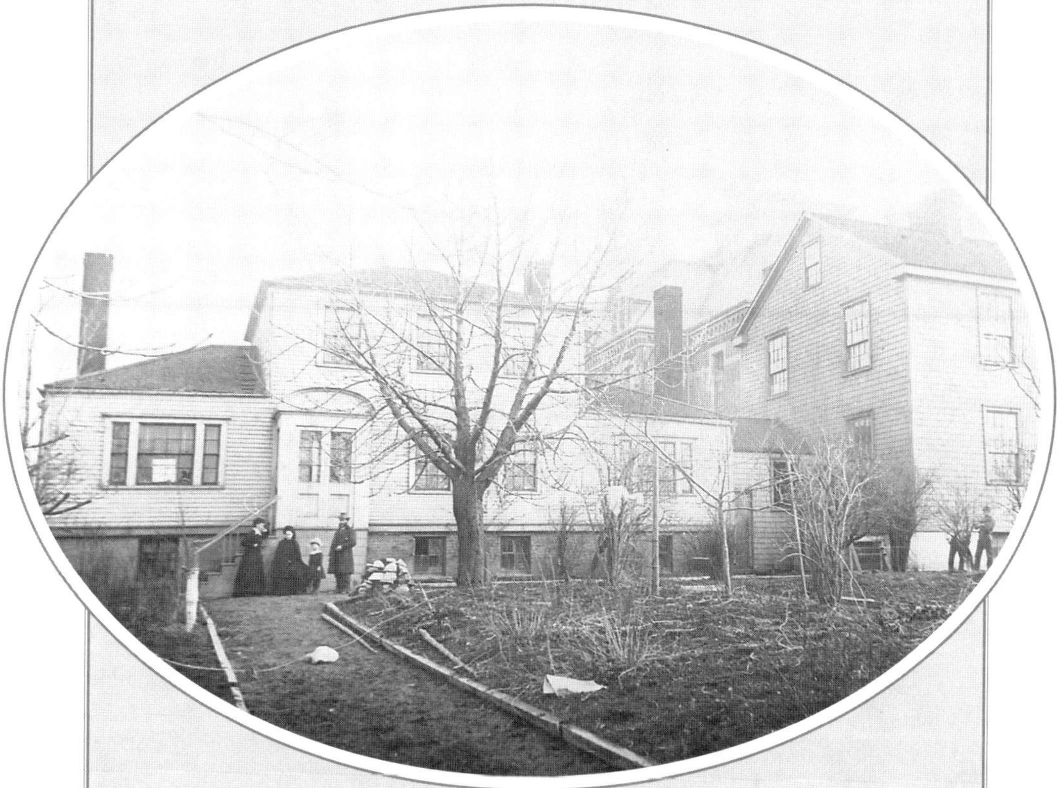

**MARINE HOSPITAL, C.1877**

In 1822, the Marine Hospital was organized "for the care of the disabled seamen." The hospital rented a house from Nehemiah Merritt until land was purchased in 1823 for a permanent hospital. Diseased mariners were quartered here, as well as at a second mariners' hospital, on Partridge Island. Those who died were buried in the marine lot in Fernhill Cemetery. In 1867 the Dominion government took over hospital operations and replaced the wooden buildings with a brick building in 1882. The old hospital is now the Turnbull Nursing Home.

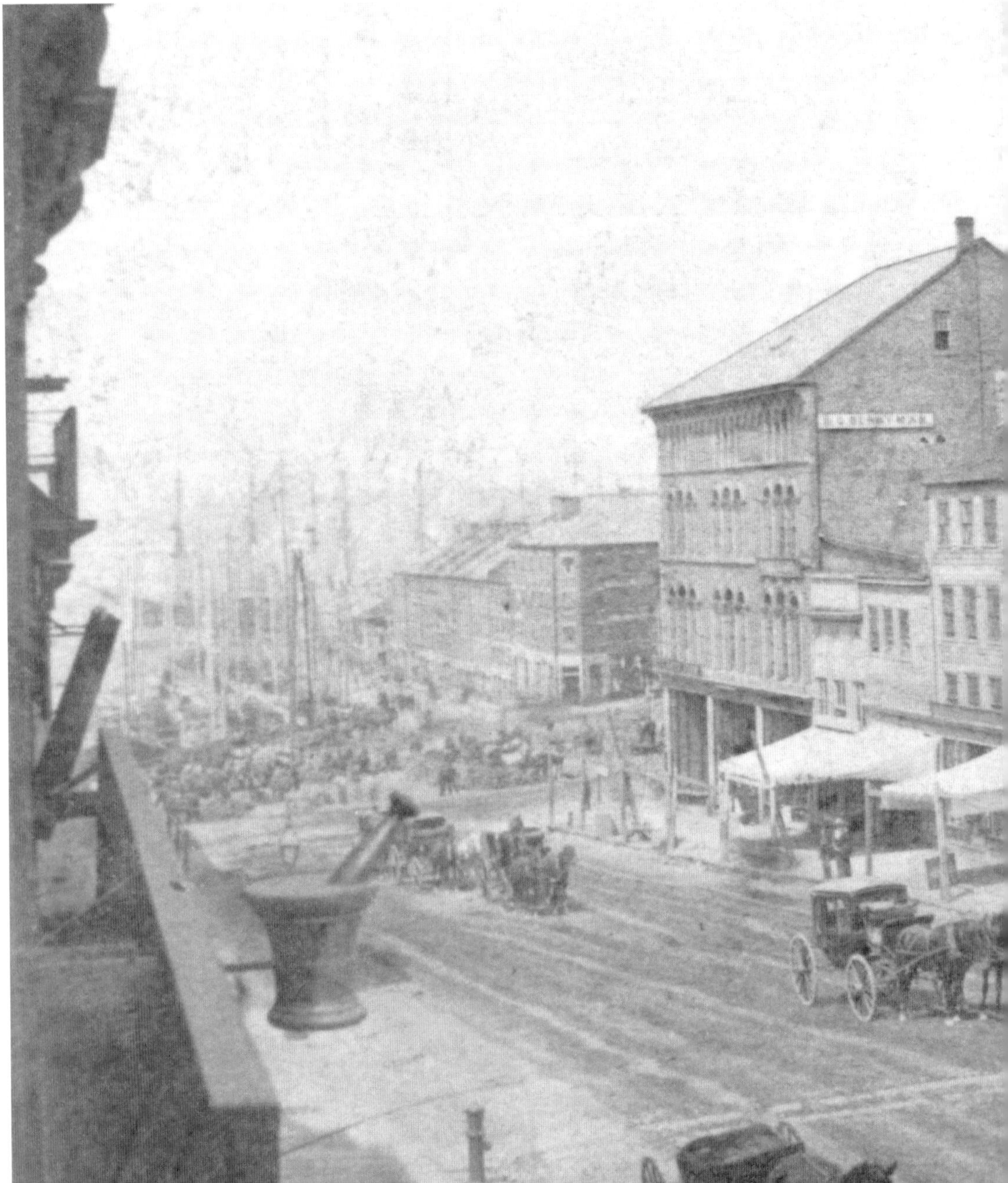

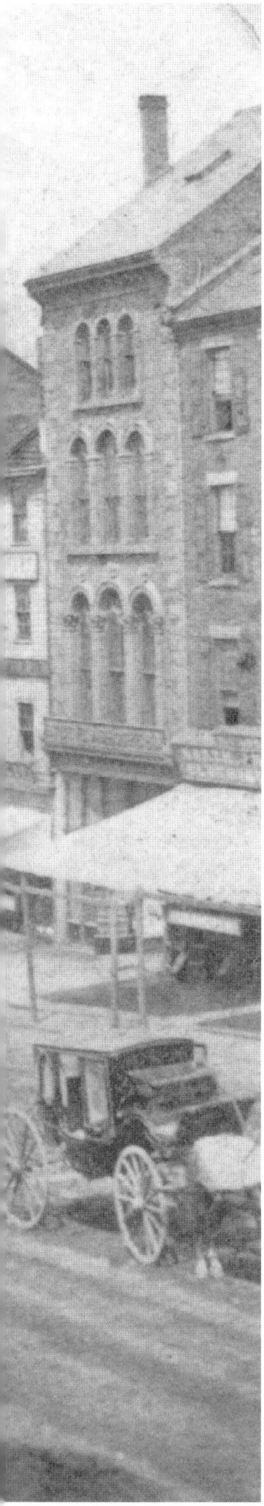

**King Street, c.1870, at left and Cartsmen at Market Slip, c.1875 (below)**

The view at left, taken prior to the 1877 fire, reveals much about the commercial centre of Saint John. First, on the left is a drugstore, indicated by the apothecary's sign, an important symbol for the illiterate. On the other side of the street, awnings keep the sun out of the windows to protect the goods. At the foot of the hill is a sea of masts, showing how important Market Slip was to the port economy. In the view below, the cartsmen at Market Square are waiting for work. The low-slung wagon is a sloven that was developed in New Brunswick to make it easier to load heavy cargo. At the top of King Street you can see the fire bell, which was built in a wooden tower painted to resemble stone. The tower burned down in the 1877 fire. The building on the left is Robinson's, where medicines were sold.

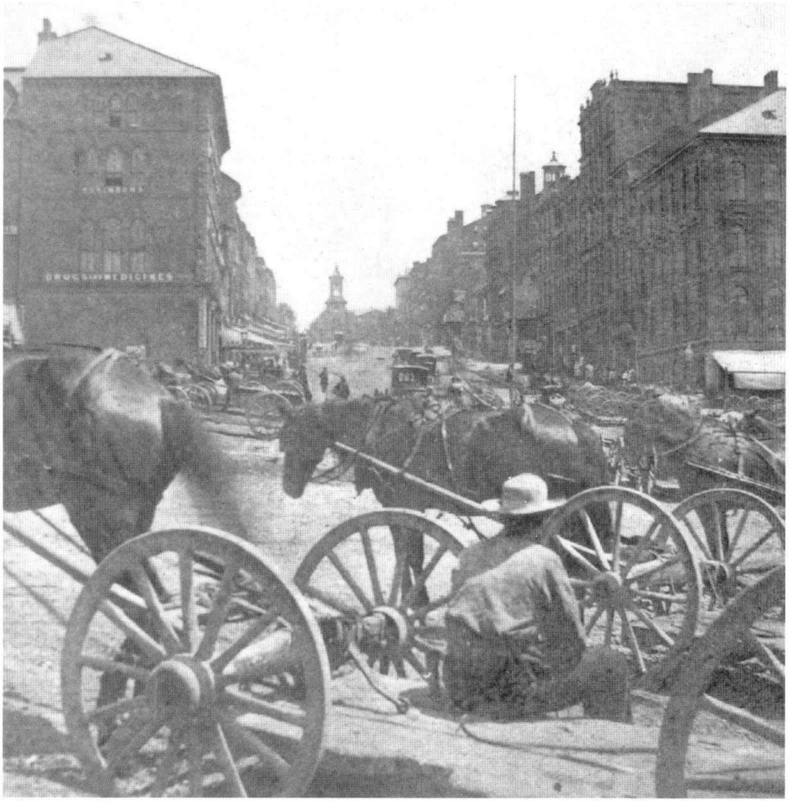

## Customs House, c.1860 (below) and 1894 (right)

The first customs house was designed by John Cunningham and built in 1841. The building was privately owned until it was sold to the federal government in 1870. In 1871 a mansard roof was added but the customs house was destroyed in the great fire of 1877. Its replacement was built between 1878 and 1881 from designs by Thomas Scott of Ottawa, and McKean and Fairweather of Saint John. That building was demolished from 1957 to 1960, and the current customs building was constructed. Through this building passed both the paperwork and goods for local businesses.

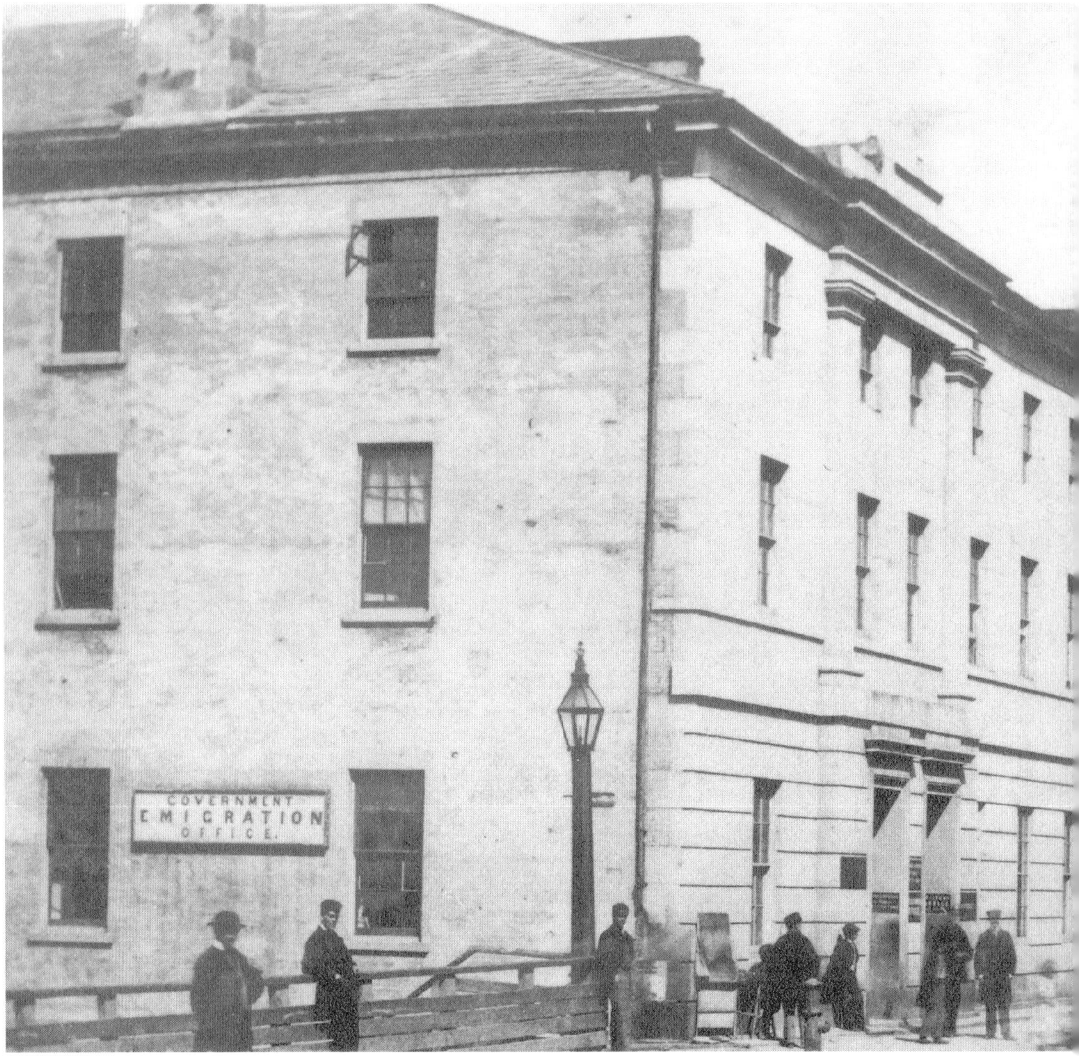

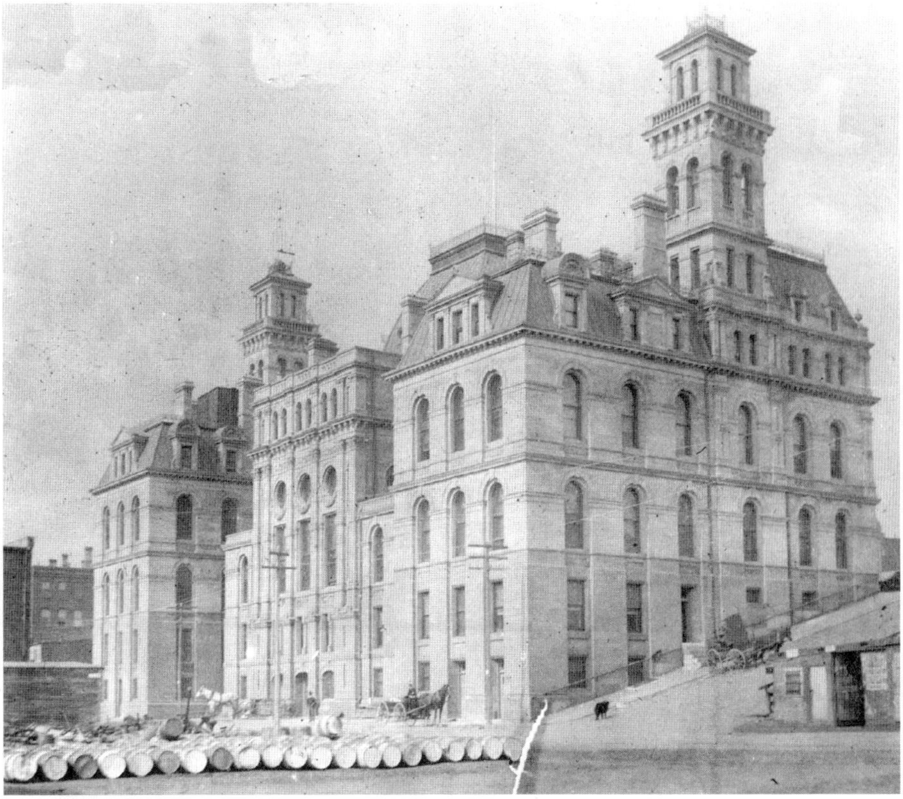

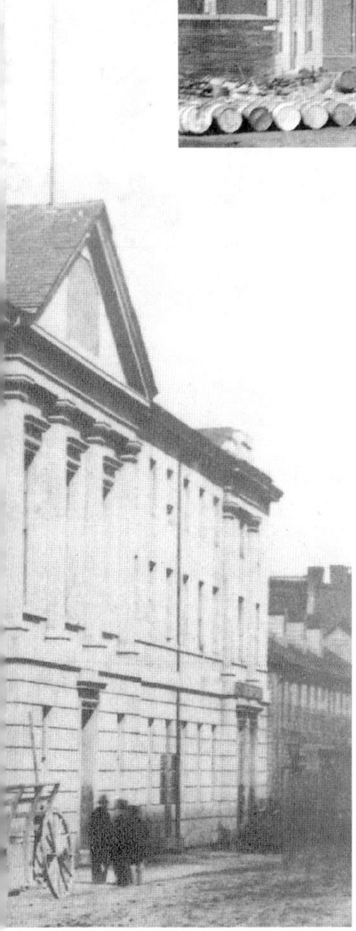

As an example, the following goods were imported by Hayward and Warwick on Princess Street:

- Austrian decorated glass lemonade set
- Austrian majolica pipe & ash trays
- Bohemian glass vase
- English bone china
- Fairy lamps, to imitate flowers
- Fancy ornaments
- French wares
- German ware
- Japanese china candlestick
- Japanese umbrella stand
- Majolica art shaded jardinieres and pedestals
- Nickle reading lamps with 10-inch white shade
- Parisian wares
- Royal Bayreuth ornamental china
- Table glassware
- Tea ware
- Tobacco jars in Doulton, air-tight covers

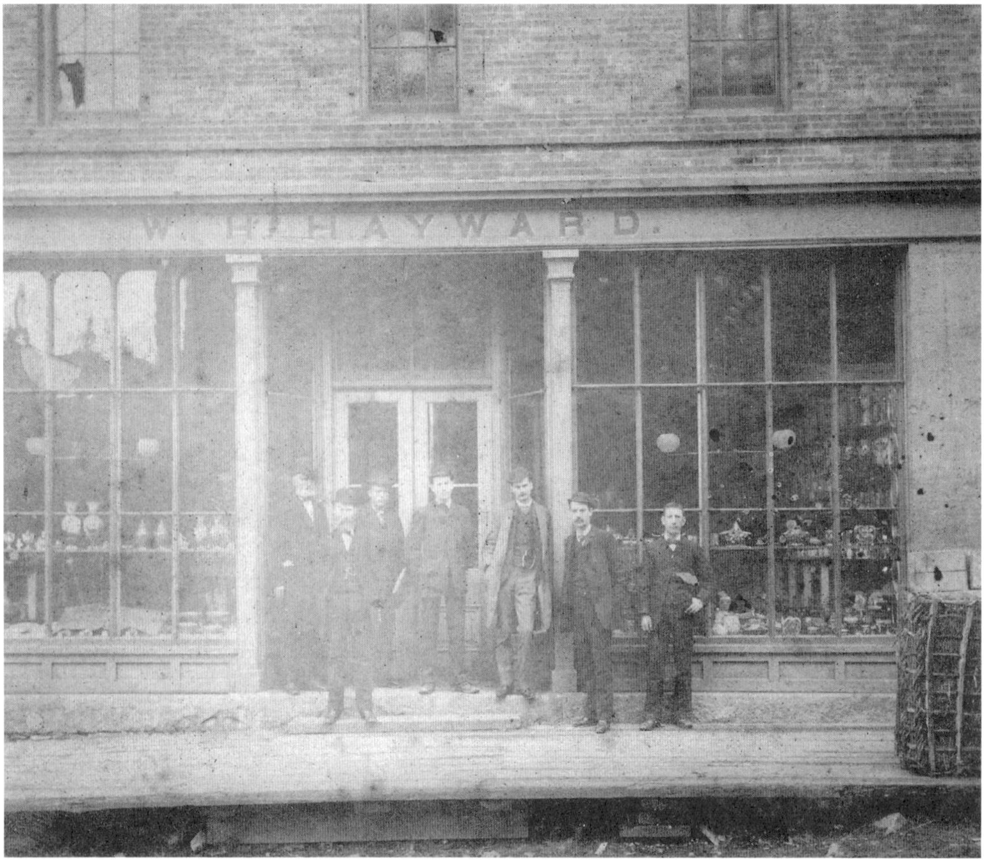


**W.H. HAYWARD, 1894**

In May 1855, William H. Hayward purchased the glass and earthenware stock of his brother-in-law William Warwick, who had started in business in 1853 on the second floor (over Haywards) at 59 Prince William Street. In 1873, the partnership between Hayward, William Warwick, and Orlando Warwick was dissolved. Six months after the Prince William Street store was destroyed in the fire of June 20, 1877, Hayward opened a new crockery store at 85 Princess Street. In 1894 a large warehouse addition was built. In 1902 W. H. Hayward, now operated by his son Harvey P., was incorporated as the W.H. Hayward Company Limited. In 1928 Hayward amalgamated with O.H. Warwick's China Store on King Street to become Hayward & Warwick Limited, the largest crockery, china, glassware, and silverware dealer east of Montreal. Today the fifth generation of the Hayward Family manages the company, making Hayward & Warwick Limited Saint John's oldest family-owned business. In 2000, the store established the Hayward China Museum on Princess Street.

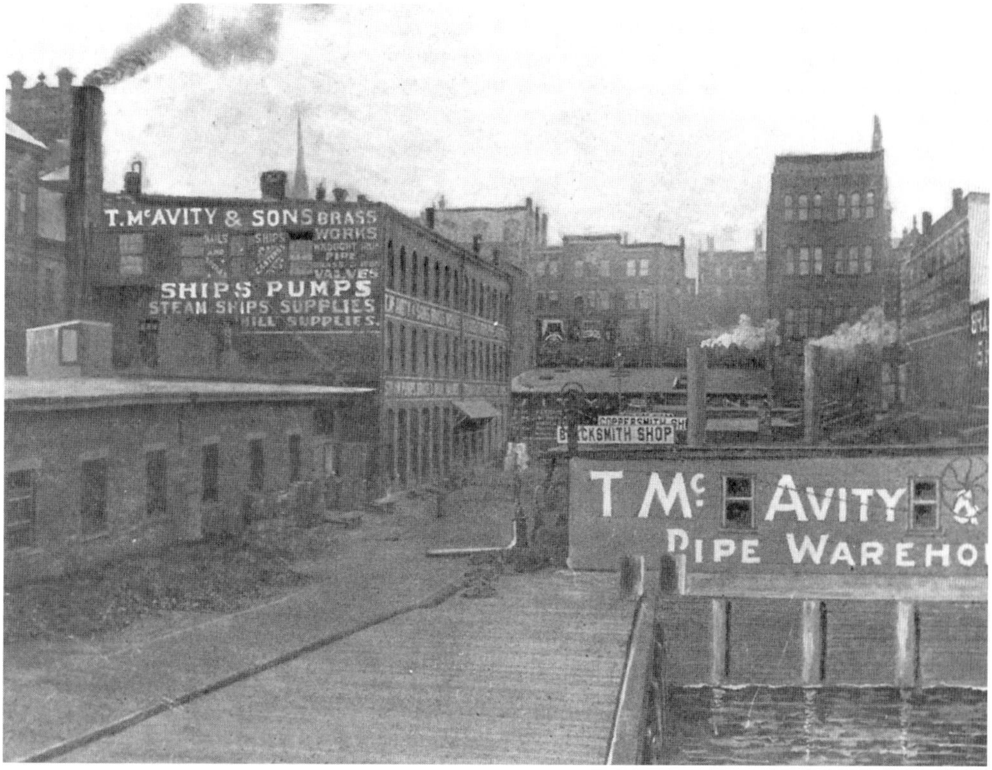


**MERRITT'S WHARF, 1899**

T. McAvity & Sons had their brass foundry on Water Street before the 1877 fire. They rebuilt in 1879, adding another building in 1882 to manufacture bells, rudder braces, ship's pumps, and various steamship supplies. They also had blacksmith and coppersmith shops and were ship and mill machinists. The second building was needed in part to handle the brass orders for the expanding locomotive trade. All these buildings were demolished before the construction of Pugsley Terminal in the 1940s. In 1916 McAvity & Sons moved all foundry operations to their new building on Rothesay Avenue.

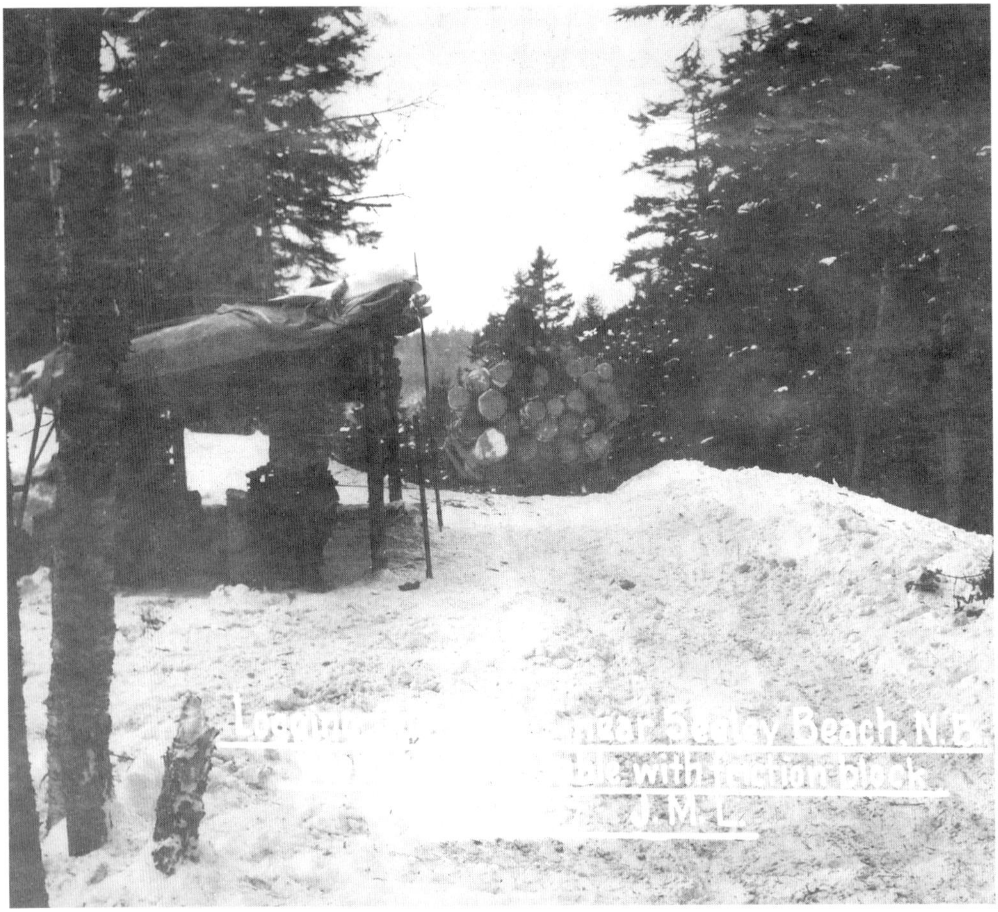


**SEELEYS BEACH, FEBRUARY 23, 1927**

The logging season began in the fall when the choppers, sawyers, and axemen headed to the lumber camps to fell trees and prepare them for hauling. In winter teamsters hauled the logs to the frozen rivers. "Wide trails had to be cut, hollows and irregularities in the land skidded over with tree trunks and even then two pair of oxen could not drag out the larger ones, so a block and tackle was used. This was called 'bowsing out'." Once the ice broke up in the spring, the logs went downriver in great log drives. River drivers would free logs from log jams and herd loose logs. The construction of the Mactaquac Dam effectively put a halt to log drives on the St. John River.

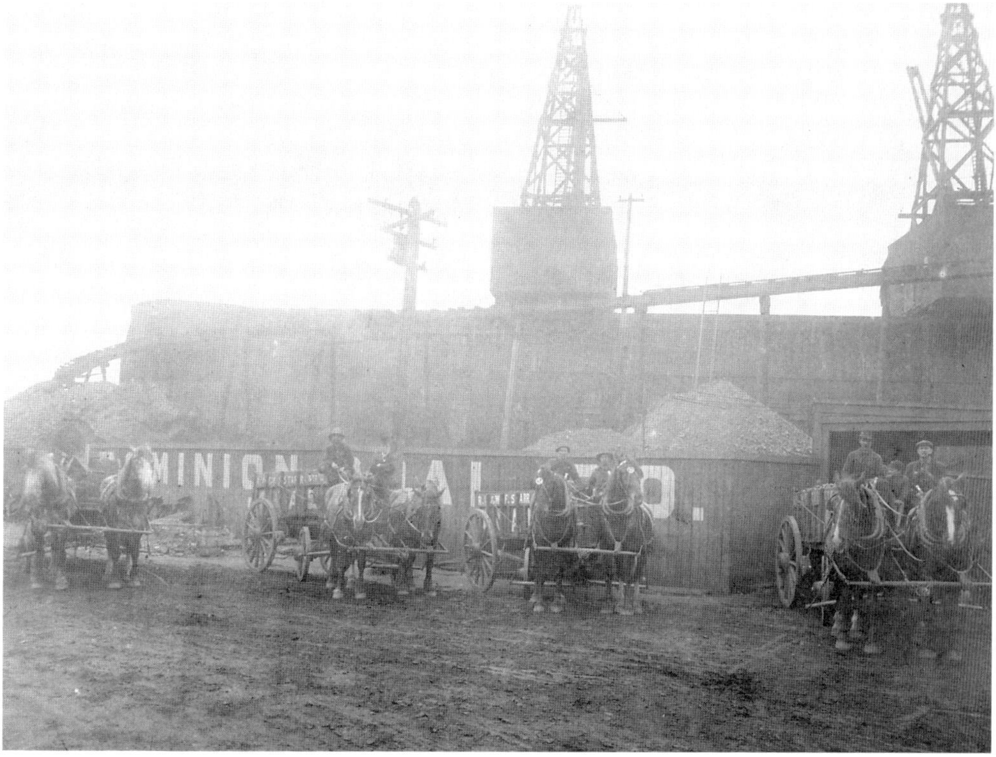

**DOMINION COAL, c.1930**

R.P. and W.F. Starr Limited started in 1863 as a general importing and commission business, selling salt, flour, meal, provisions, sugar, molasses, tea, and tobacco, from their premises at Hare's and York Point wharves and the old Cudlip and Snider's coal yard. Their father, W.J., was involved in insurance and coal, importing the latter from the UK, Nova Scotia, and the USA. In 1893, the Starrs became associated with the Dominion Coal Company, the largest coal company in Saint John, and the only one with coal pockets "by which thirty teams can be loaded at once, in less time then it takes to tell, and all coal is automatically screened and freed from dust." These coal pockets were added in 1903 to R.P. and W.F. Starr Limited. The pockets handled up to 300,000 tonnes of coal per year and employed up to four hundred men. R.P. and W.F. Starr also operated their own separate wholesale and retail coal business, selling 50,000 tonnes of coal annually, using forty teams of horses and 200 men. With offices on Smythe Street, Prince William Street, and, later, Union Street, the company delivered coal until August 1952.

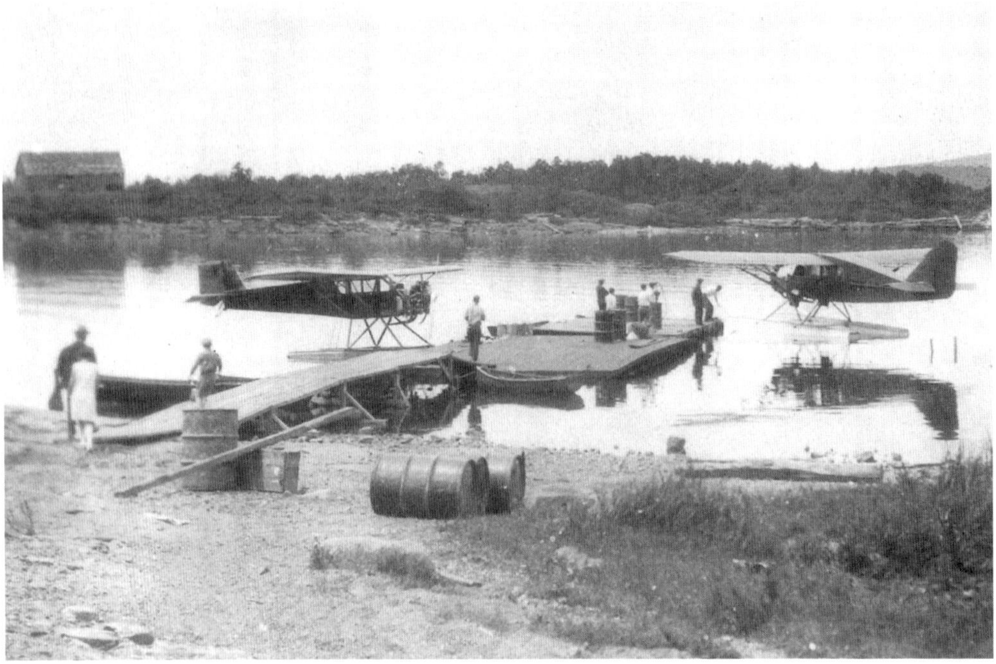

**Millidgeville Seaplane Base, c.1935**

Saint John's municipal airport was in Millidgeville from 1928 until 1951. From this airport operated the Saint John Flying Club, Atlantic Airways, and, during World War Two, the Royal Canadian Air Force. The seaplane base shown here operated from Brothers Cove near the Royal Kennebecasis Yacht Club.

## Chapter 7

# River Boats, Harbour Ferries and The Boston Boat

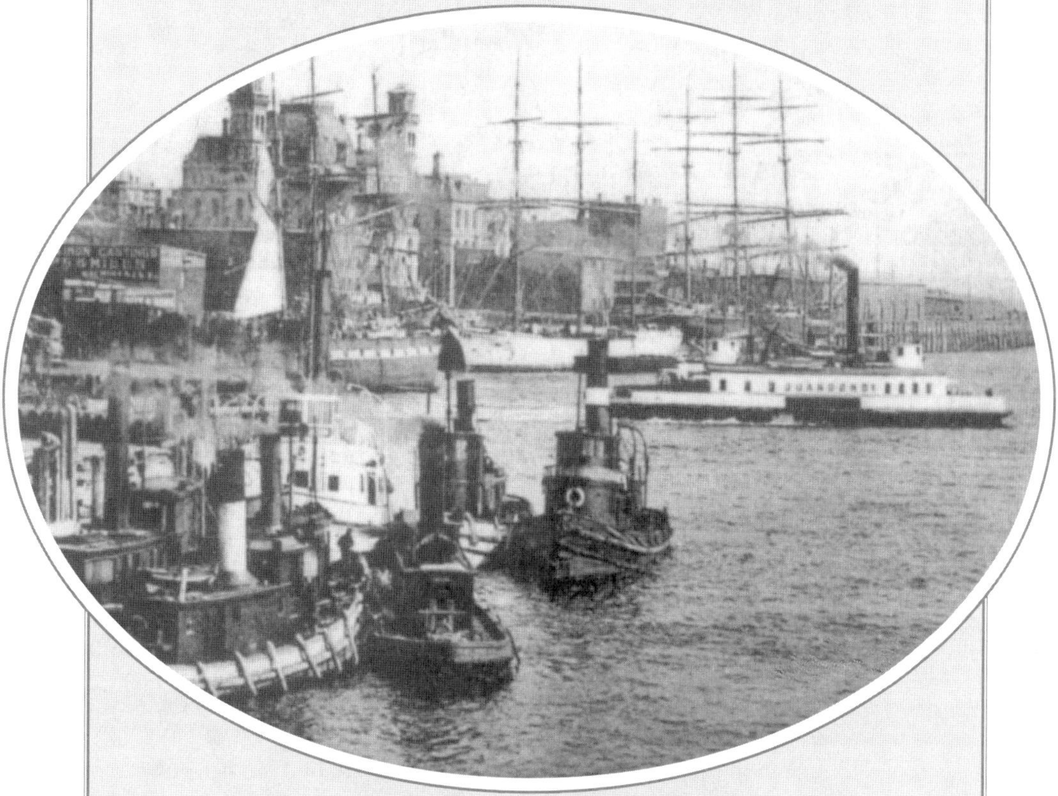

**HARBOUR FERRY *OUANGONDI*, C.1905**

In 1911, the harbour ferries carried 2,002,226 foot passengers and 107,448 teams of horses. The next year, these numbers increased to 2,167,931 foot passengers and 111,594 teams, and in 1913, to 2,490,233 foot passengers and 120,786 teams. In the latter year, ticket sales totalled $49,719, with a net profit of $1,331.98. In 1907, the Ludlow Street United Baptist Church described the ferry *Ludlow* as a floating rum shop because of an upriver trip taken by some British journalists. There was also a river ferry between Indiantown and Milford. One such ferry was the *E. Ross*, built in 1892 by Elijah Ross, a member of the famous Paris Crew.

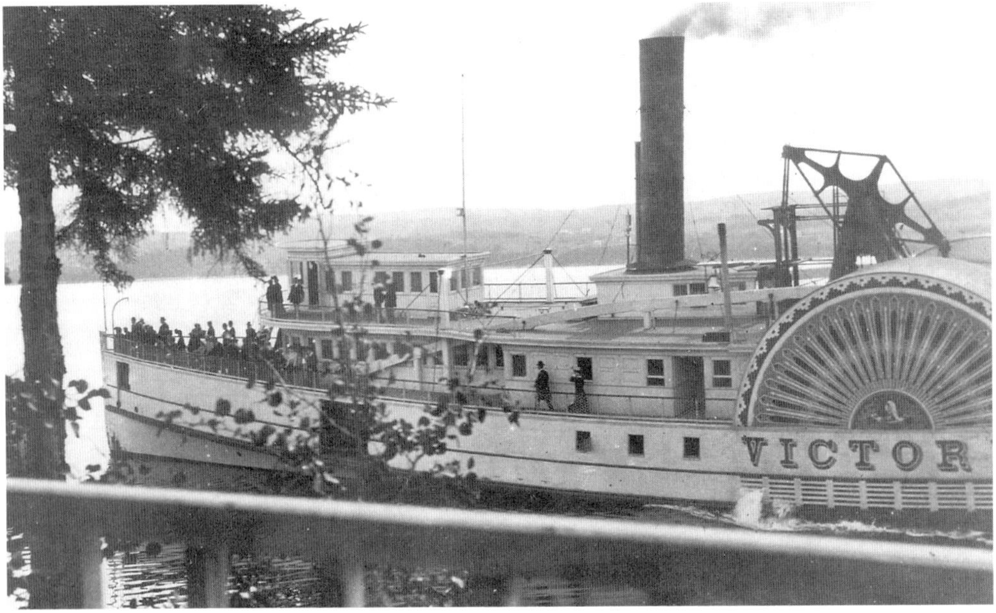


***VICTORIA*, c.1900**

To commemorate the sixtieth anniversary of Queen Victoria, the side-paddle steamer built in Saint John in 1897 by Edward McGuiggan was named *Victoria.* The joinery was by George Beatteay; the frame was built of spruce, the bottom was birch and spruce to the gunwales, the stern was fashioned from hemlock, and the rudder was oak. *Victoria's* main salon was elegant and spacious, with gold-leaf decorations surmounting the windows. The floor was covered with deep-pile carpeting, and there were solid mahogany chairs and couches upholstered in plush. A soda fountain extended across the forward end of the dining saloon. The *Victoria* operated primarily between Saint John and Fredericton, and on occasion she sailed moonlight excursions. On one picnic outing to Brown's Flat, she carried 952 passengers. John Dunham wrote a poem about the *Victoria*, part of which goes, "Now there was the glorious '*Vic*'; Whose answer to helm was quick. She e'er did contrive, While the river she'd ride, All rivals to handily lick." She was the premier steamer on the St. John at the time, which also saw the *David Weston* and *Majestic* servicing the same route. During the winter of 1911 she was sold to the Saint John River Steamship Company, and by 1915 her primary owner was E.C. Atkinson of Fredericton. In the early months of 1916 the *Victoria* burned to the water's edge and was deemed a complete loss.

***BEATRICE E. WARING*, c.1905**

TOP RIGHT

This riverboat *Beatrice E. Waring* was built in Carleton in 1903 by Alward N. Harned. The 140-foot stern-wheeler had a very short life, having been lost to fire in 1906. Sailing under the Springfield Steamship Company flag, she operated on the Belleisle-St. John run. With fourteen heated staterooms, *Beatrice E. Waring* was the first steamer to be outfitted with electricity. She was named after the general manager of the company, who was the daughter of William L. Waring, the steamship inspector for Saint John. William Waring, his wife Charlotte and their daughter Beatrice owned both the *Beatrice E. Waring* and the *May Queen.* Sometime after 1903, Beatrice Waring married Hugh Bailey and moved to British Columbia.

BEATRICE E. WARING, C.1905

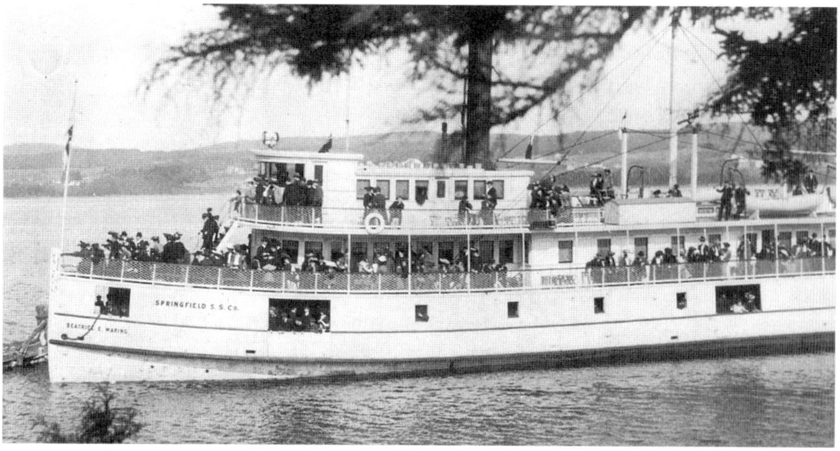


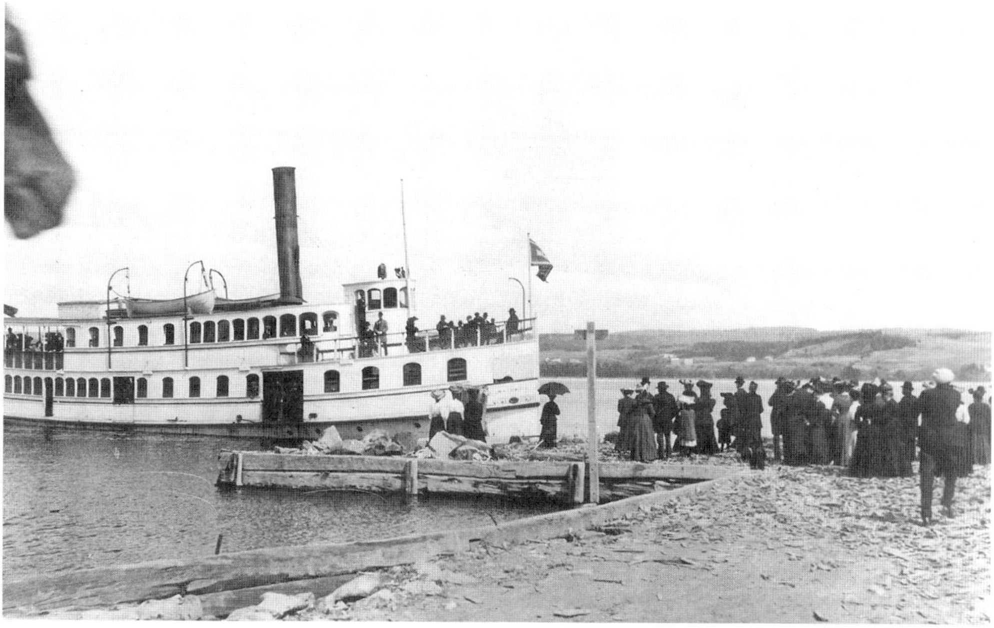

**MAJESTIC, C.1905**

ABOVE

The steamer *Majestic* was built in Toronto in 1899 and remained on her run until 1942. This steel-hulled, coal-burning steamer first appeared on the St. John River in 1902, and over the next fourteen years she established a reputation for the accuracy of her timetable. Based in Saint John she operated on the four runs: Gagetown, Fredericton, Wickham, and Coles Island. Like most steamers, this one suffered her share of misadventures. In 1912, after her superstructure was extensively damaged in a fire, the wheelhouse was raised from the saloon deck to the hurricane deck. By the time the *Victoria* was withdrawn from service, the *Majestic* was operating under the Crystal Stream Steamship Company, which was controlled by D.J. Purdy, and by 1929 she was sailing under the flag of Eastern Canada Coastal Steamships. The *Majestic* made her last trip in November 1942 and ended her days as a decaying derelict on the shore at Nauwigewauk.

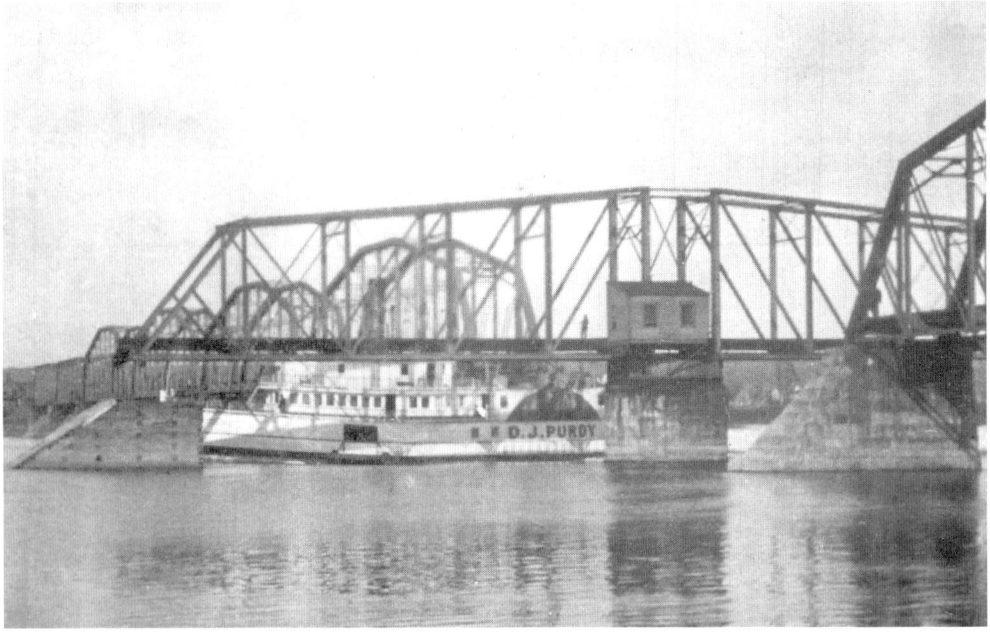


**STEAMSHIP *D.J. PURDY*, C.1920**

The *Purdy* was built using the hull of the fire-damaged *Sincennes* in 1912, and she operated on the Washademoak. She had steel "feathering-float" paddle-wheels which allowed for a smaller paddle-wheel, thereby saving space on the saloon deck. She was withdrawn from service in 1923. She is seen here going past the swing-gate bridge at Fredericton. In 1924 the motorship *D.J. Purdy* went into service on the Saint John-Fredericton route. She was the last of the river steamers in service, retiring in 1946. Virginia (Lynch) Dunbrack remembers Purdy's early years on the river: "The public wharf at Brown's Flat was where we all congregated daily to take the sun, swim, go and play tennis, and socialize. The most exciting event of the day was the arrival of the river boat, which usually discharged people and fresh produce. Some of the more daring divers climbed up to the top deck of the boat, and dove off as it was pulling away from the wharf."

**NEW FERRY, APRIL 10, 1933**

TOP RIGHT

This photo was taken the day before the launch of the *Loyalist*. Built by Shelburne Shipbuilders Limited, she was christened by Elizabeth Bruce, daughter of the company's president, on April 11. The new ferry arrived in Saint John on April 27.

**HARBOUR FERRY *WESTERN EXTENSION*, C.1900**

BOTTOM RIGHT

From 1870 to 1910, this ferry operated as the extension of the railway from the west side of Saint John Harbour to the east side. The vessel on the right is the *Alert* of Saint John. After the *Victoria* inaugurated ferry service in Saint John Harbour in 1839, other harbour ferries joined suit: *Lady Coldbrook* (1850s), the *Forty Second* (1850s), *Ouangondi* (1870-1908), *Ludlow* (1905-1933), *Governor Carleton* (1911-1933), and *Loyalist* (1933-1954). The typical timetable for the ferry would see the service start at 6 A.M. and finish at midnight with 20-minute trips. Sunday service started at 8 A.M. and was a 30-minute trip.

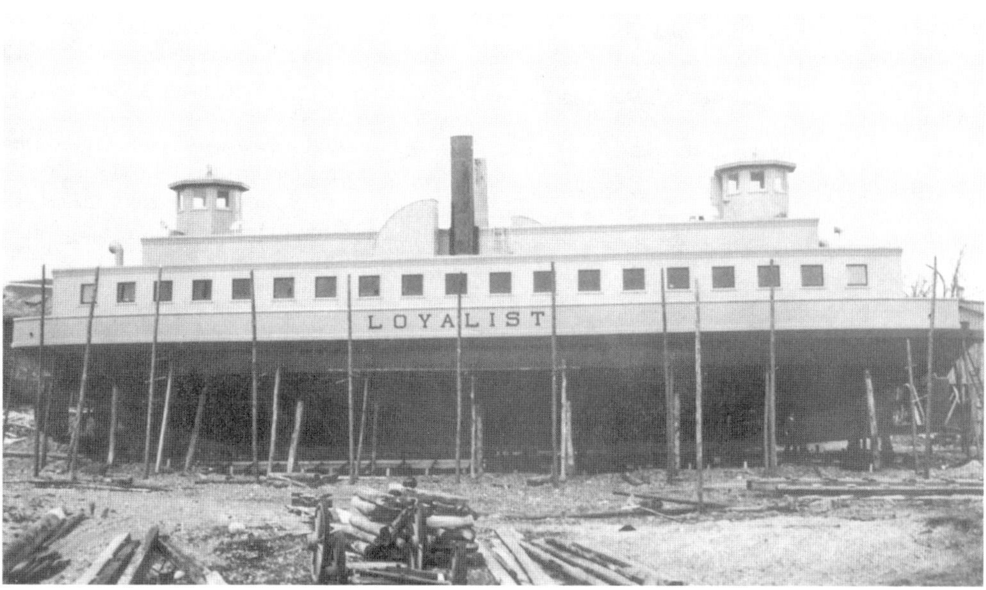


NEW FERRY, 1933 (ABOVE) AND THE HARBOUR FERRY *WESTERN EXTENSION* (BELOW)

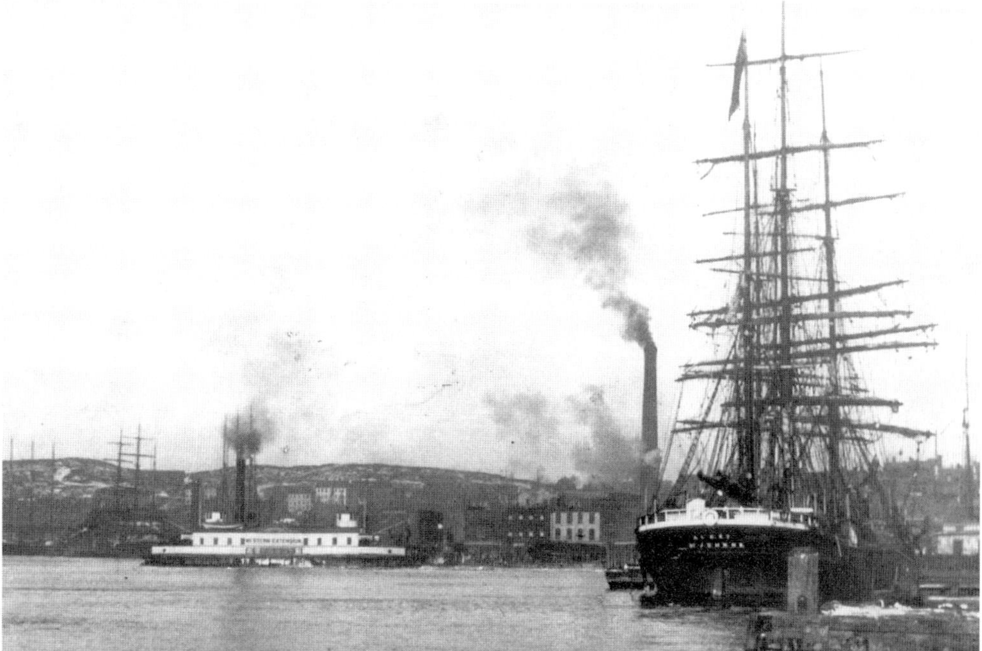

**FERRY ENGINEER, DECEMBER 1946**

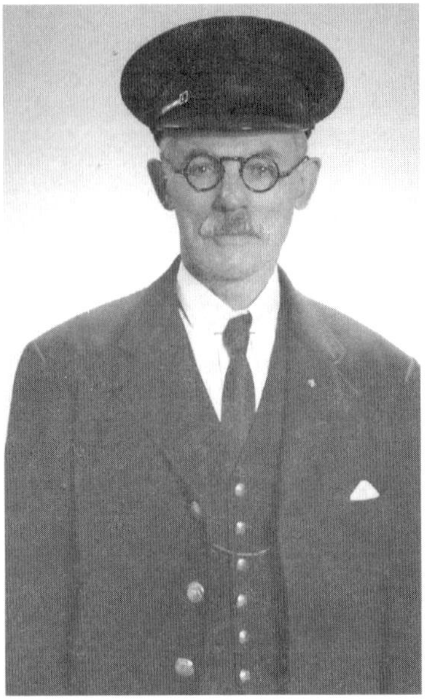

Arthur Ross was appointed shore engineer before the launch of the *Loyalist* in 1932. Part of his job was to keep the ferry slip free of ice floes during the winter: "The Engineer and his assistants commenced the work of clearing the slip at 4 o'clock this morning. They shoved numerous ice cakes and a gigantic tree back into the harbour stream." On one winter occasion Ross had to let go of the ferry side to prevent being crushed between the *Loyalist* and the dock; he almost drowned. On another occasion he suffered severe head injuries and a cracked rib when he fell on the west side footbridge. His ferry nicknames were "The Lightning Express," "the Flying Arrow," and "the R-100". He was still at work when this photo was taken in 1946 at aged seventy-two. He died on January 22, 1951.

**ACROSS THE HARBOUR OR BUST, C.1935**

BELOW

During efforts to provide the best ferry service for west side residents, Councillor Ingraham was immortalized by this Stuart Truman cartoon. The caption read: "'YOU'RE ON THE SPOT,' remarked the mayor, smiling, to Councillor Ingraham of West Saint John when the councillor arose on Thursday morning to address the determined delegation from his own community which demanded a

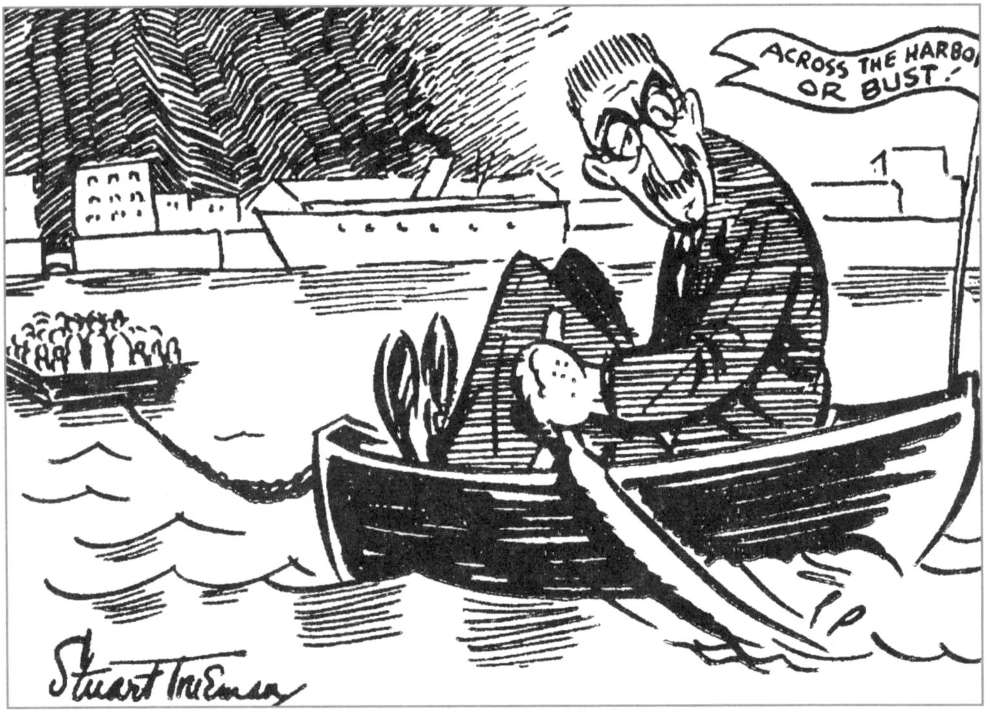

complete ferry service. Councillor Ingraham, undaunted, gave a good speech which left the delegates satisfied with the firm belief that he'd get them across the harbour safely or he'd know the reason why, and the conference, which might have produced combustion, wound up like disarmament conferences which they could. Incidentally, a suggestion advanced jestingly or not by J. Harry Driscoll was that the ferry be submerged in the Public Works Department, where no one would ever hear of its deficit. More serious was his idea that the ferry should be drummed up as a tourist attraction, to fatten revenues by inducing visitors to take the cruise across the harbour."

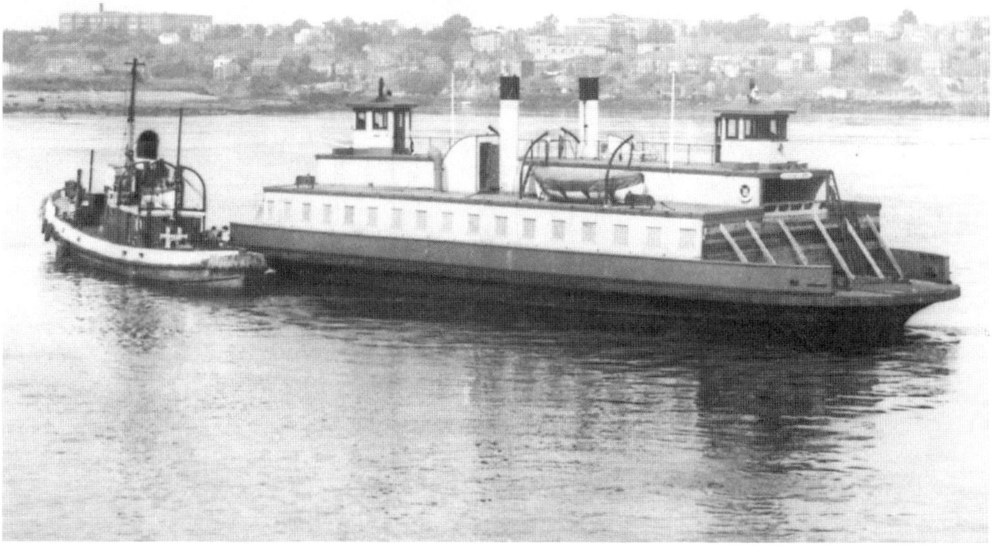

**Chatham Bound, 1954**

On July 31, the *Loyalist* was towed by the *Ocean Kiwi* from Saint John to Chatham to replace the *Frances Ullock* on the Chatham run. The *Loyalist* was replaced in 1961 by the ferry *Romeo & Juliette* (which was eventually put on the Millidgeville service). Although Common Council decided in October 1951 to remove the ferry from service, extensions kept the ferry in Saint John until 1954.

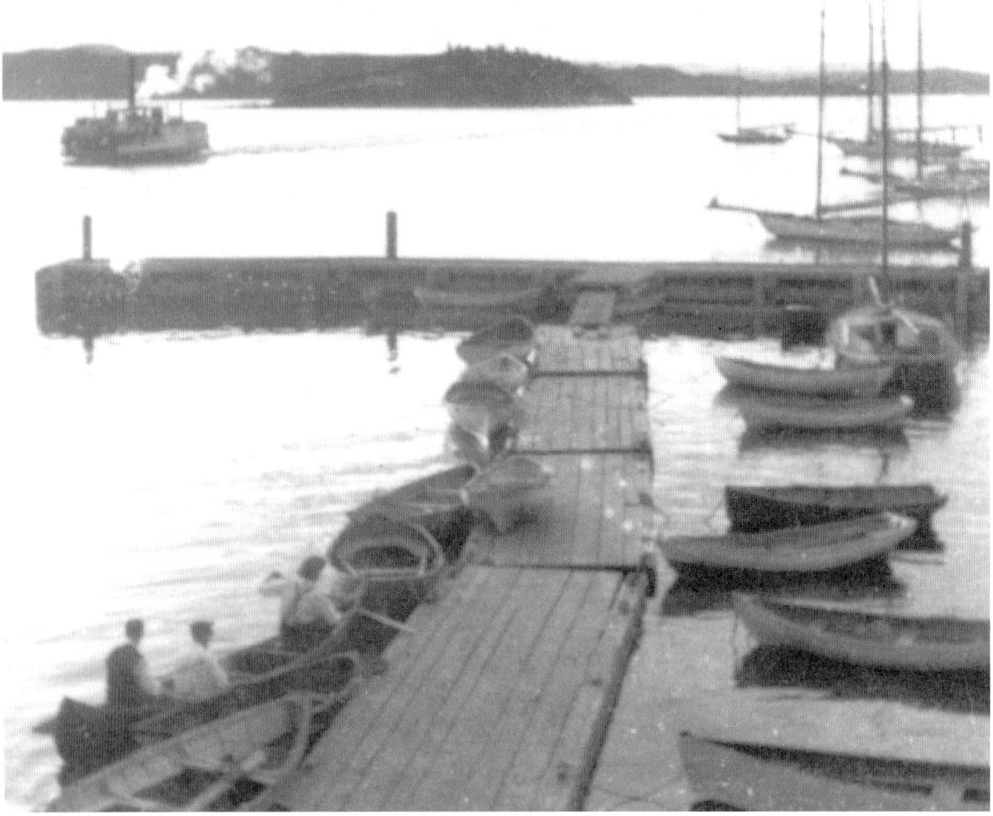

**MILLIDGEVILLE FERRY, C.1910**

Pictured above is the *Maggie Miller* near the Royal Kennebecasis Yacht Club. The Millidgeville ferry had served that community and residents of the Kingston Peninsula since the 1800s. In 1892 the first *Maggie Miller* started her run and remained in service for about forty years, charging fares of ten cents for each passenger and twenty cents for each horse team and teamster. In 1934, *Maggie Miller II* replaced the first vessel. Fares were dropped when the New Brunswick Department of Highways made ferries part of the toll-free road system.

**BAY FERRY *GRAND MANAN II*, C.1925**

TOP RIGHT

The *Grand Manan II* and the *Grand Manan IV* were built at the Saint John Drydock and operated between Blacks Harbour, Grand Manan, and Campobello Island. The *Grand Manan III* was formerly a warship, HMCS *Elk* which had been commissioned in Halifax in September 1940. She served in Bermuda, Nova Scotia, and Newfoundland. After being paid off on August 4, 1945, she was sold to Coastal Transport Limited where she remained until 1968. The ferry service is still operated by Coastal Transport Limited.

**GONDOLA AND REEDS POINT FERRY, C.1930**

BOTTOM RIGHT

Waiting to board the *William A. Pitt II* are Hickey Road residents Margaret Ellen Arthurs, her sister and brother, Beatrice and Andrew Christopher, Audrey Christopher, and Francena Estabrooks.

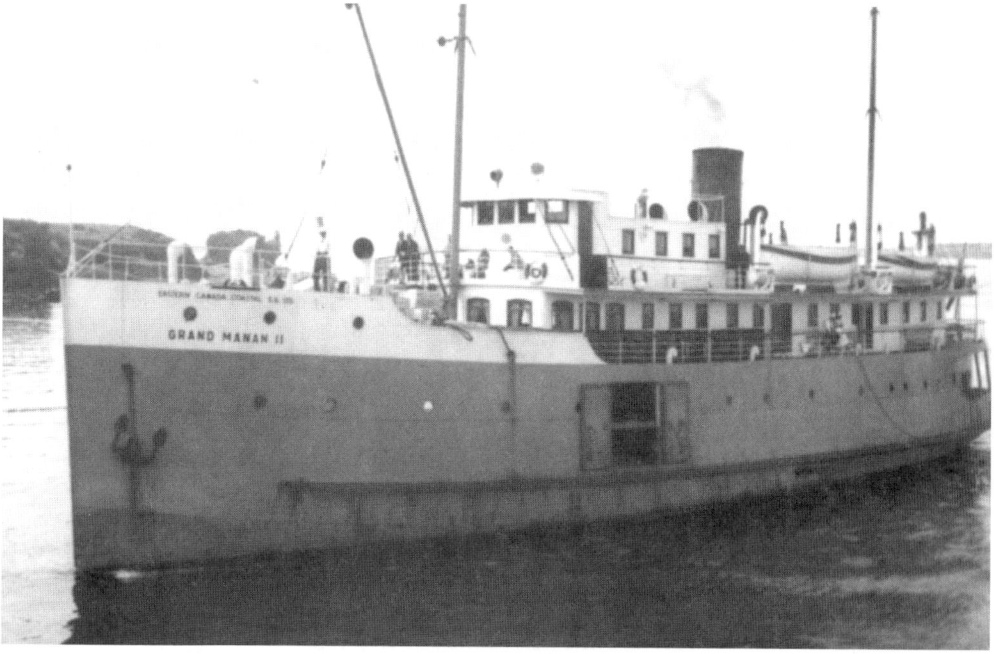


THE BAY FERRY *GRAND MANAN II* (ABOVE) AND THE GONDOLA AND REEDS POINT FERRY (BELOW)

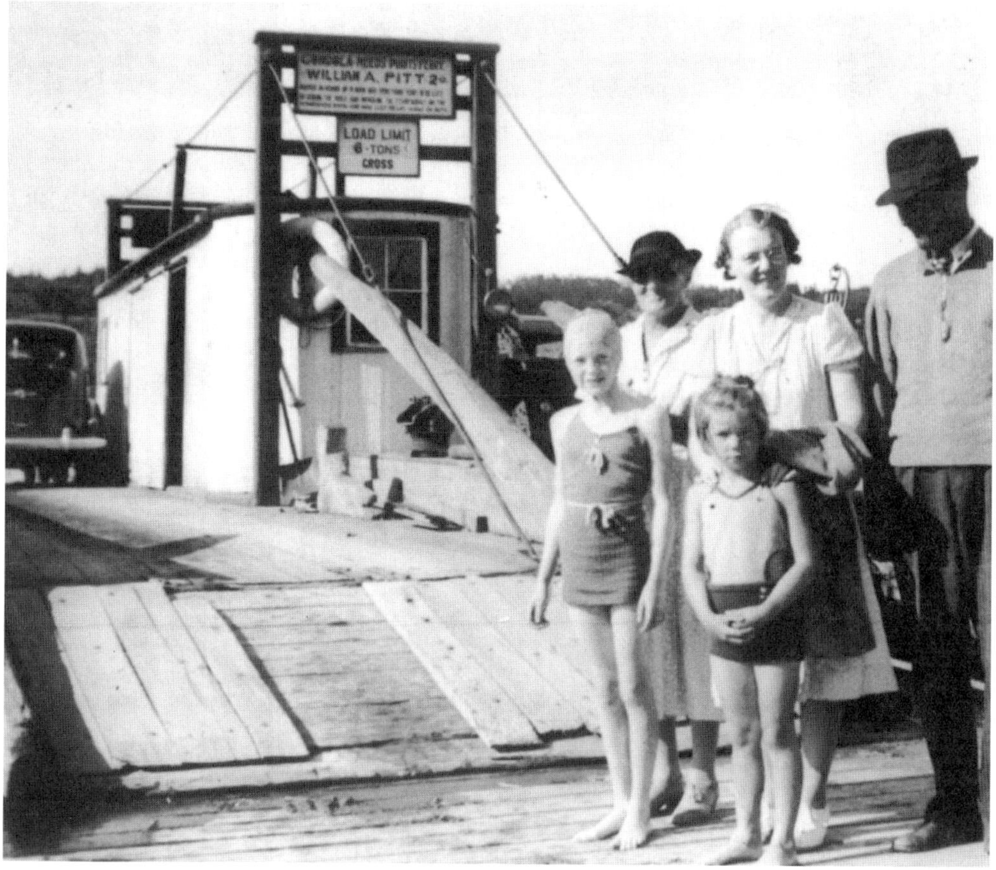

## *Calvin Austin*, c.1910

The *Calvin Austin*, shown entering Saint John Harbour, was built by the Delaware Shipbuilding Yard in Bath, Maine, in 1903 for the Eastern Steamship Company. Her maiden voyage was on June 10, 1904. After the Halifax Explosion on December 6, 1917, the *Austin* went to Halifax to assist in delivering supplies to the residents of that devastated city. The ferry service between Saint John and Digby started in 1784 with the *Sally*, which was shortly joined in competition by the *Mary Ann* and the *Matilda*, and in 1815 by the sloop *Hairm*. Owners of these vessels were from both Saint John and Digby. In 1827 the steamer *Saint John* made her first run between Digby and Saint John. Ferries to follow included

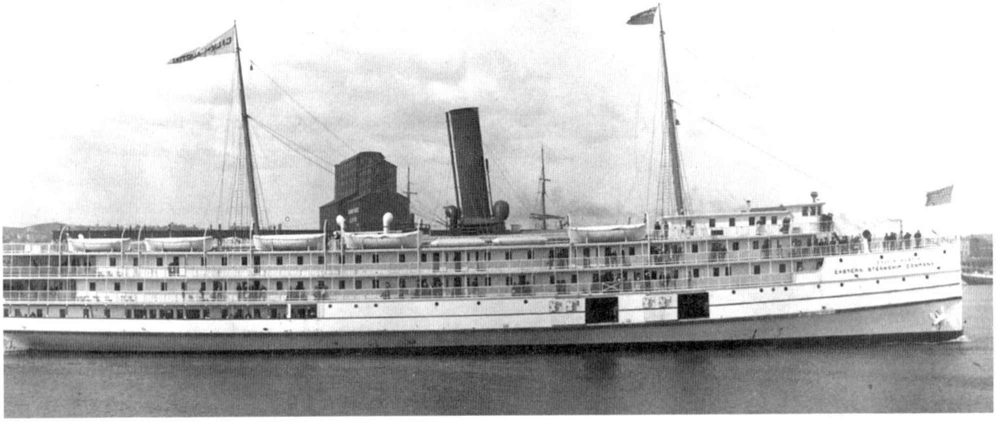

the *Henrietta, Maid of the Mist*, and in 1834 the *Royal Tar*, which was lost in Penobscot Bay in 1836. Other bay ferries included the *Maid of Erin*, the *Fairy Queen*, the *Pilot*, and the first *Empress*, which ran until 1884. The SS *Secret* then operated until the Saint John steamer *Dorcas* took over in 1888, but she was unsuitable and, as no other private operator was prepared to take over the service, the federal government steamer *Lansdowne* took over the route until 1889 when she was replaced by the *Monticello*. In 1895 the Dominion Atlantic Railway put the SS *Prince Rupert* on the route, and after the Dominion Atlantic was acquired by the Canadian Pacific Railway in 1911, the *St. George* was placed in service in 1913. The *St. George* was replaced by the second *Empress* in 1916, followed in 1930 by the *Princess Helene*.

## SS *Saint John*, 1932

As she loomed out of the fog surrounded by a cordon of escort boats, our namesake vessel, the SS *Saint John*, arrived at her home port on May 3, 1932. To the tunes of "O' Canada" and "Yankee Doodle," she was welcomed by a crowd of some ten thousand people. Built at the Newport News Shipyard, and christened with water from the Reversing Falls, she and her sister ship *Acadia* each held 744 passengers. Their speed was 20 knots and each cost $3.2-million dollars. Under the Eastern Steamship Company, the *Saint John* carried passengers and cargo between Saint John, Yarmouth, Boston, and New York. The overnight service to Boston cost $10 one way. The *Saint John* offered dancing under the "rainbow-

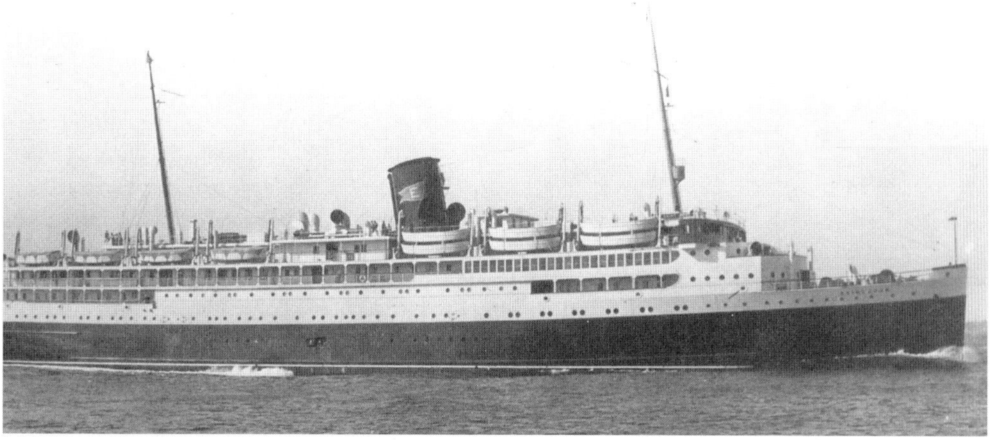

hued dome of the Terrace Ball Room panelled in silver and ebony," the great blue and gold dining hall, the Elizabethan smoking room, library, music room, and comfortable staterooms for as low as $1.50. In the plush interior hung paintings and murals depicting Saint John Harbour in 1604 and in 1932. The *Saint John* and the *Acadia* were purchased by the US Navy in April 1941. *Saint John* was commissioned as the submarine tender USS *Antaeus* (AS-21) on May 17, 1941, and she served for eighteen months in the Caribbean. She was redesignated as the miscellaneous auxiliary AG-67 in September 1942 and ferried troops between the Caribbean and Canal Zone ports until December 1944. Then she went to the New York naval shipyard in Brooklyn and was converted to the hospital ship USS *Rescue* (AH-18) on January 18, 1945. Equipped with beds for 792 patients, she left in February for the Pacific, where she earned her first battle star at Okinawa and her second star as a member of the US Third Fleet engaged in air strikes against Japan. As a fleet unit, she sailed into Tokyo Bay and soon was engaged again in coastal operations. This time, however, she steamed up and down the coast of Japan transporting thousands of released Allied prisoners to Yokohama. On her first homeward voyage she stopped at Guam to disembark repatriated prisoners of war. She arrived back in New York in October 1945 with 770 patients, among them 498 POWs. After other Pacific runs she was decommissioned at Seattle, Washington, in April 1946 and returned to the War Shipping Administration two months later. After sitting for twelve years as part of the West Coast Reserve Fleet, the SS *Saint John* was scrapped in Belgium on January 14, 1958.

**_PRINCESS HELENE_, C.1950**

The *Princess Helene* replaced the *Empress* in 1930. Built at Dunbarton, Scotland, in 1930, *Princess Helene* was designed to carry five hundred passengers and fifty automobiles. On August 8, 1949, the *Helene* was hit by a flash fire, causing $40,000 damage to twenty-eight automobiles and her 106-ton cargo of sugar, wrapping paper, cotton waste, and assorted foodstuffs. It took firefighters four hours to bring the fire under control. The *Helene* listed heavily to port, and tugs stood by to assist as the fifty overnight guests were evacuated safely. The next day the *Helene* resumed service, with cleanup and painting being done on the days immediately after the fire. Canadian Pacific had the following to say of the *Helene*: "Built like an ocean liner, the *Princess Helene* gives speed, spaciousness and comfort to the Saint John-Digby service. Public rooms are large, airy and bright and are equipped with comfortable furniture." In 1953 the one-way fare for a car with one passenger was $12.00. One-way passenger fare was $2.60. The *Helene* was outdated by 1963, so she was sold to a Liberian company on July 11, 1963, and became the car ferry *Carnia*. In 1967 she was sold to International Cruises S.A. of Greece who converted her to the cruise ship *Carnia II* for the Mediterranean. She was scrapped in 1977.

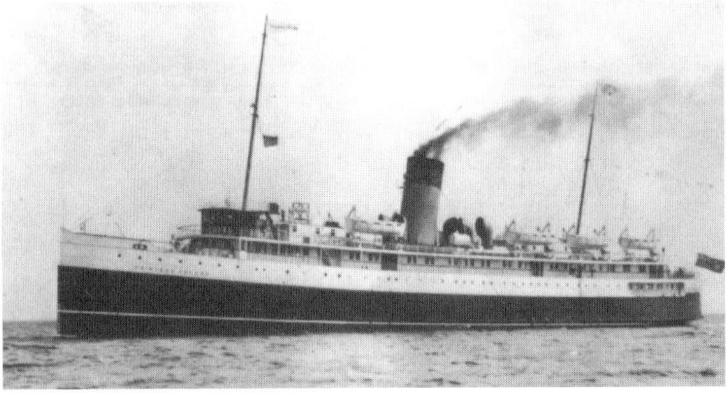

**_PRINCESS OF ACADIA_, 1970**

In 1963, the Canadian Pacific Railway bought the *Acadia*—the former *Princess of Nanaimo* from the West Coast—to serve the Digby run. By 1969, Canadian Pacific and the federal government agreed on a new ferry for Saint John. In 1971, *Acadia* was replaced by the *Princess of Acadia II* and her terminal moved to Sand Point on the West Side. The new *Acadia* was built at the Saint John Drydock at a cost of $8 million, and her maiden voyage was on June 1, 1971. She was owned by Canadian Pacific from 1971 until September 1, 1976, when she was taken over by Canadian National and operated by Marine Atlantic. On April 1, 1997, Bay Ferries Limited took over the ferry and continue to operate the service.

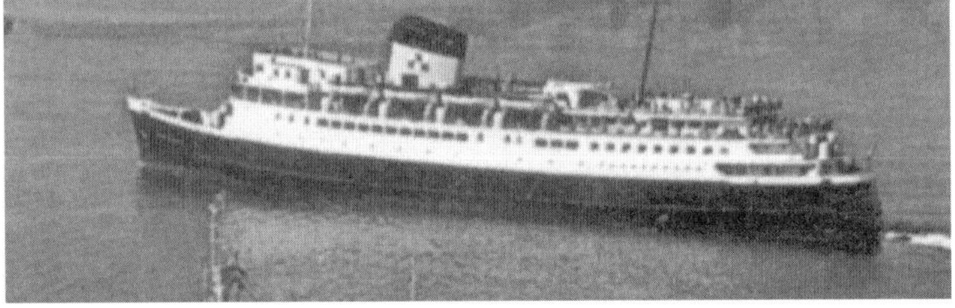

## Chapter 8

# *Harvesting the Sea*

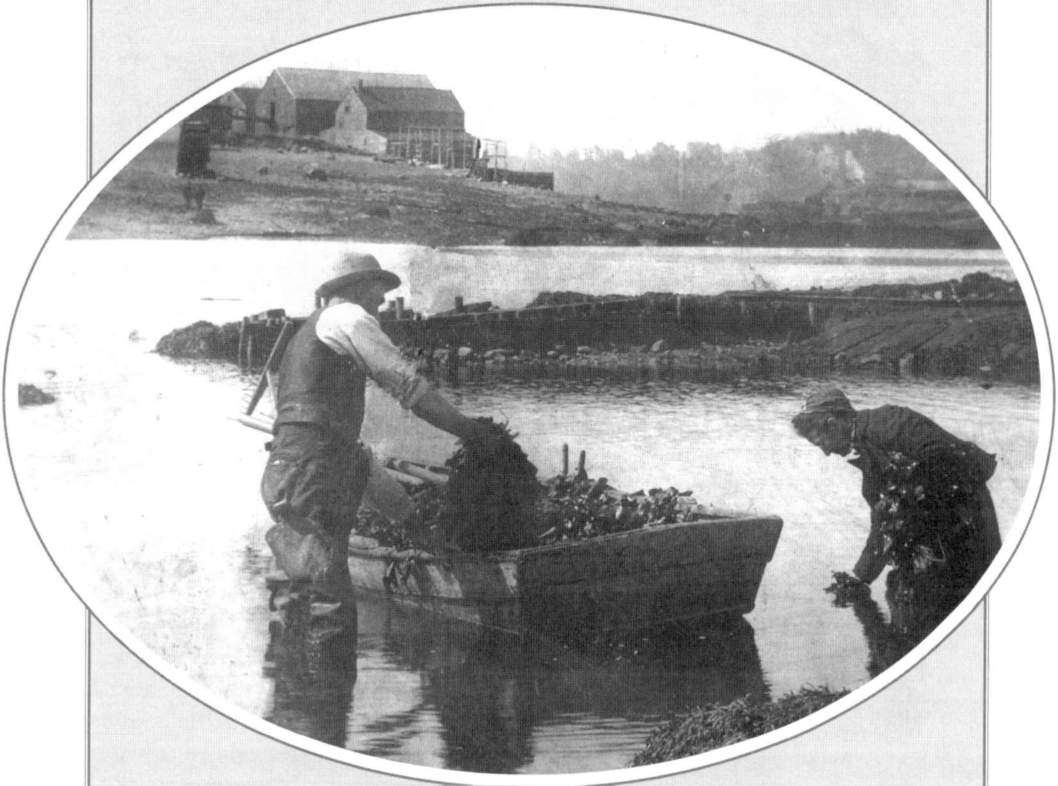

**GATHERING DULSE, BUTTERMILK CHANNEL, C.1890**

Navy Island residents Andrew and Ceylon Lamoreau are picking dulse in Buttermilk Channel for sale later at the Saint John city market. At low water, island residents could walk across Buttermilk Channel. During the port expansion in the 1930s this channel was filled in and Navy Island was obliterated.

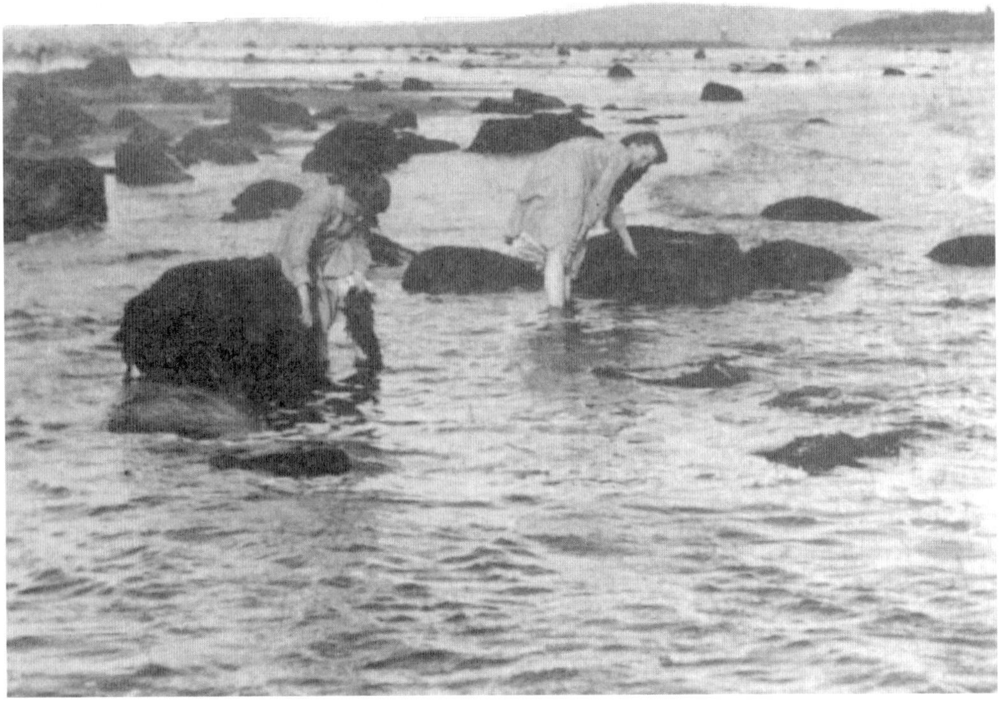

**Gathering Dulse, Bayshore, 1904**

This stereoscope view was sold with this writeup printed on the back:

> "You are below the city, where the river enters the bay. Even if the tides of Fundy were not famous, you would know it must be salt water that is lazily rolling in; the sea-weed draperies covering those rocks tell the tale of the ocean's intimacy. How much they look like the shaggy pelts of big beasts, swimming and playing with each other in the shallow water! The old tales about the sudden and enormous rise of the tides along the bay have been greatly exaggerated. Twice a day the steadily recurrent impetus comes from the surging Atlantic far outside, and the waters roll in higher and higher. Up at the bridges just above the town of St. John, there is a difference of some twenty-five feet between high and low tide, but seldom more than that, and the height increases gradually—not all at once. The place to see a really formidable 'bore' or tidal wave is away up at the head of the bay, on the Petitcodiac River, near Moncton. There the incoming tide, after battling with the out-going river-current, does conquer with a sudden rush, and roll on with a wave or wall from two to (sometimes) ten feet high, as advance-guard of the flood. Before long, the waters which you see now just lazily and experimentally lapping that reach of sand will cover not only the sand but the rocks as well. Boats must needs keep to a known channel on their way up the river. Notice that lighthouse away over there at the bend in the shore: New Brunswick skippers know it well."

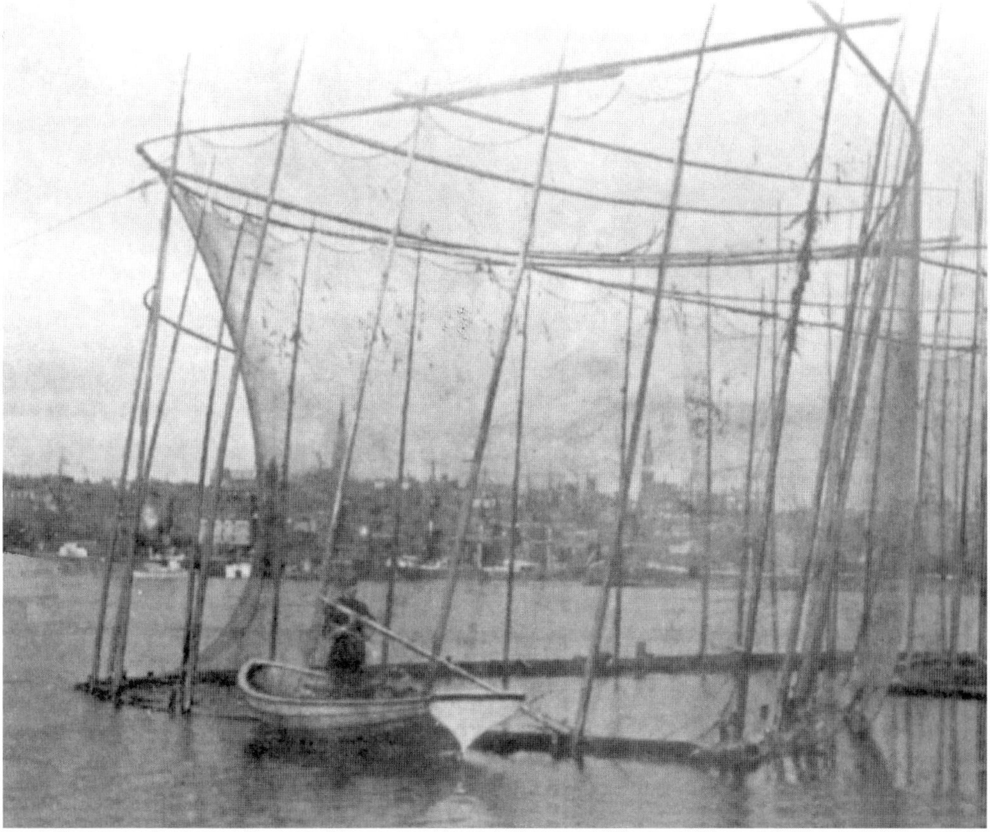

**Sand Point Weir, 1904**

The tides in the Bay of Fundy worked to the fishermen's benefit. As the tide receded, it was relatively easy to pluck fish from the net. Fishermen, however, had to contend with many misadventures, such as this 1935 incident: the hull of the harbour ferry *Governor Carleton* broke her moorings and ripped through Robert Wilson's fishing weir on the Strait Shore. Saint John's fishing community was centred in the South End, the Strait Shore, and Riverview Drive, where there are only a few fishing sheds left today. In 1896 a report on the fishery stated:

> "The harbour has valuable fisheries and the neighbouring bay yields cod, hake, halibut, salmon, shad, mackerel, herring, haddock and lobsters, that are caught, cured and shipped all over Canada, to the West Indies the United States and elsewhere."

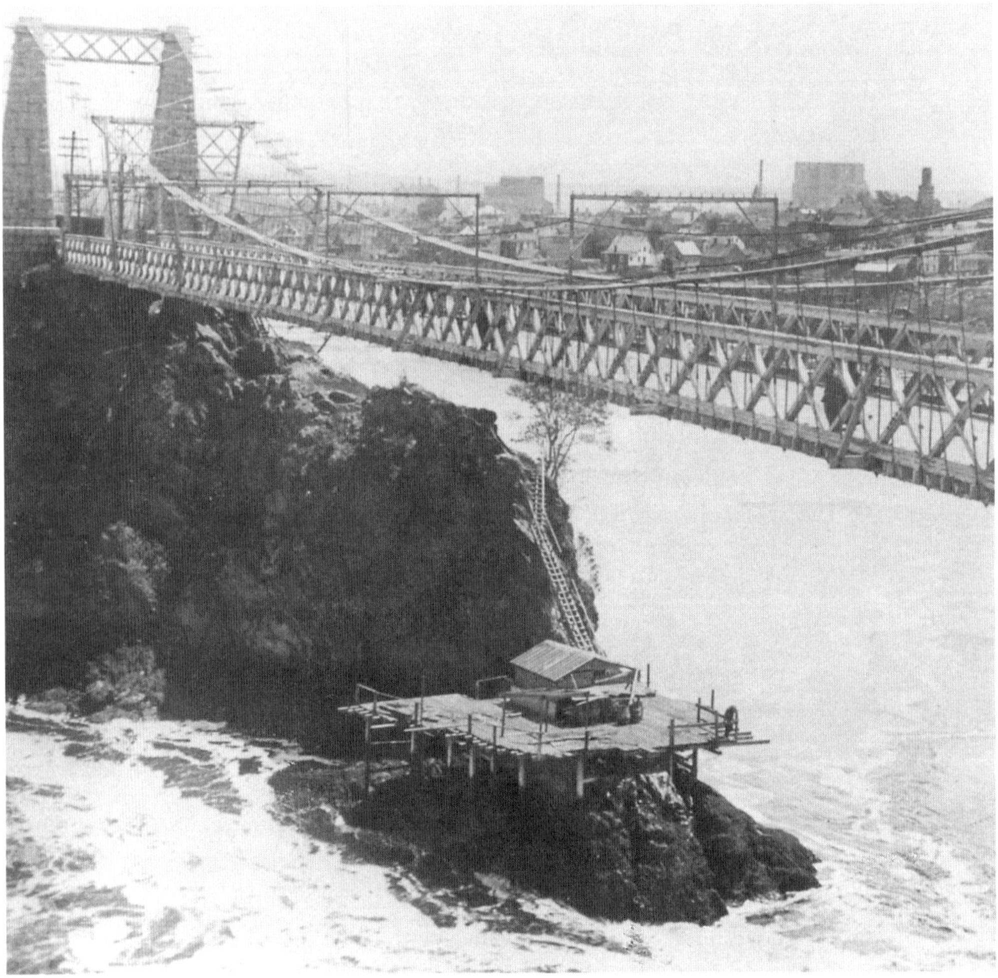

**SPLIT ROCK, C.1905**

The platform being built on Split Rock below the bridge in this picture was probably used for fishing. In the *Times Globe* on Saturday, May 26, 2001, David Goss quotes local fisherman Jack Sweet about fishing at the Reversing Falls:

> "I grew up on the corner of Watson and Water Street. I fished the harbour mostly for shad and salmon. We'd go down by Murray Stackhouse's shed on Water Street. We'd lay there at slack water and take our turn … drifting down by the Hilyard's reef and out into the harbour. Then you'd take your net up and you'd go on the other side by Lord's wharf. Then you'd take your turn again, up and down. The first boat there got to go; if you got there before me, it was your turn. I'd give you space to get your net out. If someone cut in, it was called 'corking'. You'd do the same thing with salmon fishing. You never got entanglements among your nets. The only thing you had to watch was an old weir that stuck up only so far in the water. Your line might get caught and you'd lose your net. Sometimes, when the men would be waiting for the tide to turn, we'd be at Giggy Humphries in the calm water just below the Trading Post. The tourists at the Post would see us, and in those days they would come right down to the edge of the falls, into what we called Deadman's Cove, and sometimes we'd tell them a few stories."

## Salmon Catch, 1930

Cutch McCallum is carrying a salmon from his net located below the Trading Post on the west side of the Reversing Falls. A cross net over the top prevented seagulls from entering the net at low tide and feasting on the catch. Multiple species of fish, including shad, herring, gaspereaux, sea trout, sturgeon, cod, and pollock, were caught in the harbour and bay.

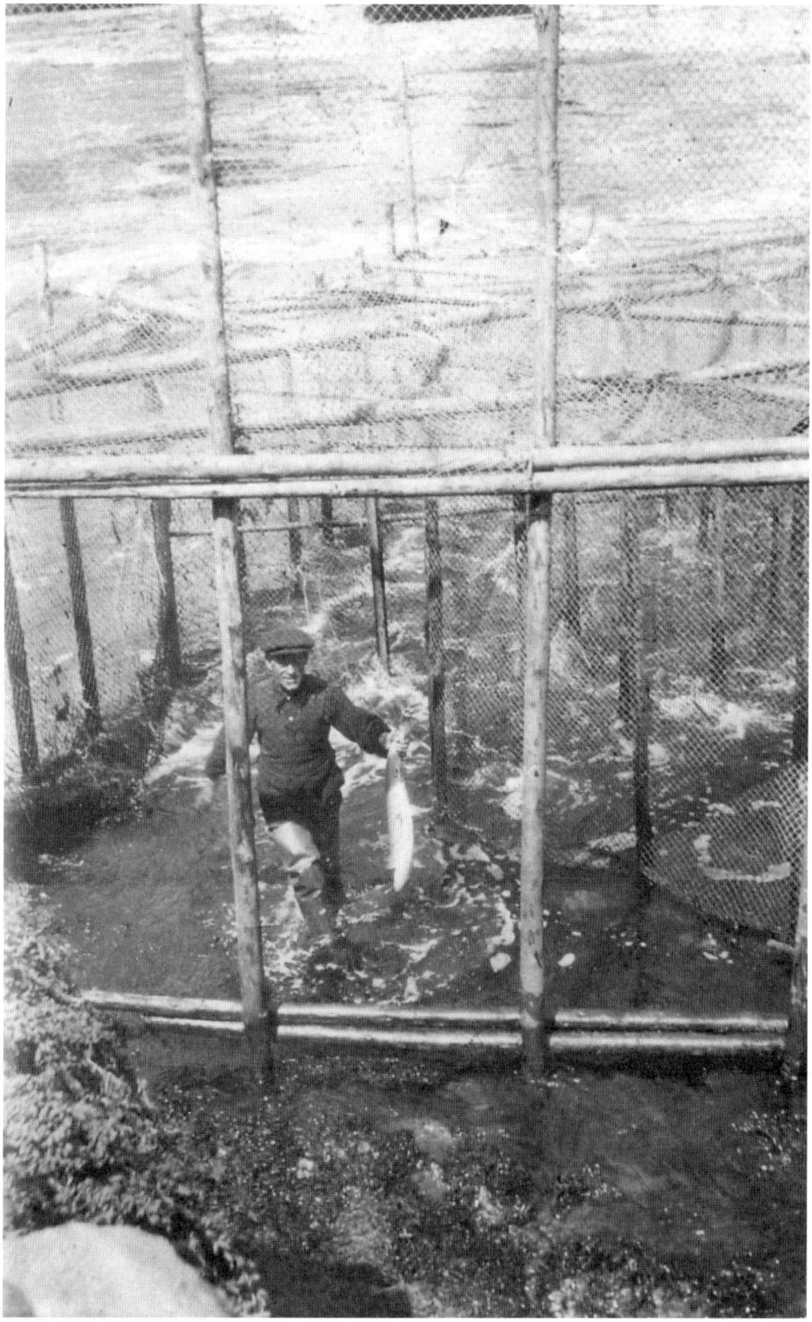

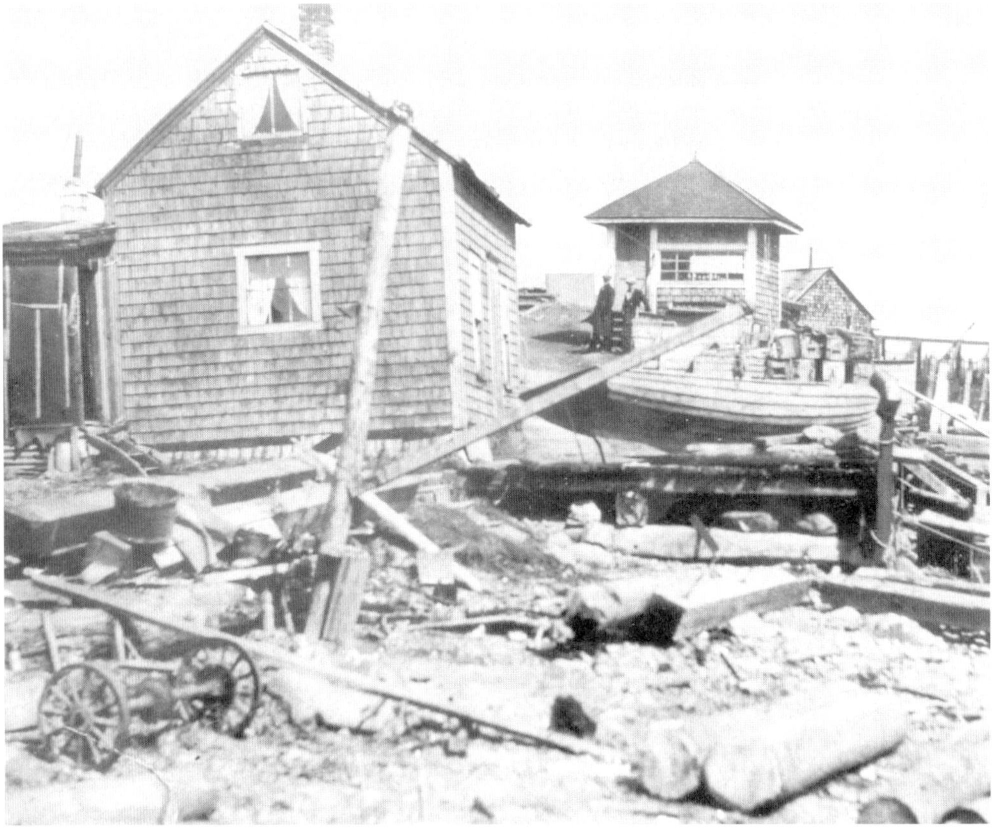

**NAVY ISLAND, 1930**

When De Monts and Champlain arrived here in June 1604 they saw Ouigoudi lined with high and small trees tied one against the other. In the centre was a large communal lodge, the council house for Chief Chkondun, who was buried on Ouigoudi. With the arrival of the Loyalists, the island became home to the fishermen. The 1785 charter for Saint John provided for the use of Navy Island by the Admiralty. This was transferred to the city of Saint John in 1835 for as long as the city made annual payments of 35 pounds sterling to the Madras School. The one provision was that the Admiralty could take possession of the island in times of war. In 1872 Francis Gills requested the use of Navy Island for a graving dock. There is an account of at least one ship being built and launched from Navy Island. When the photograph above was taken, Navy Island was covered with weather-beaten homes, such as Fred Lord's 75-year-old home of "three-inch deals on end…[and] … beaches strewn with fishing gear and traps, logs, big boats and little boats, rough jutting wharves, an atmosphere which belies that the island is really part of the city." In 1930 the National Harbours Board issued eviction notices to the eight families (forty-five people) then living on Navy Island. The families evicted were: Fred Lord and family, Amos Cogswell and wife, William Guthrie, Charles Lord and family, Roy Lord and family, James Donovan and family, Edward Bannan and family, and Stephen Benson and family. Within two years Buttermilk Channel was filled in and Navy Island became part of the west side docks.

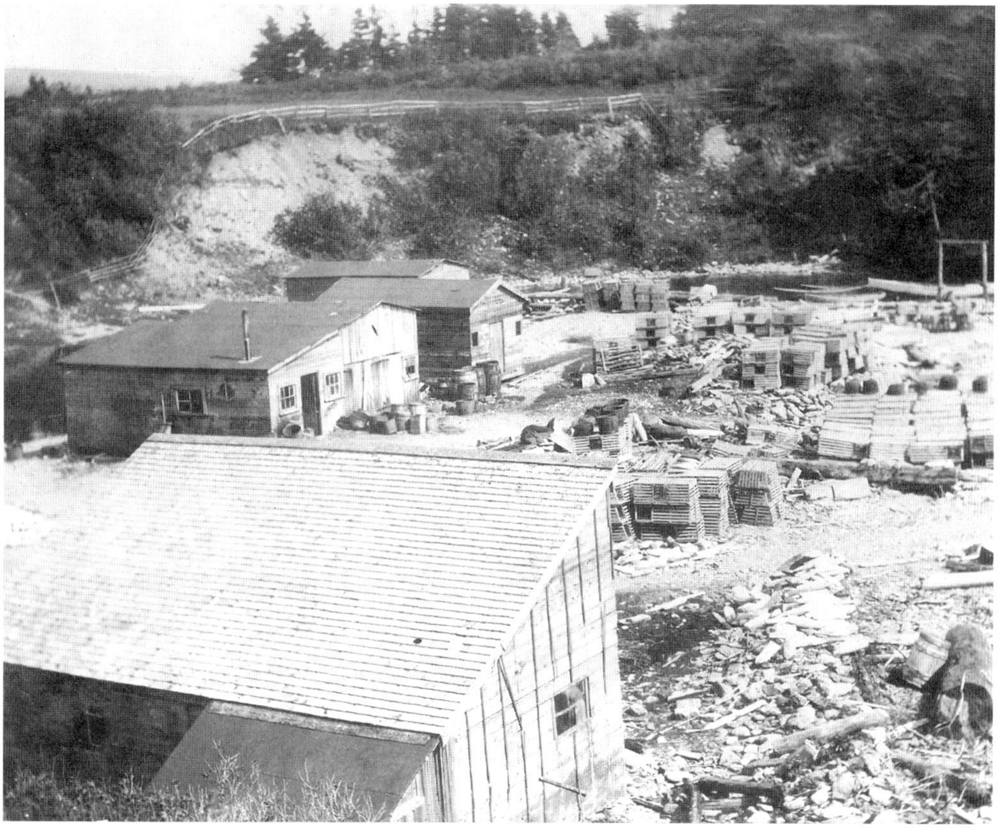

**THOMAS'S CREEK, JUNE 30, 1922**

This image of fishing sheds, lobster traps, and boats can be quite misleading. This photo, taken from an album of St. Martins photographs, is identified as Thomas's Creek. This appears to be MacCumbers Beach, where Huttges's canteen is located, but St. Martins residents Olive Hennessey (age 98), Miriam Davidson (age 85), and Barbara McIntyre have never heard of Thomas's Creek. Plus, lobster was not known to be fished from Mac's beach.

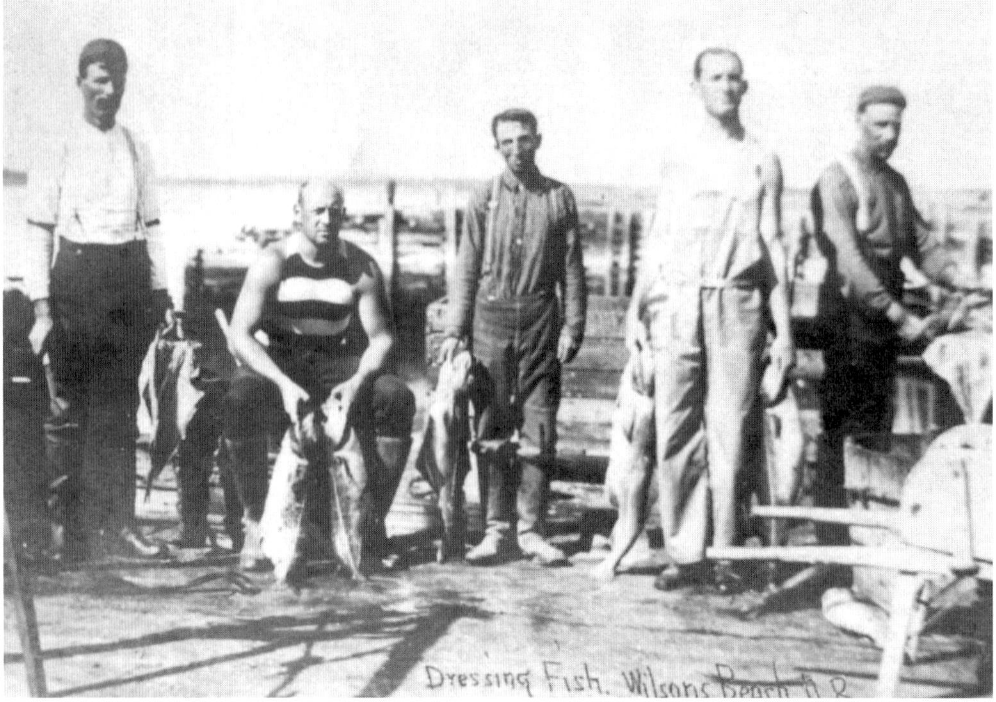


**Dressing Fish, Campobello Island, c.1910**

Cod are being dressed at Wilsons Beach by (left to right): James Brown, Dr. John Manning, Ollie Brown, Mr. Ayres from Baltimore, and Emmerson Brown. The island's first fish weir was erected in 1840 to trap herring. Hand-lining and trawl-fishing for groundfish continued to provide a living to many islanders. Fish-drying flakes and smokehouses still dot the shores from the time when the manufacture of wooden boxes for shipping fish was a significant industry.

**Charlotte County Fair, 1930**

TOP RIGHT

The Maple Leaf Hall at Wilsons Beach, Campobello was the scene of the annual fish fair. In the photo we see smoked cod, fish barrels, model boats, and ships' flags. The only person identified is Elmer Mitchell, at left.

**Riding a Fish, c.1932**

BOTTOM RIGHT

Is riding your tuna to the cannery a Maritime custom? Archie Leslie of Nor'west Harbour, Deer Island fished his entire life as had his father Alvah. The Bay of Fundy fishery is more than an industry, it is a way of life. Archie married Mabel Eaton, also of Deer Island, and they lived most of their lives on the island. Archie retired around 1967 and died in 1975; Mabel died in 1991. Both are buried at Mount Hope Cemetery on Deer Island. The children shown next to Leslie are cousins Lois Dunham and Elizabeth Leslie. The weir in the background was named 'Henry.' Did fishermen name their weir out of a sense of pride, ownership, or as an aid for navigation?

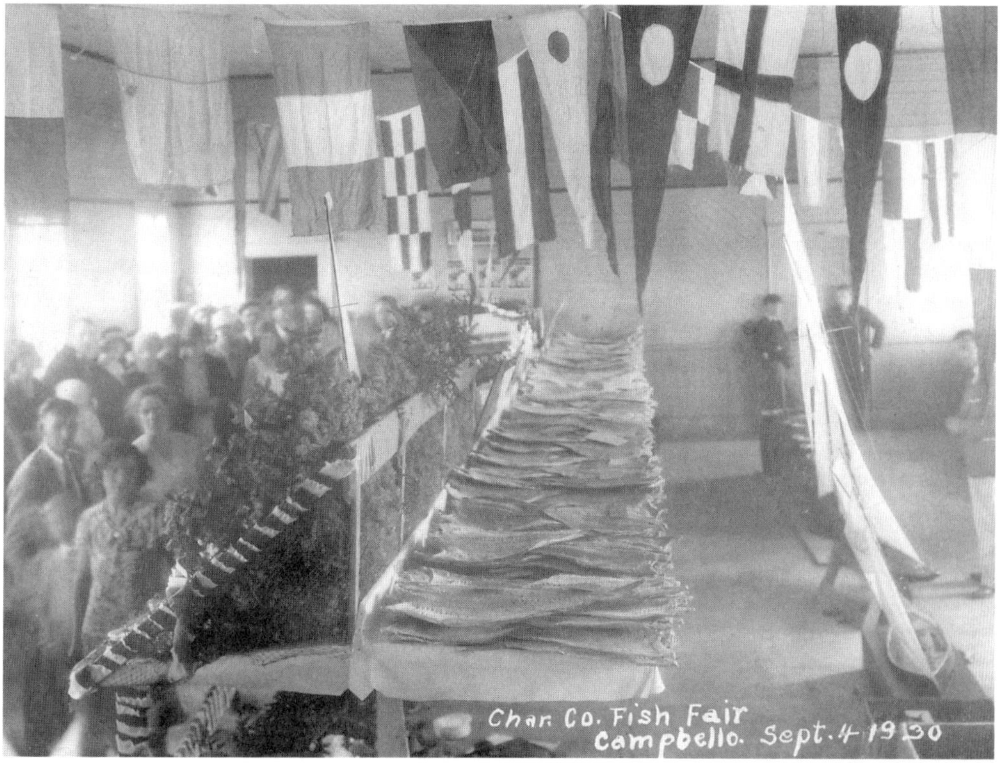


CHARLOTTE COUNTY FAIR (ABOVE) AND RIDING A FISH (BELOW)

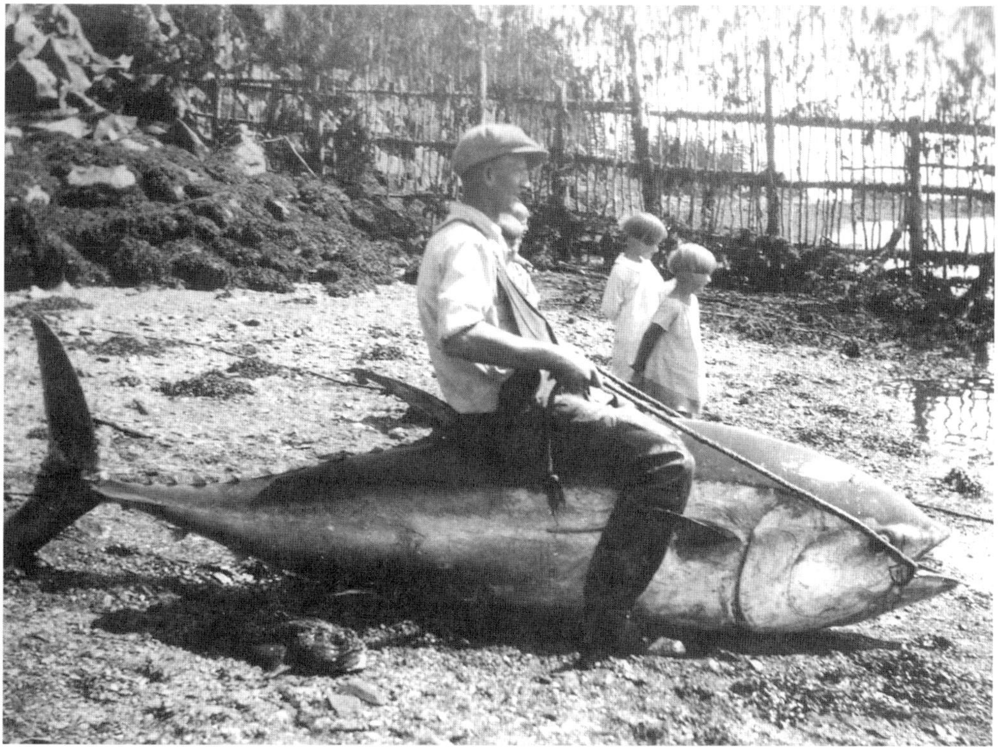

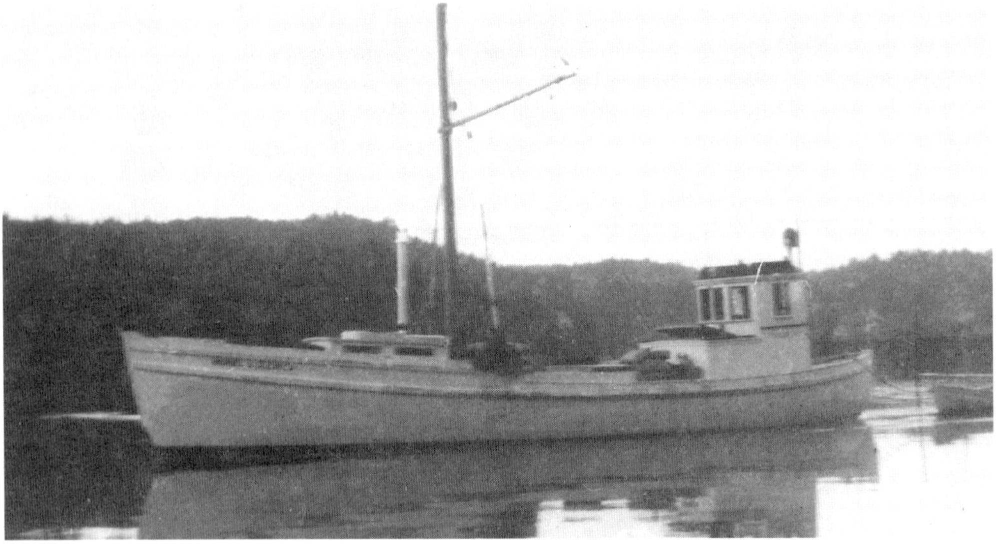

**Herring Carrier, c.1932**

The *Muriel & Glenita* was the boat Archie Leslie used until he retired. Then remodelled as a 50-foot cruiser and renamed the MV *Jojurogomi*, in 1975 she was offered for sale by its owners up the St. John River.

**Asa Brown, c.1930**

TOP RIGHT

In 1982, 90-year-old Asa Brown recalled that Morris Fletcher built the first of 25 boats that he used while he was a fisherman:"I went over and asked him, 'How much would you build me a boat for? I don't want one very big, I want her built 26-foot-long and 6-foot-wide.' He said, 'Oh, should be over a hundred dollars.' He built her and painted her. And I went over after and 'Well, now,' I said, 'You said it'd be over a hundred dollars. It don't want to be too damn much over a hundred dollars, cause I ain't got very much over a hundred.' Well, he said, 'I'm going to be as good as my word. A hundred and one dollars'."

**Jackson Brothers' Wharf, 1944**

BOTTOM RIGHT

This wharf scene was repeated at multiple coves and harbours along the Bay of Fundy. At Wilsons Cove the Jacksons operated a store and Imperial gas station, in addition to their fishplant. There are several people shown aboard the boats, including a woman and a boy. In 1945 this wharf and several boats were destroyed in a storm. The wharf was rebuilt in 1946.

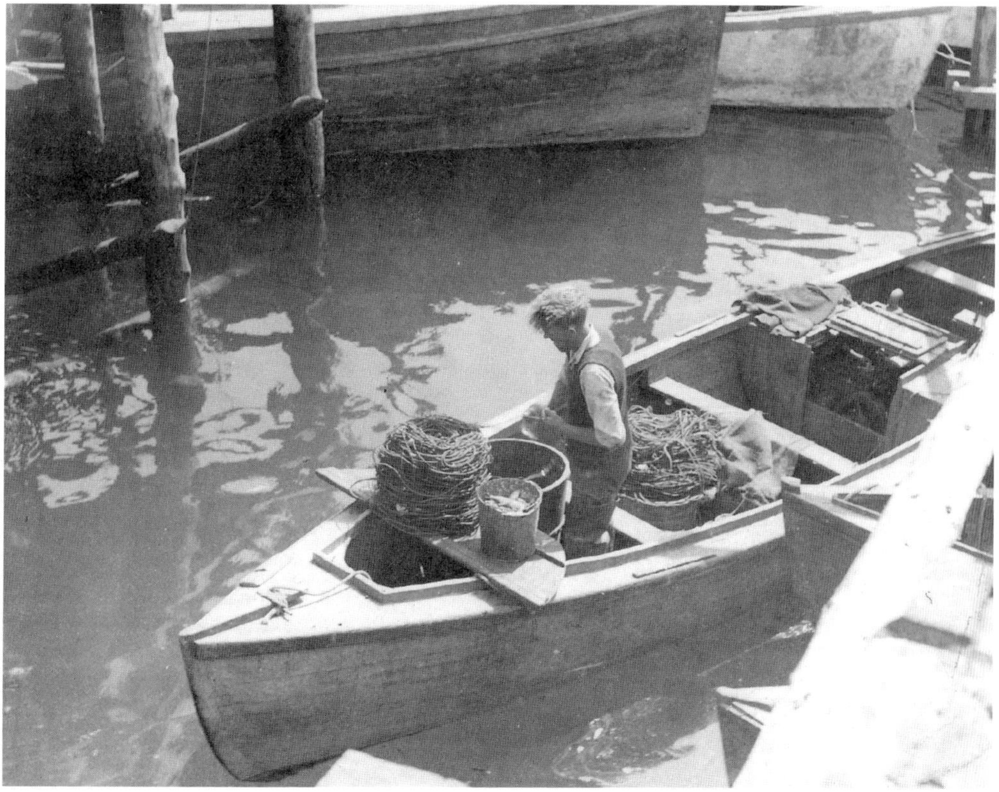

ASA BROWN (ABOVE) AND JACKSON BROTHERS' WHARF (BELOW)

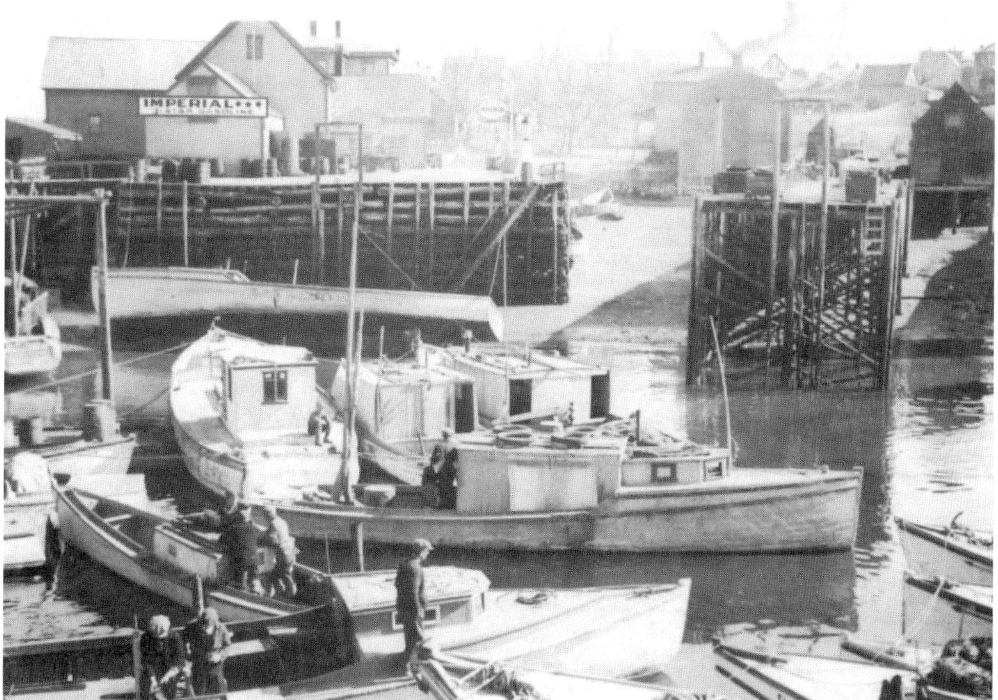

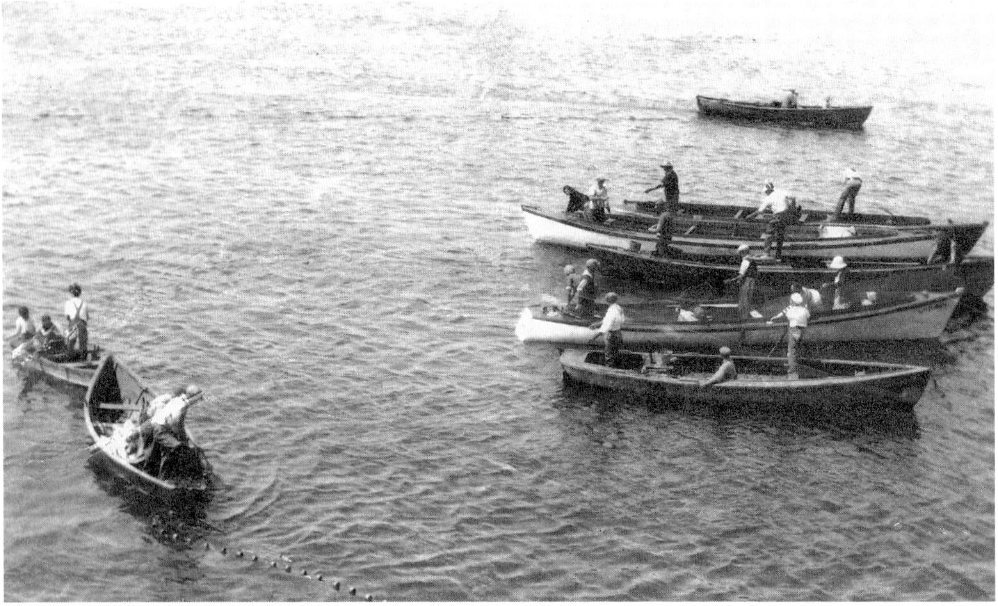

SEINING POLLOCK, CAMPOBELLO ISLAND (ABOVE) AND DRESSING COD AT JACKSON BROTHERS (BELOW)

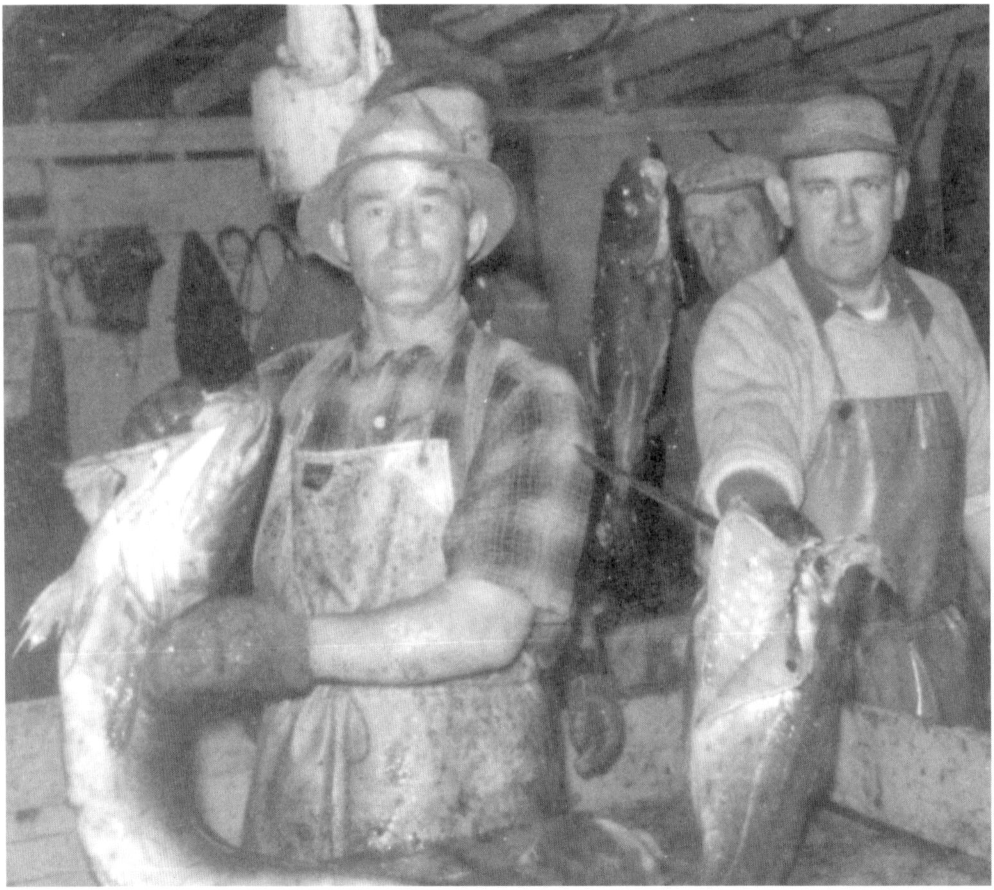

TOP LEFT

## Seining Pollock, Campobello Island, c.1930

The harvesting of pollock, lobster, scallops, clams, sea urchins, herring, cod, mackerel, and pen-raised salmon, and other fishing-related occupations remain the mainstays of Campobello's economy.

BOTTOM LEFT
AND BELOW

## Dressing and packing cod, May 1960

At Jackson Brothers in the photo at bottom left, Eldon Lank and Ralph Malloch, with Cal Tinker in the background, are shown dressing cod caught in the Bay of Fundy. Below, John Mitchell and Calvin Linkes are packing cod. Owned by Keith and Donald Jackson and their sister Margie Newman, Jackson Brothers closed in the fall of 2000. Cod is still hand-lined in the bay today.

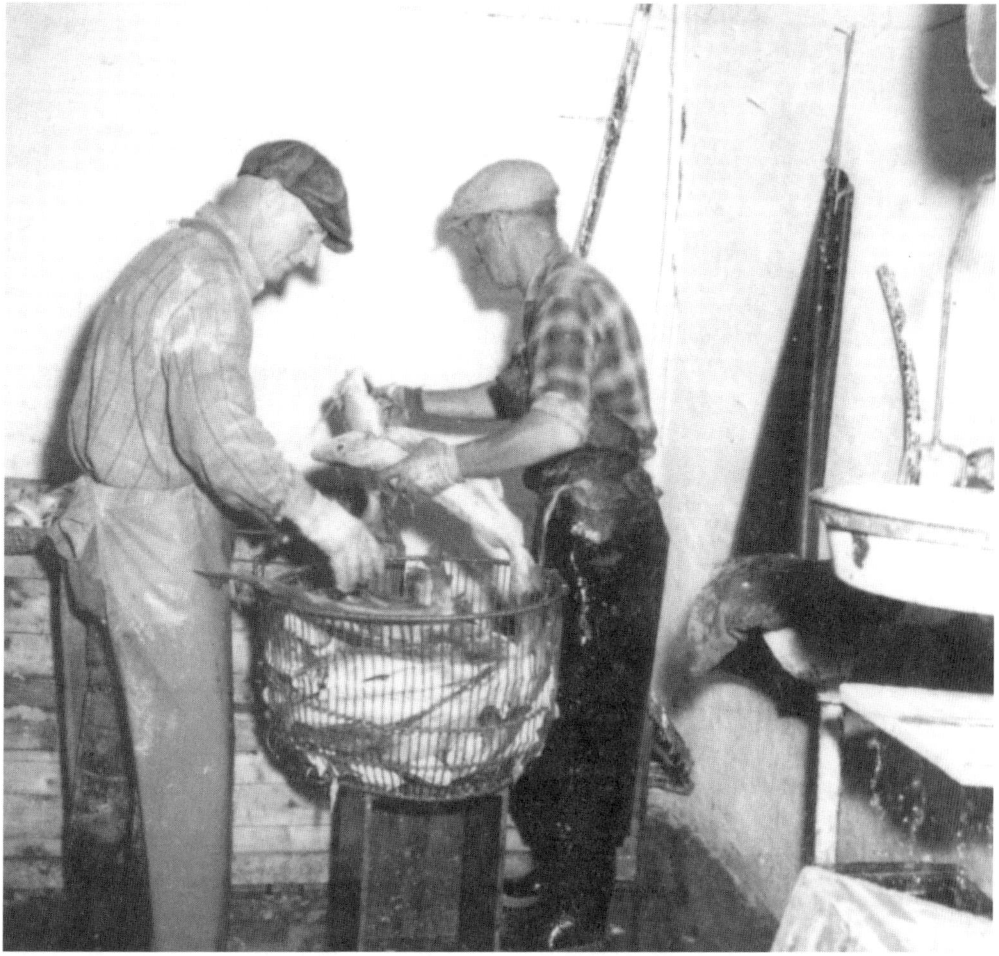

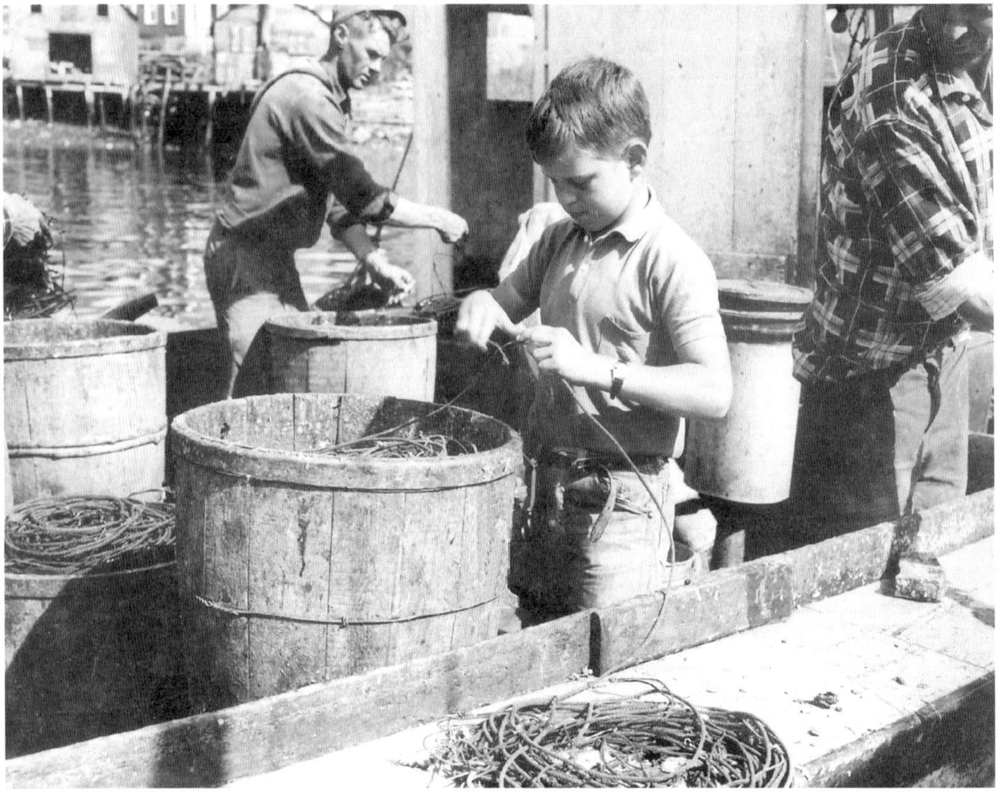

*HAZEL & MILDRED*, **1965**

Aboard the 45-foot line-trawler *Hazel and Mildred*, members of the Malloch family repair trawls before another trip. Douglas is in the foreground, his uncle Stewart is at left, and his father Whitman is on the right. Also aboard was his grandfather William and uncle Walter.

**COURTENAY BAY SARDINES, AUGUST 1954**

TOP RIGHT

Today many people think of Courtenay Bay as the place with the causeway, the Saint John Shipyard, the potash terminal, the fertilizer plant, or even the former location of an Irving Oil terminal. In 1963 the Irvings built the causeway for Saint John in exchange for reclaimed land to the north of the causeway. Few probably remember the herring runs into Courtenay Bay, as shown here when the "sardine fleet" invaded the bay. In 1910 the mudflats of this same bay were the site of Saint John's first airplane landing.

**MARKET SLIP, c.1953**

BOTTOM RIGHT

These fishing boats are now a thing of the past. Pollution, over-fishing, and physical changes to Market Slip and other areas of the port led to a decline in the number of people fishing the harbour and bay. At the end of North Market Slip a truck is dumping something into the harbour. The offices of Irving Oil were in the building at right. Today the only visible reminders of Saint John's once viable harbour fishing industry—a few fishing sheds—can be found on Riverview Drive.

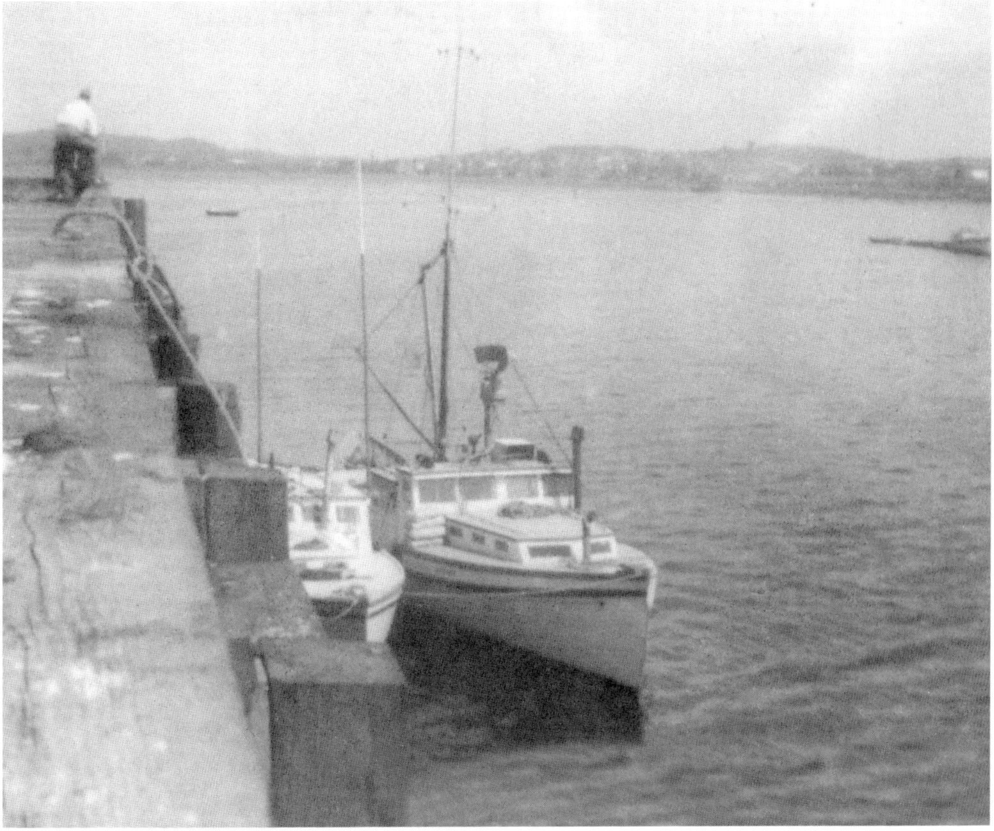

COURTENAY BAY SARDINES (ABOVE) AND MARKET SLIP IN SAINT JOHN (BELOW)

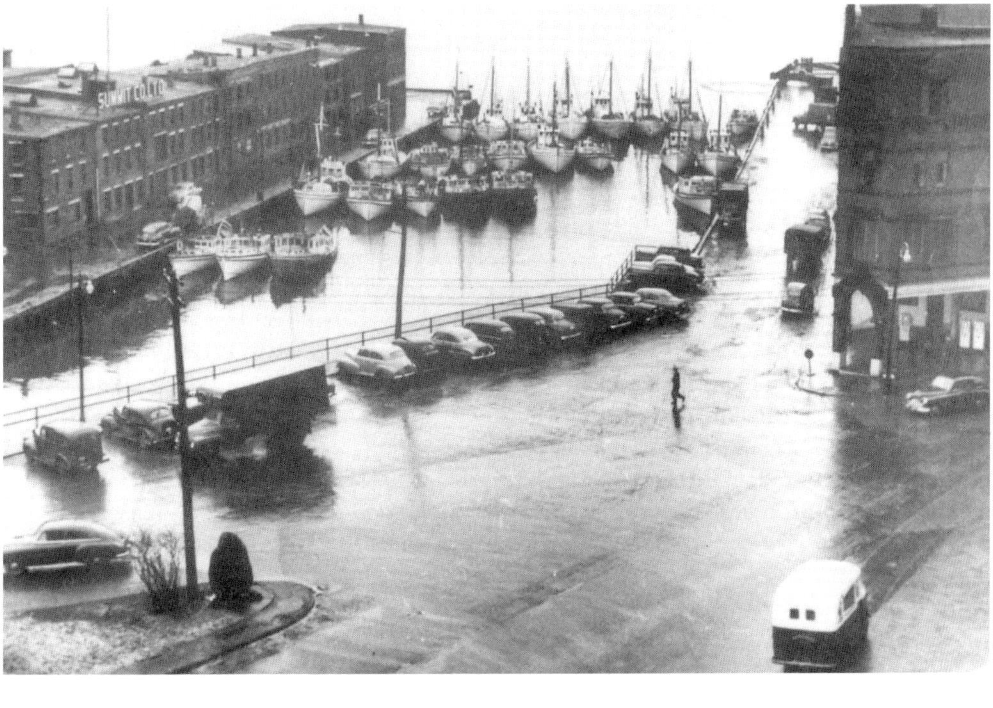

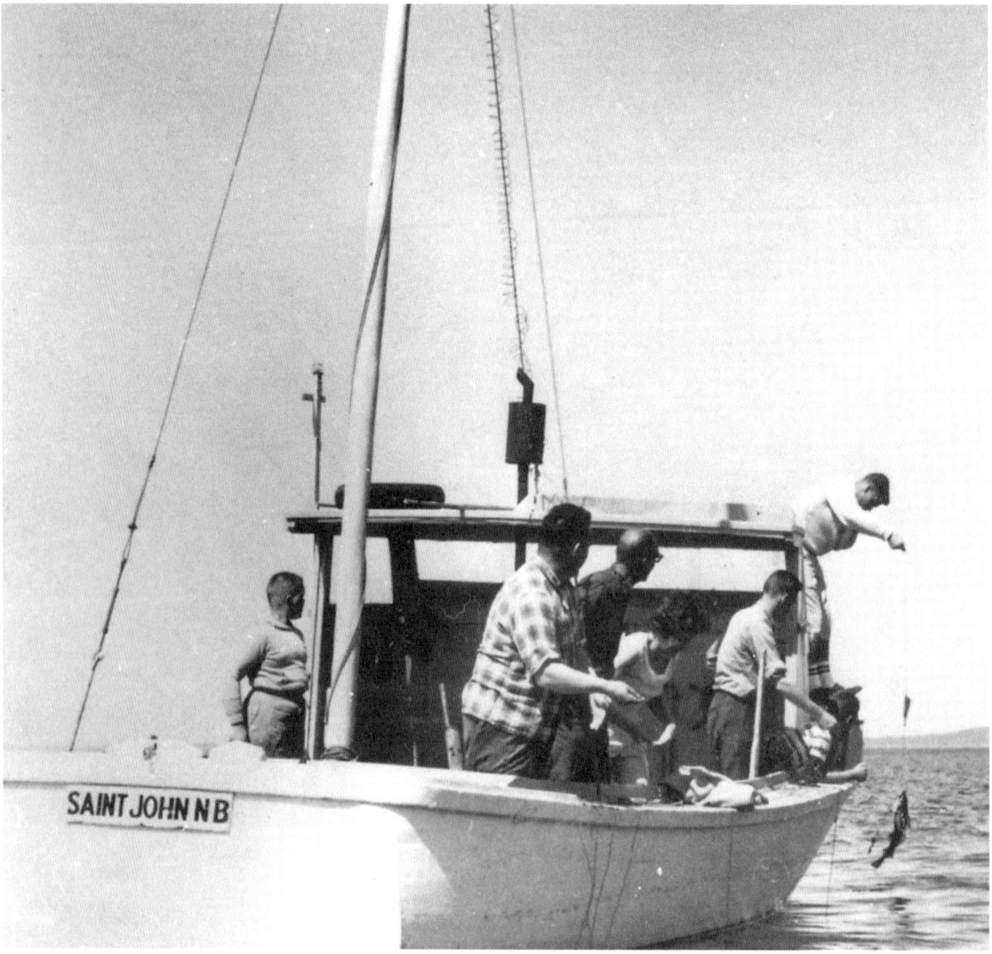


**Recreational fishing, c.1955**

A growing tourist industry after World War Two did not neglect the possibilities of Bay of Fundy fishing. In 1947 the local newspaper wrote: "Our harbor is colorful and holds unlimited appeal, particularly for inlanders. We don't capitalize on this fact, have not set aside spots from which they can view the harbor from pleasant surroundings, have no boat on which they can tour the harbor and perhaps go out around Partridge Island. Within a few miles of Saint John there is lots of deep sea fishing—but nobody here makes a business of taking out deep sea fishing parties. Similarly, a vacationist who is staying in the city has difficulty finding a day's fresh water angling without travelling too far away, unless he happens to have friends to show him where to go. We have not earmarked any handy lakes or streams for persons with non-resident anglers' licenses." Today, tourism promotes whale watching and adventure activities such as kayaking.

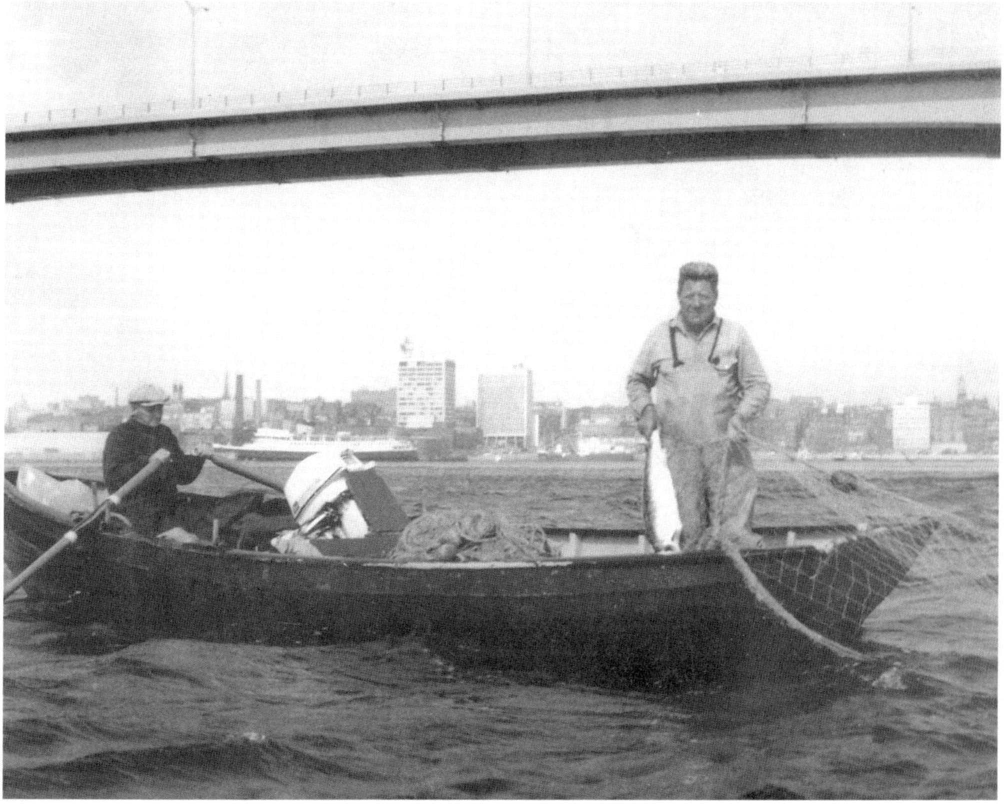

**Salmon mystery, 1970**

In 1971 the New Brunswick Publishing Company used this photo for their company calendar. Murray 'Mousie' Gray is shown manning the oars and his partner Walter 'Squeeze' McGuire is holding the salmon. If you look closely, you will see that the salmon has no head. Fishing was not good that day, so the men resorted to buying a salmon from the City Market for this pose. Salmon fishing is a thing of the past for Saint John Harbour, although the occasional salmon is still caught—by accident! In this view the Harbour Bridge had just been built, and, in the background, the new city hall can be seen. The *Princess of Acadia* is shown at her old slip.

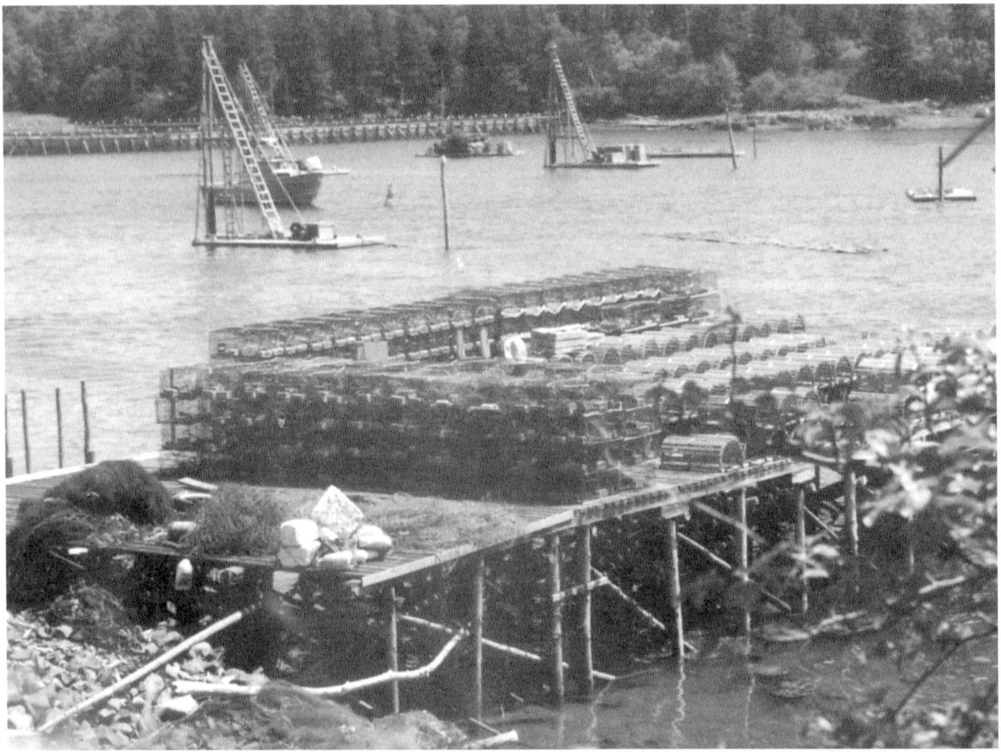

**Leonardville, Deer Island, 1999**

Here lobster traps—both metal and wood—have been readied for another season. Lobster remains a vital part of the Bay of Fundy fishery. For over two hundred years, Fundy fishermen have caught lobster for both domestic and international markets. In 1929 the *Fundy Fisherman* of Blacks Harbour carried this article: "Lobster of Many Colors Caught at Marblehead—Joseph's proverbial coat of many colors has nothing on an alleged member of the lobster family that was caught Tuesday by Ralph Connors, Marblehead lobster fisher. Oldtimers who gathered en masse to examine the strange fish vow that never in their long and varied careers have they gazed on such an oddity. Blue and gray featured the queer find." This northern lobster was photographed in Cobscott Bay by Shelly Corey of World Beneath Photos in Maine.

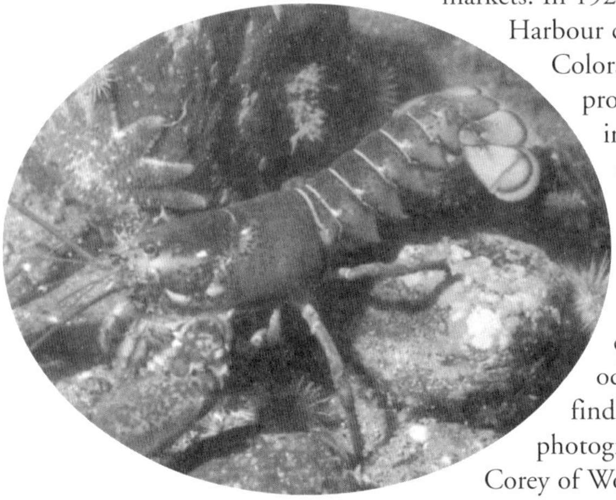

*Chapter 9*

# *Pleasurable Pursuits*

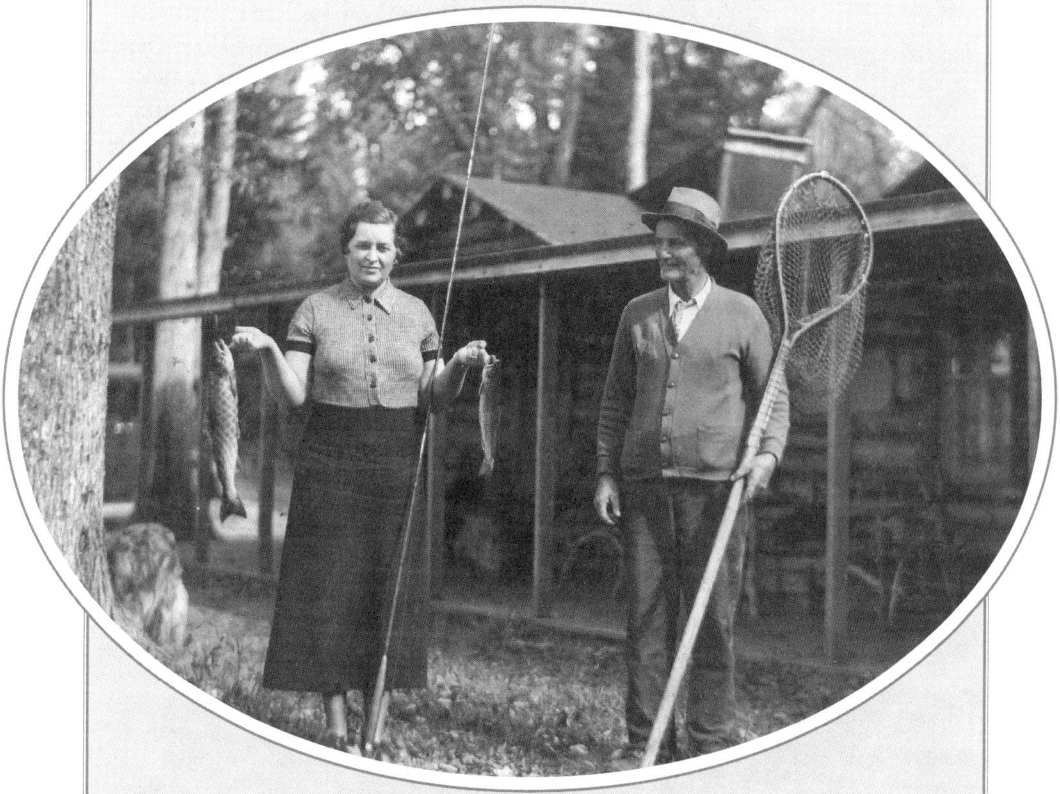

**GUIDE AND FISHING CAMP, C.1920**

Since the mid-nineteenth century, New Brunswick advertised itself as a sportsman's paradise for both fishing and hunting. Trout and salmon were the two species promoted for recreational fishing. The American market has always been the focus for much of the twentieth-century tourist advertising. Several generations of New Brunswickers have made their livelihoods as guides or lodge owners.

## Blue Rock, 1906, (below) and McLaren's Beach, 1894 (bottom)

Leslie and Margaret Green stand on the rocks at Bluc Rock Beach. In the 1890s a popular seaside attraction was developed at the base of Blue Rock Hill, alternately known as Blue Rock or Beatteay's Beach but by 1914 the area had disappeared because of port expansion. The Green girls were daughters of Herbert Green of 51 Mecklenburg Street, manager of R.H. Green and Sons, Germain Street engravers and printers. Further along the shore by Duck Cove was McLaren's Beach, shown in the photo below. These men are probably having a clambake. McLaren's once had several cottages (some shown in the background), two canteens, changing rooms, and, until the 1950s, a bus service. The last canteen was destroyed in the 1976 Groundhog Day gale.

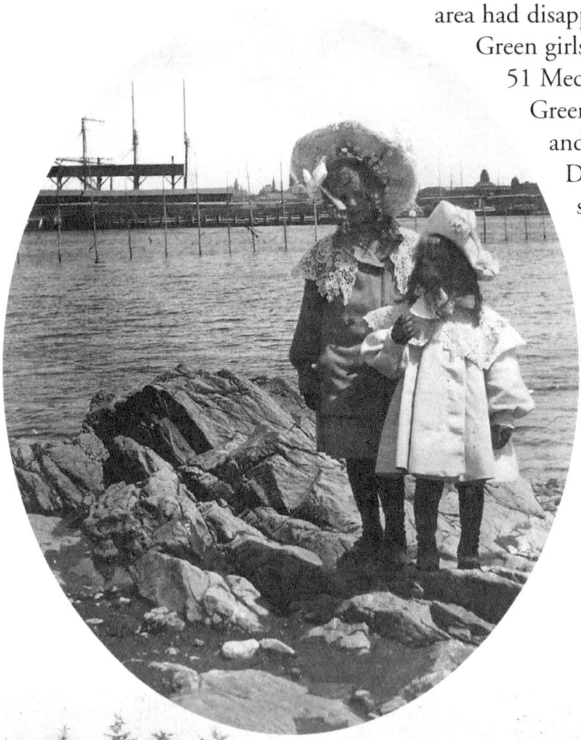

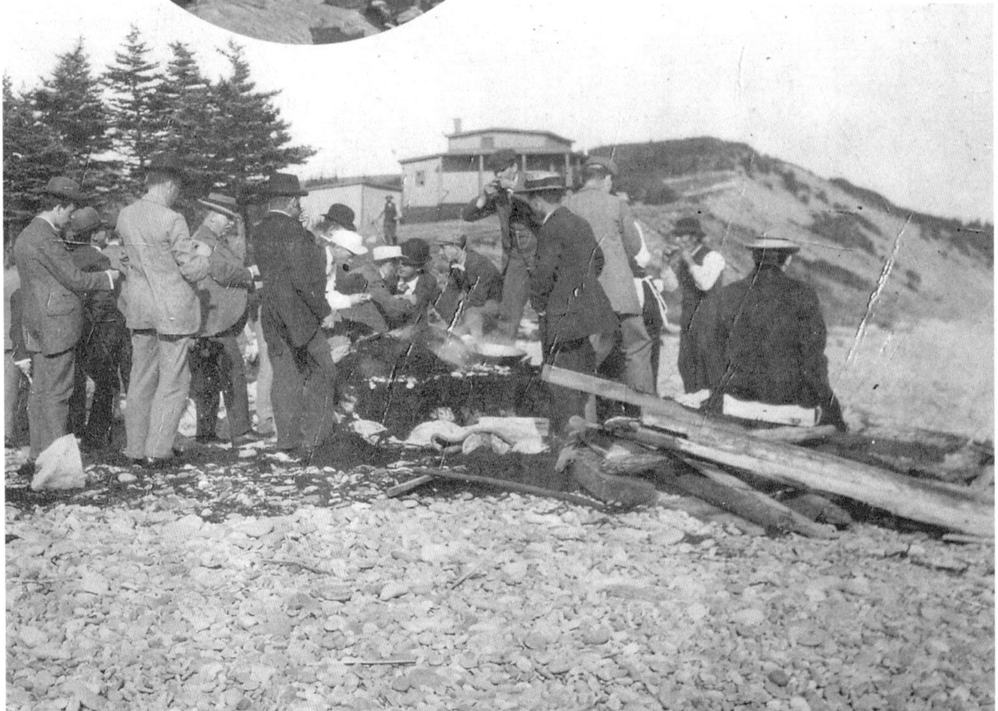

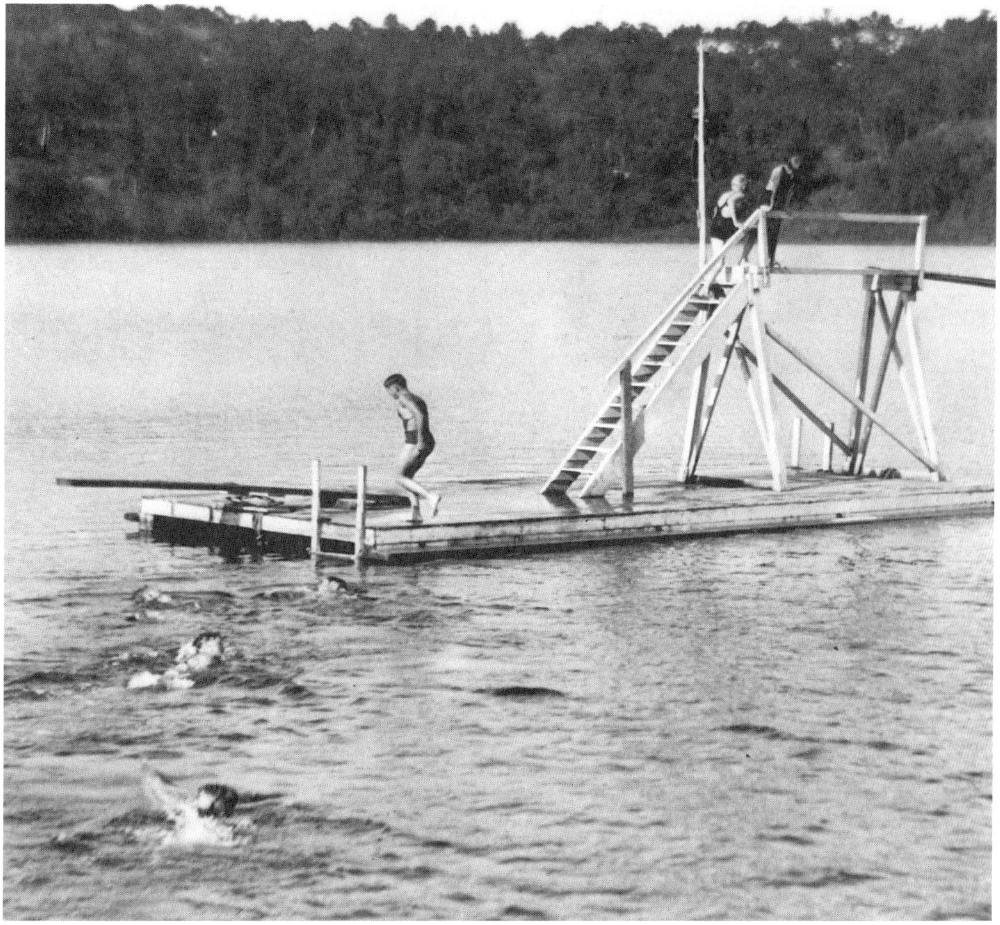

**Lily Lake Swimming, c.1920**

In 1899 Downing Vaux, the landscape architect who designed New York's Central Park, prepared a development scheme for Rockwood Park. Included were plans for riding and walking trails, an arboretum, a zoo, fishing, boating, and skating, but no plan for swimming because Saint John locals and visitors have been swimming at Lily Lake since before the 1830s.

## Captain Arthur W. Hilton, 1904

Captain Hilton of Yarmouth, Nova Scotia was master from 1889 until 1904—a time when it was common for shipmasters to take their families on extended voyages. Captain Hilton (middle) is shown here with some friends at Cartageina, on the southeast coast of Spain, and below with his daughter Marion aboard the *Abysinnia*. The bark *Abysinnia,* at 1,127 registered tonnes, was built in Saint John in 1885 by Oliver Pitfield. She sailed under the Taylor Brothers Fleet, who sold her in 1904 to Italian owners.

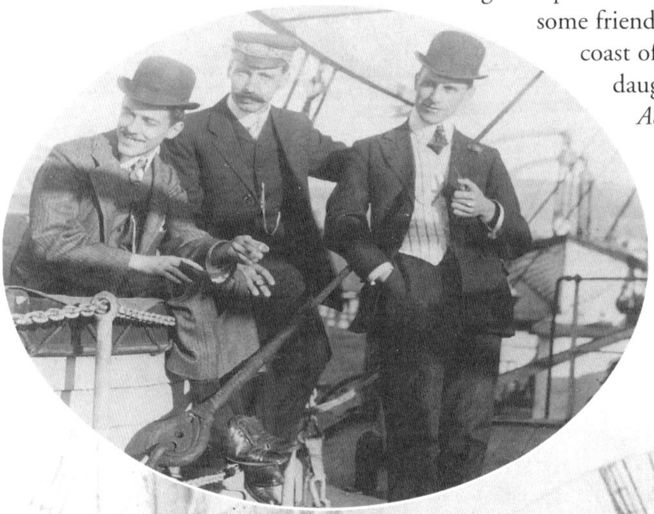

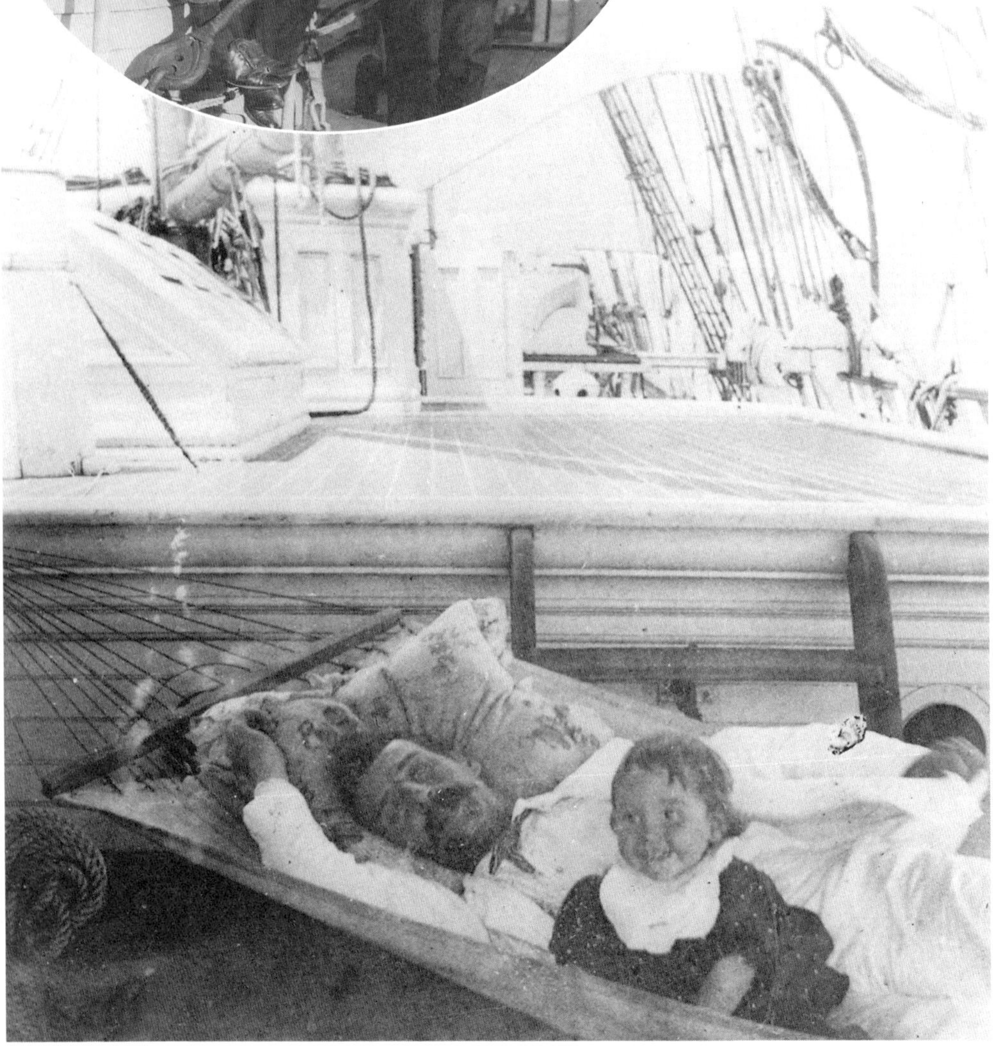

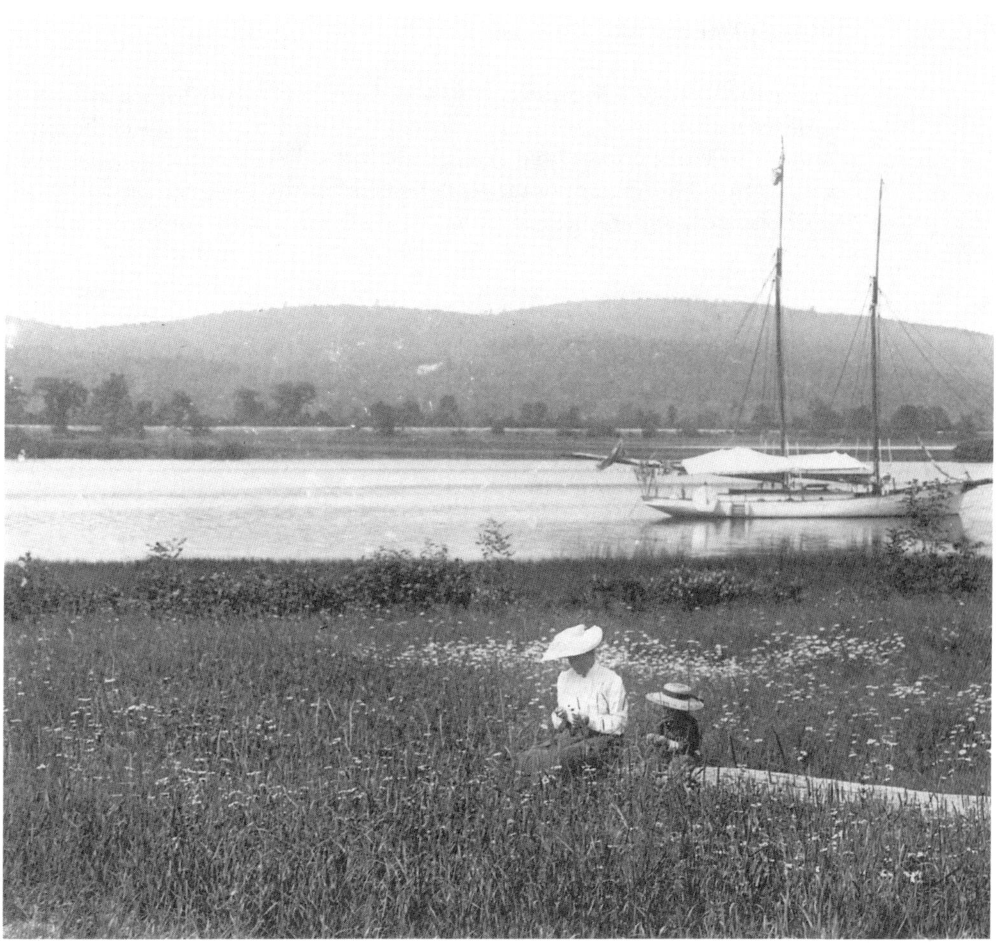

**Along Kennebecasis River, c.1920**

In 1998 Virginia (Lynch) Dunbrack recalled what life was like on the rivers in the 1920s and 1930s: "The river, which served for many years as a commercial waterway, is now used mostly by pleasure craft, except for small car ferries, which in some locations are still the only way to get either yourself or your car across the river." She also said, "Having lived in Saint John most of my life except for a few years away, I feel that I, and my fellow citizens of this city, are very fortunate to have access to both the fresh water of the river, and the salt water of the Bay of Fundy—and as the icing on our cake, we even have some fresh water lakes right within the city limits—What more could a person ask?"

## Girls camping and fishing, c.1920

In the 1920s, Edith Kees, who later married Gordon G.K. Holder, was actively involved with St. James Anglican Church in the south end. The girls in the photos here are believed to be from that church, with Edith in the group, on a canoe trip. During this trip some of the girls dressed in "native costume," possibly in an early twentieth-century attempt to understand how Mi'kmaq women lived. On the fishing expedition shown at bottom the girl at the right is the only one with a proper fishing rod; the others are using alder branches as poles. The male guide is holding a trout.

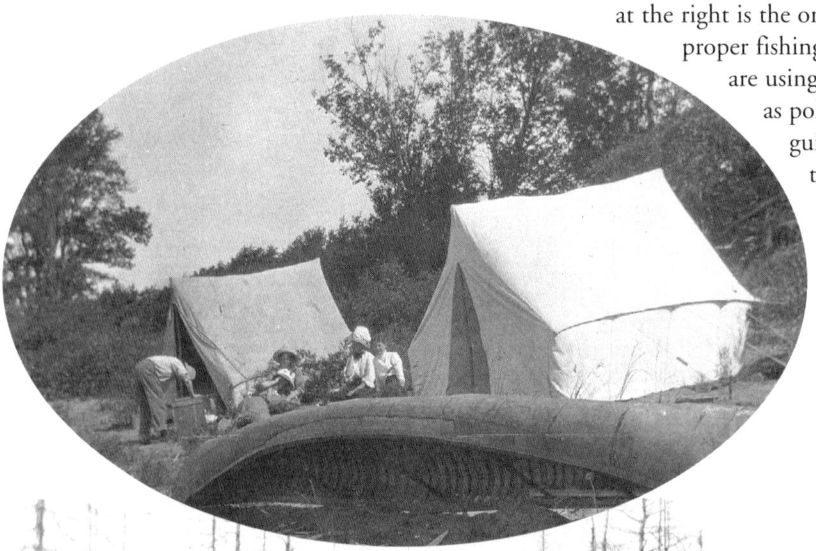

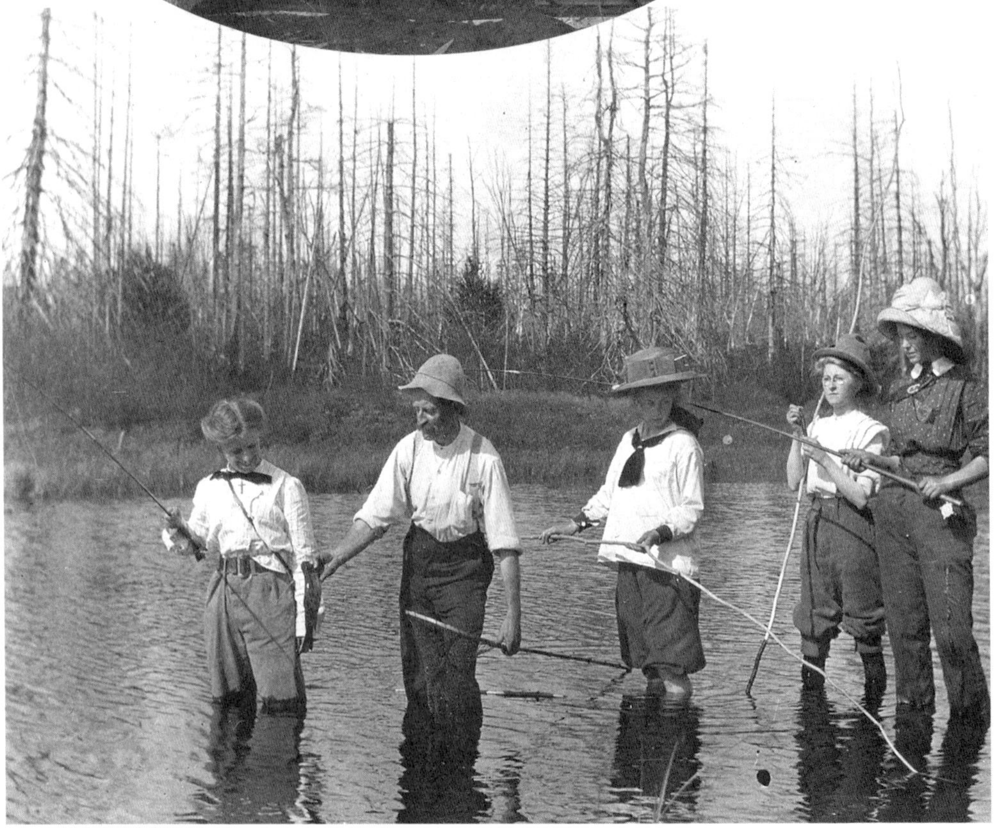

## First Fish, Little River, 1962

Growing up in the Rifle Range in the early 1960s provided ample angling opportunities for Harold Wright (below) and his father Doug. At six, Harold's first fishing trip was to Dark Lake in Rockwood Park. Subsequent trips were to Long Lake and Little River near the fish hatchery. This is Harold's first trout, at over a pound, caught in Little River downstream from the fish hatchery.

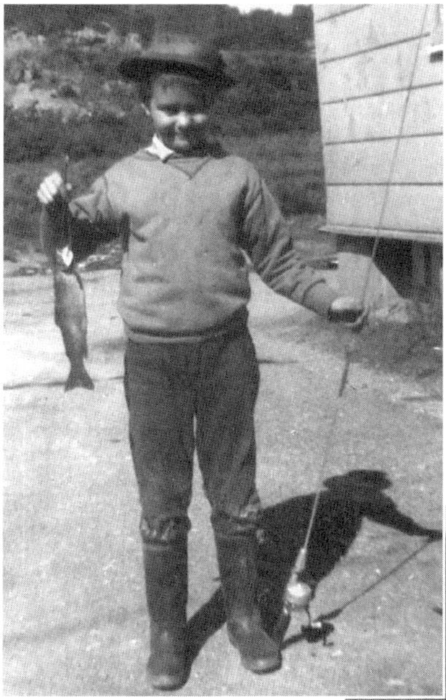

## Gondola Point, 1974

Generations of New Brunswickers have spent weekends and summers at the cottage. For many years Everett and Mae Robertson owned a cottage in Gondola Point, where friendly neighbours and the convenience of beach rights on the Kennebecasis River made for enjoyable times. Their daughters Deborah, pictured below, and Gail spent many hours in the water and on the beach, enjoying respite from the hot, humid weather.

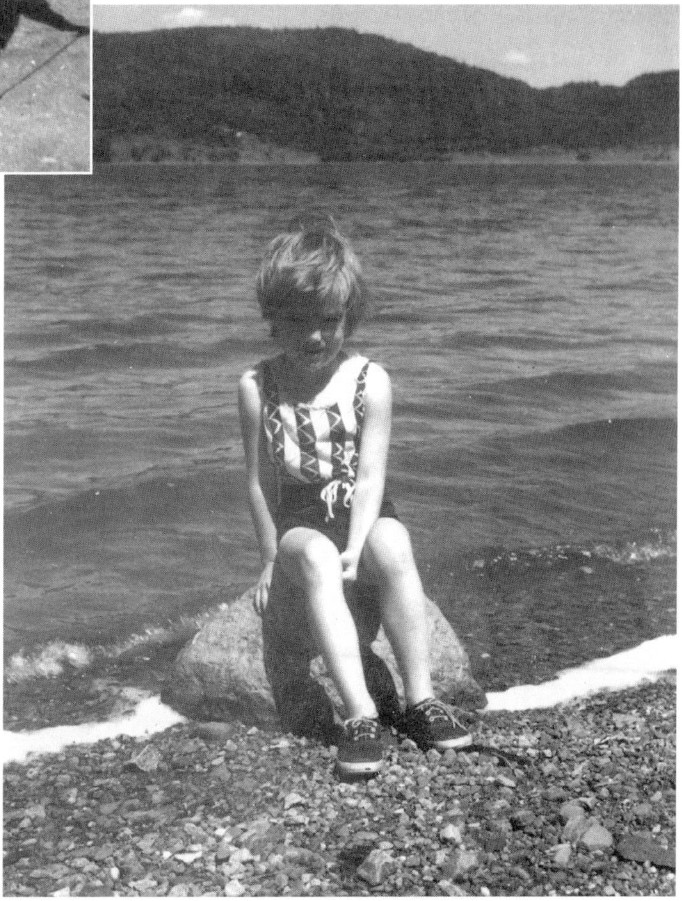

HAROLD WRIGHT OF HOWARD COURT (ABOVE) AND DEBORAH ROBERTSON AT GONDOLA POINT (RIGHT)

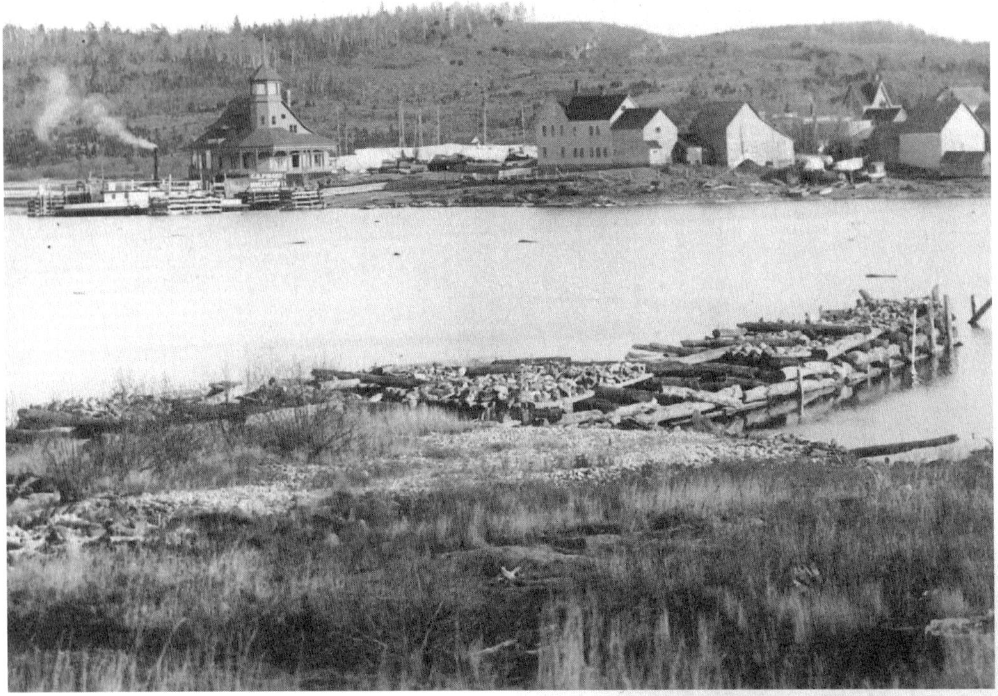

THE NEW CLUBHOUSE OF THE ROYAL KENNEBECASIS YACHT CLUB, C.1910 (ABOVE) AND A YACHT RACE C.1920 (RIGHT)

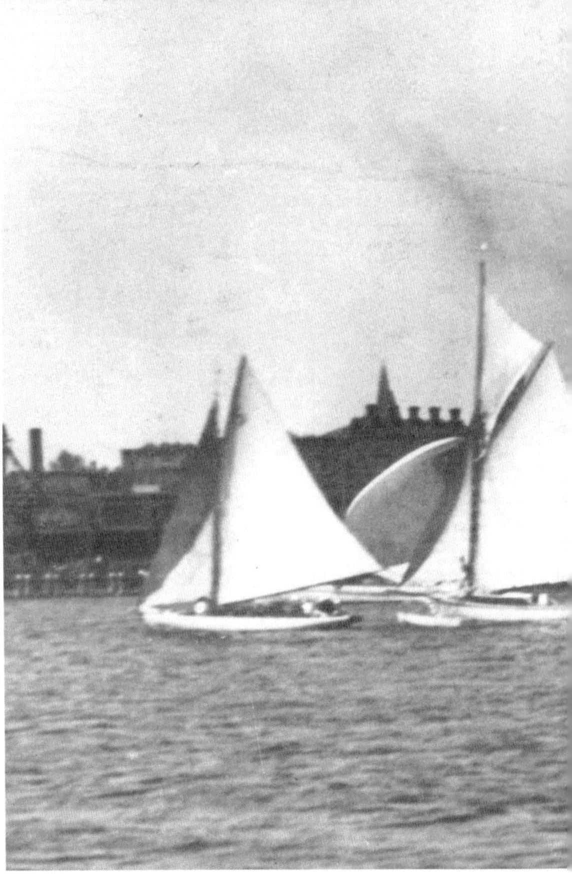

## Royal Kennebecasis Yacht Club, c.1910, and Yacht Race, c.1920

The Royal Kennebecases Yacht Club (RKYC) was formed in 1894 and received its royal charter in 1898. The new clubhouse was opened in August 1901. Designed by prominent local architect F. Neil Brodie and built by John Duffy, the building was "the most commanding structure in the suburban hamlet, and the one architectural feature of that locality." The original exterior finishes were light-green-coloured siding with deep-red roof trim, lattice-work and dark-green trim. The ferry *Maggie Miller* is shown arriving at her slip at the foot of Millidge Avenue. The RKYC has for decades held river, harbour, and bay races with a trophy and bragging rights as the prize. The vessels below are entering the inner harbour just past the sugar refinery.

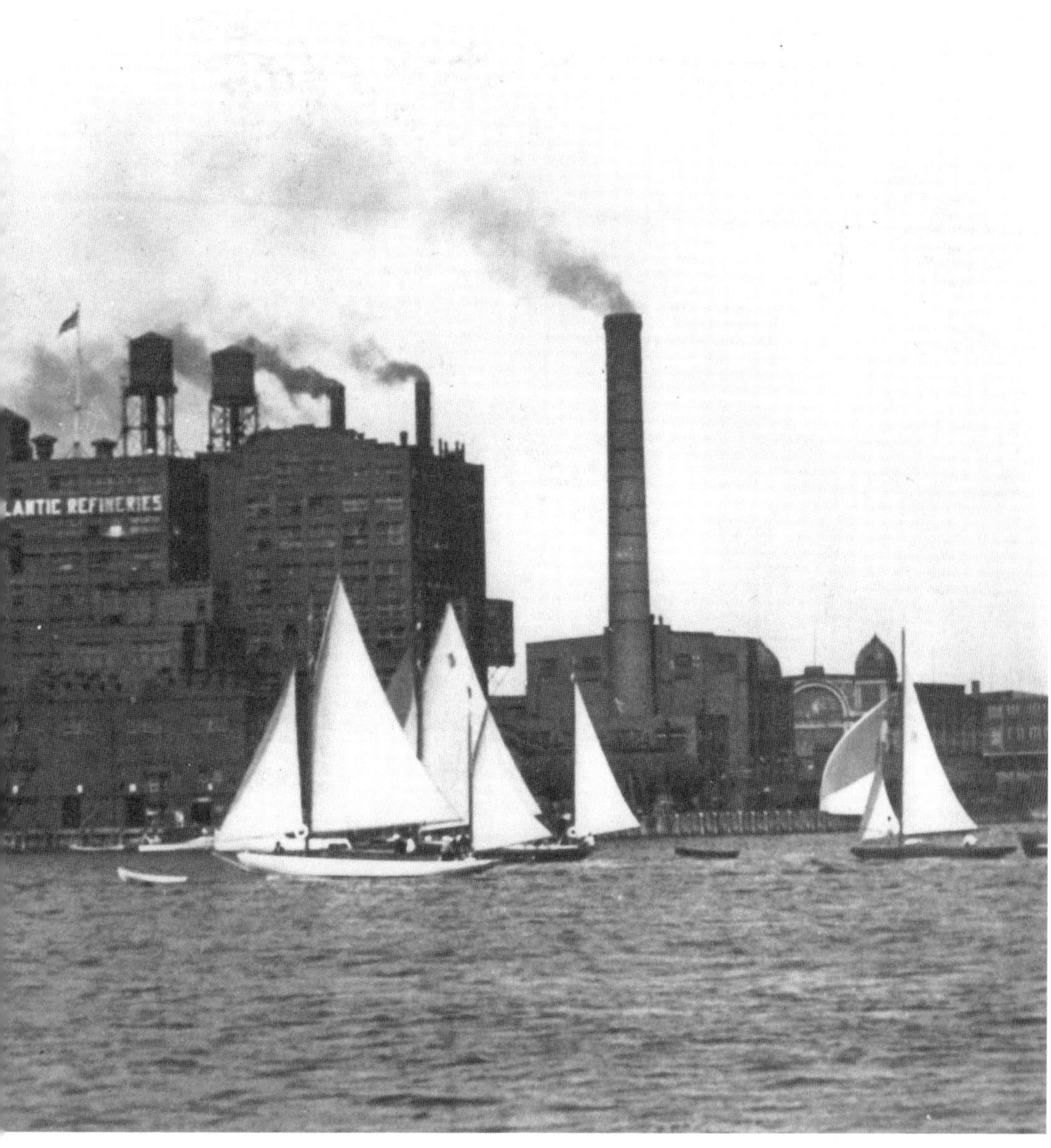

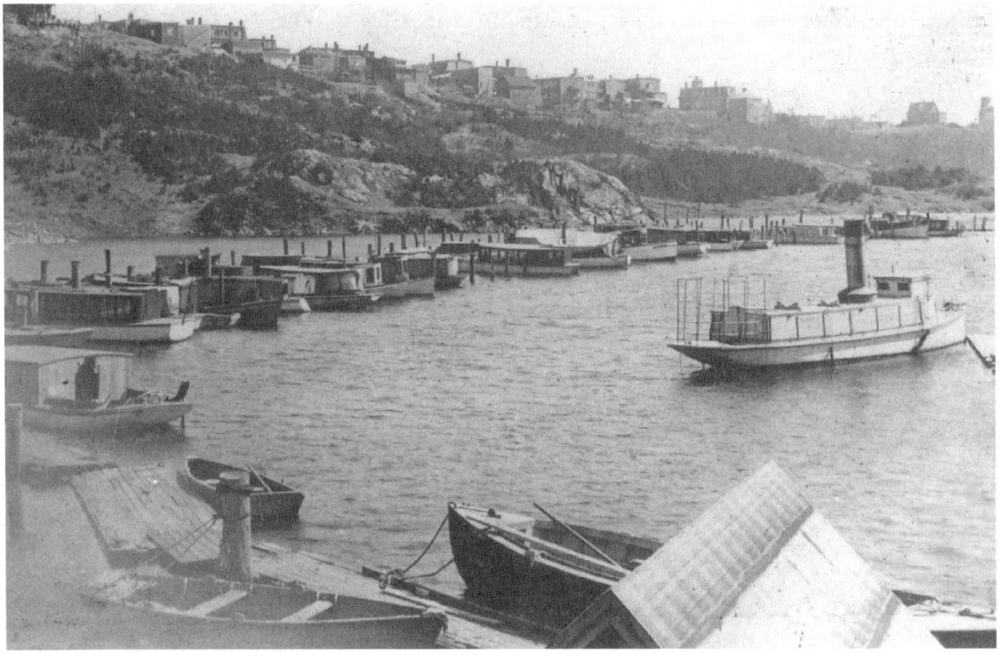

**MARBLE COVE, c.1930**

The Saint John Power Boat Club was founded in April 1910, and its first commodore was S.P. Gerow. The clubhouse was on Cedar Street. Since July 1911, the club has held annual cruises upriver or down the bay. The first cruise was to St. Andrews and Passamaquoddy Bay. A favourite was a cruise to Belyeas Point.

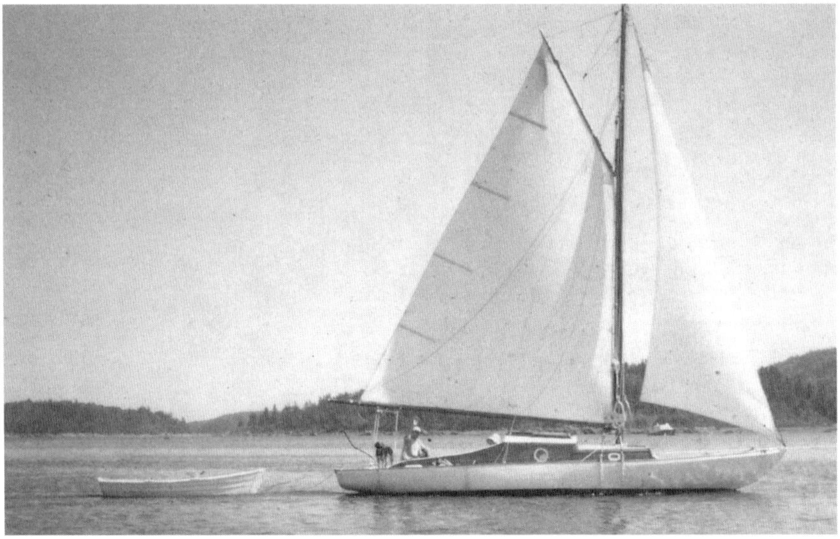

***SAVITAR*, c.1950**

The sloop rig *Savitar* was built in Boston in 1895 by the Fore River Engine Company. Designed by C.C. Hanley of Boston, the sloop's original owner was William Lovitt of Yarmouth. The sloop's rigged sail area was 750 square feet, overall length was 32 feet, the beam was 10 feet, and she registered net 3.45 tonnes. Colonel Gordon G.K. Holder is shown here at the tiller.

### *Ethel M.*, c.1950, and Belyeas Point, c.1935

Fred J. Watts (front row, second left) was skipper of the *Ethel M.* Pictured are executives of Air Canada on their way to Crystal Beach. The boat was sold to an owner in Maine before 1975. Below, The Carleton Cornet Band, under Bandmaster Thomas Lanyon, played for members of the Saint John Power Boat Club for many of their annual cruises.

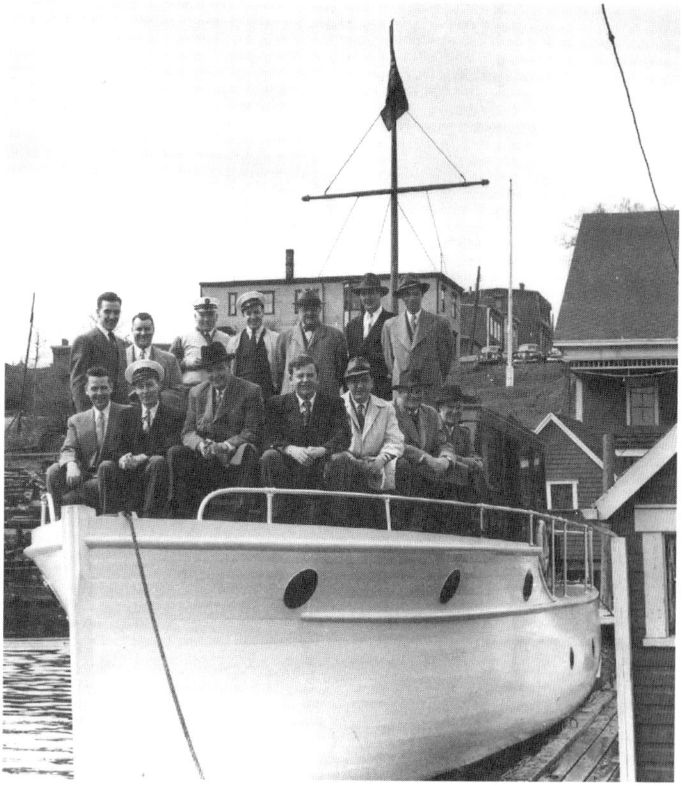

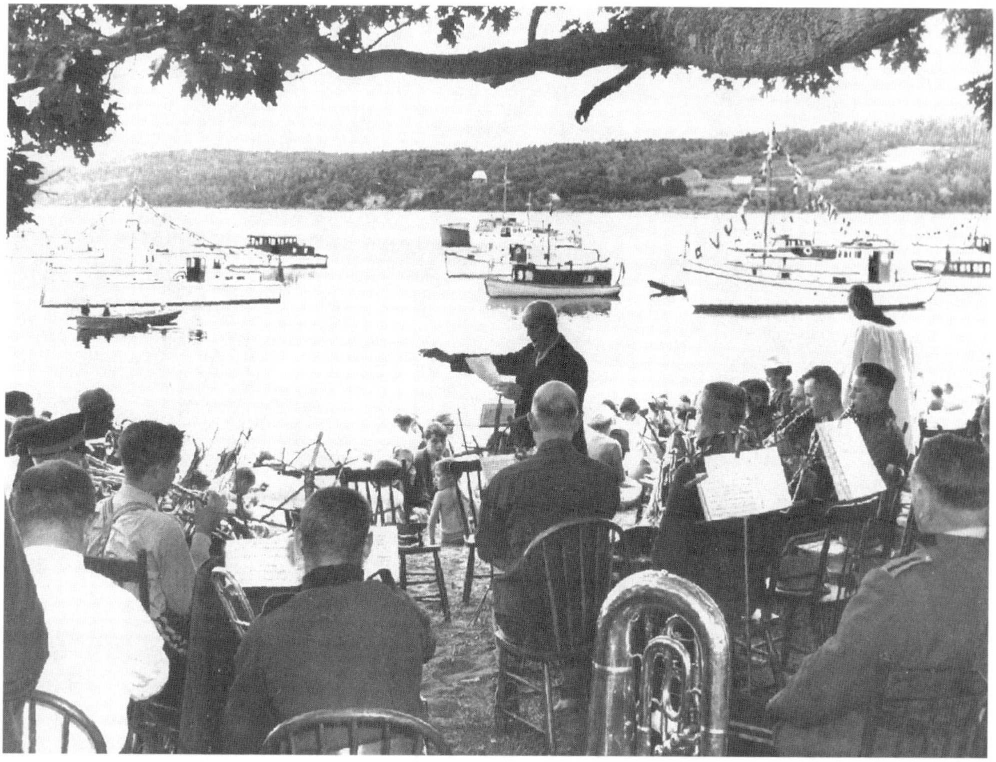

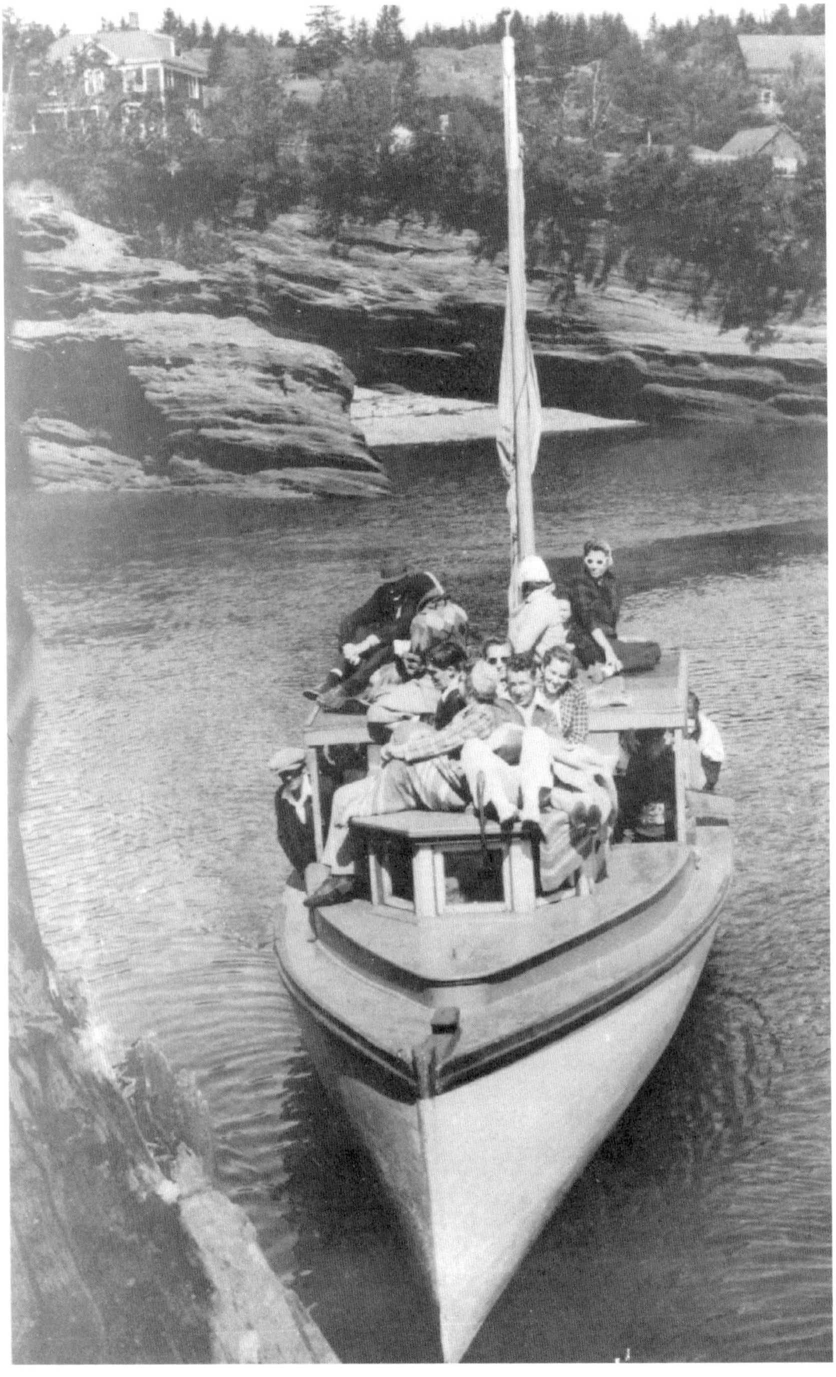

**St. Martins, c.1939**

This may be Bill Holland's boat near Echo Cove just within the Quaco Harbour breakwater. Some of the people on the boat are Otis McLeod, Maurice McIntyre (who later became a well-known Saint John schoolteacher), Crena Allen, and Harry Pibus (who was killed during World War Two).

## Chapter 10

# *Immigration*

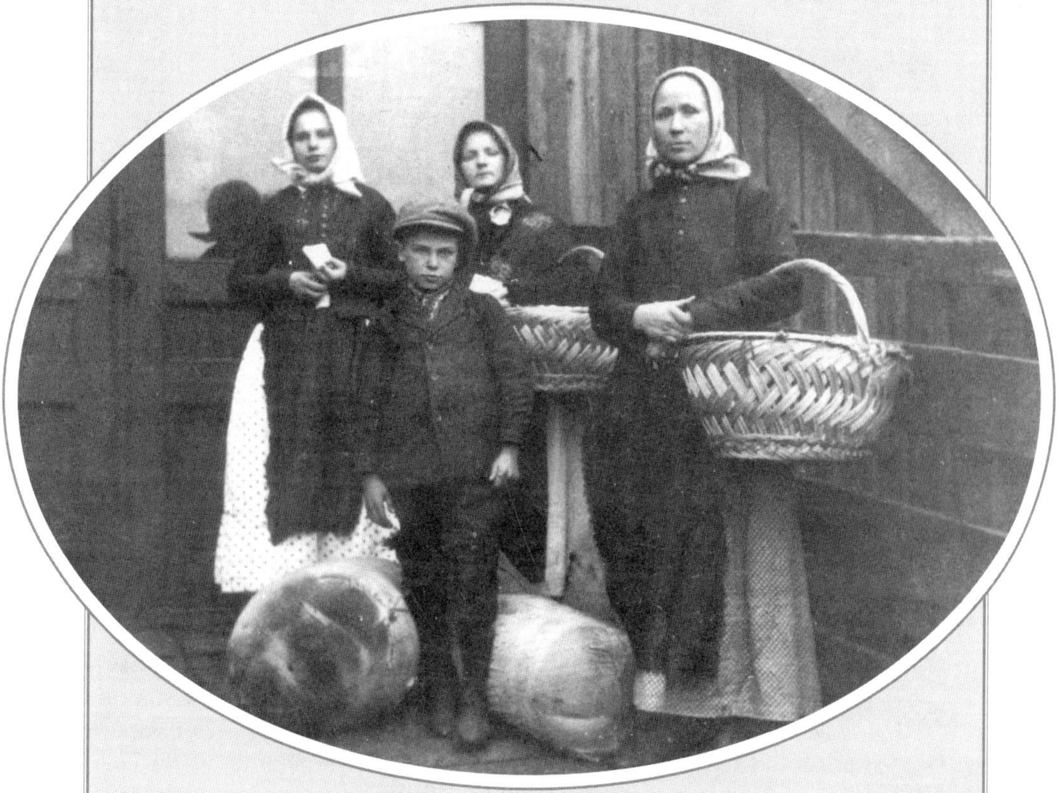

**IMMIGRATION SHED, SAINT JOHN, 1918**

The war years saw a steep decline in immigration to North America, but as the war drew to a close, the numbers increased as thousands of displaced persons sought homes away from the destruction of the European battlefields. This building was destroyed in the 1931 port fire.

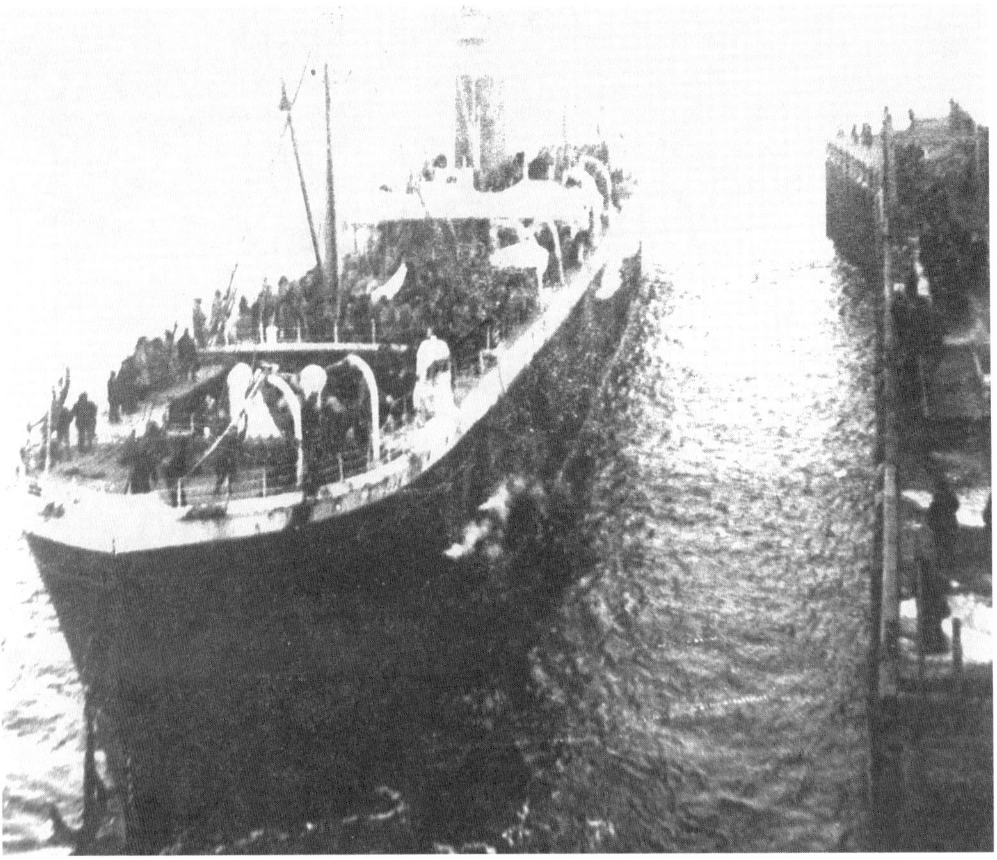

***Lake Superior* Carrying Russian Immigrants, 1901**

Several times during the 1901-1902 immigration season, the *Lake Superior* brought thousands of eastern European immigrants, including Peter Virigen, leader of the Doukhobors, to Saint John. During this immigration season there was an outbreak of smallpox which killed immigrants on Partridge Island such as two-year-old Teddy Harlow, as well as residents of Saint John. The *Lake Superior* tied up at Sand Point after the infected immigrants were removed to the Partridge Island hospitals. In December 1895, when the federal government provided a subsidy to turn Saint John into Canada's winter port, the Beaver Line *Lake Superior* was the first ship to call on the port.

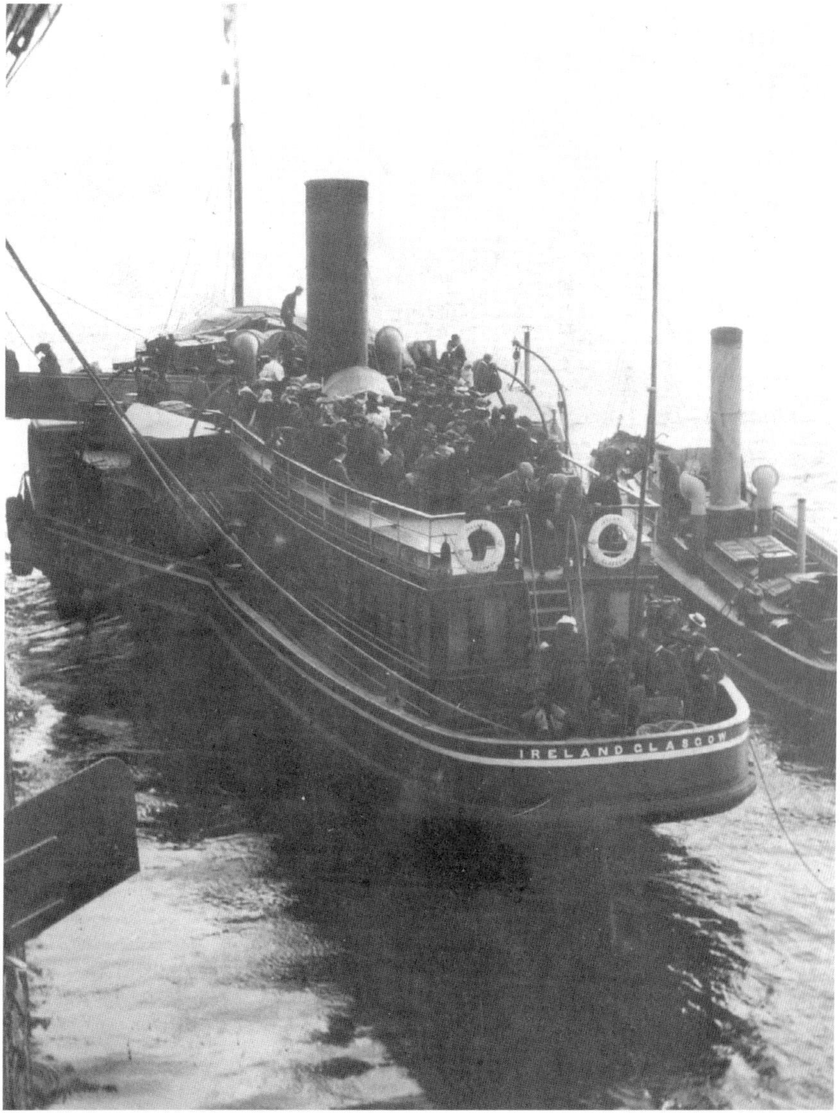


**BOARDING THE SS *IVERNIA* HOMEWARD BOUND, 1904**

In October 1904, some Saint John residents, including the Green Family, boarded the SS *Ivernia* in Liverpool, UK, for the return trip to Saint John. Also aboard were many English and Irish immigrants determined to find a profitable new life in Canada.

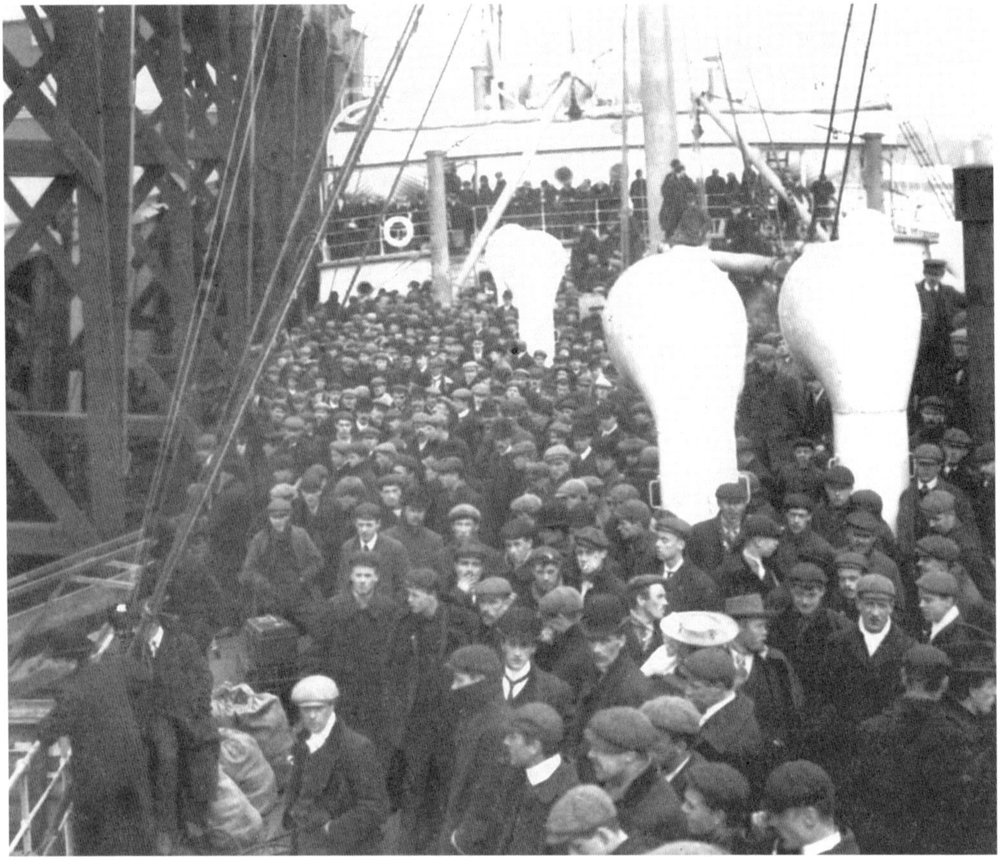

**Sand Point Immigrants, 1906**

In 1908 the Saint John Board of Trade described the city as the ideal stopping-point for the "right" kind of immigrant: "Of late years in the British Isles the ears and eyes of the over-crowded population have been directed to Canada… . Today in St. John and other towns in the Province and on its farms or in its forests there is work for thousands of men who today are tramping the streets of London and other large cities in Britain, or who are existing as laborers on starvation wages in the agricultural districts in the old country. Any man who is not a weakling or an 'unemployable' can find work here."

TOP RIGHT

**Partridge Island Quarantine Station, December 19, 1934**

The 1785 Royal Charter set aside Partridge Island for use as a quarantine station for both immigrants and mariners. In 1830 the first hospital was built, coinciding with the first two deaths of Irish teenagers. By the time the island was closed in 1941, thirteen hospitals and six graveyards had been established. From left to right (west to east) are the detention hospital, barn, smallpox hospital, general hospital, quarantine staff residence, assistant lightkeeper's residence, bacteriologist's laboratory, three lightkeepers' residences, the lighthouse, first-class hospital,

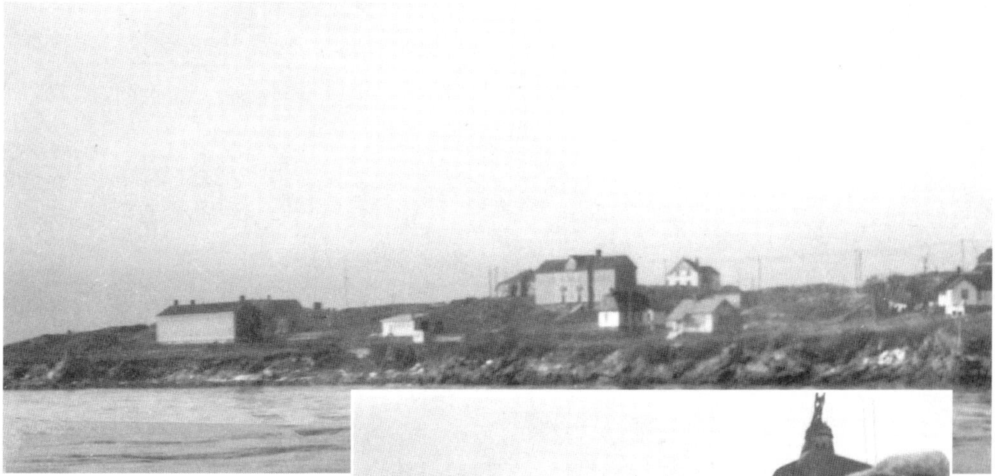

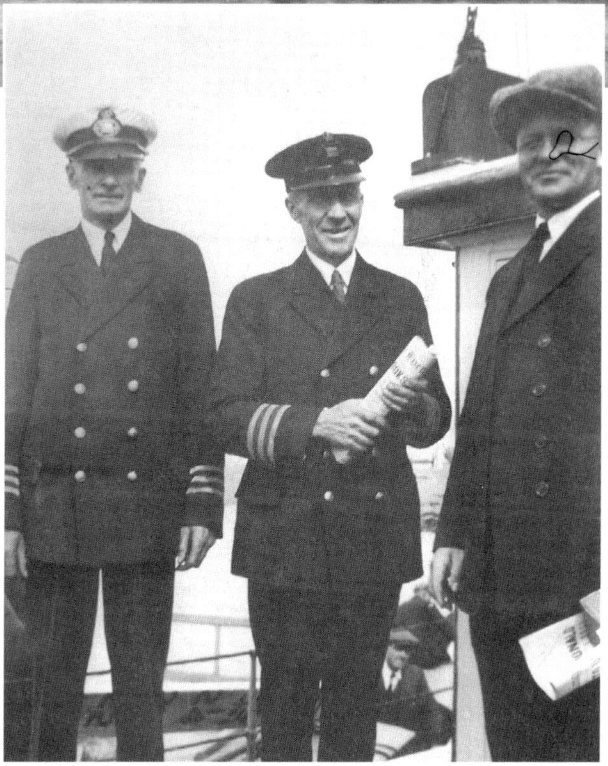

marine hospital, doctor's residence, second-class hospital, disinfecting plant and wharf. All of these buildings have been demolished.

### PARTRIDGE ISLAND QUARANTINE STAFF, c.1932

Left to right in the photo at right are: Captain George Kinghorn, Ossie Heans, and Dr. Douglas Reid. George Kinghorn was born in Digby and, as a youth, fished off Newfoundland. During World War One, he was mate on the Saint John tug *Neptune*, and in 1932, he became skipper of the *Salucan III*, the doctor's boat for Partridge Island. He remained skipper until 1954, then worked in the Department of Health office until his death in 1958. Ossie Heans was engineer of the *Salucan* from the early 1930s until 1954. When the *Salucan* exploded and burned in the 1930s, he was blown from the boat onto the wharf and suffered severe burns. He recovered and continued working, dying in the 1960s. Douglas Reid was born in Truro and graduated from Dalhousie Medical School in 1924. During World War One he served with distinction in the army and was severely wounded. He was appointed quarantine medical officer on Partridge Island in 1928, and in 1936 he was appointed chief medical officer for the Lancaster Veterans' Hospital. In 1946, Dr. Reid transferred to Ottawa where he died on August 18, 1956.

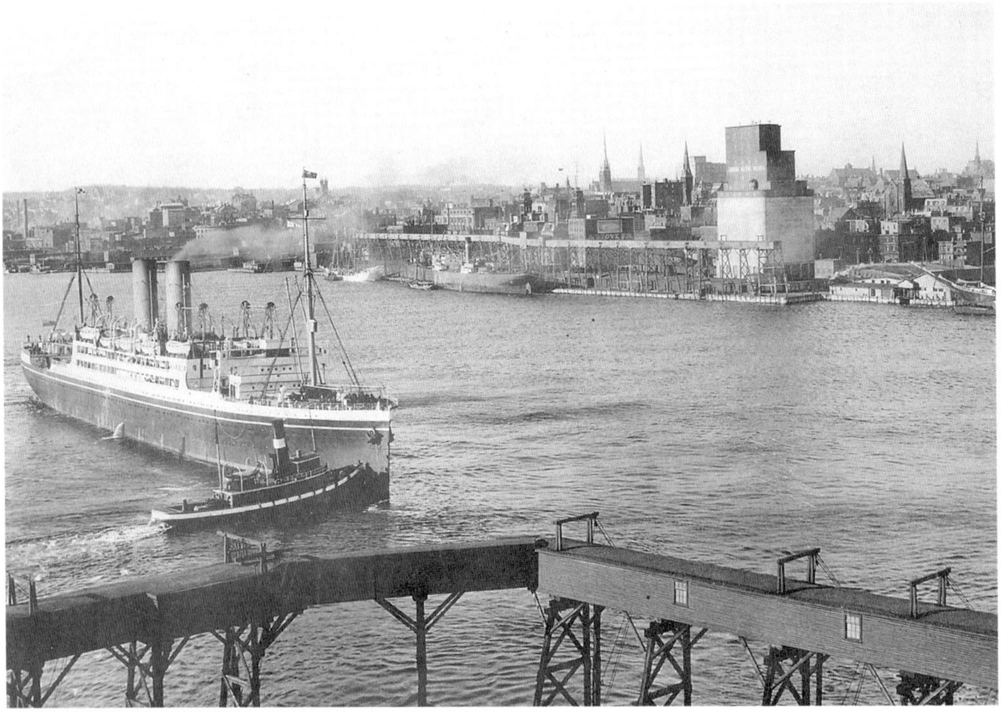

**CP SHIP DEPARTING SAINT JOHN HARBOUR, 1925**

This is probably the *Montcalm III.* After discharging passengers and taking on cargo and new passengers, she is being pushed into the main channel of the harbour by the tug. The *Montcalm III* entered the Canadian Pacific Steamship service in 1922. In 1939 she was requisitioned by the British Admiralty and converted to an armed merchant cruiser. She was purchased by the Admiralty in 1942 and survived World War Two. A wide array of vessels appear in the background: tugs, sailing vessels of many kinds, scows, and steamships. To the left of the CNR grain elevator is the McLarey Building. Note the huge STOVES sign painted on the side of the building. In front of the grain elevator and in the foreground are the grain conveyors.

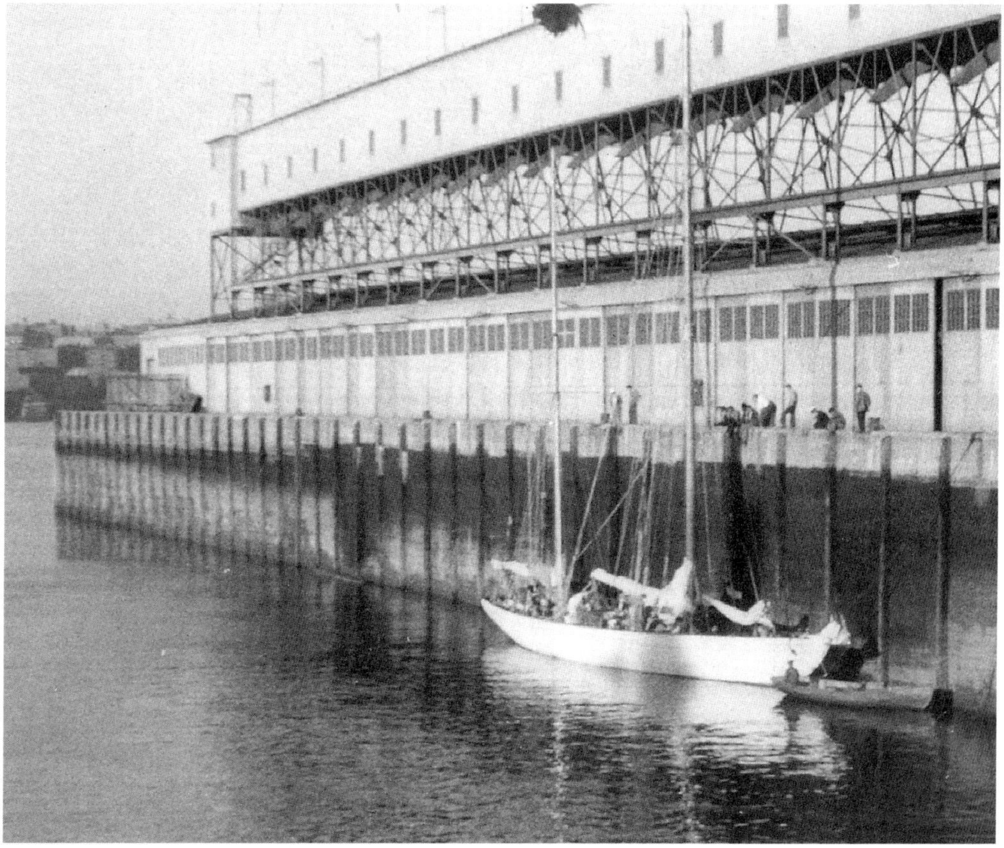

**Estonian Refugees, 1957**

The arrival of 42 Estonian refugees made international headlines as Captain Eugene Kommissar sailed the 60-tonne yacht *Atlanta* three thousand miles from the Canary Islands to Saint John with them aboard. Four children and seventeen women were in the group, including Captain Kommissar's wife and their two-and-a-half-year-old daughter Molle. *Atlanta* sailed from Sweden to England and then to the Canary Islands, taking three months. Here the yacht is shown tied up at Pier 2 on the west side. Captain Kommissar and a few others considered making Lancaster their new home.

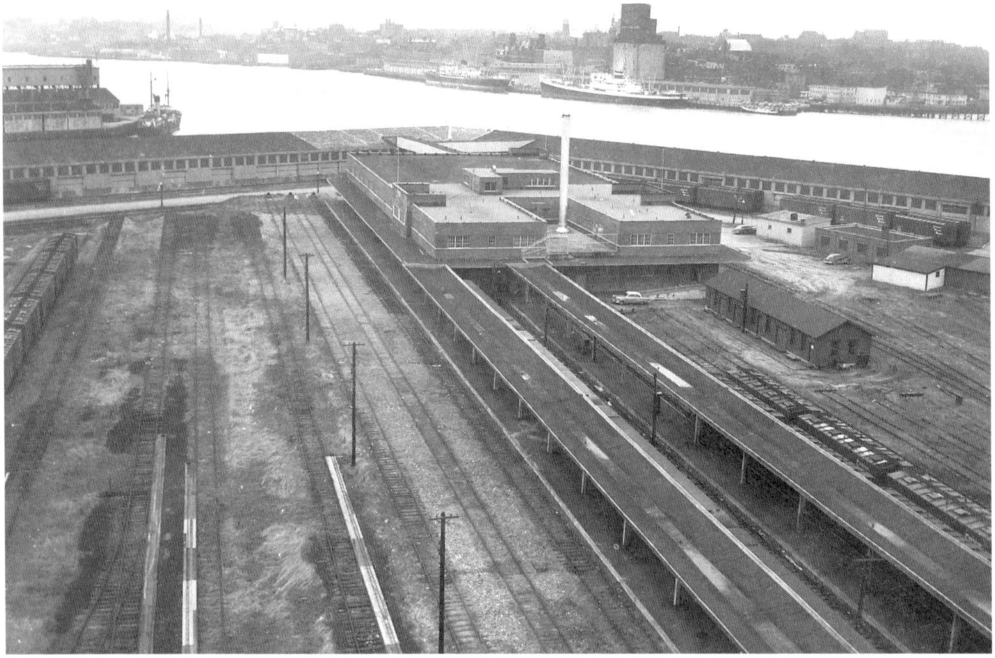

**IMMIGRATION BUILDING, PORT OF SAINT JOHN, DECEMBER 3, 1956**

In June 1931 the immigration building burned in the port fire, so Canadian Pacific passenger and immigrant traffic was rerouted to Halifax. In 1945, plans were completed for a new customs and immigration building. The EGM Cape and Company of Montreal was awarded the $1-million contract and site clearing was underway by February 9, 1948. The building was ready for immigrants on December 9, 1950. At the ribbon-cutting ceremony, some three hundred future citizens of Canada looked on. The immigrants had arrived just a few hours previously on the Canadian Pacific *Empress of Canada*, which was the first ship to deliver passengers through the new terminal. Medical, immigration, and customs staff conducted their examinations in the new terminal, and later the passengers left by special trains for their destinations across Canada and the United States. While their hand luggage was placed in special cages on the second floor, arriving immigrants reached the building through an enclosed ramp from Sheds 9 and 10, went to the doctors' offices for examinations, then proceeded to the large section of the second storey reserved for immigration authorities. The second floor also housed a large, fully-equipped kitchen and cafeteria-type diningroom, separate detention rooms for men and women, quarters for deportees, and detention cells for persons awaiting deportation. Immigrants went downstairs where the general waiting rooms, customs departments, and baggage sections were located. Canadian Pacific and Canadian National Railways had offices on the ground floor, where there were also steamship ticket offices. A 25-bed hospital on the third floor consisted of four wards and included a recreation room, an emergency operating room, a dispensary, and outdoor recreation grounds. The immigration building was demolished in 1997.

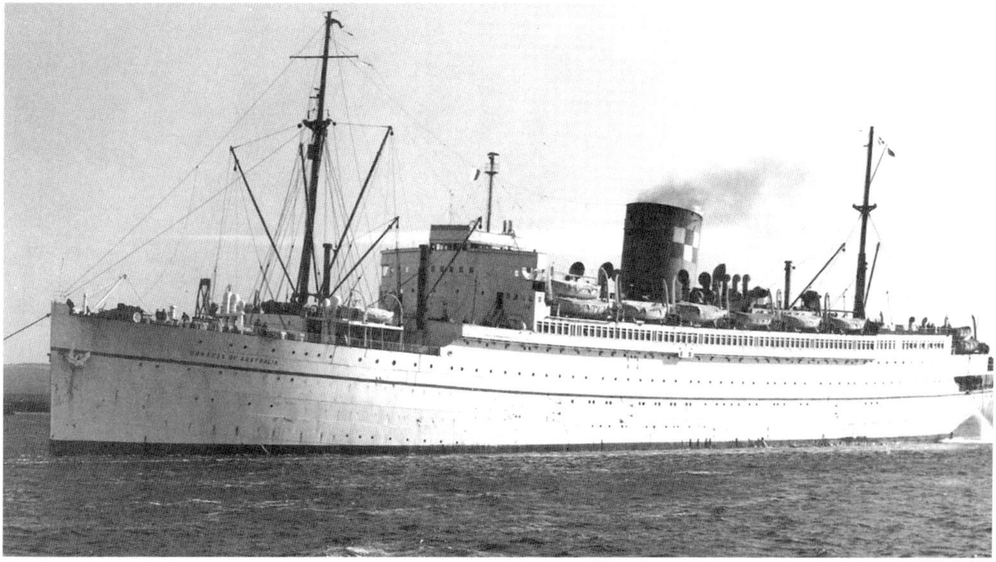

**EMPRESS OF AUSTRALIA II, 1954**

The first *Empress of Australia* was a World War One reparation named the *Tirpitz* of the Hamburg-Amerika Line. She was renamed *Empress of China III* in 1921, then *Empress of Australia* on June 2, 1922, and she served as a troopship during World War Two. Launched in 1924 as the French Liner *De Grasse*, she was sold to the CPR in 1953 and renamed *Empress of Australia II*. She remained with the CPR until being sold to Fratelli Grimaldi, Genoa, in 1956.

**BEESLEY FAMILY, MARCH 26, 1959**

The *Empress of France* brought the Beesley family to Saint John. They are shown here, from left to right: Catherine, Michael holding Andrew, Michelle, and Philip. The Beesley family was assigned tourist cabin C59 aboard the *Empress* under command of Captain S.W. Keay. In 1989 Michael Beesley wrote about this voyage:

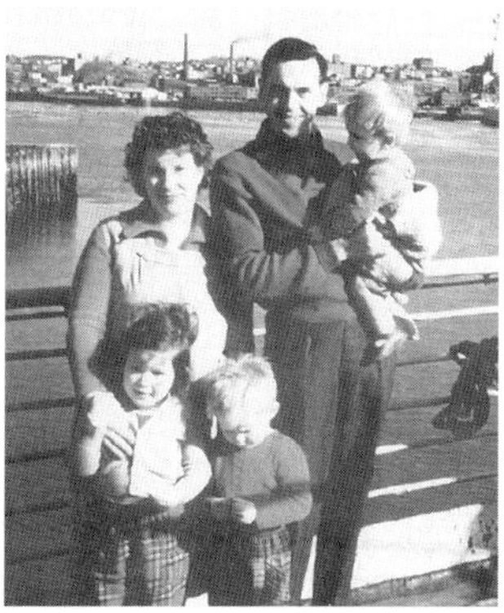

"My wife was born in Hitler's Germany and came to England as a refugee child in 1938. I am half French, half English; both my parents had in their younger days spent some years in Canada. We were married in Ceylon where I was employed for three years as an engineer, and our first child was born there just before our return to England in 1954. We were greatly attracted to Canada. Late in 1958, we finally made our big decision to emigrate. My wife's brother and sister-in-law had already emigrated to Canada some time earlier, and were established in Toronto, and we had very helpful correspondence with them about general conditions and prospects. After negotiating with my employers, I received the offer of a job in Hamilton, Ontario, if we would pay our own way over. We accepted, and booked our passage as economically as possible through CP Steamships, timing our departure so that the youngest of our three children would be just less than one year old and thus travel for only 10% of adult fare. We travelled by train from Newcastle to Liverpool to embark on the *Empress of France*, armed with last minute purchases of baby diapers, and accompanied by 28 pieces of luggage."

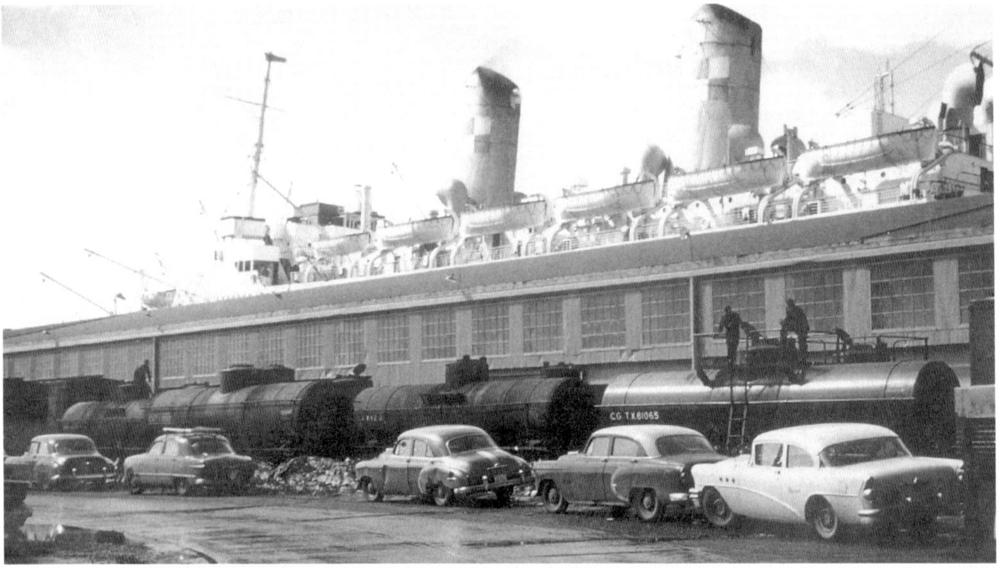


**The *Empress of France*, port of Saint John, March 26, 1959**

This is a final view of the *Empress of France* looming over the immigration building before the departure of the 17-car CPR boat train. Michael Beesley's account continued:

> "We sailed on March 17th, 1959, and should have arrived March 24th, but in fact because of weather and head winds on the journey, it took two extra days, and we finally docked on the morning of March 26th, our young son's first birthday. Just before docking, we learned that those of us travelling on to Montreal, Toronto or other western points would leave by train in the afternoon. We simply didn't know what else would happen, where we could go in the interim, or what we would do with our confused young children and our mountain of luggage. It was at this point that the ladies of Saint John stepped in to help the new arrivals in such a memorable way. As soon as the ship docked, they came onboard, armed with passenger lists, and actually sought out each family by name to offer their help. They made a special effort for us and for others with youngsters, and explained that we could wait in the immigration building and that they would look after the children for as long as it took to clear through the Customs and Immigration formalities and board our train. Sure enough, when we got ashore and entered your building, they had a large area setup with chairs, rugs, toys, coloring books, babysitters, coffee and the children were taken off our hands and well looked after, until some hours later when we could get onto the train. We were really overwhelmed with their kindness towards us, and the general friendliness of the atmosphere, in such vivid contrast to the dourness and grayness of the England we had just left behind, and giving us a truly memorable welcome to our new homeland."

The *Empress of France II* was originally named the *Duchess of Bedford* when she was launched in 1928. She was the first of the four Duchess boats to sail the Atlantic. The *Duchess* served as a troopship during World War Two. She was renamed the *Empress of France II* in 1948 and served until 1960.

## Chapter 11

# *Changes to the Harbourfront*

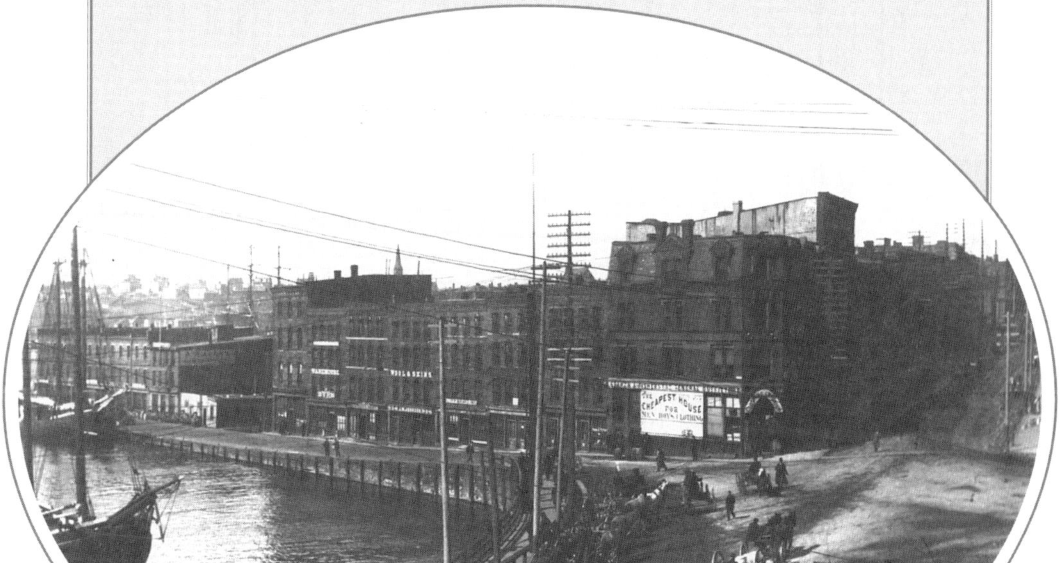


**MARKET SLIP, 1901**

The façades of seven of these post-1877 fire buildings are all that remain in this springtime view of Market Slip. A close look shows ice floes at the head of the slip. At the corner of Nelson Street, a building sign for A.W. Adams is visible. J.M. Johnson's store has a Wool & Skins sign on the building front. At the Clothing Emporium on the corner of Dock Street, the sign advertises Seamen and Fishermen's General Outfitting. The cartsmen with their slovens at Market Square are waiting for cargo.

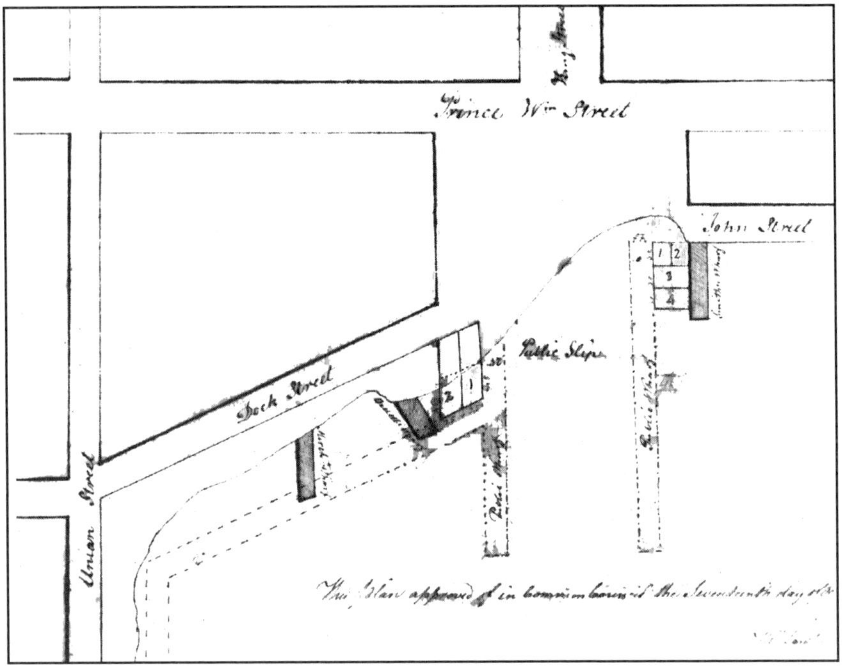


**Wharf Plans, October 17, 1788**

This drawing shows the construction plans for the public wharves for the Public Slip at Upper Cove, later renamed Market Slip. The only unfamiliar name shown is St. John Street, which was later renamed Water Street. Barely visible is the street which parallels that street, Ward Street, named after John Ward, the "Father of Saint John." The two private wharves coming off Dock Street are Merritt's on the left, and Beddell's on the right. Behind lots one to four on St. John Street is Smith's wharf. Market Slip has changed considerably over the past two hundred years.

**Mill Pond, 1863**

TOP RIGHT

The area to the left of centre is where Harbour Station is today. Part of this area was once a pond, and the road in the background, now called Station Street, was once Pond Street. Centuries ago the water actually went all the way along Rothesay Avenue (originally called Marsh Road) to Glen Falls, and the Portland Bridge crossed the pond. When the pond was filled in, Mill Street replaced this bridge. Many of the buildings shown here still stand: the Cathedral on Waterloo Street is at the left, and Stone Church is at the right. There is a burned-out building at bottom right.

**York Point, 1863**

BOTTOM RIGHT

York Point was the Irish-Catholic neighbourhood of Saint John. To the right out of the image was where Lloyd's Graving Dock was located and at the right was the warehouse where the "Great Fire" of 1877 started. Note all the lumber piled on the wharf, ready for shipment. The wooden wharves, combined with the cargo and the close proximity of all the wood-frame houses, provided the perfect setting for fire on June 20, 1877. The church to the left of centre is the original Trinity Church.

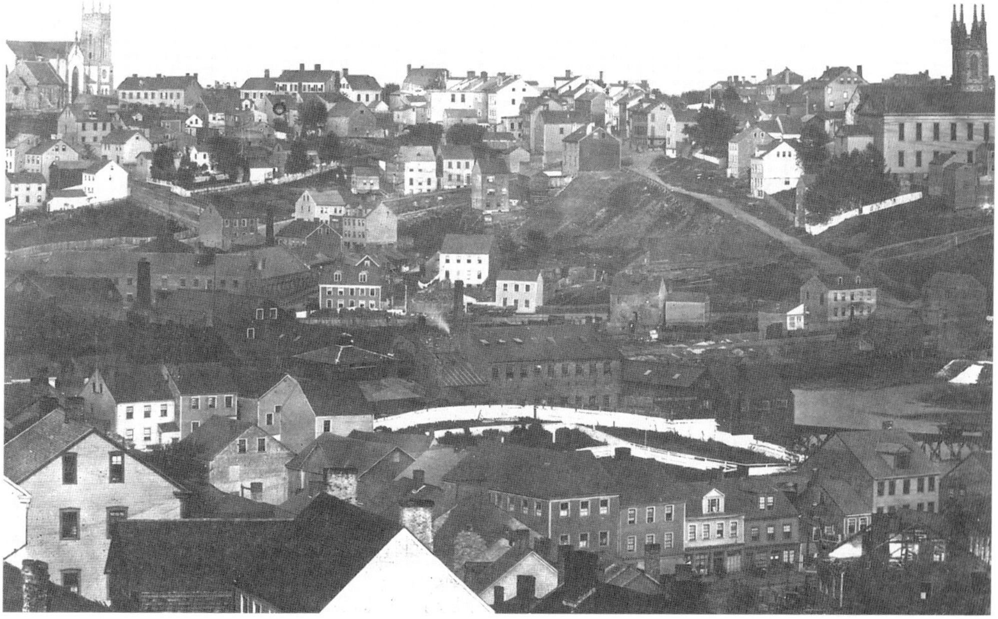

MILL POND IN 1863 (ABOVE) AND YORK POINT IN 1863 (BELOW)

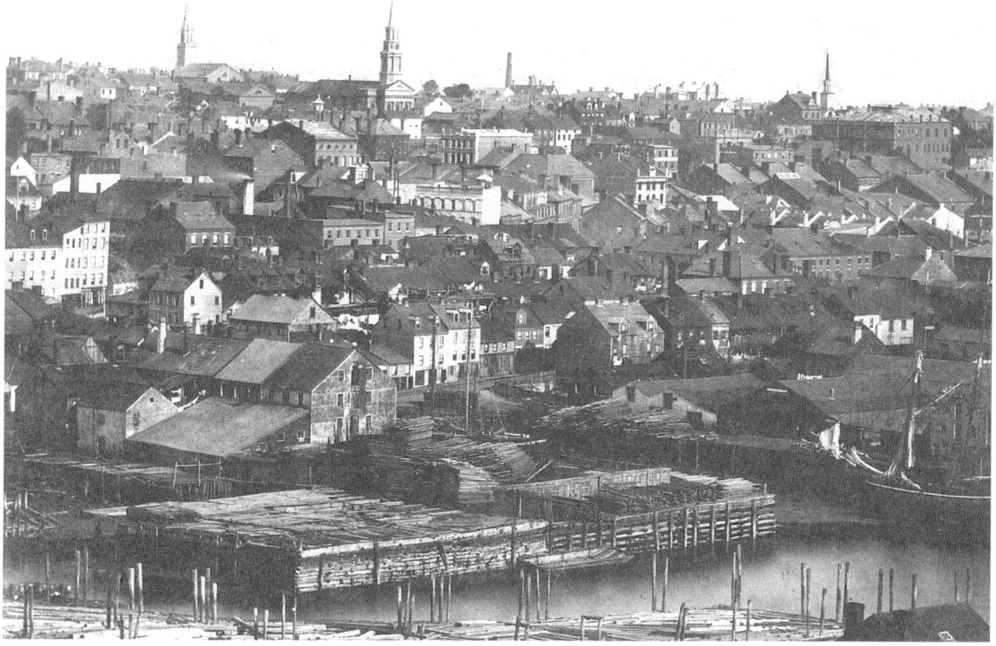

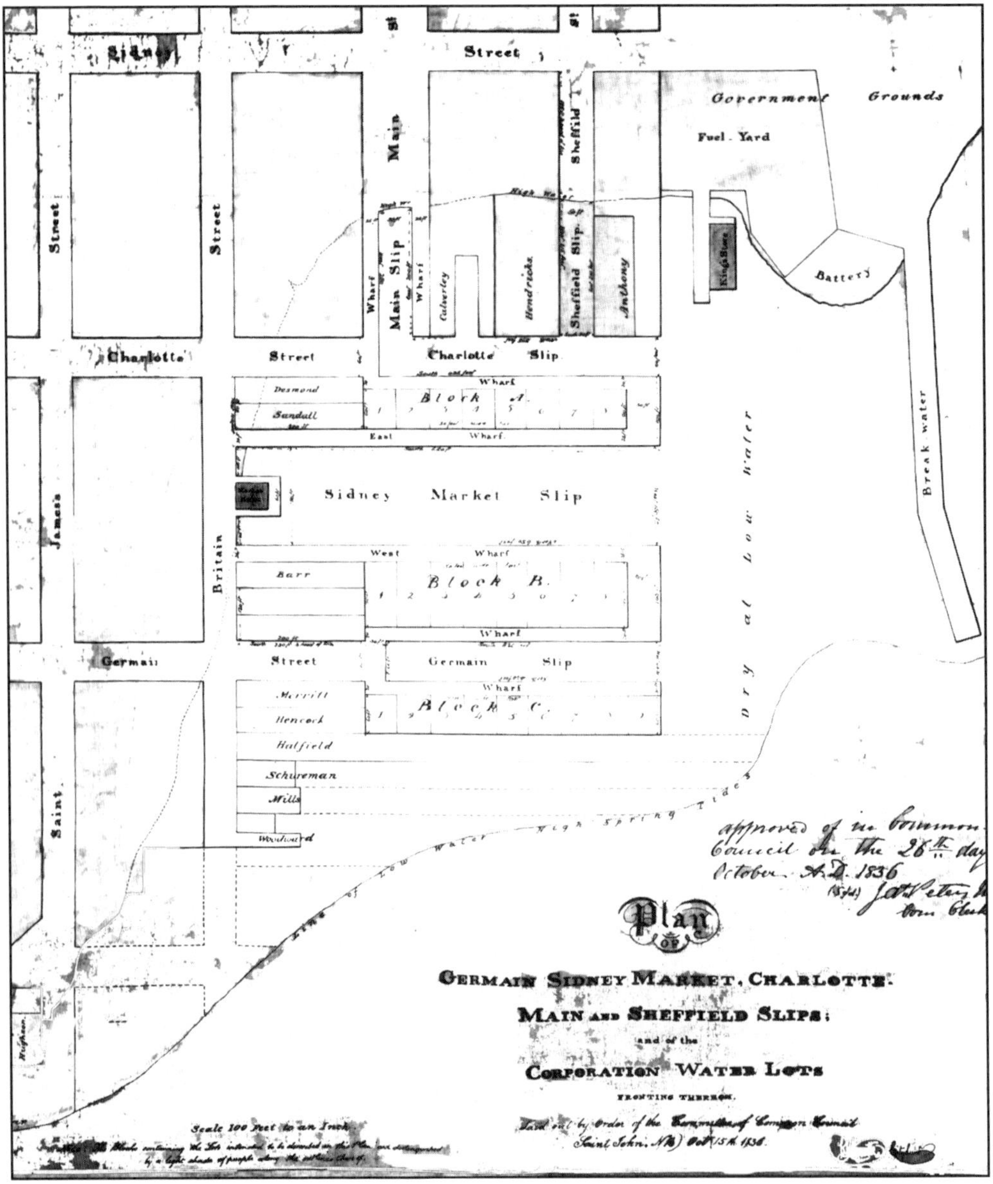


## Lower Cove, October 15, 1836

This drawing shows the Germain, Sidney [sic] Market, Charlotte, Main (Broad) and Sheffield slips in 1836. Prince William Street did not extend to St. James Street, nor did Germain and Charlotte streets extend to Main (now Broad) Street. There was a breakwater and an artillery gun battery in the area of today's Lantic Sugar Refineries. At Reeds Point, the wharf was leased by Hughson, while the wharves along Britain Street were leased to Woodward, Mills, Schureman, Hatfield, Hencock, Merritt, Barr, Sandall, Desmond, Calverley, Hendricks, and Anthony.

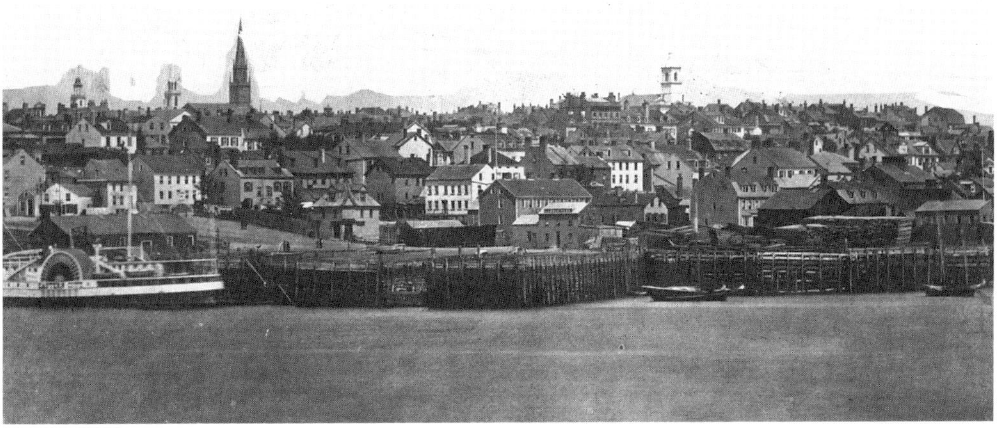

**REEDS POINT, 1863**

Reeds Point was named for the prominent Reed family, involved in shipbuilding, shipping, lightkeeping, and piloting. The point was also the site of the ferry terminal for both the Boston boat and Digby ferry. The Reeds Point lamp, commonly referred to as "the three sisters," is shown at the foot of Prince William at St. Patrick's Square. All of the buildings shown here were destroyed in the 1877 fire. In addition to the fishing sheds on the wharves, wood and coal yards also once stood here. Note the lumber on the wharves.

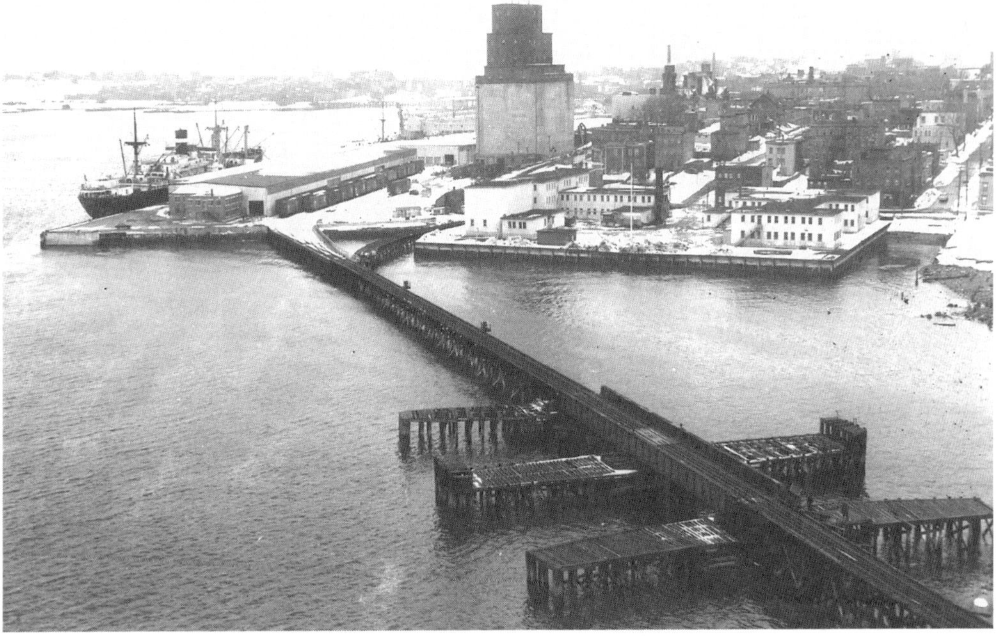

**LOWER COVE, c.1955**

The CN Rail trestle across Lower Cove included a swing-bridge that allowed small boats to enter the cove. In front of the CN grain elevator are the white buildings of the former HMCS *Brunswicker*. In the 1980s this cove was filled in to create the 7.4-hectare Lower Cove Terminal. Lower Cove was one of two landing sites for the American Loyalists in 1783.

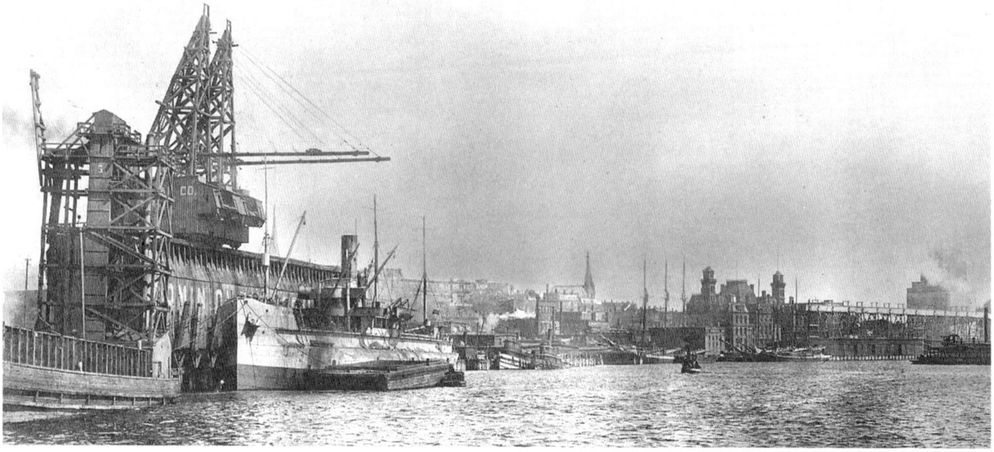

DOMINION COAL POCKETS C.1920 (ABOVE) AND LONG WHARF, C.1952 (BELOW)

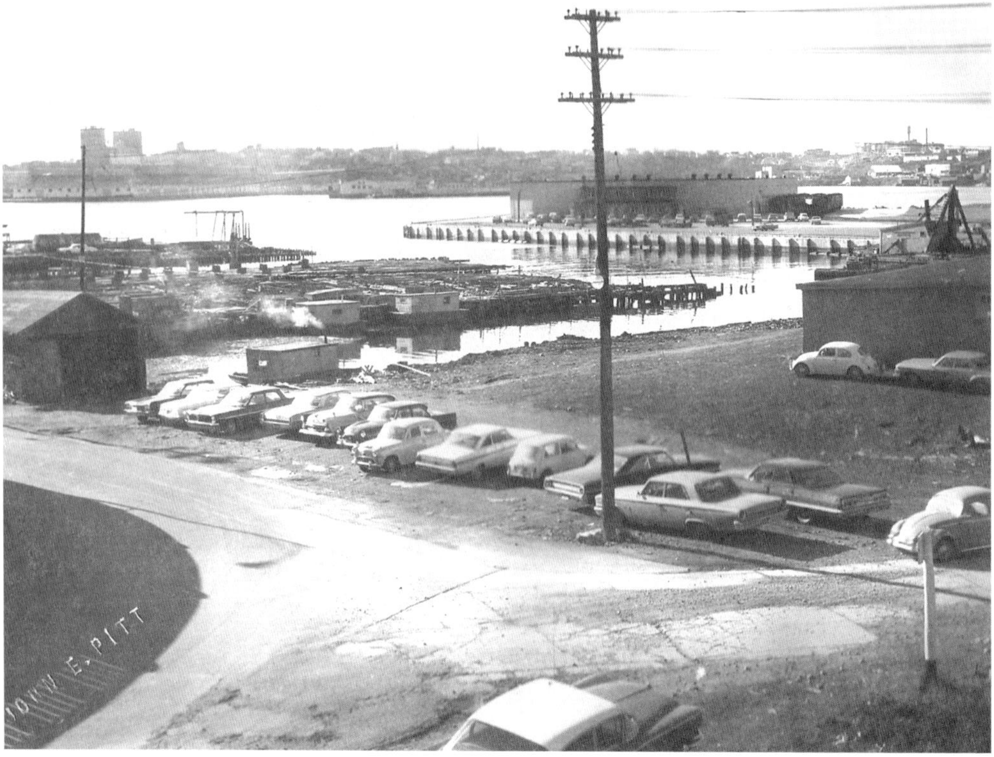

PHOTOS AT LEFT

## Dominion Coal Pockets, c.1920, and Long Wharf, c.1952

A collier is being unloaded. "Among other ships making the port during the week-end were the collier *Rockwood Park*, a regular visitor at the port, from Sydney, NS." A barge is in front of the collier on her port side, two tugs are tied up at the face of South Market Slip, and the harbour ferry *Ludlow* is approaching the Princess Street slip. Several schooners are tied up near the Customs House. At the extreme right is the Boston boat, either the *Yarmouth* or the *Calvin Austin*. When Starr shut down their coal operation in 1952, their property was appraised for sale. What remains of their wharves is shown in the centre, with the two small workboats tied up. At the right, a dredge is working in Long Wharf and the warehouse for Red Rose Coffee is visible.

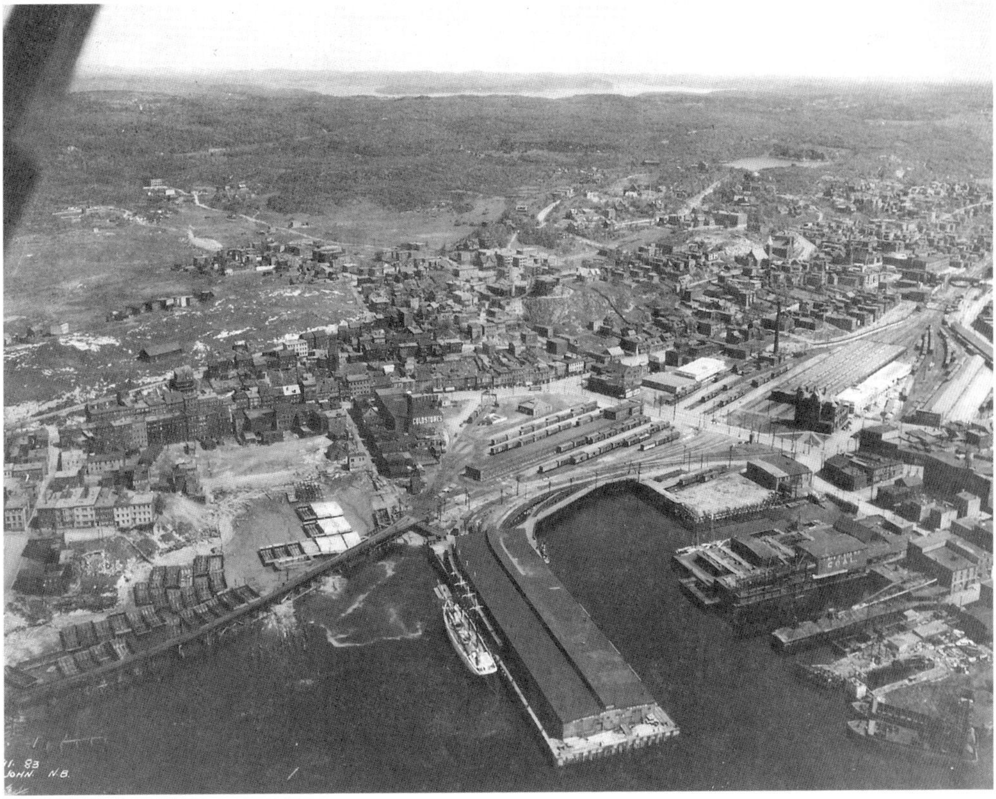

## Long Wharf, 1930

With Fort Howe and Portland Place in the background, we see a remarkably changed harbourfont. To the left of Long Wharf are the remnants of the mill pond, with numerous lumber scows and the rail trestle. At the head of Long Wharf is the cold-storage plant on Main Street and numerous rail lines crossing Mill Street. Today the ICR Union Depot still stands, with many rail sheds and warehouses on Pond Street. The Estabrooks Tea Plant is visible with the Starr Coal Company buildings and coal cars at the right.

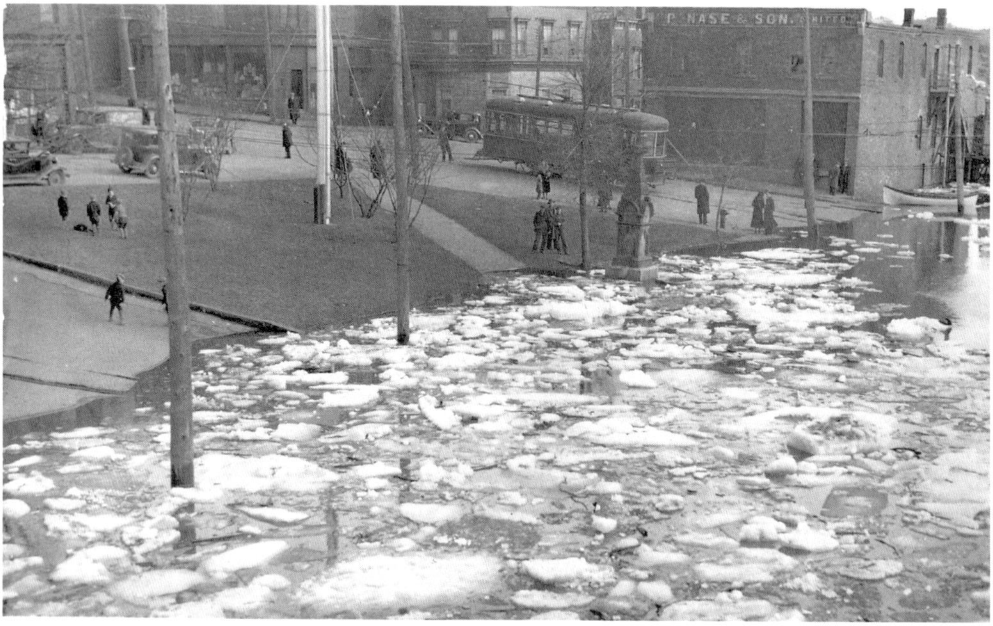

**Indiantown Flood, March 1936**

Streetcar tracks continue into the water in this image of the annual spring freshet in Robertson Square. Many merchants had to use boats to row to their businesses. The drinking fountain in the square was erected in 1883, a gift of ex-Portland councillor and Mrs. James T. Kennedy of Marble Street, in memory of their son, Wilmont Kennedy, who died on October 30, 1877.

**Harbour from Portland, c.1952**

TOP RIGHT

The Dominion Coal pockets at York Point are shown being demolished to make way for the new Princess Helene terminal. At the right is Portland Point, showing the reef where the *Beaverhill* went aground. Remnants of Navy Island are still visible, and out toward Partridge Island are several fishing weirs where the Princess of Acadia terminal now stands.

**Market Slip and Courtenay Bay, c.1932**

BOTTOM RIGHT

This remarkable aerial view of the centre of Saint John offers many clues to the marine heritage of the area. In Courtenay Bay there is one boat, probably at anchor. Behind the York cotton Mill are the remnants of a wharf, while at the head of the bay at Marsh Creek lie the skeletal remains of a wooden boat. In this view the 1930 addition to the Admiral Beatty Hotel has been completed, as was the 1929 addition to the NB Tel equipment building next to the Pythian Castle on Union Street. At Market Square we can see the many buildings which were torn down in the late 1950s to construct the coast guard base. McAvity's Water Street warehouses and brass plant are shown at the foot of Princess Street.

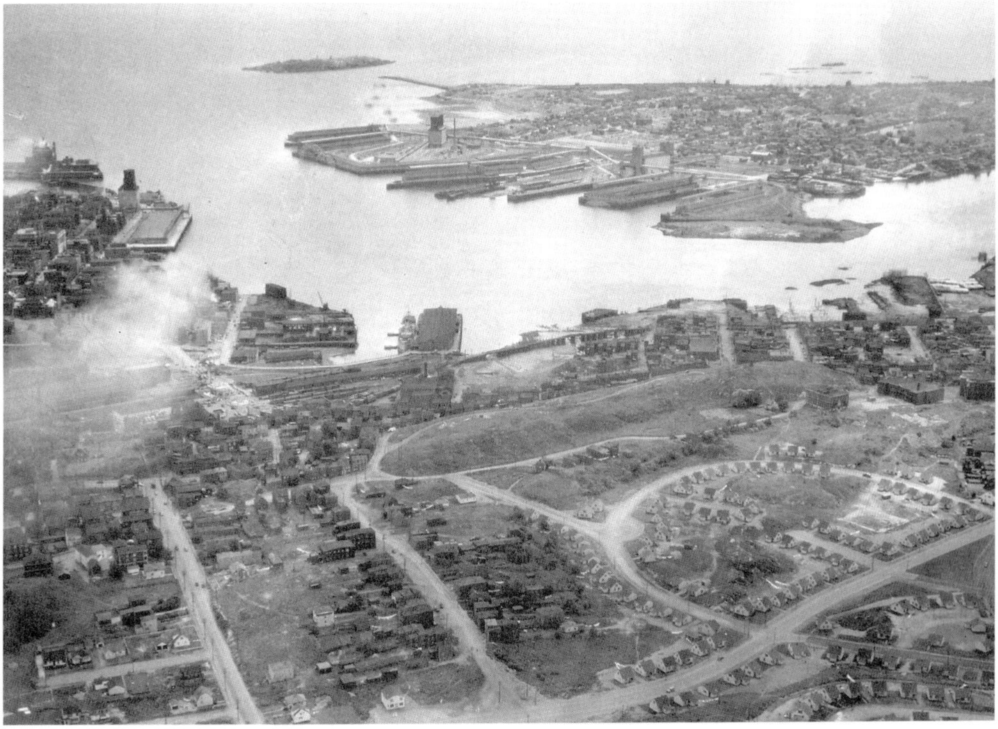

HARBOUR FROM PORTLAND C.1952 (ABOVE) AND MARKET SLIP AND COURTENAY BAY, C.1932, (BELOW)

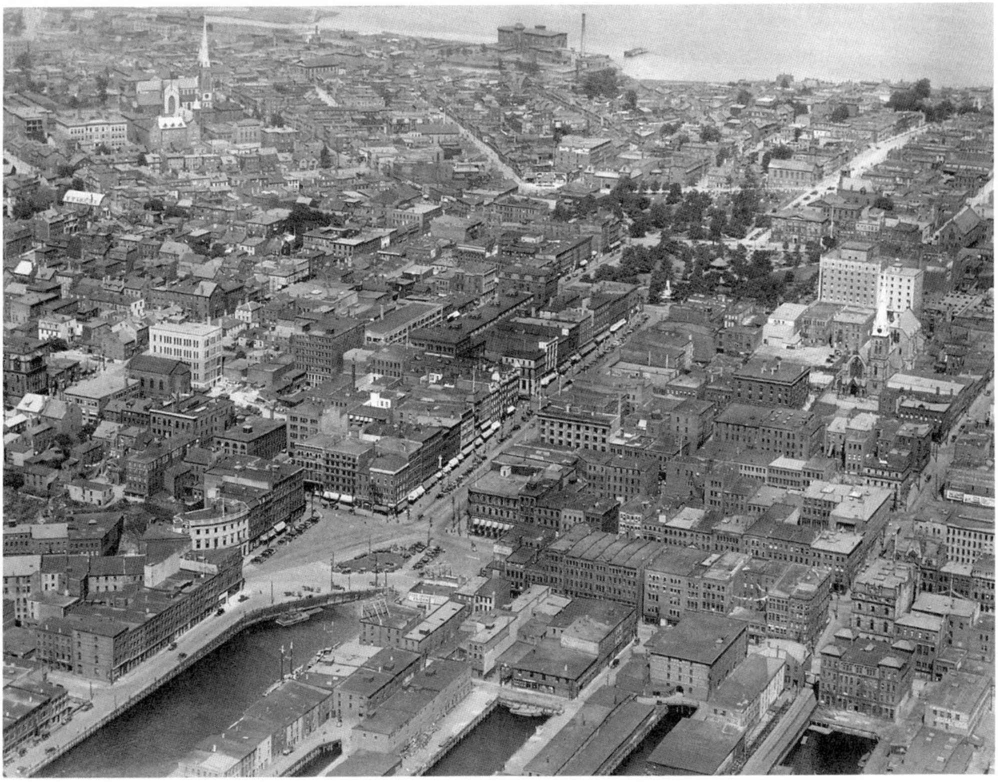

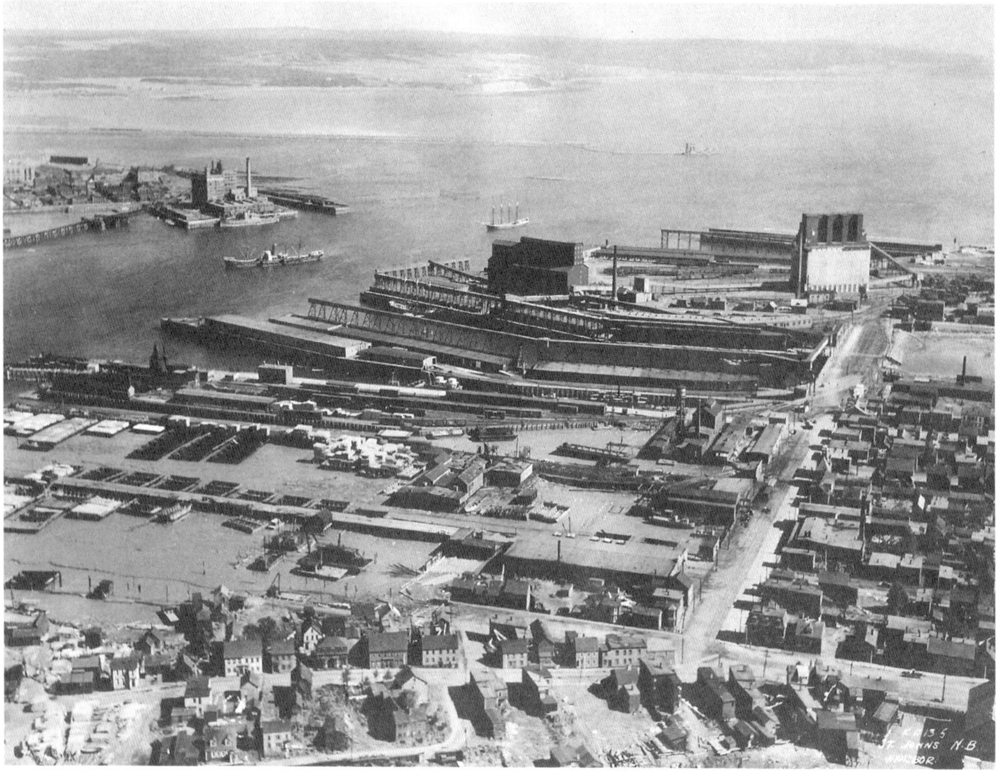

***Frederick C. Elkin*, c.1930**

The *Frederick C. Elkin* is entering the harbour just in front of the Atlantic Sugar Refineries. In the foreground we see timber scows on mudflats. The port facilities from the centre to the concrete grain elevator at the right were destroyed in the 1931 port fire.

**Coffer Dam, July 1930**

TOP RIGHT

To facilitate harbour improvements, a coffer dam was built from Navy Island to the area of Rodney Slip. Water was pumped from the area, the seabed excavated, and bedrock dynamited. In February 1930 the dam was breached, setting back the construction schedule.

**Coffer Dam, 1932**

BOTTOM RIGHT

The Coffer Dam was rebuilt and construction resumed. Several interesting things are evident here: the fishing community on Navy Island, the donkey engine, rail cars and the track running along the top of the coffer dam, and the Dominion government wharf at the lower right (now the site of DMK's Marine operation). On the other side of the harbour are the *Princess Helene* ferry at Reeds Point, Lower Cove with its rail trestle, and the Atlantic Sugar Refineries.

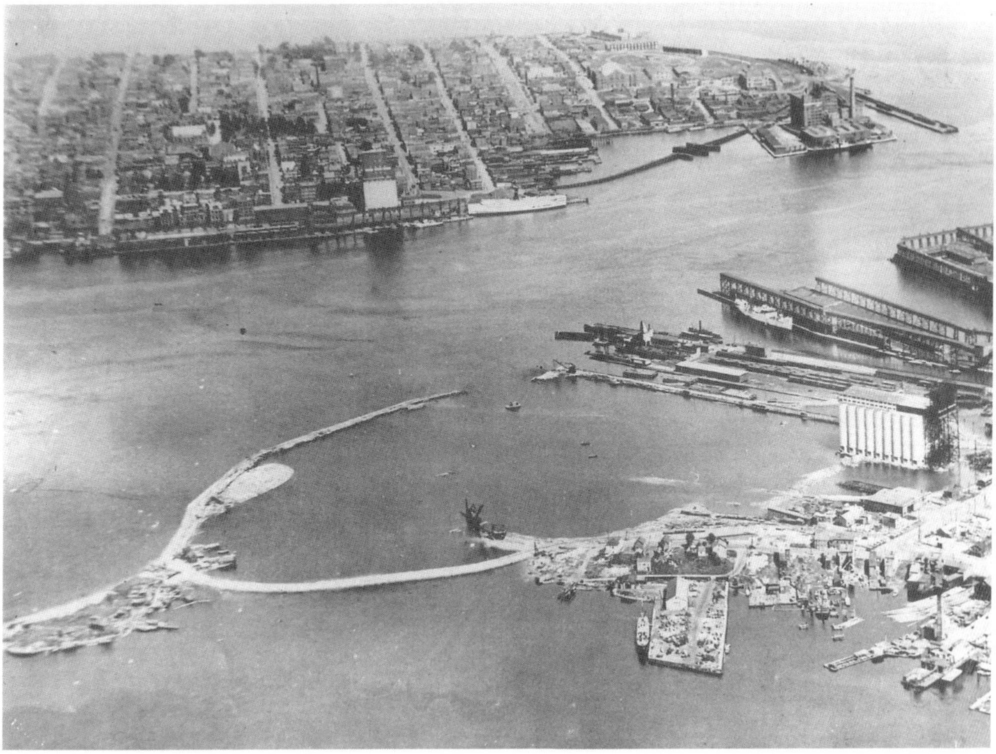

COFFER DAM IN 1930 (ABOVE) AND IN 1932 (BELOW)

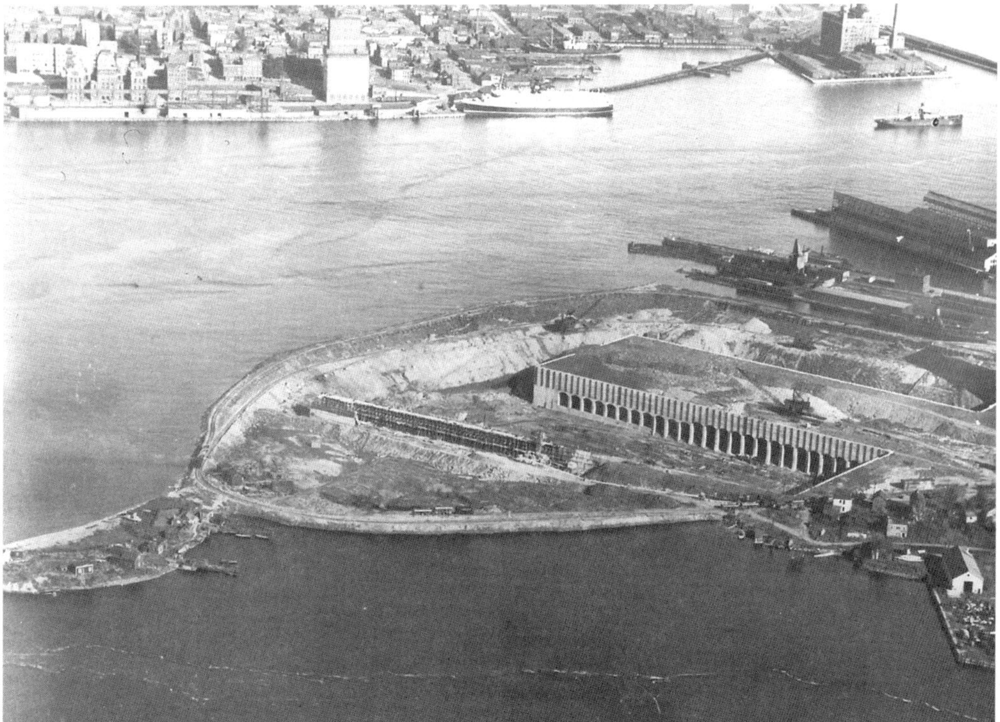

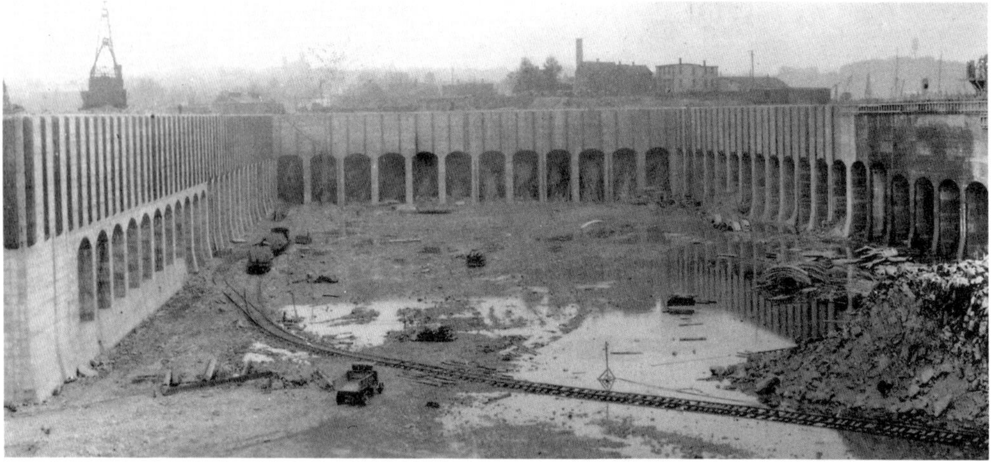

**PIERS 1 AND 2, c.1932**

At right is bedrock remaining to be blasted and removed. The small dumptruck and the small rail cars would have made thousands of trips to remove this debris, most of which was used to fill in the Carleton Mill Pond at the foot of St. John Street.

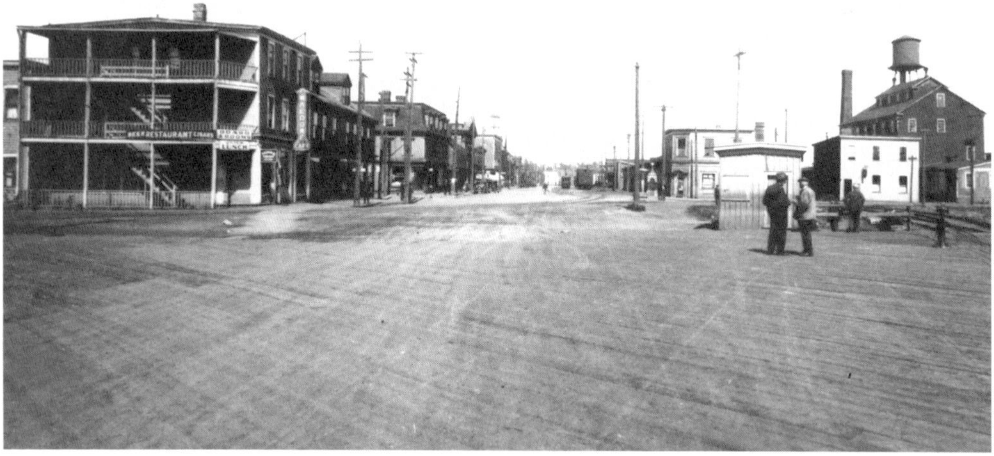

**UNION STREET, JULY 31, 1928**

In June 1906, as the federal Board of Works was dredging the west side of Saint John Harbour, clearing space for the cribs for Clark's Wharf, there was the danger that this work could cause a cave-in on Union Street. The street had been settling for nearly a year because of the dredging. Work was proceeding when on August 2, the street began to cave in. By August 7 the cave-in was so bad that the street was closed and the CPR was forced to move portions of its track. There were a lot of competing interests for Union Street property in 1928: at the left was the Waldorf Cafe and Hotel, and at the next corner was Susie Murphy's lunch counter. In the centre are shown a streetcar, a rail car, and the Band of Mercy Fountain (which now rests in front of the Carleton Community Centre). During the 1930s' port expansion, Union Street was obliterated.

**CLOSE QUARTERS, 1918**

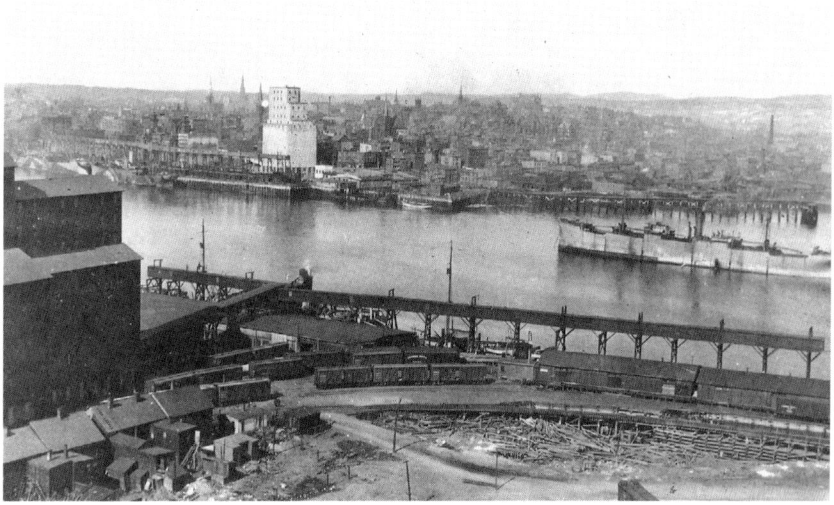

The image above shows Protection Street in the foreground, with Reeds Point and Lower Cove across the harbour. The arrival of the CPR in 1889 meant that the homes on Protection Street had to share their neighbourhood not only with grain elevators, but also with tracks and boxcars. The entire area was destroyed in the 1931 port fire. Across the harbour at the left can be seen two camouflaged ships, another reminder of wartime.

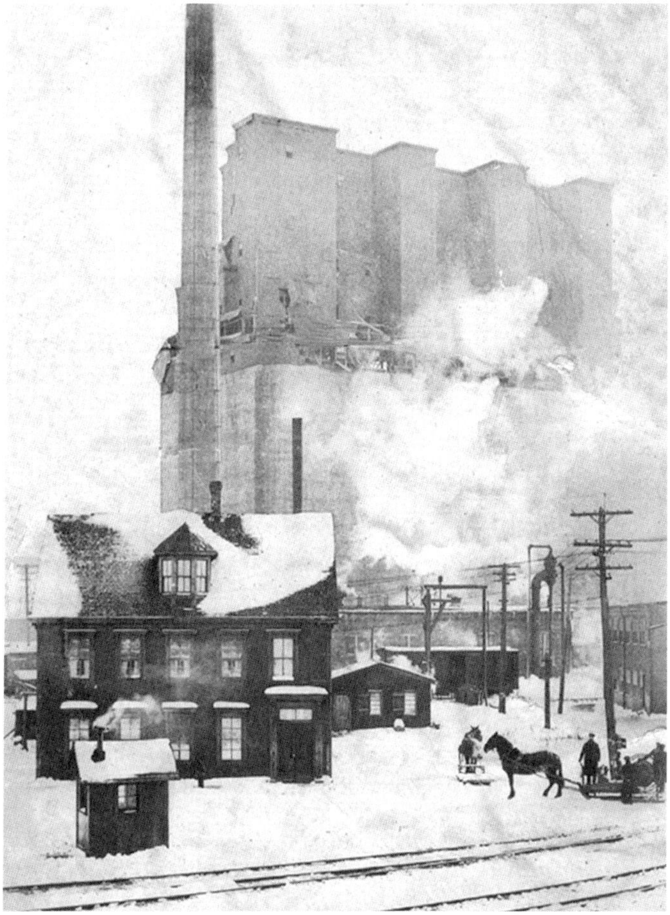

**ST. JOHN STREET, C.1930**

AT LEFT

In the background of the St. John Street image at left is the new CPR grain elevator, demolished in the 1990s. The sleigh at the right is a hosecart for the fire department and the firemen are standing next to Call Box #117. Behind the house is the smokestack of the CPR blacksmith and cooper shop.

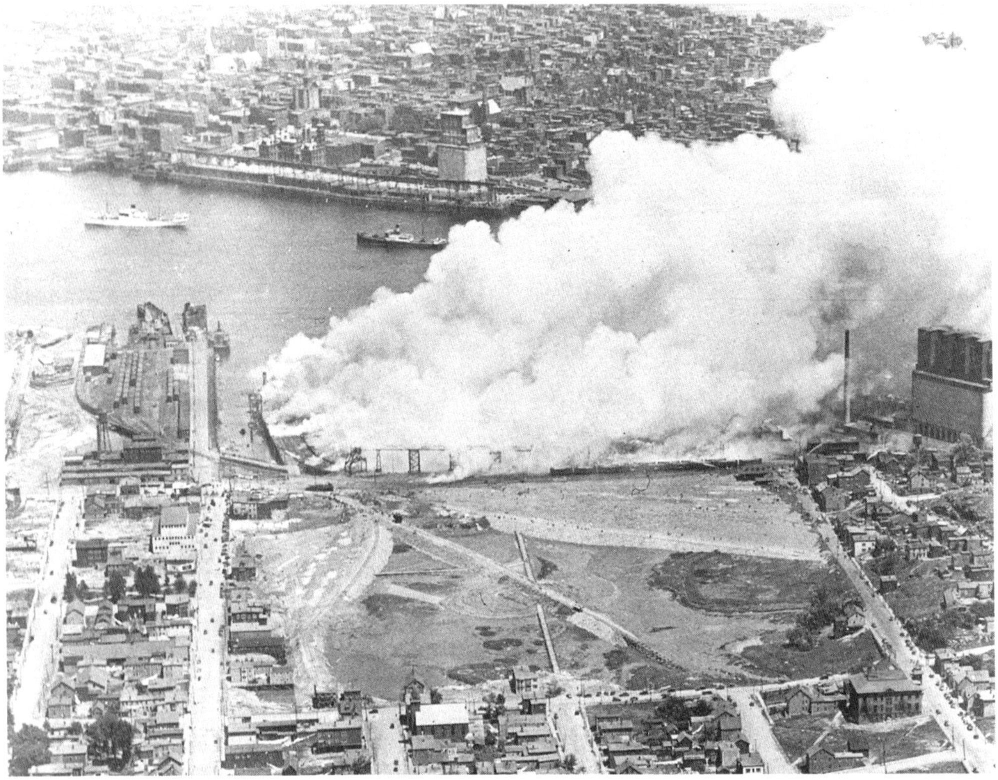

**PORT FIRE, 1931**

At 11:00 A.M. on June 22, fire broke out in a bathroom at the eastern end of Shed No. 7. The steamer *Gundersen* of the United Fruit Company was in the process of unloading a cargo of bananas, and a large quantity of packing straw was in the shed. Within fifteen minutes fire pumpers from Beaconsfield and the King Street West stations were on the scene. The new King Street pumper was driven right into the shed, but it was quickly surrounded by flames and abandoned. By 11:30, Shed No. 7 and the pier were engulfed and flames were spreading to adjoining structures. The SS *Gundersen* was moved into midstream to keep it from burning, but the pilot schooner *Glooscap* and the CPR steamship *Empress* were destroyed despite attempts to save them.

***OCEAN HAWK*, JUNE 22, 1931**

TOP RIGHT

In addition to Saint John's firefighting forces, the *Ocean Hawk* was requisitioned as a fireboat. She took up position at the eastern end of Shed No. 7 and extinguished the burning ruins of the wharf. After the fire, the hull of the *Empress* was converted to a coal barge.

**GRAIN CONVEYORS, JUNE 22, 1931**

BOTTOM RIGHT

The fire destroyed seven houses on Protection Street, two grain elevators, and overhead conveyors, CPR rolling stock, the immigration and customs buildings, a fertilizer plant, the cattle shed, and shed numbers 1-7 and 14-17, as well as the associated wharves. One life was lost, the accountant for the United Fruit Company.

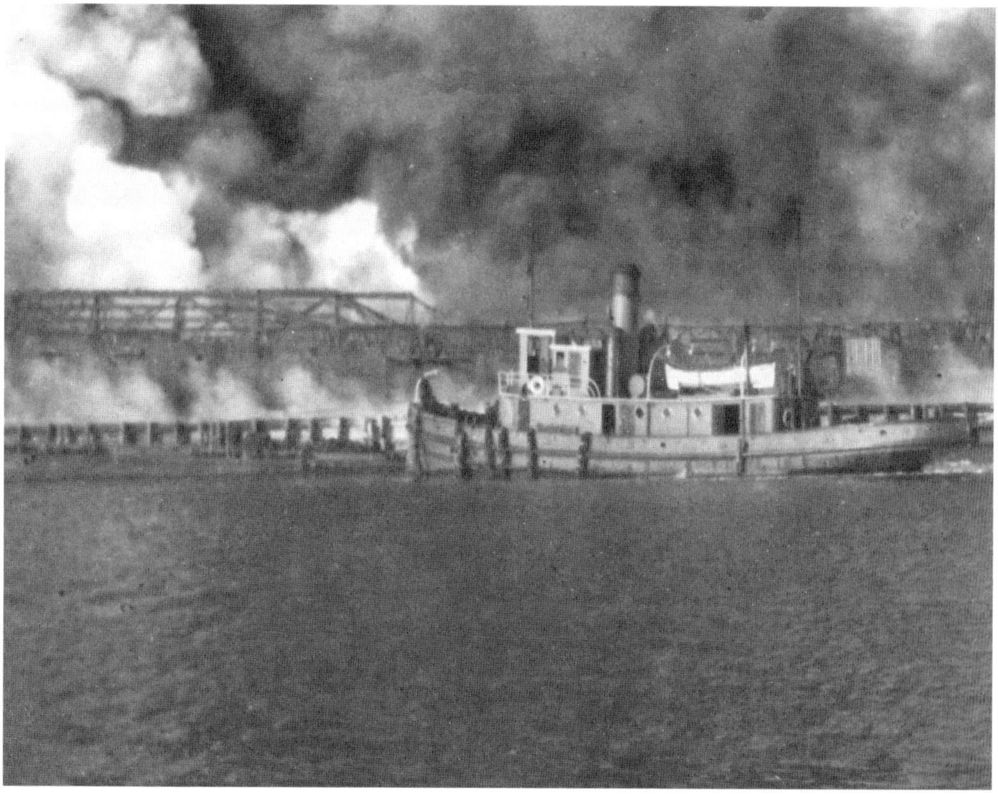

THE *OCEAN HAWK* (ABOVE) AND GRAIN CONVEYORS (BELOW) DURING THE FIRE OF 1931

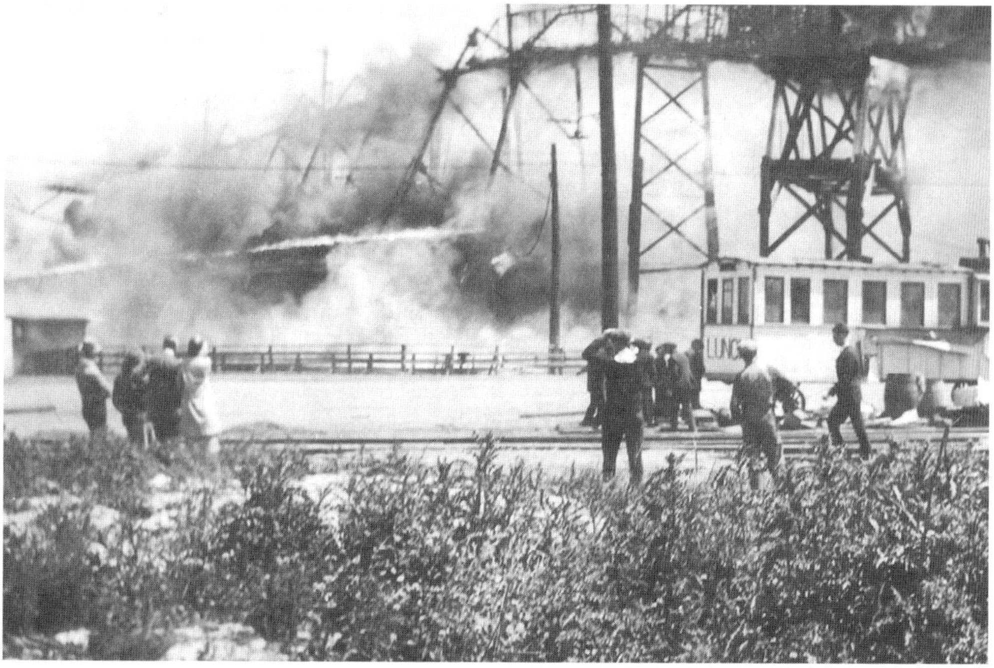

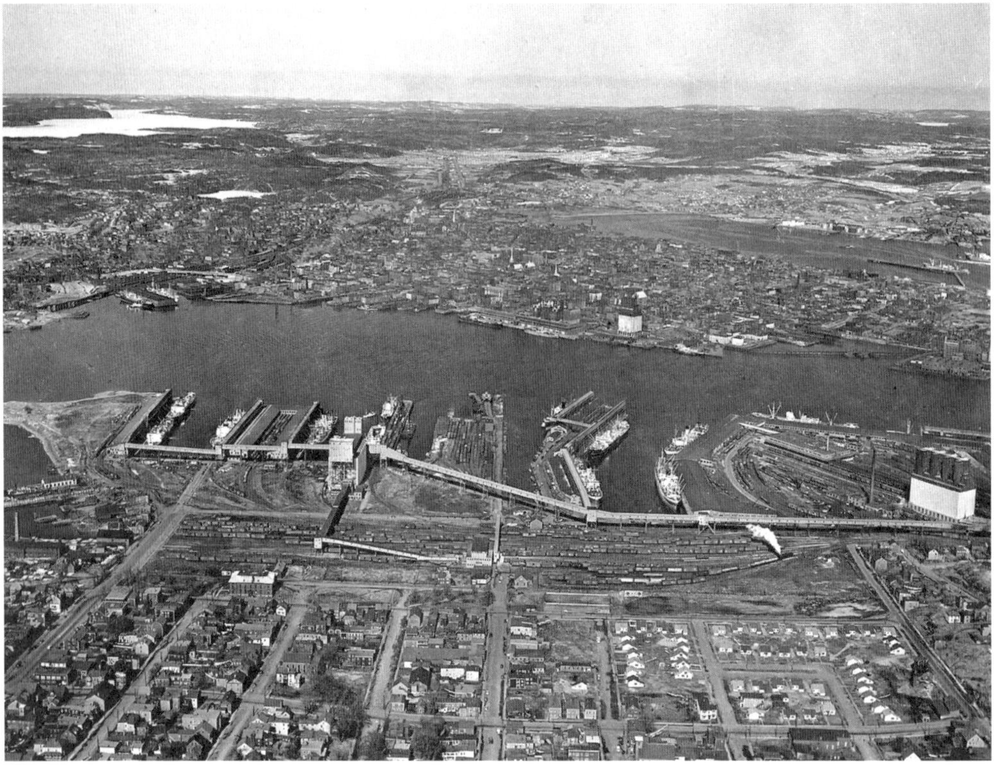

**SAINT JOHN HARBOUR, 1950**

Very little of the harbour as it appears in this photograph from 1950 remains. Starting on the west side of the harbour, Navy Island remains, but is now the site of the Forest Products Terminal. The Harbour Bridge crosses over the island, the CP grain elevator has been demolished, and, from Pier 3 to the partially dismantled grain elevator at the right, the piers and grain conveyors have been replaced by the container terminal. On the east side of the harbour, Long Wharf has been expanded to Portland Point, the Dock Street power plant is gone, and Market Slip to Princess Street is now occupied by the coast guard base, which will close after 2002. At the lower cove, the white buildings of HMCS *Brunswicker* are still visible, but the cove was filled in during the 1980s. Atlantic Sugar Refineries is shown at the right. At this time, the causeway through Courtenay Bay had not yet been built.

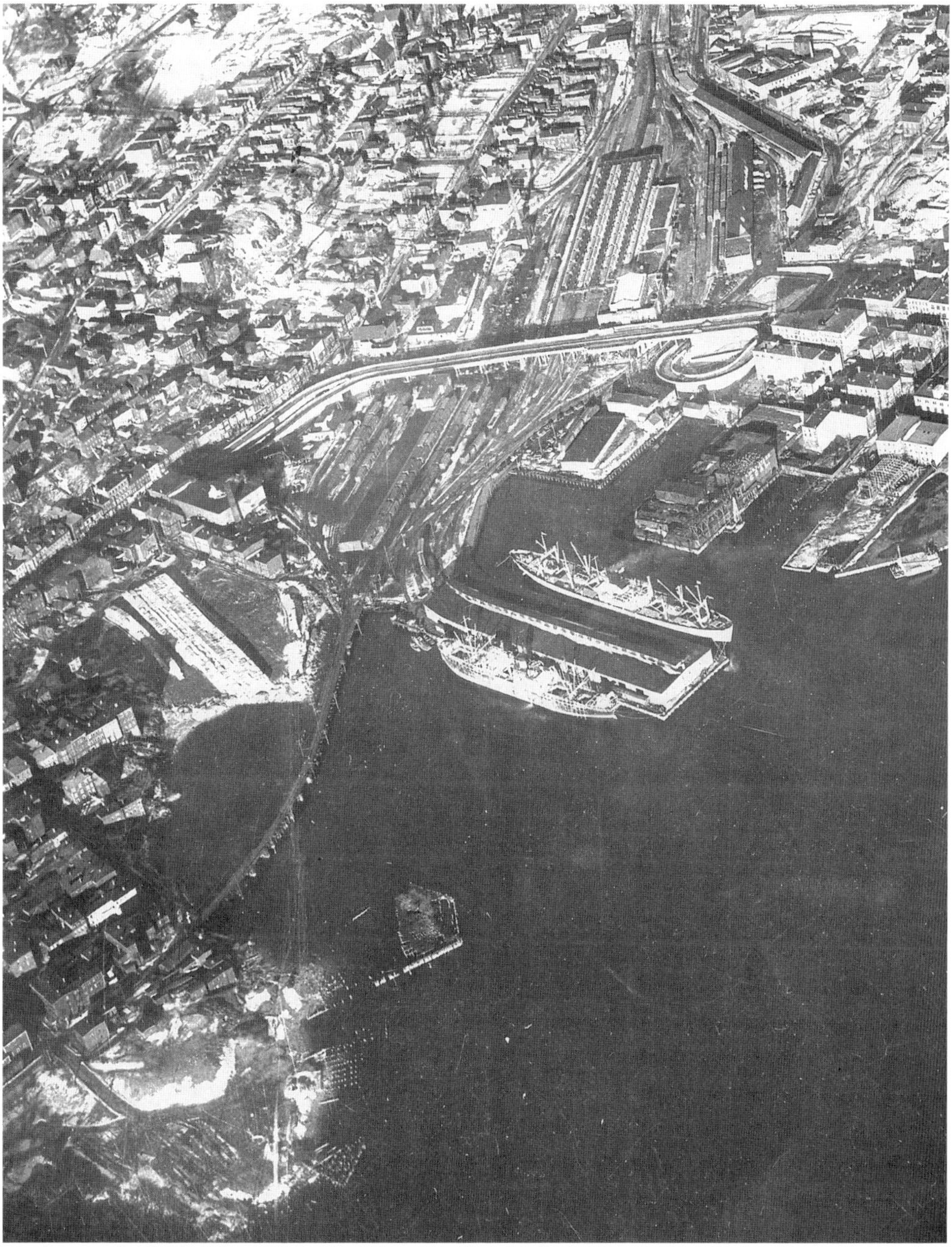

**Long Wharf, 1950**

This image clearly shows the close relationship between the harbour, industry, and the residential section of Saint John. At bottom left is Portland Point showing, the remnants of wharves, and the almost-finished viaduct. The Union Station, the Red Rose Tea and Coffee buildings, the Starr Coal Company, and the Dock Street power plant are visible as is the foundation for the YMCA at top right. Almost everything shown here was later destroyed or rebuilt through urban renewal, port expansion, or the Market Square development.

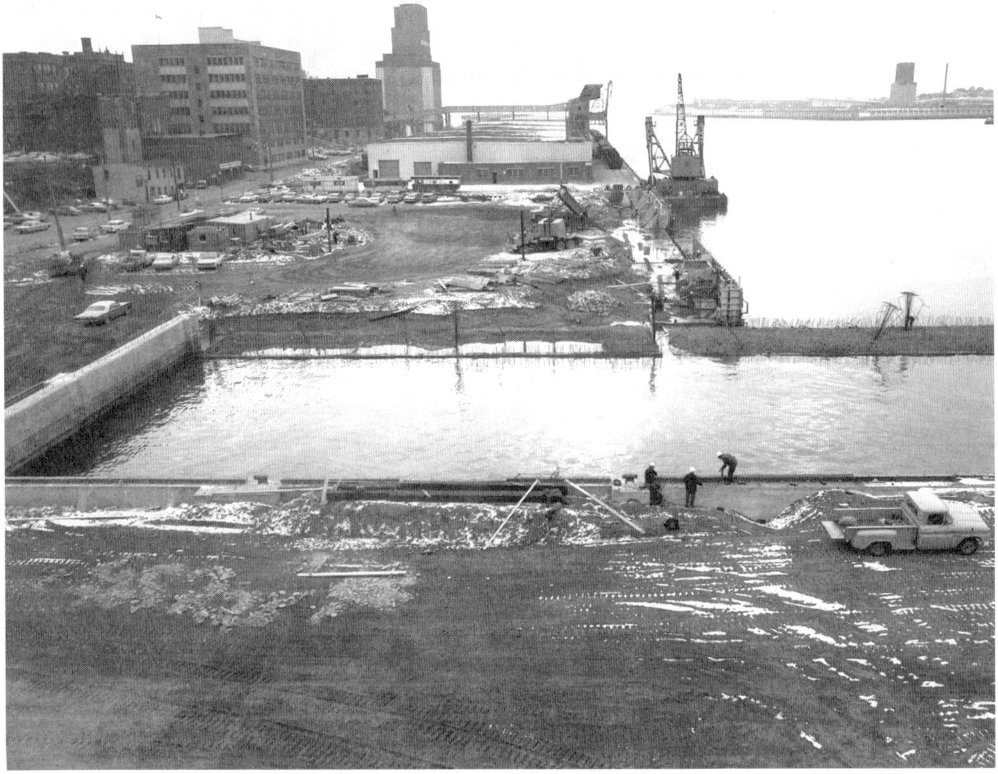

**Princess Street Slip, c.1959**

In 1957, the G.P. Porter Company of Montreal received the contract for underwater excavation of the new wharf facilities for the Department of Transport. The three-year project involved the deep-water berth for coast guard ships, a new wharf, and an administration and stores building. In 1958 Foundation (Maritime) Limited of Halifax was awarded the second contract: to place seven concrete cribs at the old ferry landing at the foot of Princess Street. This second phase, shown here, was completed in February 1960. Phase 3 was the construction of the office and stores building, which today comprises the Saint John Coast Guard Base.

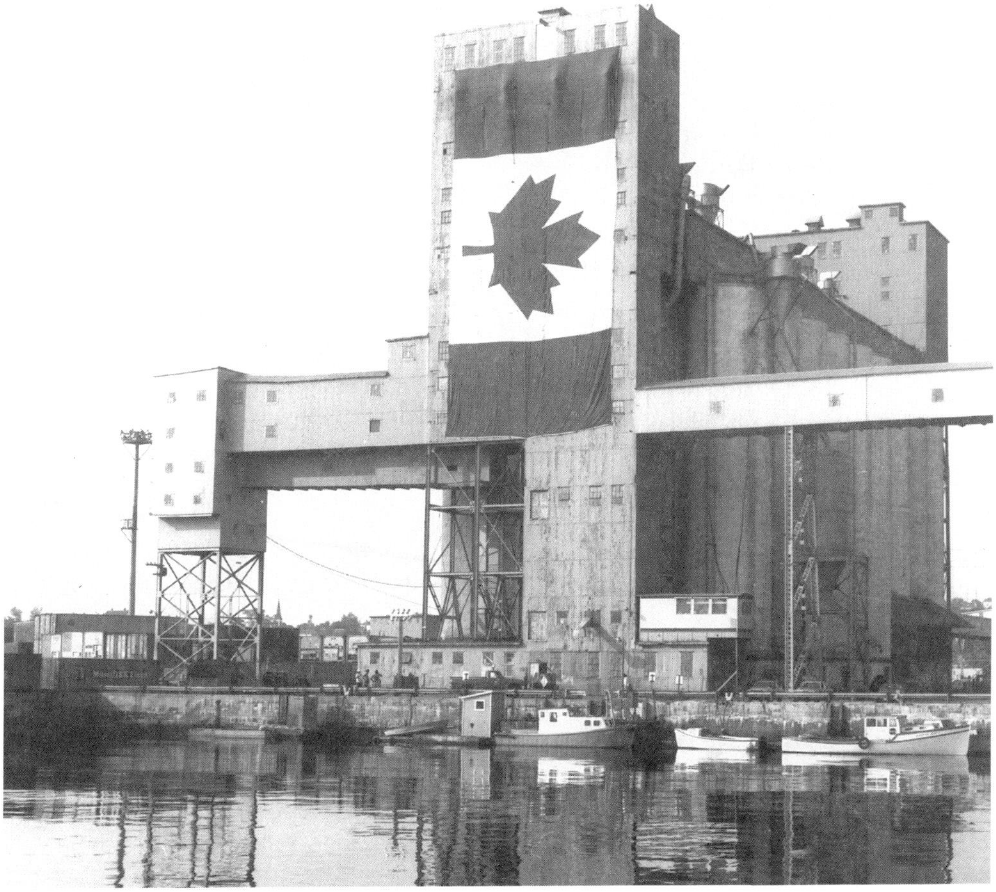

**Pier 3 Grain Elevator, July 1, 1985**

To celebrate Saint John's bicentennial, the country's largest Canadian flag was flown from this grain elevator. After grain shipments were halted in the 1980s, the elevator was demolished and a new paper shed was built in its place. The boat in the centre is the National Harbours Board workboat *Lady LaTour*, and the fishing boat at the right is believed to be the *Mandy and Jean II*.

# *Historic Image Sources*

Betty Mabey: 47, 116
Deborah Stilwell: 137 bottom
Denise Hendershot: 31
Gerry Thompson: 60, 72
Gordie Halvorsen: 64 bottom
Harold E. Wright: 5 top, 137 top
Hayward & Warwick Ltd.: 96

Heritage Resources: title page, xiv, 1, 2 ,3, 4, 6, 7, 8, 9, 10, 12, 13, 14, 15, 16, 17, 18, 19, 20, 21, 22, 23, 27, 28, 30, 32, 33, 34, 35, 36, 37, 38, 39, 40, 41, 42, 43, 44, 45, 48, 49, 50, 51, 52, 53, 54, 56, 57, 58, 59, 61, 62, 63, 64, 67, 68, 69, 70, 71, 73, 74, 75, 76, 77, 79, 80, 81, 82, 83, 84, 85, 86, 87 bottom, 88, 89 bottom, 90, 91, 92, 93, 94, 95, 97, 98, 99, 101, 102, 103, 104, 105, 106 bottom, 107, 108, 109 bottom, 111, 112, 113, 114, 115, 117, 118, 119, 127, 128, 129, 131,132, 133, 135, 136, 138, 140, 141, 143, 144, 145, 146, 147, 148, 149, 151, 152, 153, 154, 155, 156, 157, 158, 159,160, 161, 162, 163, 164, 165, 166, 167, 168, 169, 170,171

The following photograph collections are represented: Arthurs, Beatteay, Beesley, Belyea, Bernard, Callaghan, Cavanaugh, Chesley, Clark, Devenne, Donovan, DOT, Flood, Fowler, French, Garbutt-Woodcock, Gilliland, Hall, Hamm, Hargrove, Hawker, Herrington, Holder, James, Jordon, LeBlanc, Legere, Leonard, Logue, Lynch, Malcolm, Meating, McIntyre, McLellan, McPherson, Miller, Nave, O'Neill, Perry, Price, Reid, Reinhart, Richards, Ring, Rourke, Seeds, Shephard, Snodgrass, Starr, Trentkowsky, Wasson
Horace Meating: 106 top
Jackson Brothers: 11, 109 top, 120, 121 top, 123, 124, 125, 126
M. Melanson: 87 top
Margaret Patterson: 121 bottom, 122
Mrs William Metz: 57 top, 142
National Archives of Canada: 25, 29, 150
New Brunswick Museum: vii, 26
Peter Maher: 100
Provincial Archives: 89 top, 110
Robert S. Elliott: 24
Ron Grant: 55
Saint John Port Authority: 65, 66, 78
San Francisco Maritime Museum: 5 bottom
Shelly Corey, World Beneath Photos: 130
Yarmouth County Museum: 134

All quoted material is from the research files of Heritiage Resources, Saint John, New Brunswick.